PHILIPPIANS, COLOSSIANS, 1 & 2 THESSALONIANS

PHILIPPIANS

by
John M Riddle

40 Beansburn, Kilmarnock, Scotland

ISBN-13: 978 1 910513 22 4

Copyright © 2015 by John Ritchie Ltd.
40 Beansburn, Kilmarnock, Scotland

www.ritchiechristianmedia.co.uk

All rights reserved. No part of this publication may be reproduced, stored in a retrievable system, or transmitted in any form or by any other means – electronic, mechanical, photocopy, recording or otherwise – without prior permission of the copyright owner.

Typeset by John Ritchie Ltd., Kilmarnock
Printed by Bell & Bain Ltd., Glasgow

Contents

Preface	7
Philippians Introduction	9
Chapter 1A	18
Chapter 1B	28
Chapter 1C	38
Chapter 1D	46
Chapter 2A	56
Chapter 2B	66
Chapter 2C	74
Chapter 3A	82
Chapter 3B	92
Chapter 3C	100
Chapter 4A	108
Chapter 4B	118
Chapter 4C	126
Colossians Introduction	136
Chapter 1	144
Chapter 1A	154
Chapter 1B	162
Chapter 2	172
Chapter 2A	180

Chapter 2B	190
Chapter 3	198
Chapter 3A	204
Chapter 3B	212
Chapter 4	220
1 Thessalonians	231
Thessalonians Introduction	232
Paul at Thessalonica	240
Chapter 1	248
Chapter 1A	256
Chapter 2	264
Chapter 2A	272
Chapter 3	280
Chapter 3A	288
Chapter 4	296
Chapter 4A	304
Chapter 5	314
Chapter 5A	323
2 Thessalonians	333
Chapter 1	334
Chapter 1A	342
Chapter 2	350
Chapter 2A	358
Chapter 3	368
Chapter 3A	376

Preface

This book represents the substance of Bible Class discussions on Friday evenings at Mill Lane Chapel, Cheshunt, between January and June 2000 in the case Philippians, between March and July 2001 in the case of Colossians, and between January and July 2003 in the case of 1 & 2 Thessalonians.

As with previous publications in the series, the original notes were written without any thought of their eventual appearance in the public domain, and the current volume, like its predecessors, does not purport to be a commentary in the usual sense of the word. While the "notes", as we call them locally, are a little more (hopefully) than "dry bones", having at least some "sinews" and "flesh", they are far from being "an exceeding great army". We allude, of course, to Ezekiel's splendid description of Israel's coming national resurrection, but whether he would have approved of the allusion remains to be seen!

Unlike, for example, the Book of Ezekiel, which is not *about* us (but certainly *for* our spiritual profit), the New Testament Epistles were decidedly written for the church. They were written for our "edification, and exhortation, and comfort". It is of course supremely important that we should be increasingly occupied with the Gospel records which bring before us the Lord of the doctrine, but this should engender an ever-deepening desire to become thoroughly acquainted with the doctrine of the Lord.

We should also remember that the Epistles address 'real life' situations. They not just theoretical treatises. How glad we should be that God's "divine power hath given unto us all things that pertain to life and godliness", whether in relation to our personal lives or to assembly life. New Testament churches were sometimes, perhaps more often than not, troubled places, and we might be forgiven for wondering why an all-wise God should allow problems and difficulties to arise so early in church history without giving His people much time, in horticultural language, to 'harden off'. Had He done so, then the apostles, men eminently qualified and authoritative to deal with those problems and difficulties, would have passed off the scene, leaving His people exposed to "the wiles of the devil". In His marvellous wisdom and foreknowledge, God allowed the storms to come so early in order that His people then, and ourselves today, often facing the same pressures, would have authoritative teaching to help them 'weather the storm'. He had in mind, not only first-century believers, but all believers in the 'church age', including ourselves.

The Bible Class at Cheshunt remains indebted to John Ritchie Ltd for their continuing willingness to publish its notes, and to Mr. Fraser Munro and his colleagues for their invaluable help in editing the material submitted to them. The Bible Class also continues to be grateful to Miss Lesley Prentice for having checked and corrected the original manuscripts, something she continues to do, and to Mr. Eric Browning for his considerable help in sending copies of current studies by Email to a wide readership.

John Riddle
Cheshunt, Hertfordshire
June 2015

PHILIPPIANS

INTRODUCTION

READ ACTS 16.6-15 & 40, PHILIPPIANS 1.1 & 4.15-23

"Paul and Timotheus, the servants of Jesus Christ, to all the saints in Christ Jesus which are at **Philippi,** with the bishops and deacons". These first-century Christians lived at Philippi. That was their **geographical** location. But they were "in Christ". That was their **spiritual** location.

There can be no doubt that these believers were very close to the heart of Paul, and that Paul was very close to their hearts. They were bound together by mutual love for each other. This epistle is the most intimate of them all. It flows with deep affection. "For God is my record, how greatly I long after you all in the bowels of Jesus Christ" (1.8). He calls them "my beloved" (2.12), and "my brethren dearly beloved and longed for, my joy and crown" (4.1). The Philippians did not lag behind in their love for Paul: "It is righteous for me to think this as to you all, because ye have me in your hearts" (1.7, JND). He prays that their "love may abound yet more and more" (1.9). Like the assembly at Thessalonica, the assembly at Philippi was born out of suffering (See Acts 16), and both were dear to the apostle. His deep desire for their spiritual health and prosperity surfaces throughout the epistle.

In our introductory study, we will endeavour to cover the following: *(1)* the city of Philippi; *(2)* the contact with Philippi; *(3)* the church at Philippi; *(4)* the circumstances of the epistle; *(5)* the contention at Philippi; *(6)* the circumstances of Paul; *(7)* the content of the epistle.

1) THE CITY OF PHILIPPI
The city of Philippi lay in what is now northern Greece, just below the Bulgarian border, and was located on the Gangites River, some ten miles inland from the port of Neapolis (modern Kavalla) on the Aegean Sea. Its only modern building when visited by H.V. Morton *(In the Steps of St.Paul,* originally published in 1936) was a watchman's hut, and what Luke describes as "the chief city of that

part of Macedonia, and a colony" (Acts 16.12) lay between ten to fifteen feet below ground level. The Via Ignatia, the famous east-west Roman highway on which the city stood, lies almost beneath the modern road. As Paul approached Philippi, he would have seen the old town, founded by Philip of Macedon (from whom the city took its name), climbing a conical hill, with the new Roman colony, founded by Caesar Augustus, at its foot on flat ground. The stone rain-gutters of the excavated market-place still functioned at the time of H.V. Morton's visit, and marble floors and bases of columns indicated the fine public buildings and temples which once lined the square.

Philip of Macedon wrested the city (it was originally called Datus or Datum, and was known as Krenides, from its numerous springs) from the Thasians around 300BC. It was near Philippi (in 41BC) that the legions of Antony and Octavius (the future Augustus) defeated the forces of Brutus and Cassius. Augustus settled his veterans in Philippi, and constituted it a Roman colony. Ten years later (31BC), after he had defeated Antony and Cleopatra at the battle of Actium, Augustus settled yet more of his veterans in Philippi. The inhabitants of Philippi therefore considered themselves Roman citizens. They practised Roman customs and used Roman coinage. They acknowledged the Roman emperor. Their names were enrolled on a register at Rome. Philippi was a replica of Rome. It was a Roman colony in Greece.

We can now see why Paul should refer to the church at Philippi as a 'heavenly colony' (3.20), where the word "conversation" *(politeuma)* means "the condition, or life, of a citizen: citizenship" (W.E. Vine).The same English word (this time translating *politeuo*) occurs earlier in the Epistle ("let your conversation be as it becometh the gospel of Christ", 1.27) where it signifies "conduct characteristic of heaven citizenship" (W.E. Vine). So the believers at Philippi were 'citizens of heaven' and owed allegiance to Christ. This is equally true of all Christians. You now know where our word 'politics' comes from. You will sometimes hear preachers quote this verse, and say that it can be translated, 'our politics are in heaven'. We know what they mean, so we won't try and be too pedantic!

It was here that the first Christian church was founded in what is now Europe, though Paul would not have known about such continental distinctions when he crossed the Aegean Sea on his second missionary journey. This brings us to:

2) THE CONTACT WITH PHILIPPI
Acts 16 now becomes compulsory reading. By closing two doors, in Asia and Bithynia, God propelled Paul towards Troas, where he received a vision: "There

stood a man of Macedonia, and prayed him, saying, Come over into Macedonia, and help us". Luke continues: "And after he had seen the vision, immediately we (so Luke was there at the time) endeavoured to go into Macedonia, assuredly gathering that the Lord had called us for to preach the gospel unto them. Therefore loosing from Troas, we came with a straight course to Samothracia, and the next day to Neapolis; and from thence to Philippi" (Acts 16.6-12). Read the rest of the story yourself. It is familiar ground, but do refresh your memory. Incidentally, military towns like Philippi did not attract Jews until they assumed a commercial importance, and that is why there was no synagogue there. That, in turn, was why the preachers went "on the sabbath" to "a riverside, where prayer was wont to be made". It was there that the Lord "opened" the heart of Lydia. It does seem that Lydia was a Gentile who had embraced Judaism. In other words, she was a proselyte.

3) THE CHURCH AT PHILIPPI
Have you ever wondered what sort of people were in fellowship at Philippi? Read Acts 16 again, and you'll get some idea! There would have been **Lydia.** She was a business woman, and **possibly** quite well off. At least, she seemed to have a house big enough to entertain Paul and Silas (That doesn't mean that everybody with their own business and their own house is well off!). Being, it seems, a Jewish proselyte, she would have repeated, "Hear, O Israel: the Lord our God is one Lord". There would have been the ***jailor.*** Perhaps what we might call a 'middle class' man. He was almost certainly a Roman citizen, in which case he may well have worshipped many gods. The Roman 'pantheon' was a temple dedicated to all the gods, of which the circular example at Rome itself is the most famous. Perhaps (a little speculation here!) there would have been the ***"damsel"*** once "possessed with a spirit of divination". She would have been as poor as the proverbial 'church mouse', and was totally dominated by Satan. In social, cultural and religious terms, they were a real 'mixed bag!' But they were all 'sinners saved by grace', and out of such unlikely material, the church at Philippi was formed by the Holy Spirit. All the believers are simply called "brethren" when Paul left the city: "And when they had seen the **brethren** (notice: all distinctions have disappeared: "there is neither Jew nor Greek...bond nor free...male nor female", Gal. 3.28), they comforted them, and departed" (Acts 16.40). They were bound together in Christ.

4) THE CIRCUMSTANCES OF THE EPISTLE
We do not have to go outside the New Testament to acquire the information we need to understand the Epistle to the Philippians. All we have to do is to read the Epistle to the Philippians! This applies equally to the other books of the

Bible. The best commentary on the Bible, is the Bible itself! So, why did Paul write to the Philippians?

The epistle was written, in the first place, as a "thank you letter'. The Christians at Philippi had sent Paul a gift. This is made very clear in the last chapter, although Paul certainly alludes to it in 1.5, 2.1 and 2.17. We are not told whether it was in cash, or in kind. The expression "the things which were sent from you" (4.18) might suggest the latter. Take time to read the relevant verses in the last chapter: "But I rejoiced in the Lord greatly, that now at the last your care of me hath flourished again; wherein ye were also careful, but ye lacked opportunity…ye have well done, that ye did communicate with my affliction…I am full, having received of Epaphroditus (he carried the letter: see 2.25-30) the things which were sent from you" (4.10-19). Paul uses very significant language to describe the gift. He calls it "an odour of a sweet smell, a sacrifice acceptable, wellpleasing to God" (4.18). (Compare Ephesians 5.2 and 2 Corinthians 2.14-16 where the two words "odour" and "sweet smell" also occur. You will need a good concordance to check the words: the connection isn't too obvious in our English Bible, so do get used to handling a concordance/lexicon). This passage puts the highest possible complexion on our stewardship. It emphasises its value Godward: the gift was "wellpleasing to **God**" (4.18). It emphasises its value manward: "ye sent once and again unto **my necessity**" (4.16). It emphasises its value selfward: "fruit that may abound to **your account**" (4.17). The gift sent to Paul demonstrated *(i)* the spiritual concern of the Philippians: "Ye have me in your heart" (1.7, RV margin); *(ii)* the spiritual appreciation of Paul. What about our concern to show fellowship to others, and our appreciation of the fellowship shown to us? We ought to bear this in mind when the time comes to take the assembly offering on "the first day of the week" (1 Cor.16.2).

Notice too that the assembly at Philippi had been consistent in their stewardship. Paul rejoiced in their "fellowship in the gospel from the first day until now" (1.5). The "first day" takes us back to Acts 16 where Paul and Silas enjoyed the hospitality of Lydia (Acts 16.15) and, later, the hospitality of the converted jailor (Acts 16.34). "Until now" refers, obviously, to the gift which Epaphroditus brought from Philippi.

What a wonderful way in which to say, 'Thank you!' But the epistle does far more than that, and Paul takes the opportunity to write to them about other matters. Sydney Maxwell *(What the Bible Teaches - Philippians)* suggests that the letter covers four main areas: he "thanks them for their **generosity**" (we have already noticed this); he "encourages them against **despondency**" (they were

Introduction

suffering for Christ's sake, 1.29); he "warns them against **disunity**" (two sisters were 'at loggerheads', 4.2: this was an internal problem); and "he strengthens them against **legality**" (the Jewish teachers weren't far away, 3.1-3: this was an external problem). We will deal with these aspects of the epistle as we meet them in future studies, but for the time being we should notice:

5) THE CONTENTION AT PHILIPPI

It is quite clear from the epistle that although danger lurked on the horizon (see 3.1-2: it was a common danger at the time), the assembly was not actually tainted by false doctrine. Paul therefore warns them in advance. But there **was** an immediate problem. A personal problem. Two sisters, Euodias and Syntyche, were 'at odds' with each other. Like Epaphroditus, they had laboured with Paul. See 2.25 and 4.3. Paul appeals to them by name (see 4.2), so you can't say that he wasn't straightforward about it. At the same time, he wasn't rude or nasty either. The manner in which Paul deals with the difficulty is most instructive. He does not use a 'heavy hand', but approaches the problem gently. We have the first reference to it in 1.27, and the second in 2.2-3. At this point, Paul draws attention to 'the mind of Christ', Who certainly looked not "on his own things", but "on the things of others". Having done this, Paul adds, "work out your own salvation with fear and trembling" (2.12), and "do all things without murmurings and disputings" (2.14 etc). The "salvation" to which Paul refers, is not salvation from sin, but salvation from the problem that had arisen. Notice, too that Paul had a larger heart than the warring parties at Philippi. The two sisters probably got on well with everyone except each other, but Paul loved them "all". Do note the emphasised word "all" in 1.1, 1.4, 1.7, 1.8, 4.23. Paul says the same about Epaphroditus ("he longed after you all", 2.25-26). Notice how Paul gets the atmosphere right before he names the two sisters: "Therefore, my brethren dearly beloved and longed for, my joy and crown, so stand fast in the Lord, my dearly beloved", and then, "I beseech Euodias, and beseech Syntyche, that they be of the same mind in the Lord" (4.1-2). So often we say the right thing, but we say it in the wrong way, or with the wrong approach. Paul sets us a marvellous example here of how we ought to approach each other!

6) THE CIRCUMSTANCES OF PAUL

He was in prison. Notice the expressions, "my bonds" (1.7, 13, 16), and "my affliction" (4.14). Whilst there are other views, it "seems best...to remain with what is generally held, and is more satisfactory to the evidence, that Philippians was written from Rome" (Sydney Maxwell). The Epistles to the Ephesians, Colossians and Philemon were evidently written during the same imprisonment (not quite like the inmates in Dartmoor: see Acts 28.16, 30). Scholars suggest that Philippians was written around AD63. Very clearly, Paul's imprisonment was not a hindrance to the spread of the gospel. Unlike materialism and worldliness, persecution does not hinder the gospel. Just listen to this: "But I would ye should understand, brethren, that the things which happened unto me have fallen out rather unto the furtherance of the gospel" (1.12). As a result, there were "saints" in "Caesar's household!" (4.22). Through Paul's imprisonment at Rome, the gospel reached the most unlikely people! His short imprisonment at Philippi in Acts 16, resulted in the conversion of the jailor! God doesn't make any mistakes in directing the movements and affairs of His servants.

Now let's have a look at the prisoner. Can you see a poor, miserable, dejected little man cowering in the corner? No, you can't!

> Two men looked through prison bars;
> One saw mud; the other - stars.

You have only to read this letter to discover the category to which Paul belonged! But Paul looked beyond the stars! He was occupied with the Creator of the stars. He was Christ-centred. Read through the epistle yet again, and notice, if you haven't already done so (how could you miss it?), that Paul is always *rejoicing!* In fact, he rejoices more in Philippians than he does anywhere else in his correspondence: see 1.4, 18; 2.2, 17-18; 3.1, 3; 4.1, 4, 10. For example, he rejoiced in the fact that the gospel was preached (1.18). He rejoiced (the word here is actually 'boast' or 'glory') at the prospect of the judgment seat (2.16). He rejoiced at the prospect of death (2.17). He rejoiced in salvation through Christ (3.1-3). He rejoiced in the care of the Philippians (4.10). Nothing had changed since he first visited Philippi when "at midnight Paul and Silas prayed, and sang praises unto God: and the prisoners heard them ('were listening', margin)" (Acts 16.25). Paul certainly had the moral right to say, "Rejoice in the Lord *alway:* and again I say, Rejoice" (4.4).

But how could he rejoice like this? After all, he was in *prison,* wasn't he? We have already noted the answer. Paul was able to rise above his circumstances in triumphant rejoicing, because Christ was everything to him. Notice, amongst other verses, the following: "For to me to live is *Christ"*, and to die is gain" (1.21); "Holding forth the word of life; that I may rejoice in the day of *Christ,* that I have not run in vain, neither laboured in vain" (2.16); "What things were gain to me, those I counted loss for *Christ*" (3.7); "I can do all things through *Christ* which strengtheneth me" (4.13).

Introduction

In an earlier epistle, Paul had said, "But we all, with open face beholding as in a glass the glory of the Lord, are changed into the same image from glory to glory, even as by the Spirit of the Lord" (2 Cor. 3.18). It is therefore not in the least surprising that Paul reflected the character of the Lord he loved and served. The very man who wrote, "Look not every man on his own things, but every man also on the things of others. Let this mind be in you, which was also in Christ Jesus" (2.4-5), was just like Him! Read, carefully, 1.22-26, 2.17 and 4.17. The 'mind of Christ is discernable in all three passages. Paul was not looking "on his own things", but "on the things of others". Just like Christ! The same mind is discernable in Timothy (2.20-21) and in Epaphroditus (2.26-30). This brings us, finally, to:

7) THE CONTENT OF THE EPISTLE

We have now set ourselves an impossible task in a few lines! Perhaps the best thing we can do is to notice some leading themes in the epistle, and then attempt a short title for each chapter. But do remember that short headings are usually quite inadequate!

a) Some leading themes

It goes without saying that the **Lord Jesus** is the leading theme of the whole epistle. He has the "preeminence" in "all things" (Col. 1.18), and we will reserve this for the chapter headings. We have already noticed that **joy and rejoicing** are prominent in the epistle. There is a strong emphasis on the **gospel,** particularly in Chapter 1. See vv.5, 7, 12, 17, 27 (twice). Further references to the gospel are found in 2.22; 4.3, 15. Philippians has been called 'the epistle of the **mind**'. Read it through again (yes, again), and see if you agree. See 1.27; 2.2, 5, 20, 3.15, 4.2, 7. Notice 4.8, "think on these things." The theme of **fellowship** is also prominent. Paul refers to "fellowship in the gospel" (1.5), the "fellowship of the Spirit" (2.1), and the "fellowship of his sufferings" (3.10). But that's only a start. The epistle mentions a "fellowsoldier" (2.25) and "fellowlabourers" (4.3), and there are others in the Greek text. We will note them as we proceed.

a) Some chapter divisions

Do remember what we said above about chapter headings! Every preacher seems to have a different set, and most of them are perfectly valid. During a visit to Cheshunt, G.B. Fyfe suggested the following well-chosen titles: **Chapter 1:** Christ, the purpose of our living. **Chapter 2:** Christ, the pattern of our thinking. **Chapter 3:** Christ, the prize of our running. **Chapter 4:** Christ, the power of our doing.

For the purpose of these studies, we will use something a little shorter. In **Chapter 1** we have the gospel of Christ. We have already noticed the prominence of the gospel in this chapter. In **Chapter 2** we have the mind of Christ. "Let this mind be in you, which was also in Christ Jesus". We have also noticed how Paul, Timothy and Epaphroditus displayed the mind of Christ in this chapter. In **Chapter 3** we have the knowledge of Christ. Paul calls it "the excellency of the knowledge of Christ Jesus my Lord". It embraces past, present and future. In **Chapter 4** we have the sufficiency of Christ. For example, "I can do all things through Christ which strengtheneth me".

This comparatively short epistle therefore covers a wide variety of subjects, but engages our hearts and minds with the Lord Jesus in every case. In fact, the epistle displays Paul's passion for Christ, and this permeates the epistle from beginning to end. It is, firstly and foremostly, a devotional letter, and whilst Paul uses very emphatic language, it is never at the expense of his deep love for them.

If our studies deepen our desire, like Paul, to "know him, and the power of his resurrection, and the fellowship of his sufferings" (3.10), they will not be in vain.

READ CHAPTER 1.1 and 1 TIMOTHY CHAPTER 3

Four significant nouns

"Paul and Timotheus, the servants of Jesus Christ, to all the saints in Christ Jesus which are at Philippi, with the bishops and deacons". This must be the first time in all the years of Mill Lane Bible Studies that we have devoted an entire study to a single verse! But the verse does contain four significant nouns, and we really must pay careful attention to them. Two of them describe us all, and two of them describe particular people. They are "servants", "saints", "bishops", and "deacons".

1) "SERVANTS"

Paul describes Timothy and himself as "the **servants** (*douloi*) of Jesus Christ". The "damsel" at Philippi recognised that Paul and Silas were "the servants (*douloi*) of the most high God" (Acts 16.17). As noted, the word "servants" translates *douloi*, meaning 'bondservants', and it has often been pointed out that this is a very fitting way to begin a letter which describes the Lord Jesus as the perfect 'bondservant'. He "took upon him the form of a **servant** *(doulos),* and was made in the likeness of men" (Phil. 2.7). The perfect Servant brought great pleasure to God. This is easily detected in Isaiah 42.1, "Behold my servant, whom I uphold; mine elect, in whom my soul delighteth". Unlike ourselves, He was never subject to the mastery of sin, but Paul speaks for *us* all in writing "But God be thanked, that ye were the **servants** of sin, but ye have obeyed from the heart that form of doctrine which was delivered you. Being then made free from sin, ye became the **servants** of righteousness" (Rom. 6.17-18). The word "servant" *(doulos)* occurs on numerous occasions in the New Testament, and should remind us, as the "servants of God" (see, for example, 1 Pet. 2.16) and the "servants of Christ (see, for example, Eph. 6.6), that we are 'not our own' but have been "bought with a price". But the "servants of Jesus Christ" are not unwilling people who complain about their lot in life. Like the Hebrew servant, they love their Master! See Exodus 21.5.

The omission of Paul's apostleship here is significant. It was unnecessary for him to assert his authority. See also 1 & 2 Thessalonians and Philemon. Compare Galatians 1.1, where he strongly emphasises his apostleship. Grave doctrinal error had infected the believers in Galatia, and this must be dealt with by an authoritative man. But Paul had every reason to rejoice over the assembly at Philippi, and the delicate problem that did exist was best resolved kindly and graciously, rather than with a heavy hand. Paul did not adopt a standard introduction when he wrote his epistles. He 'tailored' his approach to suit the circumstances at the time.

Notice, too, that Paul, the experienced servant of God, happily associated himself with Timothy, a younger and less-experienced man: "Ye know the proof of him (Timothy), that, as a son with the father, he hath served with me in the gospel" (2.22). Compare Moses and Joshua in the Old Testament. Older Christians should be deeply concerned about preparing younger Christians for future responsibilities, and younger Christians should be deeply concerned about their spiritual growth "in grace, and in the knowledge of our Lord and Saviour Jesus Christ" (2 Pet. 3.18). We should notice, however, that while Paul makes no distinction between himself and Timothy here, thereafter he speaks alone. Hence, "*I* thank my God upon every remembrance of you" (1.3). Paul also had the following to say about Timothy: "I trust in the Lord Jesus to send Timotheus shortly unto you, that I also may be of good comfort, when I know your state. For I have no man likeminded, who will naturally (genuinely) care for your state" (2.19-20). Paul and Timothy were "likeminded" fellow-servants, and this gave Paul the moral right to urge Euodias (Euodia) and Syntyche to "be of the same mind in the Lord" (4.2).

2) "SAINTS"

The Epistle is addressed to "all the **saints** in Christ Jesus which are at Philippi, with the bishops and deacons". Compare 4.21, "Salute every **saint** in Christ Jesus". Very clearly, "all the saints" means 'all the Christians', so there is no question of 'canonising' people! Paul wrote to "the church of God which is at Corinth, to them that are sanctified in Christ Jesus, called *to be* **saints** (omit the italicised words: see also Rom. 1.7), with all that in every place call upon the name of Jesus Christ our Lord, both theirs and ours" (1 Cor. 1.1-2). These Christians were not acting in a very 'saintly' way, but that did not alter their divinely-given position. They were "called...saints". The two words, "sanctified" *(hagiasmos)* and "saints" *(hagios)*, both refer to holiness, which can be defined as 'separation to God', or 'set apart for God'. The word "saints" is, literally, 'holy ones'. The "saints" have a marvellous future (2 Thess. 1.10).

"We should remember that whilst the word "saints" describes our position before God, it should also govern our daily conduct". Sydney Maxwell (*What the Bible Teaches – Philippians*) explains the words "to all the saints in Christ Jesus which are at Philippi" as follows: "In Christ Jesus" suggests their position and security; "at Philippi" reminds us of their responsibility and testimony. That very nicely sums up the position and practice of "saints". The fact that Paul addresses the letter to "all the saints...at Philippi", rather than 'the church of the Philippians' (compare, for example, 1 & 2 Corinthians etc), stresses the intense personal joy and interest which he had in each of them. It is not, strictly speaking, a 'church epistle'.

3) "BISHOPS"
Paul addresses the Epistle to "all the saints which are at Philippi, with the **bishops** and deacons". Whilst we are all "servants" and "saints", we are not all "bishops" and "deacons". But this does not minimize the importance of the subject. Paul deals in detail with "bishops" and "deacons" in 1 Timothy 3. As we shall see, "bishops" are elsewhere called "elders" in the New Testament. Even a most cursory reading of the chapter will show that both "bishops" and "deacons" are far removed from the ecclesiastical dignitaries which abound in Christendom. The Authorised Version does, however, use language which requires some investigation. For example, "the office of a bishop" (1 Tim. 3.1), and "the office of a deacon" (1 Tim. 3.10). As you read 1 Timothy 3, it will become very clear indeed that both "bishops" and "deacons" have to fulfil some very stringent conditions. The reason becomes obvious when we remember that, in the first case, Paul is dealing with those who exercise **care** in the assembly, and in the second, with those who **serve** in the assembly. Whether it is **caring** or **serving**, the highest spiritual qualities are required. Responsibility **for** the assembly, and responsibility **in** the assembly, are no light matters.

We will deal with the subject of "bishops" in the following way; *(a)* their titles; *(b)* their work; *(c)* their appointment.

a) Their titles
i) "Bishops". The word "bishop" in our Authorised Version translates the Greek word *episkopos*. It is made up of *epi,* over, and *skopeo,* to look or watch. So, literally translated, the word means 'overseer'. Now let's look at the various places in the New Testament where *episkopos* occurs:

- "Paul and Timotheus, the servants of Jesus Christ, to all the saints in Christ Jesus which are at Philippi, with the **bishops** and deacons" (Phil. 1.1).

Chapter 1A

- "This is a true saying, If a man desire the office of a **bishop**, he desireth a good work. A **bishop** then must be blameless" (1 Tim. 3.1-2)

- "For this cause left I thee in Crete, that thou shouldest set in order the things that are wanting, and ordain elders in every city, as I had appointed thee: if any be blameless, the husband of one wife, having faithful children not accused of riot, and unruly. For a **bishop** must be blameless, as the steward of God" (Titus 1.5-7).

- "And from Miletus he sent to Ephesus, and called the elders of the church. And when they were come to him, he said unto them...Take heed therefore unto yourselves, and to all the flock, over the which ('in the which', JND) the Holy Ghost hath made you **overseers**" (Acts 20.17, 28).

These four passages yield at least four immediate lessons, all of which simply consist in noting what the Scriptures say for themselves:

- The plurality of "bishops" is emphasised in Philippians 1.1. Not one bishop presiding over a number of churches, but a plurality of bishops in one church. Proverbs 11.14 gives at least one reason for this: "Where no counsel is, the people fall: **but in the multitude of counsellors there is safety**". See also Proverbs 15.22; 24.6.

- The word "bishop" or "bishops" in the first three references above (Phil. 1.1; 1 Tim. 3.1-2 becomes "overseers" in the last reference (Acts 20.28). The lack of uniformity in the Authorised Version evidently arises from the fact that the translators were charged, amongst other things, to keep 'the old ecclesiastical words'. The "overseers" in Acts 20.28 are not "over" the flock in any hierarchical sense, but 'in' the flock. It is not a case of 'clergy and laity'.

- The "overseers" are not appointed by democratic processes, but by the Holy Spirit (Acts 20: 28). This is very important, and we will refer to this again later.

The word *episkopos* also occurs in 1 Peter 2 with reference to the Lord Jesus Himself: "For ye were as sheep going astray; but are now returned unto the Shepherd and **Bishop** of your souls" (v.25). You will also notice, that in two of the above passages (Titus 1.5-7) and Acts 20.17, 28) the "overseers" (we'll use this word for a little while) are also described as -

ii) "Elders." The word in our New Testament translates the Greek word *presbuteros*, meaning, literally, 'an old man'. But don't get too alarmed over this definition! There are in fact three passages where *episkopos*, or a kindred word, and *presbuteros* occur together:

- "For this cause left I thee in Crete, that thou shouldest set in order the things that are wanting, and ordain **elders** in every city...for a **bishop** must be blameless" (Titus 1.5-7). Do notice that Paul does not say 'ordain elders in every **assembly**, but in "every **city**". Perhaps this stresses their standing in the community.

- "And from Miletus he sent to Ephesus, and called the **elders** of the church (so they were a recognised body of people: it wasn't a case of calling 'a brethren's meeting'). And when they were come to him, he said unto them...Take heed therefore unto yourselves, and to all the flock, over the which (in the which) the Holy Ghost hath made you **overseers**." (Acts 20.17-28).

- "The **elders** which are among you I exhort...feed the flock of God which is among you, taking the **oversight** thereof" (1 Pet. 5.1-2) The word "oversight" (*episkopeo*') describes the work rather than the person *(episkopos)*, but the point is clear. The two words, bishop and elder, describe the same person. It is also worth mentioning at this juncture that the body of elders is called "**the presbytery**" *(presbuterion)* in 1 Timothy 4.14.

iii) Overseers and Elders. The use of two words to describe the same men is certainly not mere duplication. The terms are not synonymous:

- The word "**overseer**" describes the man's **ministry.** It stresses his **duty.** Notice in this connection that the word "visitation" (see Luke 19.44; 1 Pet. 2.12) and the phrase "the office of a bishop" (1 Tim. 3.1) translate *episkopos*. So an overseer is someone who visits!

- The word "**elder**" describes the man's **maturity**: it stresses his **dignity.** An elder is not necessarily an old man in years: but he must be a man with experience and maturity. He must not be "a novice", referring to a new convert (1 Tim. 3.6).

b) Their work
Let's say straight away, that overseers or elders are people who work. They are not non-executive directors: in fact, they are more like working-directors, although the word 'director' is not really suitable at all! Paul put it like this: "And we beseech you, brethren, to know them which **labour** among you, and

are over you ('take the lead among you', JND) in the Lord, and admonish you" (1 Thess. 5.12); "If any one aspire to exercise oversight, he desireth a good **work**" (1 Tim. 3.1, JND). It is the work of the overseer that is stressed in the following:

- "If a man desire the **office of a bishop**" (1 Tim. 3.1) or, literally, 'If any one seeketh **overseership**' *(episkopos)*. W.E. Vine observes that "there is no word representing 'office'". It is a work, not a position.

- Referring to Judas Iscariot, "his **bishoprick** *(episkope)* let another take" (Acts 1.20). "Bishoprick" sounds rather grand! But it simply means 'oversight'.

- "The elders which are among you I exhort...Feed the flock of God which is among you, taking the **oversight** *(episkopeo)* thereof." (1 Pet. 5.1-2).

So far we have been rather technical. Now the time has come to get to grips with the actual work. Paul puts it as follows: "If a man know not how to rule his own house, how shall he **take care of the church of God?**" (1 Tim. 3.5). If you want to find out what this means, turn up Luke 10. Yes, the 'Good Samaritan!' "But a certain Samaritan, as he journeyed, came where he was: and when he saw him, he had compassion on him, and went to him, and bound up his wounds, pouring in oil and wine, and set him on his own beast, and brought him to an inn, and **took care of him.** And on the morrow when he departed, he took out two pence, and gave them to the host, and said unto him, **Take care of him**" (Luke 10.33-35). The words are exactly the same. So there's no doubt about the work. It is caring for people, and especially when they've taken some hard knocks. 'Taking care' of people involves shepherding and stewardship.

- **Shepherding.** Notice the expressions "**feed** the church of God" and "**feed** the flock of God" (Acts 20.28; 1 Pet. 5.2). The word "feed" means more than giving food. It is really 'shepherding the church of God' or 'tending the church of God'. The Lord Jesus, as the "Good Shepherd", is the perfect example for all assembly overseers. Read John 10. God loves shepherds. Think about Abel, Joseph, Moses, David and Amos for a start. **You** can supply the appropriate references!

- **Stewardship.** Acts 20.28 and 1 Peter 5.2 also emphasise the responsibility of the overseers: "feed the church of **God**...feed the flock of **God**". They are responsible to **the Lord.** Hence, "a bishop (overseer) must be blameless, as **the steward of God**" (Titus 1.7). An elder is not responsible **to** the flock, but he is responsible **for** the flock.

Whilst elders must not be "lords over God's heritage", or "not as lording it over your possessions" JND, they are to be esteemed "very highly in love for their work's sake" (1 Pet. 5.3; 1 Thess. 5.13). When Paul says, "*know* them which labour among you, and are over you ('take the lead among you', JND) in the Lord, and admonish you", he means 'recognise and acknowledge them' as spiritual leaders.

c) Their appointment
They are certainly appointed, but not by a church synod, or by 'a show of hands!' Read Acts 20.28 again: "Take heed therefore unto yourselves, and to all the flock over the which ('in the which') **the Holy Ghost hath made you overseers**". So they are appointed and equipped by the Holy Spirit. But weren't these men chosen by the apostles, and doesn't this mean that because we do not have apostles today we cannot therefore have elders today? People who espouse this view refer to Acts 14 where Paul and Barnabas were travelling home after completing the outward leg of the first missionary journey: "And when they had preached the gospel to that city (Derbe), and had taught many, they returned again to Lystra, and to Iconium, and Antioch, confirming the souls of the disciples...and when they had **ordained them elders in every church**, and had prayed with fasting, they commended them to the Lord, on whom they believed" (Acts 14.21-23). The word "ordained" simply means 'chosen', literally, 'to stretch out the hand'. But how did they know who to choose? The answer is quite simple: they chose those men who exhibited the necessary qualifications. These qualifications were later listed in 1 Timothy 3 and Titus 1. Paul and Barnabas were able to discern fitness for eldership. They were not voted into office, or chosen by some democratic process. Their own lives and ability bore witness to their calling.

This is very important. It is not a case of choosing a brother 'to fill the gap'. Or choosing a brother who 'would make a good elder'. Or choosing a brother who, because of professional qualifications, would 'be an asset on the oversight'. It is a case of recognising a brother because he is already doing the work, because he is already displaying a shepherd heart, and because he is already marked by the necessary spiritual and moral qualities. All too often, a brother is asked to 'join the oversight', and is then expected to commence the work of overseership. The correct order is the exact reverse: a brother is already acting as an overseer, and is therefore recognised by the assembly for what he is already doing.

4) "DEACONS"
Keep 1 Timothy 3 open. We have already noticed that the first part of the chapter (vv.1-7) deals with those who exercise *care* in the assembly. They are

described as "bishops", or better, "overseers". As we have seen, they are also called "elders" elsewhere in the New Testament. The second part of this chapter deals with those who **serve** in the assembly. They are called "deacons", or better, "servants". In fact the word "deacon" is simply an Anglicised version of the Greek word *diakonos*.

The Greek word *diakonos* occurs frequently in the New Testament, and it might be helpful to look at some of the different ways in which it is used, before dealing with its relevance to the local assembly. As we have already noticed, another Greek word *(doulos)* is often translated "servant" in our New Testament. W.E. Vine *(An Expositary Dictionary of New Testament Words)*, explains the difference: "*Diakonos* views a servant in relationship to his work; *doulos* views him in relationship to his master". The Lord Jesus is never called the bondservant of men, but He is described as the bondservant of God (Phil. 2.7). But when the Lord Jesus said to His disciples, "I am among you as he that serveth" (Luke 22.27), He used *diakoneo*". (The verb is *diakoneo*: the noun is *diakonos*).

a) It is used to describe different classes of servants
It is used to describe domestic servants, civil rulers, the Lord's servants, and the Lord Jesus Himself.

- **Domestic servants.** "His mother saith unto the **servants,** Whatsoever he saith unto you, do it...the **servants** which drew the water knew..." (John 2.5, 9).

- **Civil rulers.** "For rulers are not a terror to good works, but to the evil...For he is the **minister** of God to thee for good" (Rom 13.3-4). This is rather striking. Since "the powers that be are ordained of God", they are accountable to Him for their service. Bearing in mind that government, with law and order, is a Divine institution, it is not surprising that the authorities are subject to relentless Satanic pressure. He attacks every Divine institution.

- **The Lord's servants.** "If any man **serve** me, let him follow me; and where I am, there shall also my **servant** be" (John 12.26); "Who then is Paul, and who is Apollos, but **ministers** by whom ye believed" (1 Cor 3.5); "If thou put the brethren in remembrance of these things, thou shalt be a good **minister** of Jesus Christ" (1 Tim 4.6); "I commend unto you Phebe our sister, which is a **servant** of the church which is at Cenchrea" (Rom 16.1); "For I speak to you Gentiles, inasmuch as I am the apostle of the Gentiles, I magnify mine **office**" *(*Rom 11.13).

- **The Lord Jesus.** "Now I say that Jesus Christ was a **minister** of the circumcision for the truth of God" (Rom 15.8); "Is therefore Christ the **minister** of sin? God forbid" (Gal 2.17).

These references serve to show that in general terms, the word "deacon" has a far wider meaning than is generally supposed!

b) It is used to describe different types of work
The word covers all forms of Christian service, whether temporal or spiritual in character. This is illustrated in Acts 6.

- **Material service.** "Their widows were neglected in the daily **ministration**"; "It is not reason that we should leave the word of God, and **serve** tables" (Acts 6.1, 2).

- **Spiritual service.** "We will give ourselves continually to prayer, and to the **ministry** of the word" (Acts 6.4). Notice the two ways in which the same root word is applied in the passage above. As Wm.Hoste *(Bishops, Priests and Deacons)* observes "Both the seven and the twelve fulfilled their respective deaconships. As the result of one, we no longer hear of murmuring among the widows; and as the outcome of the other, "the word of God increased; and the number of the disciples multiplied in Jerusalem greatly" (Acts 6.7).

c) It is used to describe service in the local assembly
This brings us back to 1 Timothy 3.8-13. The word is used here to describe those who undertake service in connection with the local assembly. Hence, "Paul and Timotheus, the servants (*douloi:* bondslaves) of Jesus Christ, to all the saints in Christ Jesus which are at Philippi, with the bishops and **deacons** (*diakonoi*)". In general, the deacons may serve in the material or spiritual realm (see Acts 6.1-4 above): they may serve in a permanent or temporary capacity: the service may be undertaken by men or women (Phebe was "a servant of the church which is at Cenchrea", Rom. 16.1). Such service would include, for example, the responsibilities of the assembly treasurer, and the Sunday School superintendent with his teachers.

It is, however, difficult to escape the conclusion, that 1 Timothy 3 refers particularly to spiritual service, and this "explains why these qualities (referring to vv.8-9) are of the same standard as that required for elders" (J. Allen *(What the Bible Teaches - 1 Timothy)*. We should notice that Paul used the word *diakonos* of himself and of others in 2 Corinthians 3.6, 6.4, Ephesians 3.7,

6.21, Colossians 1.7, 23, 25, 4.7, 1 Thessalonians 3.2. These references cover Gospel preaching and Bible teaching, and include local men labouring locally. Referring to 1 Timothy 3.8 & 12, and 1 Timothy 4.6, J. Allen observes, "gifted by the Lord and responsible to him, they exercised a ministry within the local assembly to the edification of the saints". We should add that whilst an elder can also act as a deacon in other areas of Christian service, deacons are not necessarily elders. The terms are not interchangeable.

Philippians 1.1 therefore emphasises the privileged position of every believer in the Lord Jesus Christ. We are all "servants" and we are all "saints". It also helps us to understand how New Testament churches functioned, by drawing attention to the work of those who cared for them ("bishops" or "overseers") and served in them ("deacons" or servants). God has never altered this pattern. It cannot therefore be bettered. But scriptural principles can never operate properly without spiritual power, and that power lies in devotion and love for Christ. A local church that has lost its passion for Christ has lost its right to exist. Remember the warning to Ephesus. Read Revelation 2.4-5.

READ CHAPTER 1.1-8

"I long after you all"

In our introduction, we entitled this chapter, "The gospel of Christ". The word "gospel" occurs six times in the chapter, and is certainly one of its leading themes. See vv.5, 7, 12, 17, 27 (where it occurs twice). In addition, we must notice the following expressions: "speak the word" (v.14), "preach Christ" (vv.15-16), and "Christ is preached" (v.18). However, a snappy title seldom conveys the entire teaching of a chapter, and that is certainly the case here!

Philippians 1 can be divided as follows. *(1)* Paul's affection (vv.1-8). We cannot fail to sense the atmosphere of these verses. They are permeated by his deep love for them. *(2)* Paul's prayer (vv.9-11). This flows out of his love for them. *(3)* Paul's imprisonment (vv.12-17). The messenger was in bonds, but the message was not! Compare 2 Timothy 2.9. *(4)* Paul's confidence (vv.18-26). He was confident about his future, whether he lived or died (vv.20-21), but he was also confident that he would be released from prison (vv.24-26). *(5)* Paul's concern (vv.27-30). He was concerned about their unity, and their stability under pressure. Read the chapter through (again), and you will find eighteen references to the Lord Jesus. He is at the centre of each paragraph. Check it out! No wonder he says, "For to me to live is Christ, and to die is gain" (v.21). Christ was everything to him. Is He everything to *us?*

In this study, we will cover the first of the five sections outlined above, and notice the spiritual warmth with which the epistle commences:

1) PAUL'S AFFECTION FOR THE PHILIPPIANS, vv.1-8
This section can be divided into four paragraphs: *(a)* his address (v.1); *(b)* his greeting (v.2); *(c)* his thanksgiving (vv.3-7); *(d)* his love (v.8).

a) His address, v.1
"Paul and Timotheus, the servants of Jesus Christ, to all the saints in Christ Jesus

which are at Philippi, with the bishops and deacons". We have already considered this verse in detail, and noted the significance of the nouns, "servants...saints...bishops...deacons". We have also noted the spiritual and geographical location of the Philippians. In the first place, they were "in Christ Jesus", with all its security, sufficiency and satisfaction. This was their permanent location. In the second they were "at Philippi", with all its pressures and opportunities. This was their impermanent location. They might move from Philippi, but they were always "in Christ". The fact that Paul writes to "*all* the saints in Christ Jesus which are at Philippi", is most important, and we will encounter this again shortly.

b) His greeting, v.2
"Grace be unto you, and peace, from God our Father, and (from) the Lord Jesus Christ". This is not the formality that it might seem at first glance. It is often pointed out that Paul unites the customary Greek greeting (*charis*) with the customary Hebrew greeting (*shalom*), reminding us that in Christ, the deepest of all human divisions (between Jew and Gentile) have been abolished. See Ephesians 2.11-22.

We should also note the order. It is "grace...and peace", not 'peace...and grace.' Peace is the result of grace! We could not enjoy either "peace **with** God" (Rom. 5.1), or "the peace **of** God" (Phil. 4.7), apart from His grace. "Grace" is what Christ **brought** (see Titus 2.11): "peace" is what He **left** (see John 14.27). Both "grace" and "peace" are ongoing. Whilst, as we have noted, "the grace of God that bringeth **salvation** hath appeared to all men" (Titus 2.11), He continues to shower grace upon us. "Grace" is a colossal word! It is used in a variety of ways in the New Testament, but perhaps one occurrence in the Authorised Version sums it up beautifully: "And in this confidence I was minded to come unto you before, that ye might have a second **benefit**" (2 Cor. 1.15). Yes, it is *charis*, usually translated "grace!" So the "grace of God" is the benefit He bestows upon us, whether in salvation, or in any other way. The same Greek word, *charis*, is also translated "liberality in 1 Corinthians 16.3. So, Paul's greeting includes his desire that his dear friends at Philippi will continue to enjoy God's richest benefits and immense liberality! In other words, His "grace"!

But there is something else here that we should notice. "Grace be unto you, and peace, from **God our Father, and (from) the Lord Jesus Christ**". (Omit the second "from"). Whilst, obviously, we distinguish the Lord Jesus Christ from the Father, the fact that the salutation names Him with the Father as "the joint source of grace and peace, is evidence that He shares with God in the divine nature" (W.E. Vine). We must never forget that the entire Scriptures, Old and New

Testaments, insist on the absolute deity of the Lord Jesus. Our great blessings of "grace" and "peace" find their source in "God our Father", and have been communicated to us by "the Lord Jesus Christ". It has been nicely said that "grace" is the fount of salvation, and "peace" is the fruit of salvation. We have been supremely blessed!

c) His thanksgiving, vv.3-7
Whilst, as here, prayer and thanksgiving are often linked in the New Testament (see, for example, Philippians 4.6 and Colossians 4.2), these verses are largely devoted to Paul's thanksgiving to God for the Philippians. Read it as follows: "I thank my God upon every remembrance of you (always in every prayer of mine for you all making request with joy), for your fellowship in the gospel from the first day until now". This highlights the main theme in this section, but it does **not** mean that we can overlook v.4! We can learn some important lessons about prayer here, as well as in vv.9-11, where Paul tells us how he prayed for the Philippians. Paul is an example here of his own teaching in the epistle: compare vv.3-4 with 4.6. We learn at least four things about Paul's thanksgiving:

i) The consistency of his thanksgiving, vv.3-4
Paul's prayer and thanksgiving flowed out of intimate fellowship with God. He **knew** God: "I thank **my** God upon every remembrance of you, always in every prayer of mine for you all making request with joy". See also 4.19, "But **my** God shall supply all your need according to his riches in glory by Christ Jesus". Paul had learnt by experience to trust Him, and had personally proved His unfailing goodness and mercy. His intimacy with God led to frequency of prayer. We cannot avoid the impression that Paul often prayed for the Philippians! "**Always** in **every** prayer of mine for you all making request with joy".

Since prayer and thanksgiving are so closely associated, we will look at these two verses together, and notice:

- **Paul was thankful in prayer.** "I **thank** my God upon **every** remembrance of you". We should be characterised by thankfulness: see 1 Thessalonians 5.18. Paul thanked God every time he thought about the Christians at Philippi! It was said of Jehoram, king of Judah, that "he departed without being desired!" (2 Chron. 21.20). But Paul certainly didn't think of the Philippians like that! Are **we** giving fellow-Christians cause for praise and thanksgiving? But "remembrance" *(mneia)* here is rather more than just 'remembering'. It is sometimes translated "mention" in the New Testament. See, for example, Romans 1.9, Ephesians 1.16, 1 Thessalonians 1.2. In each case, prayer is involved. See also 2 Timothy 1.3. So it is **prayerful** remembrance. We remember lots of people, but do we remember them **prayerfully?**

- **Paul was earnest in prayer.** We know this from the words he uses in v.4: "Always in every **prayer** of mine for you all making **request** with joy". In both cases, he uses the Greek word *deesis* which means 'supplication'. (The usual word for prayer is *proseuche*). The two words, 'prayer' and 'supplication', are distinguished in 1 Timothy 2.1, "I exhort therefore, that, first of all, supplications, prayers, intercessions, and giving of thanks, be made for all men". The word 'supplication' means 'an asking' or 'an entreaty', and is often used in circumstances of particular need. See, for example, Luke 1.13, Romans 10.1 and James 5.16, where the word translated "prayer" (AV) is actually 'supplication' *(deesis)*. How earnest are **we** in prayer?

- **Paul was comprehensive in prayer.** "Always in every prayer of mine for you **all**". He embraced all the believers at Philippi. The little word "all" occurs five times in the first eight verses of the epistle. See also 4.23. This is particularly significant in view of the breakdown of fellowship between Euodias and Syntyche. Both sisters had an 'exception clause' in their affections! They could not say, with Paul, "I long after you **all** in the bowels of Jesus Christ". Euodias excluded Syntyche, and Syntyche excluded Euodias. Do **we** have any similar restrictions? Do we pray for **everybody** in the assembly?

- **Paul was joyful in prayer.** "Always in every prayer of mine for you all making request with **joy**". Prayer should never be a tiresome duty! Are we **glad** to pray? Paul's joy in the Philippians reminds us that our lives should bring joy to the hearts of those who exercise pastoral care in the assembly. See Hebrews 13.17, "Obey them that have the rule over you ('your leaders', JND), and submit yourselves: for they watch for your souls, as they that must give account (that is, give account of their work), that they may do it with **joy,** and not with grief: for that is unprofitable for you". Are we contributing to the joy of our assembly elders, or do we make things difficult for them?

ii) The reason for his thanksgiving, v.5
"For your fellowship in the gospel from the first day until now". This is, literally, "your fellowship **unto** the gospel" (W.E. Vine) and is elsewhere translated "your fellowship in furtherance of the gospel" (RV). The word "fellowship" *(koinonia)* can best be defined with reference to three of the Lord's disciples: "James and John, the sons of Zebedee, which were **partners** *(koinonos)* with Simon" (Luke 5.10). There you have it! "Fellowship" is 'a sharing in

common', or 'a partnership'. It has been described as, "fellows in a ship - all rowing together"! Greek students can throw up their hands in horror if they like, but it does illustrate the meaning very well indeed! So the Philippians acted as Paul's partners in his gospel work. Their "fellowship in the gospel" is described in Chapter 4. Paul talks about the *"**first day**"* in vv.15-16, "Now ye Philippians know also, that in the beginning of the gospel, when I departed from Macedonia, no church communicated with me (*koinoneo*, 'had fellowship with me', RV) as concerning giving and receiving, but ye only. For even in Thessalonica ye sent once and again unto my necessity". (Paul went from Philippi to Thessalonica). As we noticed in our introduction, the "first day" takes us back to the hospitality of Lydia and the jailor (Acts 16.15,34). Paul talks about *"**until now**"* in 4.14, "Notwithstanding, ye have well done, that ye did communicate with ('have fellowship with', *sunkoinoneo*) my affliction". This refers, of course, to the gift sent to Paul at Rome via Epaphroditus (4.18).

This is the first reference to "the gospel"" in this chapter. From later references, we learn that Paul's gospel work involved old and young (see 2.22), and brothers and sisters (see 4.3). Whilst Timothy, Euodias, Syntyche, and others, laboured with Paul in the 'front line', the Philippians were also involved through their gifts and support. It was all part of "fellowship in the gospel". How active is *our* "fellowship in the gospel?" Are **we** doing everything possible to advance the gospel, whether by actual involvement in the work, or by practical support of the work? In this way we become "fellow-helpers to the truth" (3 John 8).

iii) The confidence in his thanksgiving, v.6
"Being **confident** of this very thing, that he which hath begun a good work in you will perform it ('accomplish' or 'perfect it') until the day of Jesus Christ". This is not surprising. After all, the Lord Jesus said "I am Alpha and Omega, the beginning and the ending" (Rev. 1.8). Paul did not appreciate the Philippians any less because their fellowship was the result of divine grace. Compare 2.13. Their fellowship was the **work of God.** He had begun "a good work" in them. This "good work" dated back to their conversion, and Paul had seen the evidence of it over the years of their fellowship with him. Compare 2 Corinthians 8.16, "Thanks be unto **God,** which put the same earnest care into the heart of Titus for you". The old hymn puts it like this:

> For every virtue we possess,
> And every victory won,
> And every thought of holiness,
> Are **His** alone.

But unlike us, God always completes His work. See Genesis 2.1-2, "Thus the heavens and the earth were **finished,** and all the host of them. And on the seventh day God **ended** his work which he had made". See Daniel 5.26, "God hath numbered thy kingdom, and **finished** it". The Lord Jesus cried, "It is **finished**", at Calvary. Paul was therefore confident that God would accomplish, or perfect, the work he had begun in His people. We can expect Him to go on working in our lives. He intends to reproduce the character of Christ in us. This involves our growth "in grace, and in the knowledge of our Lord and Saviour Jesus Christ" (2 Pet. 3.18). It involves "reproof...correction...instruction in righteousness; that the man of God may be perfect, throughly furnished unto all good works" (2 Tim. 3.16-17). Naomi told Ruth that Boaz would not "be in rest, until he have **finished** the thing this day" (Ruth 3.18). His love for Ruth led him to work tirelessly for her greatest blessing. God's love for us leads Him to do exactly the same for us as well.

His work in us in this way will continue until the "day of Jesus Christ". (Why not construct a little message around the expressions, "the **servants** of Jesus Christ", v.1; "the **day** of Jesus Christ", v.6; "the **bowels** of Jesus Christ", v.8; "the **Spirit** of Jesus Christ", v.19). "The day of Jesus Christ" refers to His return for us, and events immediately following, in particular, the "judgment seat of Christ".

It is important to distinguish between the various 'days' mentioned in the New Testament. There are four:

- **'Man's day'.** See 1 Corinthians 4.3, where "man's judgment" (AV) is better translated 'man's day'. We live, at the moment, in 'man's day'.

- **"The day of Jesus Christ"**, elsewhere called "the day of Christ" (Phil. 1.10; 2.16); "the day of our Lord Jesus Christ" (1 Cor. 1.8); "the day of the Lord Jesus" (1 Cor. 5.5; 2 Cor. 1.14); "that day" (2 Tim. 4.8) These passages all refer to the Lord's coming and to His review and reward of our work for Him. This will take place in heaven.

- **"The day of the Lord".** Unlike "the day of Christ", this refers to events on earth, and includes divine judgment on wicked men, together with the millennial reign of the Lord Jesus. See 1 Thessalonians 5.2, and 2 Thessalonians 2.2 where it is very important to notice the RV/JND translation "'that ye be not soon shaken in mind...as that the day of the Lord is present". The Old Testament prophecies abound with references to "the day of the Lord".

- *"The day of God"*. This expression occurs in 2 Peter 3.12, and refers to the eternal state.

Paul's reference here to "the day of Jesus Christ" therefore reminds us that we can expect God to continue the work of His grace in our lives until the Lord Jesus comes, and we stand before Him to 'receive the things done in the body' (2 Cor. 5.10). Until then, we must "labour (make it our aim), that, whether present or absent, we may be accepted (well-pleasing) to him" (2 Cor. 5.9).

iv) The justification for his thanksgiving, v.7
"Even as it is **meet** (righteous) for me to think this of you all, because I have you in my heart ('because ye have me in your heart', JND/RV margin); inasmuch as both in my bonds, and in the defence and confirmation of the gospel, ye all are partakers of my grace". The alternative rendering, "because ye have me in your heart", is "equally possible so far as the grammar is concerned" (W.E. Vine).

Paul's thanksgiving to God for the Philippians was not mere sentiment. It was justified because of their love for him ("ye have me in your heart", see above) and their fellowship with him ("ye all are partakers of my grace"). It was therefore only right that he should be thankful to God. The consistent love and fellowship of the Philippians meant that Paul could do nothing else but rejoice. We must therefore notice:

- **Their love for Paul.** "Ye have me in your hearts" (see above). There was nothing superficial about their affection for him. (Compare the attitude of Reuben in Judges 5.15). Christian fellowship is far more than people sharing a common interest. We are not members of a religious club. Christian fellowship flows from mutual love. This is the hallmark of fellowship. "By this shall all men know that ye are my disciples, if ye have love one to another" (John 13.35).

- **Their fellowship with Paul.** They were 'partakers of his grace'. Paul uses two now-familiar words. The word "partakers" *(sunkoinonos)* means 'partners'. They had fellowship *(koinonia)* with Paul in what he calls "my grace" *(charis)*. We have already discussed *charis*, but here it refers to two privileges given to Paul: the "grace" of suffering for Christ, and the "grace" of serving Christ.

So far as the former is concerned, Paul refers to his "bonds". The words "my grace" include the privilege and honour of suffering for Christ: "For unto you it is given *(charizomai)* in the behalf of Christ, not only to believe on him, but also to suffer for his sake" (1.29). As W.E. Vine points out, "the trying nature of their circumstances was not an evil to be deplored, but a privilege and honour conferred upon them by God". The Christians at Philippi shared Paul's privilege of suffering for Christ. See also Hebrews 13.3.

As far as the latter is concerned, Paul refers to his service, and describes it as "the defence and confirmation of the gospel". The word "***defence***" translates the Greek word *apologia,* hence our English word 'apology'. But Paul certainly didn't apologise for the gospel! The word *apologia* means 'a speech in defence'. See, for example, 1 Corinthians 9.3, "Mine ***answer*** to them that do examine me is this"; 2 Timothy 4.16, "At my first ***answer*** no man stood with me"; 1 Peter 3.15, "Be ready always to give an ***answer*** to every man that asketh you a reason of the hope that is in you". Paul's "defence" of the gospel is therefore his explanation and vindication of the gospel. He cogently argued the case. Like the man born blind, our "defence" of the gospel begins with our experience of salvation: "One thing I know, that, whereas I was blind, now I see" (John 9.25). But we should be making progress. See, again, 1 Peter 3.15. This involves clarity and simplicity. We will not make a very good case for the gospel if we do not present the message in an understandable way! The word "***confirmation***" *(bebaiosis)* means 'to make firm, make secure' (W.E. Vine). The verb also occurs in Hebrews 6.16, but the noun *(bebaioo)* occurs in various places in the New Testament. Its use in 1 Corinthians 1.6, 8 ("confirmed"), 2 Corinthians 1.21 ("stablisheth"), and Colossians 2.7 ("stablished"), suggests that the word is used in connection with establishing believers in the faith. So Paul was involved in explaining the truth of the gospel to unbelievers, and establishing the truth of the gospel firmly in the minds of believers. W.E. Vine sums it up in saying that "the gospel both overthrows its enemies, and strengthens its friends".

d) His love, v.8
"For God is my record, how greatly I long after you all in the bowels of Jesus Christ". We must notice three things here:

i) The sincerity of his love. He also appeals to God in this way in Romans 1.9, 2 Corinthians 1.23, 1 Thessalonians 2.5, 10. Paul lived with the words, "Thou God seest me", ringing in his ears. Can **we** call on God to witness the sincerity and the reality of statements we make? One of the things that God hates is a "lying tongue" (Prov. 6.17).

ii) The strength of his love. "I long after you all". The words "long after" *(epipotheo)* mean 'to yearn after, long for greatly' (W.E. Vine). Paul's desire was shared by Epaphroditus. See 2.26. Prayer for God's people will be accompanied by a desire to see them! We have already noticed that there were no exceptions in Paul's love: "I long after you **all**".

iii) **The source of his love.** "In the bowels of Jesus Christ". The word "bowels" *(splanchnon)* refers, literally, to the intestines, and is used in that way in Acts 1.18. The word occurs in 2 Corinthians 7.15, where it is translated "inward affection". It also occurs in Luke 1.78, where the AV "tender mercy" carries the marginal note, "bowels of the mercy". (See also JND). Paul's deep desire to see his brethren at Philippi was not just a human emotion: it was an expression of divine love, engendered in his heart by the Lord Jesus. God expects us to display our "bowels of compassion" in practical fellowship. See 1 John 3.17.

READ CHAPTER 1.9-17

"And this I pray"

As we have already seen, Philippians Chapter 1 may be divided into five sections: *(1)* Paul's affection (vv.1-8); *(2)* Paul's prayer (vv.9-11); *(3)* Paul's imprisonment (vv.12-17); *(4)* Paul's confidence (vv.18-26); *(5)* Paul's concern (vv.27-30). Our current study therefore coves the second and third sections of the chapter. Like the opening paragraph, they are packed full of spiritual vitamins. Following our paragraph numbering, we come then to

2) PAUL AT PRAYER, vv.9-11
The atmosphere in which he prayed for them is described in v.8: "For God is my record, how greatly I long after you all in the bowels of Jesus Christ". Paul's prayer for the Philippians flows out of his deep love for them. We should notice that although he is in prison, his first concern is for the spiritual growth of his dear Philippian brethren. His personal situation is relegated to second place! His own interests are subordinated to the interests of other people, and this occurs time and time again in the epistle. Paul was an example of his own ministry when he said, "Look not every man on his own things, but every man also on the things of others" (2.4). But, and this is even more important, he displayed the very character of the Lord Jesus Himself. The Lord Jesus certainly did not look "on his own things, but...on the things of others" as the verses which follow (2.5-8) illustrate so clearly. The 'mind of Christ' lies at the heart of Paul's teaching in this epistle. R. McPike, writing in *The Believer's Magazine, June 1962*, puts it like this: "In living close to God we are made aware of His interest in others...this inevitably leads the soul to intercession for those with Him who are the objects of divine affection...Too seldom is this spirit of unselfishness manifest amongst us today. How much we lose in our utter unconcern for those who are bound up with us in bonds eternal!"

When we come to Paul's imprisonment (vv.12-17), we shall see that, even there, Paul is more concerned for others than he is for himself! For further examples of Paul's unselfishness in this way, see Ephesians 6.18-20; Colossians 2.2-4;

2 Thessalonians 3.1-2. Notice, in each case, what he puts first in his requests for prayer.

Note the progression of the prayer: "And this I pray, that...that ye...that ye..." A.G. Muir, also writing in *The Believer's Magazine, October 1971*, comments as follows: "Paul's ultimate design is now about to be stated. Line upon line as a master-builder he has set forth his plea: his prayers make sense; he understands spiritual processes; his own tidy mind and the orderliness and reasonableness of his requests would be impressive at the "throne of grace". He knew God's will, and adjusted his prayer to coincide". Paul's prayer contains three requests which may be summarised in the following way: *(a)* increasing love (v.9); *(b)* intelligent choice (v.10a); *(c)* integrity of character (vv.10b-11).

a) Increasing love, v.9
"And this I pray, that your love may abound yet more and more in knowledge and in all judgment". He prays for increasing **depth** in their love, and increasing **discernment** in their love.

i) Increasing in depth
"And this I pray (*proseuchomai*: the scholars call this the 'durative present, meaning, 'I keep on praying'), that your love may abound **yet more and more** in knowledge and in all judgment". It is very wonderful to notice that Paul uses the word for divine love *(agape)* here. (The New Testament also uses the word *phileo*, which "more nearly represents tender affection", W.E. Vine). The existence of that love in the hearts of God's people dates from their conversion. See 1 John 3.14, "We know that we have passed from **death unto life,** because we love the brethren". See also 1 Peter 1.22. Read Romans 5.5, "The love of God is shed abroad in our hearts by the **Holy Spirit which is given unto us**".

But the existence of that love in the hearts of the Philippians was not enough for Paul. He prays that it will "abound yet more and more!" Compare 1 Thessalonians 4.9-10: "But as touching brotherly love *(philadelphia)* ye need not that I write unto you: for ye yourselves are taught of God to love one another. And indeed ye do it toward all the brethren which are in all Macedonia: but we beseech you, brethren, that ye increase more and more". Paul did not expect God's people to 'stand still' or 'mark time' when it came to Christian love! In fact, he expected them to be 'on the move' in every way! Read 1 Thessalonians 4.1.

But for whom is their love to "abound yet more and more?" This is not stated, neither is it necessary to know. Love for God, and love for His people, cannot be disassociated. "Every one that loveth him that begat loveth him also that is begotten of him. By this we know that we love the children of God, when we love God and keep his commandments" (1 John 5.1-2).

ii) Increasing in discernment
But love is to "abound yet more and more **in knowledge and in all judgment**". (Compare Prov. 1.4; 2.11). Christian love is not just emotion, and it is not without principle: it is an intelligent love. Our love for God will be marked by an increasing desire to please Him **by understanding and practising His will**. The Lord Jesus said, "If ye love me, keep my commandments" (John 14.15). As A.G. Muir observes, such abounding love will be subject to the "governing, mellowing, enhancing values of knowledge and judgment". We have an example in this epistle: "Beware of dogs, beware of evil workers, beware of the concision" (3.2). We know that "love rejoiceth not in iniquity, but rejoiceth in the truth" (1 Cor. 13.6). It has been nicely said that love is like a strong flowing river guided by the banks of knowledge and judgment.

The word "**knowledge**" translates *epignosis,* and we can do no better than quote W.E. Vine here. "*Epignosis,* like the simpler form, *gnosis,* is always acquired or experimental knowledge. *Gnosis* is knowledge, true or false (1 Tim. 6.20). *Epignosis* is always true knowledge; it may be either full knowledge or increasing knowledge, but it is always knowledge in the spiritual sphere. God's knowledge, mentioned but twice in the New Testament (Rom. 11.33; Col. 2.3), is *gnosis*, not *epignosis*, for there are no gradations in it: it is absolute. Compare Psalm 139.6". The word "**judgment**" means 'discernment' or 'perception', and W.E. Vine helps us again here: "Not intellectual acuteness, but moral sensitiveness seems to be the meaning. This is confirmed by the use of the verb in Luke 9.45 ("they perceived it not"), and of a cognate noun in Hebrews 5.14, "having their **senses** exercised..." Paul uses such 'discernment' or 'perception in Phil. 3.18-19. J.B. Lightfoot suggests that "while '**knowledge**' deals with general principles, '**judgment**' is concerned with practical applications".

b) Intelligent choice, v.10a
Such intelligent love, which desires to know and practise God's will, puts us in a position to "approve things that are excellent". W.E. Vine writes: "Love (the denial of self-interest) and knowledge (full acquaintance with what God has revealed of His will and His ways in working out His will) and discernment (sensitiveness to moral values) must each be in exercise if the Christian is to perceive the difference between what pleases God and what pleases Him not, and if he is to be 'filled with the fruits of righteousness'".

The word "**approve**" *(dokimazo)* means, "to prove a thing whether it be worthy to be received or not" (R.C. Trench). It occurs in Romans 12.2 with reference to the will of God. That is, to approve after trial. The word is used, for example, of proving the five yoke of oxen (Luke 14.19), and of examining ourselves in view of the Lord's supper (1 Cor. 11.28). The word "**excellent**" *(diaphero)* is, literally, 'to differ or to be different from', and is used of the stars in 1 Corinthians 15.41, and of a child under age in comparison with a servant in Galatians 4.1. We are faced with so many options, so many alternatives, so many views, so many suggestions, and we can only distinguish between them with reference to God's word. It is only there that we can discover His will.

The words, "That ye may approve things that are excellent", are also found in Romans 2.18, "And approvest the things that are more excellent". Compare 1 Thessalonians 5.21, "Prove *(dokimazo)* all things; hold fast that which is good". J.A. Bengel suggests that Romans 2.18 refers to the ability to discern **supreme things:** "prove and embrace not merely good in preference to bad, but the best things among those which are good." Some of the "more excellent things" are listed in 4.8-9: "Whatsoever things are true...honest...just...pure". Compare 2 Peter 1.8, 9, 10, 12, 15. Philippians 3.5-8 lists things which are not "excellent". The ability to "approve things that are excellent" leads to:

c) Integrity of character, v.10A-11
"That ye may be sincere and without offence till the day of Christ; being filled with the fruits of righteousness, which are by Jesus Christ, unto the glory and praise of God". Let's look at it like this:

i) Its characteristics
Positively: "sincere *(eilikrines)*", meaning 'unalloyed' or 'unmixed': literally, 'tested by sunlight'. It is said that market traders used to disguise broken vases by filling the cracks with wax, and that the only way to find out whether there were hidden defects in them was to hold them up to the sunlight. The sun would show the existence or otherwise of the wax! (The English word "sincere" comes from the Latin, *sin serum,* meaning 'without wax'). The word "sincere" refers to "internal disposition, the absence of impure motives" (Sidney Maxwell, *What the Bible Teaches - Philippians*). The Christian who is "sincere" will have no time for 'sharp practice' or for spiritual manoeuvring.

Negatively, "without offence", meaning 'no occasion of stumbling', possibly in the passive sense, that is, not being stumbled. But see 1 Corinthians 10.32, "Give none offence, neither to the Jews, nor to the Gentiles, nor to the church of

God"; 2 Corinthians 6.3, "giving no offence (occasion of stumbling) in anything, that the ministry be not blamed". As to ourselves, we must be "sincere": as to others, we must be "without offence".

ii) Its continuity
Paul prays that they will be "sincere and without offence till ('with a view to') **the day of Christ**". (See our comments on 1.6). That is, until the Lord Jesus returns, and we "appear before the judgment seat of Christ; that every one may receive the things done in his body, according to that he hath done, whether it be good or bad" (2 Cor. 5.10). In other words, we are expected to live in this way consistently until the Saviour comes to take us home to heaven. Do notice that Paul does not say, 'till the day we die', but "till the day of Christ". We ought to live in expectation of the Lord's return.

iii) Its climax
"Being filled with the fruits (singular, 'fruit') of righteousness, which are by Jesus Christ, unto the glory and praise of God" or "Being **complete** as regards the fruit of righteousness" (JND). S. Maxwell points out the contrast between v.10 and v.11: "In v.10 they are to be without alloy and without offence. In v.11, they are to be filled with the 'fruit of righteousness'." As A.G. Muir observes: "All spiritual teaching resolves itself into a test of character and of conduct. Exposition evaporates if it is not exemplified: Christianity cannot be theoretical or detached". These are weighty words. The Lord Jesus censured the religious hierarchy that "sat in Moses' seat", because "they say and do not" (Matt. 23.3).

We should notice the **fruit:** "righteousness". That is the character of the fruit: it is practical righteousness. The **source:** it is "by Jesus Christ": He produces the fruit. See John 15.4-5. The **object:** it is for "the glory and praise of God". In the words of H.C.G. Moule: "This is the true goal and issue of the whole work of grace. To Him are all things, to 'Whom be glory for ever. Amen' (Rom. 11.36)". The great object of Paul's prayer is the glory of God. This is its *grand finale*.

To summarise, Paul's prayer (v.4, 9-11) was **thankful** ("I thank my God"), **consistent** ("always in every prayer of mine"), **comprehensive** ("for you all"), **joyful** ("making request with joy"), **confident** ("being confident of this one thing"), and **purposeful** ("and this I pray").

3) PAUL IN PRISON, vv.12-17
This section proves that "the word of God is not bound" (2 Tim. 2.9). The

messenger was in chains, but not the message. We must notice *(a)* the progress of the gospel (vv.12-14); *(b)* the motives of the preachers (vv.15-17).

a) The progress of the gospel, vv.12-14

"But I would ye should understand, brethren, that the things which happened unto me have fallen out rather unto the furtherance (*prokope:* 'a striking forward') of the gospel". Paul's circumstances had advanced, rather than hindered, the progress of the gospel. This emphasises the sovereignty of God in ordering the lives of His people. (Compare Acts 8.1-4; 11.19). Paul recognised that "As for God, his way is perfect (Psalm 18.30). See, for example, Ephesians 3.1, "I Paul, the prisoner of **Jesus Christ**"; Ephesians 4.1, "I therefore, the prisoner of **the Lord**". (Ephesians was written at the same time as Philippians). Paul was like Joseph in this respect: "God hath caused me to be fruitful (referring to Manasseh and Ephraim) in **the land of my affliction**" (Gen. 41.52). Paul's zeal was undiminished by reason of his imprisonment. The gospel was preached in new places (v.13), and by new people (v.14).

i) The gospel preached in new places, v.13

"So that my bonds in Christ are manifest in all **the palace,** and in all other places". Paul refers here to gospel preaching in relation to **unsaved** people. The words, "in all the palace" *(praitorion)*, evidently refer, not to Caesar's palace, but to the 'praetorian guard' (RV). We might call it 'the Imperial Guard'. The word *praitorion (praetor* means 'a general') was certainly used of a building (see, for example, Mark 15.16: the word "palace" is *praitorion* in, for example, John 18.28, 19.9, but the verse does suggest a body of people. Hence the rendering, "in all the praetorium and to **all others**" (JND, but see his marginal note), or "throughout the whole praetorian guard, and to all the rest" RV). However, the technicalities involved do not alter the fact that through Paul's imprisonment, the gospel reached people who might not have otherwise heard it. There seems to be an obvious connection between the 'praetorian guard' and the "saints... that are of Caesar's household" (4.22). He was the "'worst of the Caesars" (W.E. Vine) as well!

There is a very important lesson here for us **all.** Paul recognised, as we have already noticed, the sovereign hand of God in his life, and used his imprisonment to preach the gospel to new people. What about **our** circumstances? The neighbourhood in which we live, the place where we work, the school where we study? Let's go further: a spell in hospital, or other uncongenial circumstances. Do we **really** believe that God orders our lives in every way? If we do, then, like Paul we will look for opportunities for "the furtherance of the gospel".

But do notice something else. It was public knowledge that Paul was not in prison because he was a criminal. The words, "so that my bonds in Christ are manifest in all the palace", are better rendered, "so that my bonds have become manifest *[as being] in Christ* in all the praetorium and to all others" (JND). According to M.R. Vincent *(Word Studies of the New Testament),* "The force of this statement lies in the fact that his imprisonment had become a matter of notoriety for Christ. His confinement as a Christian would stir attention and enquiry. All who came in contact with this prisoner would soon discover that he was in chains, not a criminal, but as a Christian". Paul's testimony was not in jeopardy because he was a bad character! See 1 Peter 4.14-16. It would have been very little use if Paul had preached the gospel whilst in prison as "a murderer, or as a thief, or as an evildoer, or as a busybody in other men's matters!" Our gospel witness must be accompanied by a godly life.

ii) The gospel preached by new people, v.14

The sovereign hand of God is seen here too! Through Paul's imprisonment, others were galvanised into action. Paul now refers to gospel preaching in relation to **saved** people. "And many ('most', RV)) of the brethren in the Lord, waxing confident by my bonds (meaning, perhaps, Paul's testimony in his bonds), are much more bold to speak *(laleo,* which could embrace both private and public speaking) the word without fear". Paul's undiminished zeal in prison was an encouragement to others. They were stimulated to witness for Christ themselves. It seems a pity that it needed Paul's imprisonment to get other people involved in gospel work, but at least it happened, and Paul rejoiced! See v.18. Some Christians **never** seem to wake up to their responsibilities!

These two verses prompt two questions. Firstly, how can I use my circumstances *in the gospel?* and, secondly, how can I use my circumstances **for the good of God's people?**

b) The motives of the preachers, vv.15-17

But not all the preachers had the same motives for preaching the gospel. Sadly, quite unbelievably, they preached for very different reasons. "Some indeed preach Christ even of envy and strife; and some also of good will" (v.15). This is amplified in vv.16-17.

i) Perverted motives, v.16

Those who preached (*kerusso*, to herald or proclaim) "Christ even of **envy** (displeasure over the advantage or prosperity of others) **and strife** (the expression of enmity)" did so out of "**contention** ('faction', RV, or a 'party spirit'), not sincerely (*hagnos*, not with pure motives), supposing to add affliction to my bonds". So they were brethren with ulterior motives. People like that always cause difficulties. They were not the false teachers of the day (the Judaisers: see 3.2), but "Christians who were jealous of Paul, and who sought to undermine his influence" (Sydney Maxwell). The whole thing smacks of rivalry. How dreadful: rivalry amongst Christians! We can almost hear their conversation: 'Paul has had the limelight for too long: now it's our turn. We'll show him that he's not the only pebble on the beach. We'll show him that we can preach too!' It was a golden opportunity for them. Paul was "in bonds", and they were free! They took the opportunity to 'kick a man when he's down', although, in actual fact, Paul wasn't 'down' at all! The Philippians were not to be like them: see 2.3.

ii) Pure motives, v.17

Those who preached Christ "of **good will**" did so "**of love,** knowing that I am set for the defence of the gospel". How refreshingly different! But what about **our** motives? Let's remember that when the Lord Jesus comes, He "will bring to light the hidden things of darkness, and will make manifest the counsels of the hearts" (1 Cor. 4.5). Motives as well as methods will be assessed.

These preachers wanted to encourage Paul because they knew how much he loved the gospel. "I am set for the defence of the gospel". We have already discussed the word "**defence**". See our comments on v.7. The word "**set**" comes from *keimai,* meaning 'to lie'. W.E. Vine explains that it is used as the passive voice of *tithemi,* to place or put, and denotes 'to be appointed'. It is translated in this way in 1 Thessalonians 3.3, "That no man should be moved by these afflictions: for yourselves know that we are **appointed** *(keimai)* thereunto". Paul was "set for the defence of the gospel" in a unique way. It was through him that God revealed the great doctrines of the gospel. It is applicable to us in a secondary sense.

But how did Paul cope with this situation? After all, the motives of some of the preachers were sufficient to break his heart! Listen to his answer: "What then? notwithstanding, every way, whether in pretence, or in truth, Christ is preached; and I therein do rejoice, yea, and will rejoice" (v.18). His love for Christ enabled him to rise above the unspiritual motives of his brethren! This saved him from despondency. See v.19, where he does not refer to deliverance **from** prison, but to deliverance **in** prison.

More of this in our next study, God willing.

READ CHAPTER 1.18-30

"For to me to live is Christ"

As we noticed in our last study, Paul did not regard his imprisonment as a disaster: "But I would ye should understand, brethren, that the things which happened unto me have fallen out rather unto the furtherance of the gospel" (v.12). The gospel was preached in new places (v.13), and by new people (v.14), even though some preachers had the most reprehensible motives. The following is taken from a collection of daily meditations entitled Springs in the Valley:

> We cannot expect to learn much of the life of trust without passing through hard places. When they come, let us not say as Jacob did, "All these things are against me" (Genesis 42.36). Let us rather climb our Hills of Difficulty and say, '**These are faith's opportunities**'.

This was certainly true as far as Paul was concerned. The prisoner is far from despondent: he is confident and rejoicing! He had the moral right to say, "Rejoice in the Lord" (3.1), and "Rejoice in the Lord **alway:** and again I say, Rejoice" (4.4). This brings us to the last two paragraphs in this chapter: *(4)* Paul's confidence (vv.18-26) and *(5)* Paul's concern, (vv.27-30).

4) PAUL'S CONFIDENCE, vv.18-26

His confidence surfaces time and time again throughout these verses. Notice the following: "I know" (vv.19, 25); "according to my earnest expectation and my hope" (v.20); "For to me to live is Christ, and to die is gain" (v.21). He expresses his confidence in three ways: *(a)* with regard to his circumstances (vv.18-20); *(b)* with regard to his future (vv.21-24); *(c)* with regard to the Philippians (vv.25-26).

a) He was confident with regard to his circumstances, vv.18-20
i) His joy in prison, v.18. "What then? notwithstanding, every way, whether in pretence *(prophasis)*, or in truth, Christ is preached ('proclaimed'); and I therein do rejoice, yea, and will rejoice". Although Paul's preaching was never tainted

with impure motives (see 1 Thessalonians 2.5, where *prophasis* is translated "cloke"), his love for the gospel enabled him to soar above the unspiritual motives of some of his brethren. Love for Christ will enable us to cope with the many difficulties we encounter, not only in the world, but amongst God's people. The Lord Jesus did not say to Peter, 'Lovest thou the work?' or 'Lovest thou the sheep', but "Lovest thou *me*?" (John 21.15, 16, 17). If we 'love the work', and it gets difficult, we might be tempted to give up. If we 'love the flock', only to find that it includes a few 'black sheep', we might be tempted to give up. But if we love Christ, we'll go on with the work, and go on with the sheep, come what may!

ii) His salvation in prison, v.19. "For I know that this shall turn to my salvation through your prayer, and the supply of the Spirit of Jesus Christ". The word "salvation" occurs three times in this epistle (1.19, 1.28, 2.12), and the context determines its precise meaning in each case. This is, of course, the 'golden rule' of Biblical exposition. It has been said that "A **text** taken out of its **context** becomes a **pretext** for anything you like to imagine!". Paul refers here, not to salvation **from** prison, but to salvation **in** prison. The verses either side make this clear. It is salvation from despondency. The very fact that "Christ is preached" by others (v.18) saved Paul from overwhelming grief that his imprisonment meant the end of gospel work elsewhere. (Just remember that **your** life and service will either encourage or discourage other Christians). It strengthened his resolve to continue to bring glory to Christ, whether in life or death (v.20).

Let's sum up the verse like this: Paul's 'salvation' from despondency in prison would be achieved:

- by the desire of others to get involved in God's service.

- by the prayers of God's people.

- by the grace and strength supplied by the Holy Spirit. Paul was not equal to the task himself.

We should remember that **we** have a part to play in encouraging others. We must pray for them. Notice that Paul did not ask for the Philippians to pray for him, as he does elsewhere (but not in the Epistle to the Galatians: think about it). The reason is quite clear: he knew that they **were** praying for them! He was assured of their prayers. He knew that he was 'in their hearts' (1.7, JND) We should remember too that **God** has a part to play in encouraging others: Paul speaks about "the supply of the Spirit of Jesus Christ". This does not mean 'supplying the Holy Spirit', but what is supplied by the Holy Spirit. There is nothing niggardly about this: the word *epichoregia* means 'a full supply' (W.E. Vine). The word also occurs in Ephesians 4.16 and elsewhere in the New Testament. The title given to the Holy Spirit here is most interesting. It is "the Spirit of Jesus Christ". This emphasises His tender sympathy. After all, the Lord Jesus knew what it was to be arrested and bound. See John 18.12.

iii) His desire in prison, v.20. "According to my earnest expectation and my hope, that in nothing I shall be ashamed (through not magnifying Christ), but that with all boldness, as always, so now also Christ shall be magnified in my body, whether it be by life, or by death". So Paul did not set his heart on release from prison, but rather that he might bring honour to Christ in prison. Notice the contrast between "**be ashamed**" and "**with all boldness**". Paul's "earnest expectation and hope" was certainly fulfilled, for in his very last epistle, written from prison, he triumphantly exclaims, "I am not ashamed" (2 Tim. 1.12). Jeremiah was told, "Be not dismayed at their faces, lest I confound thee before them" (Jer. 1.17). The word "boldness" *(parrhesia)* really means 'freedom of speech, unreservedness of utterance' (W.E. Vine). It is also used, amongst other places, in Hebrews 4.16. Here, in Philippians 1, it means 'bold testimony'. Paul's great desire was that "through the instrumentality of his body, the vehicle of expression and action, Christ shall be magnified" (Sydney Maxwell).

But what about the word "magnified?" Quite obviously, we cannot possibly make the Lord Jesus any greater! He is infinite! But to so many people, the Lord Jesus is insignificant and remote. Magnification turns something which seems quite insignificant into something of consuming interest. It also reveals hitherto unseen glories and beauty. To 'magnify' (it means to 'make great') Christ, therefore, is to bring Him near to people, and to reveal His glories. God can put our bodies to the most wonderful use, can't He? He can do it through the way we live, and He can do it through the way we die. That was Paul's desire. "That…as always, so now also Christ shall be magnified in my body, whether it be by life, or by death".

Do notice the references to the Lord Jesus: **"Christ** is preached" (v.18); "The Spirit of **Jesus Christ**" (v.19); "**Christ**….magnified" (v.20). This brings us to:

b) He was confident with regard to his future, vv.21-24
Paul's desire that Christ "shall be magnified in my body, whether it be by life, or by death", leads him to contemplate life and death. Neither filled him with dread. He looked life and death in the eye with perfect confidence; "For to me

Chapter 1D

to live is Christ, and to die is gain". Paul looks at life and death generally (v.21) and particularly (vv.22-24).

i) Generally, v.21
- *"For to me to live is Christ"*. Paul has referred to those who preached "Christ even of envy and strife" and "contention" (vv.15-16). They had a hidden agenda, and preached Christ "in pretence" (v.18). But while some of his brethren wished only to promote themselves, Paul could say, "For to *me* to live is Christ". His consuming passion was Christ, and only Christ. Christ's interests, Christ's honour, Christ's glory, and Christ's will, were everything to Paul. It was life itself. What about *our* ambitions? What about *our* motives? For some Christians, 'to live' is business, sport, study, family. But for Paul "to live" was **Christ.** Compare Galatians 2.20.

But the statement, "for to me to live is Christ", means even more than the pursuit of His interests. Paul's life **expressed** Christ. As we shall see, his very willingness to continue "in the flesh" because it was "more needful" for them, was nothing less than the mind of Christ Himself. See 2.4-8. We have to confess that *our* lives are, at best, a pale reflection of Christ. Christ-likeness is an ongoing process. It is described in 2 Corinthians 3.18, "But we all, with open face beholding as in a glass the glory of the Lord, are changed into the same image from glory to glory, even as by the Spirit of the Lord".

- *"And to die is gain"*. Death meant the greatest "gain" of all. It involved being "absent from the body", and being "present with the Lord" (2 Cor. 5.8). "The apostle speaks of his death as gain because he would enjoy a state in which his union with Christ would be greater than what he was enjoying here" (W.E. Vine). This is why Paul includes "death" in the list of benefits in 1 Corinthians 3.21-22, "All things are yours; whether Paul, or Apollos, or Cephas, or the world, or life, or **death,** or things present, or things to come; all are yours". Death is a benefit to the Christian because it brings them into the very presence of Christ Himself, and Paul was ready to go!

ii) Particularly, vv.22-24
He now weighs the issues of life and death in connection with service on earth. "But if I live in the flesh, this is the fruit of my labour: yet what I shall choose I wot not. For I am in a strait betwixt two, having a desire to depart, and to be with Christ; which is far better: nevertheless to abide in the flesh is more needful for you". Paul is describing *his* desires here, but we must remember that his future was subject to the will of **God.** Let's look at it like this:

- **What would it mean for him to live?** "But if **I live** in the flesh, this is the fruit of my labour". As it stands, this is not particularly easy to understand! One thing is perfectly clear, and this is that Paul does not use the word "flesh" (it occurs again in v.24) in any sinister sense. See, for example, Romans 8.8. "If I live in the flesh" simply means, 'if I am alive on earth!' (This just underlines the importance of referring to the context of a word or verse in the Bible!). The words, "this is the fruit of my labour", are best understood with reference to Paul's future service. Perhaps we could paraphrase v.22 as follows: 'If I live in the flesh, this means fruitful service'. W.E. Vine explains it in this way: "If his life here were continued, it would consist of labour for Christ, and fruit thereby for Christ".

But this left Paul in a dilemma. "Yet what I shall choose I wot not ('what I shall choose I do not know'). For I am in a strait betwixt two (although one thing remained constant: see v.20), having a desire to depart, and to be with Christ; which is far better". So

- **What would it mean for him to die?** It would mean departing and being "with Christ, which is far better". Paul uses some very significant language here.

- "I am in a **strait**", meaning that he was under pressure from both sides. On one side was the prospect of continuing fruitful labour for Christ, and on the other was the prospect of being with Christ. The word "strait" (*sunecho*, 'to hold together') is used in 2 Corinthians 5.14 ("For the love of Christ **constraineth** us": 'holds us fast'), and Luke 22.63 ("And the men that **held** Jesus mocked him, and smote him").

- "Having a **desire** to depart", signifies a 'craving' or 'longing' (W.E. Vine). It is used in Luke 22.15, "With desire I have desired to eat this passover with you". We should note that the word "desire" is more often used in a bad sense in the New Testament.

- "Having a desire to **depart**". Whilst Paul expressed a desire to "depart" *(analuo)*, but confidently expected release from his first imprisonment (see V.25), the time for his "departure" *(analusis)* eventually did come. See 2 Timothy 4.6, "The time of my **departure** is at hand". It means to unloose, to undo, or to break up, and was used in various ways. It was used for unmooring a ship in preparation for sailing, so Paul was ready to set sail on the sea of eternity. It was used for striking a tent in preparation for a journey, so Paul was ready to quit the "earthly house of this tabernacle", and commence the most exciting journey of all! It was used as a military term for breaking camp, so Paul was ready for the victory parade!

- "To be **with Christ,** which is **far better**". Sidney Maxwell is worth quoting in full here. "'To be with Christ' surely indicates that death introduces the saint immediately into the presence of the Lord Jesus. It is a grave error to teach that saints sleep as to their souls, and have no consciousness of anything until the Lord comes. It is only the body of the saint that is viewed as sleeping, never the soul". How did Paul know that it was "far better?" Perhaps he was thinking of his experience described in 2 Corinthians 12, when he was "caught up into paradise, and heard unspeakable words, which it is not lawful for a man to utter" (v.4). He later speaks about "the abundance of the revelations" (v.7). But for Paul, the chief consideration was not what would be better for **him,** but what would be better for **them.** So

- **What would it mean to them for him to live?** " Nevertheless to abide in the flesh is more needful for you". This is astounding. Paul put the needs of his dear Philippian brethren first! Who could blame Paul for wanting to "depart, and to be with Christ?" We have only to think of the persecution he endured. See, for example, 2 Corinthians 11.23-28. If ever a man had the right to think of himself, it was Paul. But he thought of others. Just like the Lord Jesus Himself!

> Others, Lord, yes, others:
> Let this my motto be,
> Help me to live for others,
> That I might live like **Thee!**

The man who said, "Look not every man on his own things, but every man also on the things of others" (2.4) was an example of his own ministry. We shall meet this again in 2.17, 2.20-21 & 2.26). But the Lord Jesus is the supreme example. This brings us to:

c) He was confident with regard to the Philippians, vv.25-26
"And having this **confidence,** I **know** that I shall abide and continue with you **all** (see vv.1, 4, 7, 8) for your furtherance and joy of faith: that your rejoicing may be the more abundant in Jesus Christ for me by my coming to you again". This is a remarkable statement of faith, since death was obviously a possibility at the time. J.N. Darby sums up the position as follows: "Paul decides as to his own fate, without troubling himself as to either what the emperor would do, or the circumstances of the time. Christ loved the assembly. It was good for the assembly that Paul should remain; Paul then shall remain". The words "abide (that is, remain alive) and continue with you", stress Paul's close association with the Philippians.

We should notice the second occurrence of the word "*furtherance*". See also 1.12. In the first case, Paul speaks as an evangelist. He rejoices in "the furtherance of the gospel". In the second case, Paul speaks as a teacher. He anticipates their spiritual advancement. But something else would happen as a result of his release from prison and anticipated visit to Philippi. "That your rejoicing (boasting) may be more abundant *in Jesus Christ* for me ('through me' or 'as to me', JND)". Once again, Paul is not thinking about himself: he wants the Lord Jesus to be glorified through his release and return to Philippi! What a way to boast! "My soul shall make her boast in **the Lord:** the humble shall hear thereof, and be glad. O magnify **the Lord** with me, and let us exalt *his name* together" (Psalm 34.2-3).

Did he go to Philippi again? 1 Timothy was written shortly after Philippians, and it is therefore interesting to read, "As I besought thee to abide still at Ephesus, **when I went into Macedonia**" (1 Tim. 1.3). Philippi was "the chief city of that part of Macedonia" (Acts 16.12).

5) PAUL'S CONCERN, vv.27-30

For the first time, a note of concern enters the epistle. "Only let your conversation be as it becometh the gospel of Christ; that whether I come and see you, or else be absent, I may hear of your affairs, that ye stand fast in one spirit, with one mind striving together for the faith of the gospel" or "Only let your **manner of life** be worthy of the gospel of Christ..." (RV). Behind these words lies the Greek word *polites*, meaning 'a citizen', or a 'member of a city or state'. Paul used the word in Acts 23.1, "I have **lived** in all good conscience before God until this day". While the expression here refers to our conduct in society, it has added emphasis in view of 3.20, where we are urged to behave in keeping with our heavenly citizenship *(politeuma)*. Our lives should commend, and be consistent with, the gospel of Christ. See, for example, 1 Thessalonians 1.5; Titus 2.10-12. But Paul had something specific in mind: "that ye stand fast in one spirit, with one mind striving together for the faith of the gospel". We may divide these verses as follows:

a) Standing fast, v.27

"That ye stand fast in one spirit, with one mind". This has been described as 'co-ordinated energy'. As we know, there was a problem in this connection at Philippi: "I beseech Euodias, and beseech Syntyche, that they be of the same mind in the Lord" (4.2). The expression "stand fast" also occurs, for example, in 1 Corinthians 16.13; Galatians 5.1; 1 Thessalonians 3.8. We are not to be "carried about with every wind of doctrine" (Eph. 4.14). It means that we must "preach the word; be instant in season, out of season" (2 Tim. 4.2). The words "in one spirit, with one mind (soul)", mean "one" in purpose and aim. With the "spirit" *(pneuma)* we have God-consciousness, and with the 'soul' *(psuche)* we have self-consciousness. J.B. Lightfoot defines the "spirit" as "the principle of the higher life", and the 'soul' as the "seat of the affections, passions".

b) Striving together, v.27
"Striving together for the faith of the gospel". Psalm 133 now becomes compulsory reading! Very little, if anything, will ever be accomplished by a company of 'irreconcilables' preaching a message of reconciliation! The words, "striving together" translate one Greek word *(sunathleo),* and it is rather interesting to discover that it is used of the two sisters who had fallen out at Philippi! "Help those women ('these women', RV) which **laboured with me** in the gospel" (4.3). It isn't difficult to deduce that *sunathleo* (meaning 'to contend along with', W.E. Vine) is borrowed from the athletic games. We are to 'strive together for **the faith of the gospel'**. That is, for the doctrine of the gospel, which must not be compromised in any way. People must know what they have to believe.

c) Suffering fearlessly, vv.28-30
"And in nothing terrified by your adversaries: which is to them ('for them', RV) an evident token of perdition, but to you of salvation, and that of God" or "And in nothing affrighted *(pturomai* means to be startled or scared) by the adversaries..." (RV). (The word "nothing" occurs four times in the epistle: it is linked with assurance (1: 20); with fear (1.28); with ambition (2.3); with anxiety (4.6). Freedom from fear has a double effect:

i) As far as the adversaries were concerned, the bold and united testimony of the believers would be "an evident token *(endeixis)* of perdition". The Greek word *endeixis* is translated elsewhere as "proof" (2 Cor. 8.24), and "declare" (Rom. 3.25-26). The witness of the Philippians would activate the consciences of the opponents of the gospel. See Acts 26.14, "It is hard for thee to kick against the pricks (goads)". The calm courage of Stephen (Acts 7) must have made a deep impact on Saul of Tarsus. "Perdition" means destruction, not loss of being, but loss of well-being. Both Judas Iscariot (John 17.12) and "the man of sin" (2 Thess. 2.3), are called "the son of perdition", meaning 'doomed to destruction'.

ii) As far as the assembly was concerned, their bold testimony was "an evident token...of salvation, and that of God". Their suffering was a God-given token, or proof, of their salvation. Compare 2 Thessalonians 1.4-6. The "salvation" of the Lord's people is set against the "perdition" of their adversaries, and since the "perdition" of the "adversaries" lies in the future, it seems reasonable to conclude that Paul is speaking here about the future "salvation" of the Philippians. It is nicely explained in 2 Timothy 2.12, "If we suffer, we shall also reign with him". We must remember that we **have been** saved, that we are **being** saved, and that we **will be** saved.

To suffer on behalf of Christ was a privilege. "For unto you it is given (*charizomai*) in the behalf of Christ, not only to believe on him, but also to suffer for his sake". Compare Acts 5.41, "And they departed from the presence of the council, rejoicing that they were counted worthy to suffer shame for his name". As W.E.Vine observes, "the trying nature of their circumstances was not an evil to be deplored, but a privilege and honour conferred upon them by God". (It is worth remembering that persecution is not necessarily physical. See Galatians 4.29, where the word is used to describe the mockery of Ishmael in Genesis 21.9). Suffering is the normal accompaniment of salvation. See 1 Peter 2.21 and 2 Timothy 3.12. But Paul wrote about this subject with deepest sympathy: "Having the same conflict (*agon,* a contest) which ye saw in me (see Acts 16), and now hear to be in me (in prison at Rome)". He knew what it was like to suffer. He did not 'traffic in unfelt truth'.

The chapter commences with "grace...and peace". This marks our relationship with **God.** It ends with "adversaries" and "conflict". This marks our relationship with **the world.** We could never cope with the "adversaries" and the "conflict", if we did not enjoy the grace of God and the peace of God.

READ CHAPTER 2.1-11

"Let this mind be in you"

The Epistle to the Philippians has been called, 'the epistle of the mind'. To start with, the Greek word *phroneo*, meaning 'to think', occurs seven times in the epistle (1.7, 2.2 (twice), 2.5, 3.15, 3.19, 4.2), and we should notice other references: for example, "***think*** on these things" (4.8), and "the peace of God which passeth all ***understanding***" (4.7). The words, "Let this mind be in you, which was also in Christ Jesus", lie at the heart of the subject. They also lie at the heart of this chapter, which may be analysed in the following way: *(1)* the necessity for the mind of Christ (vv.1-4); *(2)* the expression of the mind of Christ (vv.5-11); *(3)* the emulation of the mind of Christ (vv.12-13); *(4)* the effect of the mind of Christ (vv.14-16); *(5)* the examples of the mind of Christ (vv.17-30).

1) THE NECESSITY FOR THE MIND OF CHRIST, vv.1-4
Paul has already emphasised the necessity for unity at Philippi. "Only let your conversation be as it becometh the gospel of Christ: that whether I come and see you, or else be absent, I may hear of your affairs, that ye stand fast in one spirit, with one mind (*psuche*, meaning 'soul') striving together for the faith of the gospel" (1.27). He now returns to the subject, "Fulfil ye my joy, that ye be like-minded, having the same love, being of one accord, of one mind" (2.2). We know from 4.2 that Paul had good reason to write in this way, all of which emphasises that disunity in the assembly, even between two people, is a very serious matter. This paragraph may be divided as follows: *(a)* the appreciation of their fellowship (v.1); *(b)* the necessity for unity (v.2); *(c)* the necessity for humility (v.3); *(d)* the necessity for selflessness (v.4).

a) The appreciation of their fellowship, v.1
"If there be therefore any consolation in Christ, if any comfort of love, if any fellowship of the Spirit, if any bowels and mercies, fulfil ye my joy…" The chapter does not begin with the "if" of uncertainty, but with the "if" of argument.

Substitute the word 'since', and you have the meaning! But what is Paul talking about here? He certainly uses some delightful expressions!

Bearing in mind that the letter was written, amongst other things, to express Paul's appreciation of their practical fellowship with him (4.10-18), and that he has already alluded to this in 1.5, 7, it is possible that he is referring here to the "things which were sent from you" (4.18). If so, what a way to say 'thank you' for a gift! He calls it:

- "Consolation *(paraklesis)* in Christ". The word means, literally, 'a calling to one's side', and signifies help and encouragement. The RV has 'comfort' here.

- "Comfort *(paramuthion)* of love". This involves a greater degree of tenderness than "consolation", and means, literally, 'a speaking closely to anyone' (W.E. Vine).

- "Fellowship *(koinonia)* of the Spiri". We have encountered "fellowship" before. It means sharing and communion. See our remarks on 1.5. But here it is "fellowship of **the Spirit**". (See also 2 Cor. 13.14). This emphasises the source of their fellowship with Paul. It wasn't a reflection of their good nature, or their charitable interest: it was engendered in their hearts by the Holy Spirit.

- "Bowels *(splanchna)* and mercies *(oiktirmoi)*" or "tender mercies and compassions" (RV). For "bowels", see our note on 1.8. The two Greek words are brought together again in Colossians 3.12, "bowels of mercies" or "a heart of compassion" (RV). They express deep inward feeling.

Now take time to look at these four expressions again, and in particular, the order in which they occur. There is an increasing depth of feeling as the verse proceeds. But Paul was not completely satisfied. His joy in them was not quite complete. So

b) The necessity for unity, v.2
"Fulfil *(pleroo,* meaning 'complete') ye my joy, that ye be likeminded, having the same love, being of one accord, of one mind". His joy would be complete when he knew that there was unbroken unity in the assembly. He calls for this in every part of the verse:

- "Be like-minded". It means 'of the same mind', and reads, literally, 'think the same thing'. Paul was not looking for an assembly of robots! There is a vast difference between unity and uniformity!

- "Having the same love *(ton auton agapon)*". Very clearly, Paul is calling for mutuality of thought and love.

- "Being of one accord *(sumpsuchos)*". It means 'fellow-souled', or 'fellow-minded (W.E. Vine). It can be rendered 'being one in soul'. We have a good illustration of this in 1 Samuel 18.1, "The soul of Jonathan was knit with the soul of David, and Jonathan loved him as his own soul". See also Judges 20 where the expression "as one man" occurs three times (vv.1, 8, 11). Compare Philippians 1.27, "stand fast in one spirit, with one mind *(psuche)* striving together for the faith of the gospel".

- "Of one mind". Literally 'minding the one thing'. We must pray that all this will be true of the assembly to which we belong. Beware of "the little foxes, that spoil the vines!" (Song of Solomon 2.15).

The results of v.2 are seen in vv.3-4. There will be no self-assertiveness (v.3), and no self-interest (v.4)

c) The necessity for humility, v.3
"Let nothing be done through strife or vainglory; but in lowliness of mind let each esteem other better than themselves". The word "strife" *(eritheia)* 'primarily denotes ambition, self-seeking, rivalry...hence it denotes party-making, taking sides for or against party leaders' (W.E. Vine). Compare 1.16: "The one preach Christ of **contention** ('faction', RV: a party-spirit), not sincerely, supposing to add affliction to my bonds". The word "vainglory" *(kenodoxia)* incorporates the word 'empty', and speaks for itself. Paul goes to considerable length in 1 Corinthians 1, to prove that "no flesh should glory in his (God's) presence", and that, "He that glorieth, let him glory in the Lord". The local assembly is the place where Christ alone is exalted. Paul likens the assembly to a temple in 1 Corinthians 3.17, and we know that "in his temple doth every one speak of his glory" (Psalm 29.9).

From self assertiveness, Paul turns to self-abnegation: "But in lowliness of mind *(tapeinophrosune)*, let each esteem (count) other better than themselves". Compare Romans 12.10, "Be kindly affectioned one to another with brotherly love; in honour preferring one another". This is what the Lord Jesus described as "poor in spirit" (Matt. 5.3). It stands in contrast to human arrogance.

d) The necessity for selflessness, v.4
"Look not every man on (or, 'to') his own things (his own interests, or his own

welfare), but every man also on (to) the things of others". This illustrates the result when we 'esteem other better than ourselves', unlike the "priest" and the "Levite" who 'looked on their own things' (Luke 10.31-32). There is no 'party-spirit' here! It reminds us that "love seeketh not her own" (1 Cor.13.5), and that "we then that are strong ought to bear the infirmities of the weak, and not to please ourselves. Let every one of us please his neighbour for his good to edification. For even Christ pleased not himself; but, as it is written, The reproaches of them that reproached thee fell on me" (Rom. 15.1-3). Paul (2.17-18), Timothy (2.19-21), and Epaphroditus (2.25-30), all looked "not...on his own things, but...also on the things of others. See 2.20-21. But the greatest example of all is provided by the Lord Jesus. This brings us to:

2) THE EXPRESSION OF THE MIND OF CHRIST, vv.5-11

"Let this mind be in you, which was also in Christ Jesus". The order is significant: "Christ Jesus" reminds us that while He is now exalted ("God hath made that same Jesus, whom ye have crucified, both Lord and Christ"), (Acts 2.36), He once 'emptied himself' (v.7). The wonderful verses that follow are more than a statement about the humility (vv.6-8) and honour (vv.9-11) of the Lord Jesus. They **do** contain very important teaching about Him, but this teaching is brought to bear on the problem of disunity and disagreement at Philippi. The Lord Jesus displayed "lowliness of mind". **He** looked not "on his own things, but...on the things of others". Having described the 'mind of Christ' towards others, Paul applies his teaching in vv.12-16. "Wherefore (in view of the perfect example of the Lord Jesus), my beloved...work out your own salvation with fear and trembling". (v.12). In this context, "salvation" refers to deliverance from the difficulty and dissension that had arisen at Philippi. Good relationships between believers can only be restored and maintained where there is humility and a genuine desire for each other's welfare. Let's now see how the Lord Jesus displayed His love and interest in others.

a) His humility, vv.6-8

These verses can be divided into two sections: **(i)** "Being in the form of God" (v.6), and **(ii)** "Being found in fashion as a man" (vv.7-8).

i) "Being in the form of God", v.6

"Let this mind be in you, which was also in Christ Jesus: Who, being in the form of God, thought it not robbery to be equal with God". While He "took upon him the form of a servant, and was made in the likeness of men" (v.7), He never 'took upon him the form of God', or was 'made in the likeness of God'. The words "**being** in the form of God" emphasise His eternal deity. W.E. Vine points out that the verb "being" *(huparcho)* "points to the existence of a person prior to what is stated of him", and gives a number of illustrations from the New Testament, including Acts 2.30.

The word "form" *(morphe)* "denotes the special or the characteristic form of a person" (W.E. Vine). W.E. Vine quotes Gifford *(The Incarnation)*: "*Morphe* is properly the nature or essence...as actually subsisting in the individual, and retained as long as the individual itself exists...*morphe Theou* ('the form of God') is the divine nature actually and inseparably subsisting in the person of Christ". The word is used again in v.7: He "took upon him the **form** of a servant".

The words that follow are equally wonderful. The Lord Jesus, "being in the form of God, **thought it not robbery to be equal with God**". The word "robbery" means a 'thing held as a prize'. The RV has "counted it not a prize ('a thing to be grasped' margin) to be on an equality with God". The New Translation (JND) has "did not esteem it an object of rapine". Bearing in mind that the entire passage presents Christ "as the supreme example of humility and self-renunciation" (W.E. Vine), the meaning of the verse becomes clear. Although the Lord Jesus was, and is, absolutely and essentially God, He did not regard the 'equality of glory and majesty with God as a prize to be held fast'. Compare the ambitions of "Lucifer, son of the morning" (Isa. 14.12). In the interests of men and women, The Lord Jesus was willing to relinquish what rightly belonged to Him. He did not, of course, resign His deity. He could not cease to be Himself! But He did resign, for a time, the majesty belonging to Him as "being in the form of God". He referred to that glory and majesty in praying "O Father, glorify thou me with thine own self with the glory which I had with thee before the world was" (John 17.5). The word "equal"" is actually plural. The Lord Jesus was, and is, '**on equalities** with God'. In every respect and in every detail, He is absolutely God.

ii) "Being found in fashion as a man", vv.7-8

In view of our Lord's eternal glory and deity, it is very wonderful that He "made himself of no reputation, and took upon him the form of a servant, and was made in the likeness of men". Had the Lord Jesus come in the full splendour of His glory and majesty, He could never have identified Himself with men and women. His glory would have isolated Him. The well-known Christmas carol puts it nicely:

> Mild, He lays His glory by,
>   Born that man no more may die;
>   Born to raise the sons of earth,
>   Born to give them second birth.

Chapter 2A

The words "made himself of no reputation""", are generally translated 'emptied himself' (see RV, JND, RSV). The verse has been used to suggest that the Lord Jesus 'emptied himself" of deity. This is called the 'kenosis' theory, from *kenoo*, meaning 'to empty'. Once again, the teaching of the section points to the correct meaning. It is introduced with the words, "Look not every man on his own things, but every man also on the things of others. Let this mind be in you, which was also in Christ Jesus". The Philippians were therefore urged, not to resign their identity, for that would be impossible, but to resign their own interests in order to promote the interests of others. The Lord Jesus is the supreme example. He 'emptied himself', not of His essential identity, for that was also impossible, but of all desire to use what was rightly His for His own advantage. He humbled Himself by coming **into** the world (v.7), and He humbled himself whilst **in** the world (v.8).

- **He humbled himself by coming into the world, v.7.** He "took upon him the form of a servant, and was made in the likeness of men". The very words, "took upon him the form of a servant", make it clear that He did not cease to be "in the form of God". In this He was so different to angels, and so different to ourselves. Angels were created to serve. "Are they not all ministering spirits, sent forth to minister for them who shall be heirs of salvation?" (Heb. 1.14). We were created, amongst other things, to serve. But the Lord Jesus "took upon him the form of a servant". W.E. Vine points out that the word "servant" *(doulos)* is significant. It is not the word for a slave *(diakonos)*. "Slave is not the proper term in regard to Christ. No man was ever Christ's master. He surrendered Himself entirely in submission to the will of His Father". This reminds us of the 'Servant' passages in Isaiah, the first of which commences, "Behold my servant, whom I uphold; mine elect, in whom my soul delighteth" (Isa 42.1). See also 50.10, 52.13, 53.11.

For the second time, we encounter the word *morphe.* The Lord Jesus "being in the **form** of God", took upon Himself "the **form** of a servant". It means exactly the same in both cases. Just as the Lord Jesus has all the characteristics and nature of God, so He has all the characteristics and nature of a servant. As servants, **we** are to "do all things without murmurings and disputings" (v.14). The perfect Servant is our example! He "came not to be ministered unto (to be served), but to minister (to serve), and to give his life a ransom for many" (Mark 10.45.) The Lord Jesus "made himself of no reputation" ('emptied himself', JND) by taking upon him "the form of a servant", and He took "the form of a servant" by being "made in the likeness of men". As "being in the form of God", He had the power and right to **command** the service of all. As taking upon him "the form of a servant""", He took the humble place of **dependance and obedience!**

The words, "was made ('becoming', RV) in the likeness (*homoioma*) of men", do not imply that He only **resembled** a man. He was, of course, a true man. See Romans 5.15; 1 Corinthians 15.21; 1 Timothy 2.5. We must contrast '***becoming** in the likeness of men*'', with "***being*** in the form of God". The words, "made in the likeness of men" remind us that He was not a **mere** man. We have already noticed that His presence here in "the form of a servant" did not mean that he ceased to be "in the form of God". He was, and is, "God...manifest in the flesh" (1 Tim. 3.16).

- **He humbled himself whilst in the world, v.8.** "And being found in fashion *(schema)* as a man, he humbled himself, and became obedient unto death, even the death of the cross". There is a great difference between "form" and "fashion". As we have seen, "form" means all that is essential and characteristic, and the Lord Jesus has the essential nature and characteristics of both God and a servant. "Fashion" refers to what is outward and perceptible: it describes His mode of appearance. He was essentially God *(morphe)*, but He made himself known in the mode and shape of a man *(schema)*.

But He humbled Himself even further: "and became obedient unto death, even the death of the cross". The Lord Jesus humbled Himself to **become** man, and He humbled himself **as** man. The words, "he humbled himself" stress that He did this voluntarily. The verb 'to humble' (*tapeinoo*, to make low) corresponds to the adjective *tapeinos*, low-lying. The Lord Jesus therefore perfectly exemplifies the "lowliness of mind" *(tapeinophrosune)* called for in v.3.

The Lord Jesus was never subject to death. His obedience to the will of God took Him "unto death, even the death of the cross" or "becoming obedient **even** unto death, yea, the death of the cross" (RV). "Obedient" is a servant word. Compare Romans 5.19, "So by the obedience of one shall many be made righteous". "The death of the cross" was "reserved for slaves and malefactors of the lowest type. It was a death on which the law of God pronounced a curse (Deut. 21.23), and which Gentile writers regard as the most foul and cruel of all punishments" (W.E. Vine). Notice that the New Testament refers to "the **preaching** of the cross" (1 Cor. 1.18); "the **offence** of the cross" (Gal. 5.11); "the **death** of the cross" (here); "the **enemies** of the cross" (Phil. 3.18); "the **blood** of his cross" (Col. 1.20).

Bearing in mind that the section commences with the words, "Let this mind be in you, which was also in Christ Jesus", we ought to pause and think about the implications for us in the passage. Notice, first of all, that Paul makes no mention of the sufferings of the Lord Jesus on account of our sin. The reason is not difficult to discover. Whilst we are called upon to emulate the Lord Jesus in humble sacrificial service, we cannot emulate His sufferings for sin. We should carefully consider the implications of the passage as follows:

- 'The mind of Christ' does not seek or maintain personal position and honour, but is willing to resign this in the interests of others: "Who being in the form of God, thought it not robbery to be equal with God, but made himself of no reputation" (vv.6-7).

- 'The mind of Christ' is to be intent on serving others: "and took upon him the form of a servant" (v.7).

- 'The mind of Christ' is willingness to be identified with the needs of others: "and was made in the likeness of men" (v.7).

- 'The mind of Christ' involves self-sacrifice for the sake of others: "and being found in fashion as a man, he humbled himself, and became obedient unto death, even the death of the cross" (v.8). Compare 1 John 3.16. "He took the lowest form of death so that no person, however low, would be outwith the reach of His service. By going to the cross, He met the crucified thief and responded to his call. He meets the needs of the lowest" (W. Sanderson, writing in the *Believer's Magazine*).

The application of these verses could be summed up in the Lord's words, "I have given you an example, that should ye do as I have done unto you" (John 13.15).

b) His honour, vv.9-11
These verses describe three aspects of his glory: *(i)* His exaltation (v.9); *(ii)* His authority (v.10); *(iii)* His acknowledgement (v.11). We must not forget that His deity was undiminished in His incarnation and that His humanity was undiminished in His exaltation.

i) His exaltation, v.10
The Lord Jesus "humbled himself", and "God also hath highly exalted him". He was "obedient unto death, even the death of the cross", and God has "given him a name ('**the** name', RV) which is above every name". The Lord Jesus could not possibly have come lower: now, He cannot possibly go higher. God has "set him at his own right hand in the heavenly places, far above all principality, and power, and might, and dominion, and every **name** that is named, not only in this

world, but also in that which is to come" (Eph. 1.20-21). So far as "this world" (age) is concerned, He will be "exalted and extolled, and be very high...so shall he sprinkle many nations; the kings shall shut their mouths at him" (Isa. 52.13-15).

We are not specifically told what name has been given to the Lord Jesus. It could be a hitherto undisclosed name. See Revelation 3.12; 19.12. It could be "Lord", and this is supported by the fact that "every tongue shall confess that Jesus Christ is **Lord**". However, Sydney Maxwell points out that "Lord" is a title, rather than a name. The name may well be "Jesus", for the following verse does say, "that at the name of **Jesus** every knee should bow". Paul himself, prostrate on the Damascus road, heard Him say, "I am **Jesus** whom thou persecutest" (Acts 9.5). It does seem appropriate that He should bear for ever, and in "the highest place that heaven affords", the very name given to Him on earth. After all, "Jesus" does mean 'Jehovah the Saviour'. God will "make him my firstborn, higher than the kings of the earth" (Psalm 89.27).

These are thrilling verses, but their context points to an important lesson. The Lord Jesus made no attempt to seek His own glory: He waited the Father's time. Compare Mark 9.9. Paul is still saying, "Let this mind be in you, which was also in Christ Jesus". We must make it our business, in humility and selflessness, to "look...on (to) the things of others". God will suitably acknowledge and reward those who put others first. The Lord Jesus taught this: "Whosoever will be great among you, shall be your minister: and whosoever of you will be the chiefest, shall be servant of all" (Mark 10.43-44). Peter puts it like this: "Yea, all of you be subject one to another, and be clothed with humility: for God resisteth the proud, and giveth grace to the humble. Humble yourselves therefore under the mighty hand of God, that he may exalt you in due time" (1 Pet. 5.5-6). The Lord Jesus is the perfect example of this teaching!

ii) His authority, v.10
"That at (or "in") the name of Jesus every knee shall bow, of things in heaven, and things in earth, and things under the earth". As W.E. Vine points out, it is "not 'at the name', as if suggesting 'at the mention of the name', but in acknowledgement of all that the name stands for and indicates". On earth, wicked men bowed in mockery; "And they smote him on the head with a reed, and did spit upon him, and **bowing** their knees worshipped him. And when they had mocked him, they took off the purple from him, and put his own clothes on him, and led him out to crucify him" (Mark 15.19-20). While the words "things in heaven, and things in earth, and things under the earth", mean creation in its totality, the expression "every **knee** shall bow" strongly suggests that this

refers to far more than inanimate creation. "Things in heaven", refers to the angelic beings: "things in earth", refers to men and women, and "things under the earth", refers to the demons. It is often pointed out that when Paul is writing about **reconciliation** (Col. 1.20), there is no reference to "under the earth". But here, he is writing about the **authority** of Christ.

Isaiah 45.23 is cited here: "I have sworn by myself, the word is gone out of my mouth in righteousness, and shall not return, That unto me every knee shall bow, every tongue shall swear". Paul also refers to this passage in Romans 14.11, "For it is written, As I live, saith the Lord, every knee shall bow to me, and every tongue shall confess to God".

iii) His acknowledgement, v.11
"And that every tongue should confess that Jesus Christ is Lord, to the glory of God the Father". On earth, men used their tongues to mock and blaspheme: "And they bowed the knee before him, and mocked him, saying, Hail, King of the Jews!" (Matt. 27.29). The religious leaders mocked Him with the words, "He trusted in God; let him deliver him now, if he will have him: for he said, I am the Son of God" (Matt. 27.43). But: *"Him hath God exalted with his right hand to be a Prince and a Saviour" (Acts 5.31).*

READ CHAPTER 2.12-18

"Work out your own salvation"

In previous studies, we suggested that Philippians 2 can be divided as follows: *(1)* the necessity for the mind of Christ (vv.1-4); *(2)* the expression of the mind of Christ (vv.5-11); *(3)* the emulation of the mind of Christ (vv.12-13); *(4)* the effect of the mind of Christ (vv.14-16); *(5)* the examples of the mind of Christ (vv.17-30). We have already noticed that the connection between the first two sections of the chapter lies in v.5, "Let this mind be in you, which was also in Christ Jesus". The Lord Jesus did nothing "through strife or vainglory". He displayed "lowliness of mind". He looked "not on his own things, but...on the things of others". The Lord Jesus was willing, in our interests, to take "upon him the form of a servant", without ceasing to be "in the form of God". He has 'left us an example, that we should follow his steps' (see 1 Pet. 2.21).

The connection between the second and third sections lies in v.12, "Wherefore, my beloved...work out your own salvation with fear and trembling". Preachers often quote the old adage: 'When you meet a **"therefore**" in the Bible, it is always important to find out what it is **there for!**' The same can be said for the 'wherefores' of the Bible! Quite obviously, Paul now expected action. The Philippians were to put the lesson into practice. They were to follow the example of the Lord Jesus. This brings us to

3) THE EMULATION OF THE MIND OF CHRST, vv.12-13
There are at least four important things to notice here: *(a)* the atmosphere; *(b)* the attitude; *(c)* the application; *(d)* the ability.

a) The atmosphere
"Wherefore, my **beloved...**" All Bible teaching, even corrective teaching, should flow from love for God's people. We must notice how Paul creates the right atmosphere for his teaching here. It is even more marked in 4.1-2, "Therefore, my brethren **dearly beloved** and longed for, my joy and crown, so stand fast in the Lord, my **dearly beloved.** I beseech Euodias, and beseech Syntyche, that

they be of the same mind in the Lord". Euodias and Syntyche had no ground for complaint when they heard their names read out! Paul had just said how much he loved them all. "Speaking the truth in love" (Eph. 4.15) is so important. Paul was obliged to say some very stern things in his first letter to the assembly at Corinth, but the very parchment on which he wrote was stained with his tears. We learn this from his second letter: "For out of much affliction and anguish of heart I wrote unto you with many tears; not that ye should be grieved, but that ye might know the love which I have more abundantly unto you" (2 Cor. 2.4).

b) The attitude
"As ye have always obeyed, not as in my presence only, but now much more in my absence..." Obedience is the key to progress and fruitfulness in the Christian life. Our Christian life began with the "obedience of faith" (Rom. 16.26). Like the believers at Rome, we were once "the servants of sin", but we "obeyed from the heart that form of doctrine which was delivered you" (Rom. 6.17). The Christian life **begins** with obedience, and it **continues** in exactly the same way. We are to be "obedient children, not fashioning yourselves according to the former lusts in your ignorance" (1 Pet. 1.14). There is no mystery about spiritual progress. It involves applying the word of God to our lives. Samuel reminded Saul that "to obey is better than sacrifice, and to hearken than the fat of rams" (1 Sam. 15.22). The hymn is so right:

> Trust and obey!
> For there's no other way
> To be happy in Jesus -
> But to trust and obey.

Obedience should not depend on who happens to be around at the time! We should obey God's word whether or not there is anyone present to supervise us. Remember what happened when Nehemiah was absent from Jerusalem. See Nehemiah 13.6. Remember what happened when Moses was absent from the camp. See Exodus 32.1-7. Mephibosheth was loyal to David, whether present or absent. See 2 Samuel 19.24. Whether he was present or absent, Paul expected the Philippians to obey his teaching. It carried divine authority. Compare 1 Corinthians 14.37.

c) The application
"Work out your own salvation with fear and trembling". This is the third reference to "salvation" in the epistle (see 1.19, 28). The context is quite different in each case. Quite clearly, the exhortation, "wherefore...work out your own salvation",

is related to Paul's description of the humility of the Lord Jesus, and that, in turn, relates to the problem at Philippi, where there was a lack of "one accord, of one mind". To "work out your own salvation" therefore refers to deliverance from the lack of unity at Philippi. This is supported by the words "work out your **own** salvation". It was something peculiar to Philippi. The problem could only be tackled effectively, when each believer had 'the mind of Christ', and looked "not on his own things, but......on the things of others". Sydney Maxwell puts it as follows: "The apostle is rather saying here, I am aware of your internal problems and I have given you an example to follow (2.5-7): now work out your salvation as an assembly".

This involves effort. The word rendered "work out" (*katergazomai*) is a strengthened form of *ergazomai*, to work, and means 'to effect by diligent labour' (W.E. Vine). Disunity must be tackled diligently. It is a serious defect, and will prove disastrous unless quickly rectified. The words, "fear and trembling" (see also 2 Cor. 7.15; Eph. 6.5, where they are also associated with obedience), describe "watchfulness against grieving God, an eagerness to avoid displeasing Him, and a reverent consciousness of His presence" (W.E. Vine). This speaks for itself, and emphasises the seriousness with which God regards disunity amongst His people. We should notice that "fear and trembling" are the very opposite to "strife or vainglory" (v.3). The former will counteract the latter.

d) The ability
"For it is **God** which **worketh** (*energeo*) in you both to will and to do of his good pleasure". So we are not left to tackle the problem of disunity as best we can. We should note that the very **will** to deal with the problem as well as the actual **work** involved, is divine. "It is God who works in you both the willing and the working, according to his good pleasure" (JND). We must remember that God is intent on finding pleasure in His people, and works in them to that end. It will spoil His pleasure in His people if their fellowship is disrupted. Once we were subject to "the **prince of the power of the air,** the spirit that now **worketh** (*energeo*) in the children of disobedience" (Eph. 2.2). What a wonderful change! The following verses describe the results when the 'mind of Christ' is emulated by His people.

4) THE EFFECT OF THE MIND OF CHRIST, vv.14-16
The effect is threefold: *(a)* on our fellowship (v.14); *(b)* on our testimony (vv.15-16a); *(c)* on our reward (v.16b).

a) The effect on our fellowship, v.14
"Do all things without murmurings and disputings". That is murmurings amongst and

against each other. Notice, "do *all* things", not 'some things!' The word "***murmurings***" translates *gongusmos* which, according to W.E. Vine, is an onomatopoeic word. (How well do you remember your 'figures of speech?' Onomatopoeia is one of them. We have a very good example in Proverbs 16.28. Think about it!). The same word occurs in John 7.12, where you can almost see little groups of people muttering to each other, and in Acts 6.1 where it refers to a complaint. (Notice how the apostles dealt with the problem: they handled it compassionately and with prayer). See also John 6.41, 43, 61. The children of Israel were given to murmuring in the wilderness. See 1 Corinthians 10.10. They "murmured against Moses and Aaron in the wilderness", but as Moses pointed out to them, "the Lord heareth your murmurings which ye murmur against him: and what are we? Your murmurings are not against us, but against the Lord" (Exod. 16.2, 8). The word is translated "grudging" in 1 Peter 4.9.

Well, we are *not* to murmur. Don't mutter and complain about things: **pray** about them! That's how we "work out our own salvation" when difficulties and dissension occur. Paul was an excellent example of his own ministry here. See Philippians 4.11, "I have learned, in whatsoever state I am, therewith to be content". No "murmurings" here!

The word rendered "***disputings***" (*dialogismos*) is rendered "thoughts" in Matthew 15.19 ("evil thoughts") and Luke 24.38 ("why do thoughts arise in your hearts": inward questioning). It also occurs in 1 Timothy 2.8 ("doubting" or "disputings", RV) and Romans 14.1 ("disputations"). The verb occurs in Mark 9.33-34. "What was it that ye disputed among yourselves by the way…they had disputed among themselves, who should be the greatest." So the word sometimes means inward questioning, and sometimes dispute. The context decides in each case. Here, it evidently refers to disputes amongst God's people. ""Murmurings" lead to "disputings". Avoid both!

b) The effect on our testimony, vv.15-16a
"*That* ye may be blameless and harmless, the sons of God, without rebuke, in the midst of a crooked and perverse nation, among whom ye shine as lights in the world; holding forth the word of life". Things must be right amongst us, otherwise our testimony will suffer. W. Sanderson calls it "a well-ordered and well-knit family of God, in the midst of the twisted and disordered world that lies around". We should notice:

i) Our testimony negatively.
What should *not* be seen in us. The word "***blameless***" (*amemptos*) is related to *memphomai*, to find fault. It is rendered "faultless" in Hebrews 8.7; Jude 24, and "without fault" in Revelation 14.5. See

also Philippians 3.6, "touching the righteousness which is in the law, blameless"; Luke 1.6 (of Zacharias and Elisabeth), "walking in all the commandments and ordinances of the Lord blameless". The word "*harmless*" *(akeraios)* means, literally, unmixed: no foreign mixture. It was used of wine unmixed with water, and of unalloyed metal. It could be therefore rendered, 'guileless' or 'sincere'. It is not the same word used in 1.10 (*eilikrines*). It is used in Matthew 10.16 ("*harmless* as doves"); Romans 16.19 ("*simple* concerning evil"). So, to sum it up, the "crooked and perverse" world in which we live should see people whose lives cannot be faulted ("blameless", and who are thoroughly genuine ("harmless"). They have no secret agendas and no double standards.

ii) ***Our testimony representatively.*** "Blameless and harmless, the **sons (children) of God**, without rebuke". As "children *(teknon)* of God", we display family likeness. The word here 'points to birth', and 'to the likeness of the begetter' (W.E. Vine) The Lord Jesus said to His disciples, "Love your enemies... that ye may be the children (*huios,* sons) of your Father which is in heaven: for he maketh his sun to rise on the evil and on the good, and sendeth rain on the just and on the unjust...be ye therefore perfect, even as your Father which is in heaven is perfect" (Matt. 5.44-48). See also Matthew 5.9, "Blessed are the peacemakers: for they shall be called the children (sons) of God". How well do *we* represent Him, and reflect His character? If there is real family likeness, we will be "without rebuke" ("irreproachable", JND). The RV has "without blemish" (*amomos* rather than *amometos*).

iii) ***Our testimony distinctively.*** "In the midst of a crooked and perverse nation ('generation', JND)". Paul is referring here to Deuteronomy 32.5: "They have dealt corruptly with him, they are not his children, it is their blemish; they are a perverse and crooked generation" (RV). It is a vivid contrast: "Blameless... harmless...sons of God...without rebuke" in a "crooked and perverse" world. What a dark background! "***Crooked***" means exactly what is says: not straight! See Luke 3.5, "the crooked shall be made straight". It is rendered "froward" in 1 Peter 2.18 ("Servants, be subject to your masters with all fear; not only to the good and gentle, but also to the ***froward***"). Not easy! But we do live in a "crooked" world, don't we? Just think about politics, business, and sport for a start. "***Perverse***" means distorted or twisted: hence turned aside or corrupted. The Lord Jesus was accused of this: "We found this fellow perverting the nation" (Luke 23.2). Elymas was guilty in this way (see Acts 13.10).

People who are "crooked" and "perverse" will inevitably be blameworthy and harmful. But the children of God must be "blameless and harmless".

Chapter 2B

iv) Our testimony positively. "Among whom ye shine as lights in the world (or 'among whom ye are seen as lights in the world', RV); holding forth the word of life". The preceding teaching forms the platform on which we stand to 'hold forth the word of life'. We are to "shine as lights in the world". This refers to our **character.** We are to 'hold forth the word of life': this refers to our **message.** The word "lights" *(phoster)* occurs again in Revelation 21.11, where the "holy city" is described as "having the glory of God: and her **light** was like unto a stone most precious, even like a jasper stone, clear as crystal". Our business in this world is to 'hold forth the word of life'. "The word of life" is, of course, the gospel. You will have no difficulty in supplying the supporting scriptures!

But the light will not shine clearly, and the "word of life" will make little impact, if we are given to "murmurings and disputings", and thus fail to be "blameless and harmless, the sons of God without rebuke".

c) The effect on our reward, v.16b
"That I may rejoice in the day of Christ, that I have not run in vain, neither laboured in vain". Paul is now looking forward to the "judgment seat of Christ". We discussed "the day of Christ" in connection with its occurrence in 1.6. (You will remember the four 'days' in the New Testament: if not, refresh your memory: see Study 3. While Paul is anticipating his personal joy over the faithfulness of the Philippians (see also 1 Thess. 2.19-20), we should ask ourselves whether or not **we** can anticipate the "day of Christ" with joy on account of **our** faithfulness. The word "vain" *(kenos)*, meaning 'empty', has "special reference to quality" (W.E. Vine). Paul looked for quality in the results of his running and his labouring. The first ("run in vain") refers to his personal qualities. Compare 2 Timothy 4.7. Are **we** running "with patience the race that is set before us?" The second ("laboured in vain") refers to his labours. These involved 'laborious toil'. The word is used of the fishermen who "toiled all night" (Luke 5.5). Paul is not saying that his reward depended on the faithfulness of the Philippians, but that he wanted to anticipate the day of reward with joy because they had acquitted themselves well in God's service.

But none of this will ever be accomplished unless we have 'the mind of Christ'. Paul now gives three examples of 'the mind of Christ' in action.

5) THE EXAMPLES OF THE MIND OF CHRIST, vv.17-24
The three examples are ***(a)*** Paul himself (vv.17-18); ***(b)*** Timothy (vv.19-24); ***(c)*** Epaphroditus (vv.25-30). We will consider the example of Paul, and leave Timothy and Epaphroditus for consideration in our next study.

a) Paul, vv.17-18

"Yea, and if I be offered upon the sacrifice and service of your faith, I joy, and rejoice with you all. For the same cause also do ye joy, and rejoice with me". Having mentioned his rejoicing at the judgment seat of Christ ("the day of Christ"), Paul now thinks of his own death in the same way. He uses remarkable language. Not 'yea, and when', but "yea, and **if**". Compare 2 Corinthians 5.1, "For we know that **if** (not 'when') our earthly house of this tabernacle were dissolved, we have a building of God, an house not made with hands, eternal in the heavens". Paul did not regard death as certain, and death for **us** is by no means certain either! The Lord is coming back! "Yea, and if I be **offered** upon the sacrifice and service of your faith". The word "offered" *(spendo)* means 'poured out', and refers to the Old Testament drink offering. Paul uses the term again in 2 Timothy 4.6, "For I am now ready to be offered" or, according to the RV, "For I am already being offered (margin, poured out as a drink offering)". In the Old Testament, wine is a picture of joy (see Psalm 104.15). Hence the four references to joy in these two verses. So Paul anticipated his death, should it occur, with joy. Only Christians can do that!

But the way in which the drink offering was used is most significant. It was offered in connection with the daily burnt offerings (Exod. 29.40-41), and in connection with the burnt offerings made at the feast of Pentecost (Lev. 23.18). The burnt offerings were major offerings, and remind us of the complete devotion of the Lord Jesus to God. The entire animal was burnt on the altar as "a sweet savour unto the Lord" (Lev. 1.17). The associated drink offering was a subsidiary offering, and reminds us of the joy of the Lord Jesus in doing His Father's will. When Paul thinks about the possibility of his death, he calls it a drink offering ('if I be poured out') which would be offered "upon the sacrifice and service of your faith". In other words, Paul rejoiced so much in the gift which had been sent to him by Epaphroditus, that he regarded his death as a subsidiary offering, when compared with the major offering of the Philippians! He says in effect, 'Yours is the greater sacrifice, in the same way that the lesser sacrifice was poured out on the greater!' Paul was not "looking on his own things", but "on the things of others". He had the 'mind of Christ'.

He uses beautiful language in describing the gift sent to him. He calls it "the sacrifice and service (it occurs again in v.30) of your faith". He looks at the gift from God's point of view. The word "service" *(leitourgia)* often refers to priestly service. (Not always: see, for example, Romans 13.6). It occurs in Hebrews 8.6, "But now hath he obtained a more excellent **ministry**"; Hebrews 9.21, "Moreover he sprinkled with blood both the tabernacle, and all the vessels of the **ministry**".

Paul is saying, 'Here is your sacrifice; it is just like the burnt offering, sweet to God, and if my death should occur, I will die with joy in view of all that you have done for me.'. He adds, in effect, 'I desire you to look at it in exactly the same way' (v.18). "Not Paul without them, nor they without Paul, but together forming one grand sacrificial service to God" (W. Sanderson).

Even in the shadow of death, when he might have been thinking about himself, Paul thought of others. The man who said, "Let this mind be in you, which was also in Christ Jesus", lived in the good of his own ministry! He was 'a doer of the word' (James 1.22).

READ CHAPTER 2.19-30

"I have no man likeminded"

These verses form part of the final paragraph in Philippians 2. For the record, here are the five sections again: *(1)* the necessity for the mind of Christ (vv.1-4); *(2)* the expression of the mind of Christ (vv.5-11); *(3)* the emulation of the mind of Christ (vv.12-13); *(4)* the effect of the mind of Christ (vv.14-16); *(5)* the examples of the mind of Christ (vv.17-30). We must now complete our consideration of the last paragraph:

5) THE EXAMPLES OF THE MIND OF CHRIST, vv.17-24
We have already noticed that Paul gives us three examples of 'the mind of Christ' in action: *(a)* Paul himself (vv.17-18); *(b)* Timothy (vv.19-24); *(c)* Epaphroditus (vv.25-30).

But is it really possible for us to have the 'mind of Christ?' After all, Paul does say elsewhere, "O the depth of the riches both of the wisdom and knowledge of God! How unsearchable are his judgments, and his ways past finding out! For who hath known **the mind of the Lord?** or who hath been his counsellor?" (Rom. 11.33-34). This doxology completes the section in the epistle which sets out God's plan for the blessing of Jew and Gentile. Paul is overcome with wonder! No human mind could have ever conceived such a plan! We can certainly never have a mind like that! But, yes, we **can** have the 'mind of Christ' **towards others.** Hence we read, "Let this mind be **in you**, which was also in Christ Jesus". We can have 'the mind of Christ' in other ways too. See, for example, 1 Corinthians 2.16, "For who hath known the mind of the Lord, that he may instruct him? But we **have** the mind of Christ". A glance at the context will show that Paul is referring here to his **preaching.** What he preached was "the mind of Christ". While we cannot possess the "mind of Christ" in its entirety, it is very wonderful that our minds can be conformed to His mind in so many ways. Now let's look at the three examples:

a) Paul, vv.17-18
"Yea, and if I be offered upon the sacrifice and service of your faith, I joy, and

rejoice with you all. For the same cause also do ye joy, and rejoice with me". We have already thought about these verses. Their gift was more important than his death! He did not look "on his own things", but "on the things of others". He had the 'mind of Christ'. But someone might have said (pure speculation here!), 'but that was the apostle Paul: we could never be like him!' Well, the next man was younger and less experienced, but he **too** exhibited 'the mind of Christ'.

b) Timothy, vv.19-24
Timothy stood out 'like a sore thumb!'. While "all seek their own, not the things which are Jesus Christ's", Timothy would "naturally care for your state". So he, too, looked "not...on his own things, but...on the things of others" (2.4). Timothy 'bucked the trend': everybody else 'looked on **their own** things', and '**not** on the things of others'. So 'the mind of Christ' is not the prerogative of older and experienced people! Now let's have a look at the details.

i) The coming of Timothy, v.19
"But I trust (hope) in the Lord Jesus to send Timotheus shortly unto you, that I also may be of good comfort, when I know your state". It has been pointed out that whilst the expression "in Christ" refers to our heavenly relationship with Him, the words "in the Lord Jesus", or "in the Lord", refer to earthly relationships and circumstances. Notice the expressions, "rejoice in the Lord" (3.1); "stand fast in the Lord" (4.1); "rejoice in the Lord alway" (4.4). We should notice Paul's confidence in the Lord, and Paul's concern for their welfare:

- **Paul's confidence in the Lord.** The words, "I trust in the Lord Jesus", show that Paul subjected everything to His will. Compare Romans 1.10, "Making request, if by any means now at length I might have a prosperous journey by the **will of God** to come unto you". See also James 4.15, "For that ye ought to say, **If the Lord will,** we shall live, and do this, or that".

- **Paul's concern for their welfare.** We catch a glimpse, more than a glimpse, of Paul's shepherd heart: "that I also may be **of good comfort, when I know your state**". The little word "also" indicates that whilst Timothy's visit would be a comfort to them, it would bring comfort to Paul as well. The words "good comfort" *(eupsucheo)* mean, literally, "to be well of soul, hence, to be of good cheer" (W.E. Vine). He wrote in similar terms to the assembly at Thessalonica: "Therefore, brethren, we were comforted over you in all our affliction and distress by your faith: For now **we live, if ye stand fast in the Lord**" (1 Thess. 3.7-8). Paul was deeply concerned about the welfare of his spiritual children. How deep is **our** concern for each other?

ii) The care of Timothy, vv.20-21

We should notice that Timothy cared for them (v.20), and that others cared for themselves (v.21):

- **Timothy cared for them.** "For I have no man likeminded, who will naturally care for your state. For all seek their own, not the things which are Jesus Christ's". Timothy was "likeminded" with Paul. "He was of one mind with Paul, in genuine sympathy with the saints at Philippi to whom the apostle was writing." (Sidney Maxwell). The word "likeminded" translates *isopsuchos*, literally, 'of equal soul'. (The word 'soul', and associated words, keep cropping up in the epistle. See our note on 1.27; 2.2; 2.19. The word "naturally" means 'truly', 'sincerely', or 'genuinely'. The words "will...care" *(merimnao)* carry the meaning of 'anxious care'. See Luke 10.41, "thou (Martha) art careful and troubled about many things". See also 1 Corinthans 7.32-34; 12.25. The word is also used in Philippians 4: 6. W.E. Vine puts it like this, "Timothy would give his undistracted attention to this matter, in real anxiety for the welfare of the saints". We must ask the question again: how deep is *our* concern for each other? Paul uses the analogy of the human body to illustrate the need for mutual care: "God hath tempered the body together, having given more abundant honour to that part which lacked: that there should be no schism in the body, but that the members should have the **same care** *(merimnao)* one for another" (1 Cor. 12.24-25).

It is the responsibility of the elders to care for the assembly. See 1 Timothy 3.5, "For if a man know not how to rule his own house, how shall he **take care** of the church of God?" Paul uses a different word here (not *merimnao* as above, but *epimeleomai,* signifying "to take care of, involving forethought and provision", W.E. Vine). It occurs in Luke 10.34-35, which illustrate the work perfectly.

- **Others cared for themselves.** "For all seek their own, not the things which are Jesus Christ's". A parallel has been drawn between this verse and Judges 5.17, "Gilead abode beyond Jordan: and why did Dan remain in ships? Asher continued on the sea shore, and abode in his breaches". These tribes certainly 'sought their own', instead of contributing to the battle against Sisera. Do **we** put our own interests first? Do we pay lip-service only to the Lordship of Christ?

iii) The commendation of Timothy, v.22

"But ye know *(ginosko:* knowledge gained by observation) the proof of him, that, as a son with the father, he hath served with me (not 'served me', but 'served with me') in the gospel". (Proverbs 10.1 tells us that "a wise son maketh a glad father"). This is a delightful verse, especially after the last one! We would all be glad of a letter of commendation like this! In the first case, the Philippians knew all about his consistency. "But **ye** know the proof of him". The word "proof" *(dokime)* means here the result of proving. He had served with Paul, and was a man of proven fitness. How are **we** progressing? Could it be said of **us**, "ye know the proof of him (or her)?" Or do others have to shake their heads in despair over us. What kind of spiritual 'track record' do **we** have?

Paul indicates two ways in which Timothy had proved himself: in his relationship with Paul, and in his relationship with his work.

- *In his relationship with Paul.* "As a son (child) with the father". Sydney Maxwell puts it nicely: "While he was Paul's fellow-worker, yet there was that filial regard for Paul by this younger man". It reminds us of the relationship between Moses and Joshua. It is very important for the various age groups to work together. On the one hand, younger people need the help and advice that can only be given by people with experience. On the other hand, older people need to be refreshed and encouraged by the energy and enthusiasm of younger people. The words, "as a child *(teknon)* with the father" also underline "the due regard for the older by the younger" (Sydney Maxwell). There is a general lack of respect in the world today, and, sadly, it often 'rubs off' on Christians.

- *In his relationship with his work.* "He hath **served** with me in the gospel" or "in furtherance of the gospel" (RV). The word "served" *(douluo)* describes the service of a bondslave. The grammar ('he did service') suggests that Paul is referring to the whole of his service at Philippi. As we have already noted, the Philippians were thoroughly aware of all this. Timothy's 'bondservice' indicates the diligent and unremitting way in which he had been engaged in the 'furtherance of the Gospe'. Could something similar be said about **us?**

iv) The confidence of Paul, vv.23-24
"Him therefore I hope to send presently (immediately), so soon as I shall see how it will go with me. But I trust in the Lord (compare v.19) that I also myself shall come shortly". While Paul did not know how long it would be before he was able to visit Philippi, he did expect to come eventually. See 1.25. He was obliged to leave the timing with the Lord. See our comments on v.19. But another man was about to leave for Philippi:

c) Epaphroditus, vv.25-30
Let's speculate again! But someone might have said, 'but that was Timothy, a friend of the apostle Paul: we could never be like him, let alone like Paul'. Well,

this man was a local brother. See 4.18. He wasn't 'a big name'. This epistle tells us all we know about him. As we shall see, he **too** had 'the mind of Christ'. So 'the mind of Christ' is not the prerogative of well-known leaders and preachers!

i) The character of Epaphroditus, v.25
"Yet I supposed it necessary (thought it necessary) to send to you Epaphroditus, my brother, and companion in labour, and fellowsoldier, but your messenger, and he that ministered to my wants". He must have been a charming man. According to J.H. Thayer, that is what his name means! It is possible that he was named after Aphrodite, the goddess of love and beauty. He had certainly become "a beloved brother in Christ". Now let's look at the Bible definition of a charming man. Epaphroditus was:

- **A "brother".** Paul calls him "*my* brother". There is something rather tender about this expression. "Brother" signifies a family relationship, but "my brother" goes a little further. "A brother is born for adversity" (Prov. 17.17), and Epaphroditus was certainly visiting brothers (and sisters) in adversity! Are **we** displaying the features of a brother or sister in Christ? You won't be a 'charming' Christian unless you do! It is so important to remember that we are "members one of another". The features of this relationship are now spelt out in detail. Epaphroditus was:

- **A "companion in labour".** He was Paul's fellow-worker *(sunergos)*. He calls Priscilla and Aquila (wife placed first here!) "my helpers (*sunergos* again) in Christ Jesus" (Rom. 16.3). We do not have precise details of the way in which the two men worked together, but the fact that they were 'fellow-workers' raises, again, the question of our "fellowship in the gospel" (1.5). Are we really committed to working together? Your personal charm will be superficial without real commitment to the service of Christ.

- **A "fellowsoldier".** Epaphroditus knew that the Christian life was a battleground rather than a playground. We must never forget that we face deadly enemies, who are intent on resisting and overcoming our testimony. Paul talks about them in Ephesians 6.12. We are 'soldiers on active service'. See 2 Tim. 2.3-4, "No man that warreth (on active service) entangleth himself with the affairs of this life; that he may please him who hath chosen him to be a soldier". Notice that Paul does **not** say here 'engageth himself', but 'entangleth himself'. Archippus was another "fellowsoldier" (Philemon v.2). Working together involves fighting side by side against a common enemy. He wants to destroy you, and your assembly.

- ***A "messenger".*** In fact, "***your*** messenger", which actually means 'your apostle'. The word *apostolos* is used here in its literal sense, rather than in its technical sense. Compare 2 Corinthians 8.23, where the word "messengers" also translates *apostolos*. Here is another feature of a charming Christian. He or she is willing to undertake service on behalf of the assembly. Epaphroditus was willing to convey the assembly gift from Philippi to Rome.

- ***A 'minister' to the needs of others.*** Yes, it is 'needs' (see RV) as opposed to "wants"!' We all have our "wants", but 'needs' *(chreia)* are rather different! We have encountered the word "minister" (*leitourgos*) before. See v.17, "Yea, and if I be offered upon the sacrifice and **service** of your faith, I joy, and rejoice with you all". See our comments. In the Greek world, the word signified public service (it is used in that sense in Romans 13.6), but the New Testament uses it particularly in connection with priestly work. See, for example, Acts 13.2; Romans 15.16. So 'ministering to the needs of others' is priestly work. We do 'as unto the Lord'. Just think about that when you next visit a sick brother or sister! Be charming! Be an Epaphroditus!

ii) The concern of Epaphroditus, vv.26-27
"For he longed after you all, and was full of heaviness, because that ye had heard that he had been sick. For indeed he was sick nigh unto death: but God had mercy on him; and not on him only, but on me also, lest I should have sorrow upon sorrow". Epaphroditus had been gravely ill (we would say, 'at death's door'), but rather than wallowing in self-pity, he was deeply concerned that his illness had caused distress at Philippi! He was "full of heaviness" (*ademoneo: to* be in distress; not knowing what to do to gain relief), not because he had been sick, but because they "**had heard** that he had been sick". He was more concerned about them, than he was about himself. In other words, Epaphroditus looked "not on his own things, but...on the things of others". Another example of 'the mind of Christ!' We should notice two further lessons here:

- The case of Epaphroditus refutes the "health and wealth gospel" preached by some today. The idea that all Christians should be bursting with good health, and that anything different only proves spiritual weakness in some way or the other, is not supported by the New Testament. See also 1 Timothy 5.23; 2 Timothy 4.20.

- The case of Epaphoditus brings to light Paul's own distress. W.E. Vine puts it as follows: "The apostle had many sorrows connected with his captivity and his physical infirmity, and bereavement would have meant still more". Although Paul rejoiced in prison, imprisonment was not a joyful experience. We must never think that great men of God were made of cast iron, and completely impervious to the trials of life. When Paul visited Corinth, he was "in weakness, and in fear, and in much trembling" (1 Cor. 2.3).

iii) The consideration of Paul, v.28
"I sent him therefore the more carefully, that, when ye see him again, ye may rejoice, and that I may be the less sorrowful". The word "carefully" *(spoudaioteros)* means 'with 'increased eagerness'. Isn't this just another example of 'the mind of Christ?' Instead of retaining the services of Epaphroditus, Paul was willing to sacrifice his own interests in order that sorrow might turn to joy at Philippi when Epaphroditus got home! Paul was looking "not on his own things, but...on the things of others". As a 'spin off' from this, Paul himself would be "less sorrowful" through knowing that the Philippians were rejoicing. We should notice that Paul does not imply that all his problems would be solved by his unselfishness in sending back Epaphroditus. He would simply be "less sorrowful".

iv) The commendation of Epaphroditus, vv.29-30
"Receive him therefore in the Lord with all gladness; and hold such in reputation (honour): because for the work of Christ he was nigh unto death, not regarding his life, to supply your lack of service toward me". This sheds a little more light on the illness of Epaphroditus. It was the direct result of "the work of Christ". He obviously 'pushed himself to the limit', disregarding his own health. The words, "not regarding his life", translate a word *(paraboleuomai)* meaning 'to throw aside'. He 'hazarded' his life. (A different word is used in Acts 15.26). Epaphroditus was to be honoured on account of his willingness to hazard his life for others. Doesn't that remind you of v.8? How far are **we** prepared to go in the service of Christ? For Epaphroditus, "the service of Christ" at that time was "to supply your lack of service (*leitourgia* again) toward me". This wasn't a criticism! It wasn't a lack of interest on the part of the Philippians, but a lack of opportunity. See 4.10. Compare 1 Cor. 16.17.

Sydney Maxwell sums up these verses nicely: "In concluding this chapter, these three men, Paul, Timothy and Ephaphroditus exemplify the spirit of the Lord Jesus in sacrifice, shepherding and suffering. They had imbibed something of the mind of Christ (2.5)".

READ CHAPTER 3.1-9

Paul's Profit and Loss Account

In business, the initials CA, stand for Chartered Accountant. Well, in this chapter they stand for 'Christian Accountancy!' Paul writes up his profit and loss account as follows: "But what things were gain to me, those I counted loss for Christ. Yea doubtless, and I count all things but loss for the excellency of the knowledge of Christ Jesus my Lord: for whom I have suffered the loss of all things, and do count them but dung, that I may win Christ (JND, 'that I may gain Christ' or 'have Christ for my gain')" (v.8). The man who had been the champion of Judaism, had become the champion of the gospel of Christ.

The chapter may be divided into three sections, each of which describes Paul's gain, and shows us why we should "rejoice in the Lord" (v.1). *(1)* He had gained a new position (vv.1-9). It can be summed up as, "*found* in Him" (v.9). *(2)* He had gained a new purpose (vv.10-16). It can be summed up as "*fellowship*" with Him (v.10). *(3)* He had gained a new prospect (vv.17-21). It can be summed up as "*fashioned* like" Him (v.21). The first emphasises the *past* ("what things were gain to me, those I counted loss for Christ"), the second emphasises the *present* ("that I may know him, and the power of his resurrection"), and the third emphasises the *future* ("we look for the Saviour, the Lord Jesus Christ"). It is a marvellous chapter! Notice that it commences with a warning against false teachers (v.2), and it concludes with an exhortation from a true teacher (v.17).

1) PAUL'S NEW POSITION, vv.1-9

Like a master jeweller, Paul sets some bright gems against a dark background. We may look at it like this: *(a)* Paul's warning against error (vv.1-3): "Beware of dogs, beware of evil workers, beware of the concision"; *(b)* Paul's confidence in the flesh (vv.4-6): "If any man thinketh that he hath whereof he might trust in the flesh, I more"; *(c)* Paul's righteousness through faith (vv.7-9): "Not having mine own righteousness, which is of the law, but that which is through the faith of Christ, the righteousness which is of God by faith".

Chapter 3A

a) His warning against error, vv.1-3
Danger loomed! Paul says "beware" three times. He introduces the subject in v.1. This isn't the last time that Paul says, "finally!" (see 4.8). The scholars tell us that it simply means 'as to the rest', and indicates a change in subject matter. We should notice the following ***(i)*** meeting the danger (v.1); ***(ii)*** identifying the danger (v.2); ***(iii)*** overcoming the danger (v.3).

i) Meeting the danger, v.1
"Finally, my brethren, rejoice in the Lord. To write the same things to you, to me indeed is not grievous, but for you it is safe". (Compare 2.12, where Paul uses the word "beloved". Here he addresses them as "brethren", emphasising the single family). Paul meets the danger in two ways:

- **He tells them what they were to do.** They were to "rejoice in the Lord" (Paul once rejoiced in himself: see vv.4-6). This seems a strange thing to do when danger threatens! But the reason becomes clear as we follow the passage. We owe everything to Him! Read vv.7-9 again. Our greatest weapon against false teaching is to rejoice in the truth. Moss will not be able to invade a lawn when the grass is growing well! Our enjoyment of Christ is our greatest defence against error. Recognition of His Lordship will always bring joy!

- **He tells them what he is going to do.** He is going to write to them about it. "To write the same things to you, to me indeed is not grievous, but for you it is safe". The words, "the same things", evidently refer to what he is going to write, rather than to what he has written. So far as **Paul** was concerned, it was not "grievous" (from *okneo,* to shrink) for him to write in this way. The RV has 'irksome', and it has been rendered, 'it is not troublesome to me'. Paul was not afraid to address the problem. He 'grasped the nettle'. All too frequently, things go wrong, and good men stay silent. Not Paul! So far as the **Philippians** were concerned, it was "safe" *(asphales).* It is sometimes rendered "certainty" (see, for example, Acts 21.34): it occurs as "sure" in Hebrews 6.19. Paul saw the danger coming, and warned the Philippians about it. Compare John 16.1-4 and 1 Thessalonians 3.4. This is very important. 'To be forewarned is to be forearmed'. The Old Testament prophets were to warn God's people of coming danger. See, for example, Ezekiel 3.16-21; 33.1-9.

ii) Identifying the danger, v.2
"Beware of dogs, beware of evil workers, beware of the concision". The word "concision" identifies the false teachers, and this is confirmed by the following verses. Paul is referring to the Jewish teachers (the Judaisers) who did their

level best to turn Gentile Christians into good Jews. There were no doctrinal disorders at Philippi, but false teaching was never far away in apostolic times. It is never far away today! The Jewish teachers led the attack on the gospel, and Paul was constantly obliged to withstand them. See, for example, Acts 15.1-5; Galatians 2.1-5; 1 Timothy 1.3-11. The gospel message proclaims that "by grace are ye saved through faith; and that not of yourselves: it is the gift of God: not of works, lest any man should boast" (Eph 2.8-9). The Jewish teachers said that salvation was through faith *plus* works, and in particular, circumcision. In other words, the work of Christ was not sufficient in itself for the forgiveness of sins. We mustn't think that this was confined to Bible times: untold numbers of people are taught exactly the same today. Just think about Roman Catholicism, but many Protestants also believe that heaven is attained by faith *plus* good works. Notice how Paul describes these false teachers:

- *"Beware of dogs"*. The word "beware", sometimes rendered "behold", carries the idea of mental vision. J. N. Darby has "see to dogs". We must be alert! It is a contemptuous reference to the Jewish teachers who regarded the Gentiles as dogs. See Mark 7.27-28, "It is not meet to take the children's bread, and to cast it unto the dogs". W.E. Vine comments as follows: "It is used to suggest defilement and savagery, and homeless, ownerless wildness, as with the prowling dogs of the east". When you think of an eastern dog, don't think about poodles and corgis! Read Deuteronomy 23.18; Psalm 59.6-7, 14-15. The word "dogs" emphasises the impurity of these men. Compare Matthew 7.6 and Revelation 22.15.

- *"Beware of evil workers"*. They are called "evil workers" probably because they detracted from the finished work of Christ, advocating justification by *works* instead of faith. They were certainly "workers". See Matthew 23.15.

- *"Beware of the concision"*. The word means, literally, 'a cutting down'. The rite of physical circumcision no longer had significance. It was just mutilation of the flesh. There is an element of sarcasm here.

iii) Overcoming the danger, v.3
"For we are the circumcision, which worship God in the spirit, and rejoice in Christ Jesus, and have no confidence in the flesh". The "we" is emphatic The danger is overcome by recognising four things:

- *"For we are the circumcision"*. What is all this about? Circumcision is first mentioned in Genesis 17, where God promised a son to Abraham and Sarah.

The New Testament comments on this as follows: "And being not weak in faith, he considered not his own body now dead, when he was about an hundred years old, neither yet the deadness of Sarah's womb: he staggered not at the promise of God through unbelief; but was strong in faith, giving glory to God; and being fully persuaded that, what he had promised, he was able also to perform" (Rom. 4.19-21). Romans 4.11 makes it clear that circumcision was the outward sign of Abraham's faith in Genesis 15.6. The removal of the flesh by circumcision was an apt symbol that Abraham had no confidence in himself, but every confidence in God. It was, literally, cutting off something natural, and that is precisely what faith does. It took place on the "eighth day" (see v.5): this suggests the commencement of something new. Think about it! Now read Philippians 3.3 again! Read also Romans 2.28.

The Jews carefully practised circumcision, but in many cases, it was a sham. See Acts 7.51, "Ye uncircumcised in heart and ears"; Jeremiah 6.10, "Behold, their ear is uncircumcised"; Exodus 6.12, 30, "uncircumcised lips". See also Jeremiah 4.4. Christians enjoy the **spiritual** significance of circumcision. It is called "the circumcision made without hands, in putting off the body of the sins of the flesh by the circumcision of Christ" (Col. 2.11).

- **"Which worship God in the spirit".** This is elsewhere rendered (RV & JND), "which worship by the Spirit of God". The word "worship" *(latreuo)* means 'religious service' and "defines any service that brings glory to God" (Sydney Maxwell). It is used in Luke 2.37; Romans 1.9, 12.1; Hebrews 9.1, 12.28. (The most frequently used word in the New Testament for worship is *proskuneo* which comes from two words, *pros*, meaning 'towards', and *kuneo*, meaning 'to kiss'. See, for example, John 4.21-24). Here, 'worshipful service' is undertaken, not in the letter or outward form, like Judaism, but with inward reality. See John 4.24.

- **"And rejoice ('glory', RV) in Christ Jesus".** The Jewish teachers gloried in something totally different. See Galatians 6.13, "for neither they themselves who are circumcised keep the law; but desire to have you circumcised, that they may glory in your flesh". They boasted in their outward ritual, but Paul boasted in Christ and in all that He had accomplished.

- **"And have no confidence in the flesh".** The word "flesh" *(sarx)* is used in 1.22 in a literal sense, but here it refers, and so often elsewhere, to 'man in his unregenerate state, whether religious or moral' (W.E. Vine). But Paul had not always thought like that, and he now takes us back to his earlier days.

b) His confidence in the flesh, vv.4-6
"Though *I* might also have confidence in the flesh. If any other man thinketh that he hath whereof he might trust in the flesh, I more". Paul had greater reason to "trust in the flesh" than the very false teachers themselves! Just look at his credentials as the leading exponent of Judaism. We can call them *(i)* his inherited credentials; *(ii)* his acquired credentials:

i) Credentials he inherited
He inherited the right ceremonial, national, tribal, and cultural credentials. He had a marvellous start in life!

- **He had the right ceremonial credentials.** "Circumcised the eighth day". He bore the covenant sign. He could not be "cut off from his people" (Gen. 17.14). Paul was not circumcised as a proselyte (in maturity), but as a true-born Jew ("the eighth day").

- **He had the right national credentials.** "Of the stock of Israel". The word "stock" *(genos)* occurs in various other New Testament passages. See, for example, Acts 4.6 ("kindred"); Acts 13.26 ("children of the stock of Abraham"); Revelation 22.16 "offspring"). As W.E. Vine observes, "His parents were not grafted into the nation, but were descended from the original stock. He was of 'pure blood'. The name 'Israel', a higher title than 'Hebrew'...suggests their calling, and indicates their dignity and divine privileges. Compare John 1.47; Romans 9.4; Ephesians 2.12". We should note that Paul does ***not*** say, 'of the seed of Abraham'. Abraham was a man of faith, not works!

- **He had the right tribal credentials.** "Of the tribe of Benjamin". See also Romans 11.1. Benjamin, with Judah, were loyal to the house of David. See 1 Kings 12.21; Ezra 4.1. Both Saul (a Benjamite), the first king, and Saul of Tarsus, displayed the tribal characteristic: "Benjamin shall ravin as a wolf" (Gen. 49.27). See, for example 1 Samuel 26.20; Acts 9.1-2. It is often pointed out that king Saul cried, "I have played the fool" (1 Sam. 26.21), but Saul, who became Paul, wrote, "I have kept the faith" (2 Tim. 4.7).

- **He had the right cultural credentials.** "An Hebrew of the Hebrews". See Acts 22 where, when he "spake in the Hebrew tongue to them, they kept the more silence". Paul addressed his audience as follows: "I am verily a man which am a Jew...brought up in this city at the feet of Gamaliel, and taught according to the perfect manner of the law of the fathers" (vv.1-3).

ii) Credentials he acquired

He acquired the right religious, practical and moral credentials. We might say that he 'had it all going for him'.

- **He had the right religious credentials.** "As touching the law, a Pharisee". Listen to him before Agrippa: "After the most straitest sect of our religion I lived a Pharisee" (Acts 26.5). The name 'Pharisees' was given to a religious school among the Jews; it is supposed to have been derived from the Hebrew word *parash,* signifying 'to separate'. They practised complete separation from all non-Jewish elements. They prided themselves on their superior sanctity of life, devotion to God, and their study of the law. The Pharisee in the temple thanked God that he was "not as other men". They were great advocates of tradition, and were punctilious in paying tithes. They were marked by formal correctness, rathen than by righteousness of action

- **He had the right practical credentials.** "Concerning zeal, persecuting (the word occurs as "follow" in v.12 and "press" in v.14) the church". Here he is again before Agrippa:"And I punished them oft in every synagogue, and compelled them to blaspheme; and being exceedingly mad against them, I persecuted them even unto strange cities" (Acts 26.11). He "made havoc of the church" (Acts 8.3). See also 1 Corinthians 15.9; Galatians 1.13-14; 1 Timothy 1.13. He had been the supreme Judaistic fanatic of his time.

- **He had the right moral credentials.** "Touching the righteousness which is in the law, blameless". As Sydney Maxwell observes, "the fact that he uses the word 'blameless' suggests that this obedience was outward. It was external righteousness. He was in this respect so like the rich young ruler who could say to the Saviour, 'all these things have I observed from my youth (Mark 10.20)'. Sydney Maxwell continues by noticing the continuing parallel between the rich young ruler and Paul. Both failed when it came to covetousness (Mark 10.21-22; Romans 7.7-9). "Blameless" does not mean 'sinless!' Very clearly, the righteousness attained by Paul was not synonymous with the "righteousness of God". See Romans 10.2-4.

In this way, Paul fully established his reasons for saying, "If any other man thinketh that he hath whereof he might trust in the flesh, I more". But he wrote off a lifetime's profit! He turned his entire profit into a loss, that he might gain the greatest profit of all! This brings us to:

c) Paul's righteousness through faith, vv.7-9

Watch "the spiritual accountant working on his ledger" (Sydney Maxwell): "But what things were gain to me, those I counted loss for Christ. Yea doubtless, and I count all things but loss for the excellency of the knowledge of Christ Jesus my Lord: for whom I have suffered the loss of all things, and do count them but dung, that I may win Christ ('have Christ to my gain')". He talks about "gain" (see also 1.21). It is actually plural, "gains", and refers to his credentials in vv.5-6. He talks about "loss", but here the word is singular. All the profits in his personal ledger were transferred to the loss column. The word "loss" *(zemia)* is translated "damage" in Acts 27.10. Paul made these entries in his ledger when he was converted, and he never reversed them.

The change was made at conversion (v.7), it had never been reversed (v.8), it had never been regretted (vv.8-9), and it had brought superior benefits (v.9).

i) The change was made at conversion, v.7
What made Paul alter his accounts so dramatically? He realised that all the entries in the credit column of his ledger were worthless when it came to salvation. Circumcision could not save him. Nationality could not save him. Religious correctness could not save him. Zeal in what he thought was a good cause could not save him. External righteousness could not save him. Only **Christ** could save him! He saw it all on the Damascus road. He counted everything in his past "loss for Christ", or 'on account of Christ'. It was either his earthly and religious credentials, or Christ. Compare the 'rich young ruler' (Matt. 19.16). He could not say, "What things were gain to me, those I counted loss for Christ". Consequently, he did not speak about "the excellency of the knowledge of Christ Jesus my Lord". Paul renounced all personal merit in favour of Christ.

ii) The change had never been reversed, v.8
Notice that whilst Paul uses the past tense in v.7, "those (things) I **counted** loss for Christ", he uses the present tense in v.8, "Yea doubtless, and I **count** all things but loss". Notice, too, that while he speaks about "**those** things" in v.7, he speaks about "**all** things" in v.8. Some thirty years lay between v.7 and v.8, but Paul hadn't changed his mind one little bit. Just think about the intervening period. 2 Corinthians 11.24-28 makes the point. "Of the Jews five times received I forty stripes save one (referring to Deut. 25.3). Thrice was I beaten with rods, once was I stoned, thrice I suffered shipwreck, a night and a day I have been in the deep; in journeyings often, in perils of waters, in perils of robbers….in weariness and painfulness…Besides those things that are without, that which cometh upon me daily, the care of all the churches". Read the whole section yourself, and then remember that none of this made Paul change his mind

about Christ! He says in effect, 'I *still* count all things but loss!' Paul certainly had not 'left his first love' for Christ. Have **we?**

iii) The change had never been regretted, vv.8-9
The passage above also illustrates what Paul meant when he said, "I count **all** things but loss". But he had no regrets. "Yea doubtless, and I count all things but loss for the excellency of the knowledge of Christ Jesus my Lord: for whom I have suffered **the loss of all things,** and do count them but dung (refuse), that I may win Christ ('have Christ to my gain)".

What makes a man willing to lose everything in this way? Listen to Paul again: "the excellency of the knowledge of Christ Jesus my Lord". For Paul, the most wonderful thing in life was to know Christ. This is clear from the words, "the **excellency** of the knowledge of Christ Jesus my Lord". The word "excellency" *(huperecho)* occurs in 4.7, and its use there explains Paul's meaning perfectly: "And the peace of God, which **passeth** all understanding, shall keep your hearts and minds through Christ Jesus". For Paul, knowing Christ surpassed everything! (*Huperecho* also occurs in 2.3, "let each esteem other better than themselves"). But this was not mere dogma. He calls Him "Christ Jesus **my** Lord". You can catch the deep devotion in Paul's heart when he wrote that! Elisabeth (Luke 1.43) and Thomas (John 20.28) both called Him "**my** Lord". Can **we** genuinely do the same? To say "my Lord" is to acknowledge personally what God has made Him (2.11).

The "excellency of the knowledge of Christ Jesus my Lord" made Paul willing to lose "all things, and...count them but dung, that I may win Christ". He regarded his national and religious assets, which were once his pride and joy, as 'refuse'. This is the man who wrote, I "profited in the Jews' religion above many my equals in mine own nation!" (Gal. 1.14). The word "dung" is plural and signifies 'bits of refuse', probably garbage thrown to dogs after a feast, which is rather significant in view of v.2! The Judaizers are now the dogs! (W.E. Vine).

The words, "that I may win Christ", are better rendered, 'that I may gain Christ' or 'have Christ to my gain'. The word "win" translates *kerdaino,* corresponding to the noun *kerdos* in v.7. It means "more than gaining the knowledge of Him; it is to gain **Him** in all His fullness" (W.E. Vine). In the words of an old hymn: "I have Christ; What want I more?" In the place of Judaism, Paul had Christ.

iv) The change had brought superior benefits, v.9
Paul had "suffered the loss of all things", firstly, "that I may win Christ" ('have

Christ to my gain'), and secondly. "be found in him, not having mine own righteousness, which is of the law, but that which is through the faith of Christ, the righteousness which is of God by faith". In the first case, he refers to the surpassing joy of having Christ Himself. In the second, he refers to the blessings of salvation. The words "found in him" describe the position and security enjoyed by every child of God. See Jeremiah 33.16; 1 Corinthians 1.30; 2 Corinthians 5.21.

When Paul itemised his assets in vv.4-6, he concluded by saying, "touching the righteousness which is in the law, blameless". While no one could point an accusing finger at him, this did not mean that he was righteous before God. He calls it "mine **own** righteousness". But now he enjoyed "the righteousness which is of **God** by faith". Faith in Christ marks 'the end of all self-effort and human attainment' (Sydney Maxwell). Once he gloried in his "own righteousness, which is of *(ek*, meaning 'out of') the law": now he rejoiced in the "righteousness which is of (*ek*, 'out of') God by (*dia,* 'by means of') faith". This is very wonderful. The very righteousness of God Himself belongs to the simple believer in the Lord Jesus. See Romans 3.21-22. The words, "through the faith **of** Christ", mean 'through faith **in** Christ'. (We are told that it is the 'objective genitive' as opposed to the 'subjective genitive'). It has often been said that Paul ceased to be like the proud Pharisee, and became like the believing publican of Luke 18.9-14.

READ CHAPTER 3.10-16

"That I may know him"

As we have noticed, this chapter can be divided into three sections, each of which describes Paul's spiritual gain, and demonstrates why we should "rejoice in the Lord" (v.1). *(1)* He had gained a new position (vv.1-19). It can be summed up as, "*found in him*" (v.9). *(2)* He had gained a new purpose (vv.1-16). It can be summed up as, '*fellowship with him*' (v.10. *(3)* He had gained a new prospect (vv.17-21). It can be summed up as, "*fashioned like him*" (v.21).

1) PAUL'S NEW POSITION, vv.1-9
We examined Paul's profit and loss account in our last study. "What things were gain to me, those I counted loss for Christ". But that did not mean that the balance sheet showed a crippling loss. On the contrary, it showed an incomparable gain. He had gained Christ! Paul had "suffered the loss of all things…that I may win Christ ('have Christ to my gain') and be found in him, not having mine own righteousness, which is of the law, but that which is through the faith of Christ, the righteousness which is of God by faith". This brings us to:

2) PAUL'S NEW PURPOSE, vv.10-16
These verses may be divided as follows: *(a)* Paul's desire (vv.10-11); *(c)* Paul's determination (vv.12-14); *(c)* Paul's directions (vv.15-16).

a) Paul's desire, vv.10-11
"That I may know him, and the power of his resurrection, and the fellowship of his sufferings, being made conformable unto his death; if by any means I might attain unto the resurrection of the dead". While there is **no** progress so far as our spiritual **position** is concerned, it is fixed and final, there **is** progress so far as our spiritual **practice** is concerned.

i) "That I may know him"
Our passage division actually interrupts a sentence, and could therefore be

Chapter 3B

criticised! However, the headings might help us to follow the development of the chapter. But vv.8-11 are really one sentence, and emphasise that our position in Christ is not an end in itself. Yes, we can certainly say, 'Jehovah Tsidkenu' (the Lord our righteousness), and that is very wonderful, but salvation is more than being right with God through Christ. Salvation involves a deepening relationship with Christ. God never intended to guide and help His people by remote control. Abraham is called "the friend of God". God spoke with Moses "mouth to mouth" (Num.12.6-8). The Lord Jesus was not a remote figure when He was on earth. Peter reminded his colleagues that the "Lord Jesus went in and out among us" (Acts 1.21). John goes further: "That which was from the beginning, which we have heard, which we have seen with our eyes, which we have looked upon, and our hands have handled, of the Word of life" (1 John 1.1).

Since all this happened two thousand years ago and, in any case, the Lord Jesus was "received up into heaven, and sat on the right hand of God" (Mark 16.19), all we can do, surely, is to learn as much as we can about Him? But Paul did not look at it like that! He did not say, 'that I may know **about** him', but "that I may **know** him". He didn't mean casual acquaintance either. The word "know" *(ginosko)* signifies "the inception and progress in knowledge". We would say, 'come to know Him better and better'. There is only one way in which we can really know someone in this way, and that is by keeping their company. The hymn says:

> Spend much time in secret
> With Jesus alone.

A biographer may know a great deal about his subject, without ever meeting the person concerned. But Paul is not writing a biography here! We can only "know" Him through reading the scriptures carefully and prayerfully, and through the ministry of the Spirit of God. To "know" the Lord Jesus is to be conscious of His presence, to be personally acquainted with Him, to be aware, instinctively, of the things that please Him, and grieve Him, and to know how He would act and react in differing circumstances. Moses prayed, "Now therefore, I pray thee, if I have found grace in thy sight, shew me now thy way, that I may know thee" (Exod. 33.13). Peter encourages us to "grow in grace, and in the knowledge of our Lord and Saviour Jesus Christ" (2 Pet. 3.18). This involves effort and determination: it does not happen automatically.

Paul now tells us **how** he wanted to "know" the Lord Jesus. He wanted to know His power, and His sufferings.

ii) "And the power of his resurrection"

Paul desired to experience the power of the Lord Jesus in his life. But why does he call it the "power (*dunamis*) of his resurrection"? The answer lies in Ephesians 1. The resurrection is the supreme demonstration of divine power. It is the power that triumphed over death. Paul calls this, "the power that worketh in us" (Eph. 3.20), and prayed that the Ephesians "may know…what is the exceeding greatness of his power to usward who believe, according to the working of his mighty power, which he wrought in Christ, when he raised him from the dead" (Eph. 1.18-19). See also Colossians 1.11, "Strengthened with all might, according to his glorious power" ('the might of his glory', JND). The man who once had every "confidence in the flesh" now tells us how much he needs the power of Christ, that is, the power inherent in His resurrection.

The "power of his resurrection" is not expressed in spectacular deeds and words, but in daily strength to go on resolutely in overcoming obstacles and difficulties. The "power of his resurrection" is power to witness in the teeth of gale-force adversity. See 2 Corinthians 1.9, "We had the sentence of death in ourselves, that we should not trust in ourselves, but in God which raiseth the dead".

We should also remember that the Lord Jesus was "quickened by the Spirit" (1 Pet. 3.18), and, therefore, to know the "power of his resurrection", is to know the power of the Holy Spirit. Equally, the fact that the Lord Jesus has been "raised up" and is "by the right hand of God exalted", has made possible the "promise of the Holy Ghost" (Acts 2.32-33). To "know him, and the power of his resurrection" is costly, which brings us to:

iii) "The fellowship of his sufferings"

We might have expected Paul to write, 'That I might know him, and the fellowship of his sufferings, and the power of his resurrection'. The order, however, reflects Paul's own experience. He first met the Lord Jesus in resurrection glory, and learned afterwards, through Ananias, "how great things he must suffer for my name's sake" (Acts 9.16). However, "the fellowship of his sufferings" is more than to "suffer for his sake" (1.29). It is suffering **with** Him, rather than suffering **for** Him as in 1.29. Quite clearly, this cannot refer to His suffering for sin. The distinction is clear from 1 Peter 2.21-24. When Paul said, "that I might know him", that included familiarity with the inner thoughts and feelings of the Lord Jesus. See, for example, John 15.18-20, "If the world hate you, ye know that it hated me before it hated you…Remember the word that I said unto you, The servant is not greater than his lord. If they have persecuted me, they will also persecute you; if they have kept my saying, they will keep yours also". The early church knew something of "the fellowship of his sufferings", and this is made clear by His own words to Paul: "Saul, Saul, why persecutest thou me?...I am Jesus whom thou persecutest" (Acts 9.4-5). They were "partakers of Christ's sufferings" (1 Pet. 4.13. (Paul deals with another aspect of "the fellowship of his sufferings" in Colossians 1.24).

The suffering and hurt that we experience brings us closer to Him, because we are aware that He knows by experience what it is to suffer at the hands of men. We experience what He experienced, and our suffering enables us to understand in some measure what it cost Him, physically and mentally, to accomplish our salvation. Paul and Silas experienced "the fellowship of his sufferings" when they were beaten at Philippi with "many stripes". He, too, had been scourged. When we are misunderstood, like Him, or rejected, like Him, we experience "the fellowship of his sufferings". In Paul's own words, "The sufferings of Christ abound in us" (2 Cor. 1.5). But to what extent was Paul prepared to suffer?

iv) "Being made conformable unto his death"
Or, "being conformed unto his death" (RV). That is, Paul was willing to go even to those lengths in "fellowship of his sufferings". Was he thinking here of Stephen, whose death he had witnessed? Stephen cried "Lord, lay not this sin to their charge" (Acts 7.60), and therefore displayed the very character of the Lord Jesus when He said, "Father, forgive them, for they know not what they do".

It is more likely that Paul is referring here to his willingness to share the complete rejection of the Lord Jesus. See 2 Corinthians 4.10-11, "Always bearing about in the body the dying (putting to death) of the Lord Jesus, that the life also of Jesus might be made manifest in our body, For we which live are alway delivered unto death for Jesus's sake, that the life also of Jesus might be made manifest in our mortal flesh". So "being made conformable to his death" ("growing into conformity to his death", W.E. Vine)) means sharing His rejection. The Lord Jesus referred to this in speaking to James and John, "Ye shall indeed drink of the cup that I drink of; and with the baptism that I am baptised withal shall ye be baptized" (Mark 10.35-40). He described "the cup" and "the baptism" in v.34, "And they shall mock him, and shall scourge him, and shall spit upon him, and shall kill him". To be "conformable to his death" is willingness "to die in the name of Him who was 'obedient unto death'" (William Trew *(Galatians and Philippians)*. Paul expressed this to the believers at Caesarea. See Acts 21.13.

M.R. Vincent looks at this rather differently, but his comments are worthy of consideration. "The most radical conformity is thus indicated: not merely undergoing physical death like Christ, but conformity to the spirit and temper, the meekness and submissiveness of Christ; to His unselfish love and devotion, and His anguish over human sin".

v) "If by any means I might attain unto the resurrection of the dead"
The word "attain" *(katantao)* signifies 'to reach' or 'to arrive at', and is used literally in Acts 27.12. It is used metaphorically in Acts 26.7; Ephesians 4.13. The word "resurrection" *(ekanastasis,* literally, 'out-resurrection') means, not a general resurrection, but 'resurrection ***from among*** the dead'.

The first thing we should say is that this cannot refer to physical resurrection. The resurrection which will take place when the Lord Jesus returns (1 Cor. 15.52; 1 Thess. 4.16) is not an 'attainment'. This passage does not teach that we have to reach a given standard of life and godliness before we can be raised from the dead! If resurrection depended on spiritual progress, we would be overwhelmed by uncertainty. Resurrection is an essential part of salvation. It is not conditional. When Paul states that "if we believe that Jesus died and rose again, even so them also which sleep in Jesus will God bring with him" (1 Thess 4.14), he does not infer or visualise that any believers will be excluded. He does not say here, 'if by any means I might be **worthy** of the resurrection of the dead'. If Paul **was** referring to physical resurrection, then the following three verses would be superfluous. There would be no necessity to say, "not as though I had already attained (a different word now), either were already perfect", or "I count not myself to have apprehended", or "reaching forth unto those things which are before, I press towards the mark…"

So what **does** Paul mean here? The whole context demands an explanation relating to personal experience **now.** This is the theme in these two verses, and in the verses that follow. W.E. Vine puts it as follows: "He desires so to live that his whole life may manifest the power of Christ as the Living One, raised from the dead. This would be the perfect fulfilment of what he has already said, "to me to live is Christ". If "being conformed to his death" means the end of ourselves, then "the resurrection of the dead" means living in complete dependence on divine power. In other words, to live as a man raised from the dead. After all, resurrection is life empowered by God! It has been suggested that 'attaining unto the resurrection of the dead' is 'living down here as we will in heaven'.

b) Paul's determination, vv.12-14
Paul had not "attained" (v.12), and he had not "apprehended" (v.13), but he was not discouraged. In the first case, he writes, "I follow after", and in the second,

"I press toward the mark". He was determined to make spiritual progress. There was nothing lethargic about him. If Paul, above all people, was obliged to speak in this way, how much more ourselves! Paul was determined "to attain" (v.12) and determined to "apprehend" (vv.13-14).

i) He was determined to "attain", v.12
"Not as though I had already attained, either were already perfect: but I follow after, if that I may apprehend that for which also I am apprehended of Christ Jesus" Let's look at it like this:

- **His assessment.** "Not as though I had already attained, either were already perfect". While the word "attained" (*lambano*, meaning, 'to obtain' or 'receive') differs from "attain" in v.11 (*katantao*, meaning, 'to reach', or, 'arrive at'), there can be little doubt that Paul is referring to his desire to "attain unto the resurrection of the dead". W.E. Vine suggests that the change of verb stresses that such an attainment is achieved "by way of help from God, and not of being entirely dependent on self-effort". The word "perfect" (*telioo*) does not mean sinless perfection, but 'to bring to completion', and describes full-growth or maturity. It is rendered "fulfilled" in Luke 2.43, and "finish" in Acts 20.24.

- **His aspiration.** "I follow after", meaning 'to pursue' or 'to speed on earnestly'. This is the second of three occurrences in this chapter of the word *dioko*. See v.3, "*persecuting* the church"; v.14, "I *press* toward the mark". W.E. Vine states that it is "a metaphor from the foot-race". (We are to "follow after" other things too: see Romans 14.19; 1 Corinthians 14.1; 1 Thessalonians 5.15; 1 Timothy 6.11; 2 Timothy 2.22). Sydney Maxwell puts it nicely: "How different is the tone of this passage. While the man has been changed by the grace of God and his pursuit is different, yet intact in this expression is all the zeal and drive of his former days. That energy, boundless in his past, is now channelled into the obsession (perhaps 'objective' might have been a little better here) of living for Christ". Does our zeal for Christ match or, better, exceed, our zeal for those interests which captivated us before conversion? How much do **we** want to know the power of Christ in our lives?

- **His aim.** He pursued this goal so that "I may apprehend that for which also I am apprehended of Christ Jesus". The word "apprehend" means 'to lay hold'. So Christ had 'laid hold' of Paul, so that he might 'lay hold of life lived in the power of the risen Christ'. He desired to grasp the purpose for which he had been saved by the grace of God. What about *our* spiritual desires and objectives? We too have been saved in order to be people who live in the power of the risen Christ. He has 'apprehended' us so that we might understand and pursue His will for us.

ii) He was determined to "apprehend", vv.13-14

"Brethren, I count not myself to have apprehended: but this one thing I do, forgetting those things which are behind, and reaching forth unto those things which are before, I press toward the mark for the prize of the high calling of God in Christ Jesus". Let's use the same approach as above:

- **His assessment.** "Brethren, I count not myself to have apprehended". The wording suggests that whilst others felt that they had reached spiritual maturity, Paul did not. As W.E. Vine observes, there was "no self-complacent carelessness" about him. It is a very dangerous thing to think that we have 'arrived' spiritually. Paul emphasises here, not so much God's purpose for him in his service, but God's purpose for him personally.

- **His aspiration.** "This **one thing** I do, forgetting (see James 1.24) those things which are behind, and reaching forth (stretching forward) unto those things which are before, I press (*dioko*, as noted) towards the mark..." (Compare John 9.25, "**One thing** I know": see also Psalm 27.4; Luke 10.42; 18.22). Paul alludes here to the games, and exhibited the concentration and single-mindedness of an athlete intent on winning the race. It was an absolute priority. Whilst it has been suggested that the "things which are behind" refers to his pre-conversion days (see vv.4-6), it seems more likely that Paul has in mind the earlier stages of his Christian life. He does not rest on past progress with smug satisfaction, neither does he ever think of turning back. "Reaching forth unto those things which are before, I press towards the mark ('goal" RV)". In athletics terms, he had his eye fixed on the tape at the end of the race. It is significant that the word "before" ("reaching forth unto those things which are **before**"), occurs in 1 Thessalonians 2.19: "For what is our hope, or joy, or crown of rejoicing? Are not even ye **in the presence of** ('before', JND) our Lord Jesus Christ at his coming?" The "things which are before" *(emprosthen)* evidently refer to the coming of the Lord.

- **His aim.** The prize! "I press towards the mark for the prize of the high calling of God in Christ Jesus". The "mark" isn't the "prize". The "mark" is a life lived in complete dependence on the power of God. Paul calls this "newness of life" (Rom. 6.4). The "prize" is the reward to be bestowed at the judgment seat of Christ for such victorious living. The word "prize" *(brabeion)* is akin to *brabeus*, an umpire, and *brabeuo*, to decide or arbitrate (W.E. Vine). See also 1 Corinthians 9.24. So there is a reward in connection with the "high calling of God in Christ Jesus". All believers participate in that calling, and therefore the prize is available to us all. Will **we** receive a reward for victorious Christian living? Notice the "high calling" (here), the "holy calling" (2 Tim. 1.9), and the "heavenly calling" (Heb. 3.1).

c) Paul's directions, vv.15-16

"Let us therefore, as many as be perfect, be thus minded: and if in any thing ye be otherwise minded, God shall reveal even this unto you. Nevertheless, whereto we have already attained, let us walk by the same rule, let us mind the same thing". We must notice that devotion cannot be commanded, or achieved by forceful measures. It cannot be compelled. Hence Paul's language here. Do notice the change from "I", some fifteen times thus far in the chapter, to "we...us...ye...our" He now applies his ministry in three directions:

- **Those who are "perfect".** A little problem arises! Paul has just told us that he was **not** "perfect" (v.12)! The context makes the apparent difference clear. In v.12, Paul is speaking about his experience. He had not fully attained life in the power of Christ's resurrection. In v.15, he is speaking about attitude. The mark of a spiritually mature mind will be a desire to "attain unto the resurrection of the dead".

- **Those who are "otherwise minded".** That is, "otherwise minded" in connection with proper spiritual objectives. Paul refers here to believers who are immature, and who do not see the need for progress. Compare 2 Peter 1.5-10. Where there is lack of understanding in this way, "God shall reveal even this unto you". He is gracious and longsuffering. But when God reveals something to us, it is important to practise it: hence what follows:

- **Those who have made progress.** "Nevertheless, whereto we have already attained, let us walk by the same rule". We must not discard what we have already learnt as believers, The words, "let us mind the same thing", are omitted by the RV and JND. The word "attained" translates *phthano,* meaning 'reached'. Preachers have often reminded us that if we want to know more about the Word of God and its teaching, then we must obey and enjoy what we already know! God will not give us further light unless we live in the light He has already given to us. But there is more here. God expects us to walk in fellowship with each other. The words, "let us walk by the same rule", are elsewhere rendered "let us walk in the same steps" (JND). The word "walk" *(stoicheo)* signifies 'walking with others', whereas "walk" in v17-18 signifies 'walking alone' *(peripatao).* Christian progress cannot be achieved if we isolate ourselves. Paul prayed that the Ephesians "may be able to comprehend **with all saints** what is the breadth, and length, and depth, and height, and to know the love of Christ, which passeth knowledge" (Eph. 3.18-19).

READ CHAPTER 3.17-21

"We look for the Saviour"

We have now reached the third of the three sections into which this chapter can be divided. Each of these describes Paul's spiritual gain, and demonstrates why we should "rejoice in the Lord" (v.1). **(1)** he had gained a new position (vv.1-9). It can be summed up as, *"found in him"* (v.9) **(2)** He had gained a new purpose (vv.10-16). It can be summed up as, *'fellowship with him'* (v.10). **(3)** He had gained a new prospect (vv.17-21) It can be summed up as, *"fashioned like him"* (v.21).

1) PAUL'S NEW POSITION, vv.1-9
The balance sheet showed a massive profit, even though Saul of Tarsus (FCA) had written off all his original assets. "What things were gain to me, those I counted loss for Christ. Yea doubtless, and I count all things but loss for the excellency of the knowledge of Christ Jesus my Lord: for whom I have suffered the loss of all things, and do count them but dung, that I might win Christ ('have Christ to my gain') and be found in him, not having mine own righteousness, which is of the law, but that which is through the faith of Christ, the righteousness which is of God by faith".

2) PAUL'S NEW PURPOSE, vv.10-16
"That I may know him, and the power of his resurrection, and the fellowship of his sufferings, being made conformable unto his death; if by any means I might attain unto the resurrection of the dead". This brings us to;

3) PAUL'S NEW PROSPECT, vv.17-21
These verses may be divided as follows: **(a)** the example to follow (v.17); **(b)** the exposure of evil (vv.18-19); **(c)** the expectation of Christ's return (vv.20-21).

a) The example to follow, v.17
"Brethren, be followers together of me, and mark them which walk so as ye have us for an ensample". At first glance, this may seem rather pretentious, but Paul is certainly not endeavouring to win disciples. He is encouraging the Philippians to share his objectives! We should notice the words used in this connection:

- **"Follower"**. The word *(summimetai)* means, literally, 'fellow-imitator" The word *mimites*, an imitator, occurs in 1 Corinthians 4.16 ("Be ye followers of me"); 11.1 ("Be ye followers of me, even as I also am of Christ"); Ephesians 5.1 ("Be ye therefore followers of God, as dear children"); 1 Thessalonians 1.6 ("And ye became followers of us, and of the Lord, having received the word in much affliction, with joy of the Holy Ghost"); 2.14 ("For ye, brethren, became followers of the churches of God which in Judaea are in Christ Jesus: for ye also have suffered like things of your own countrymen, even as they have of the Jews"); Hebrews 6.12 ("That ye be not slothful, but followers of them who through faith and patience inherit the promises"). None of these passages suggests that we should become the disciples of an earthly leader. Paul was at pains to demolish the very idea at Corinth. See 1 Corinthians 1.11-13; 3.21-23.

Quite clearly then, Paul urges the Philippians to be his 'fellow-imitators, by 'following after' (v.12), by 'reaching forth' (v.13), and by 'pressing toward' (v.14). In fact, 'fellow-imitators' of Paul in his entire outlook, as outlined in vv8-16. Paul's entire outlook was Christ! The words 'fellow-imitators' also suggest a unity of desire. We must do this together. Just think of the spiritual power of an assembly where all the believers have the same spiritual objectives!

- **"Mark"**. The verb *(skopeo)* means "to look at, behold, watch, contemplate" (W.E. Vine). It also occurs in Philippians 2.4 ("Look not...") and in Romans 16.17 where Paul warns against "them which cause divisions and offences contrary to the doctrine which ye have learned; and avoid them". There, it is "mark" so as to avoid. But here, it is "mark" so as to follow. (The same word is translated "take heed" in Luke 11.35, and "considering" in Galatians 6.1). The relevant noun *(skopos)* is used in v.14, "I press toward the mark". That is, "a mark on which to fix the eye" (W.E. Vine). We noticed in our previous study that whilst the word "walk" in v.16 signifies 'walking with others', the word "walk" in vv.17-18 signifies walking alone.

- **"Ensample"**. The word *(tupos)* means a mould, a pattern, or a model. The believers at Thessalonica were a 'model' ("ensamples", AV) to "all that believe in Macedonia and Achaia" (1 Thess. 1.7). Two important lessons emerge. Firstly, the need for us to **imitate** a godly example and, secondly, the need for us to **set** a godly example. Let us stress again that the word *peripatao* ("walk") emphasises that it is a godly **personal** example.

We should notice that the following two verses are in brackets (JND agrees, but the RV does not), and it does make good sense to link v.17 with vv.20-21.

However, it also makes good sense to omit the brackets, and follow the verses in the order in which they occur. The word "walk" clearly links v.17 with vv.18-19.

b) The exposure of evil, vv.18-19
"For many walk, of whom I have told you often, and now tell you even weeping, that they are the enemies of the cross of Christ: whose end is destruction, whose God is their belly, and whose glory is in their shame, who mind earthly things".

First of all, who are these people? They are certainly distinct from the party described in 1.15, and from the Jewish teachers described in 3.1-3. They are strikingly similar to the people described in 2 Peter 2.9-22, and Jude 4. Sydney Maxwell calls them "the antinomian traitors", which, mercifully, he then defines: "The class of people in view profess to be followers of Christ, but use it simply as a cloak for their own impurity. Although they spoke of the cross, they were bereft of its power in their lives. They 'turned the grace of God into lasciviousness', and are well described in Jude 4". ('Antinomian' means "against the moral law" and refers to people who "maintain that, for Christians, the law is set aside by the gospel", *Nuttall's Standard Dictionary*. In other words, once you are saved, you can do as you like!). We must notice the following:

i) It was desirable to many
"For **many** walk..." This is not surprising. Any 'religion' which gives God a nod of recognition, and then frees people to do as they please, is bound to be popular. Compare 2 Peter 2.2, "And **many** shall follow their pernicious (licentious) ways; by reason of whom the way of truth shall be evil spoken of". Both Enoch and Noah "walked with God" (Gen. 5.22; 6.9), and in both cases, it was a lonely path. Do not expect popularity if you "press toward the mark for the prize of the high calling of God in Christ Jesus". You are likely to be dismissed as 'an oddity', or worse.

ii) It was dealt with by Paul
"For many walk, of whom I have **told you often,** and **now tell you** even weeping..." The imperfect tense is used here, so that we could translate, 'I kept on telling you'. Paul did not let the matter rest. It was quite insufficient to mention the danger once, and then leave it. Peter did not apologise for reminding people of things they knew. Read 2 Peter 1.12-15. It is very important to 'go over old ground'. Dangers don't just go away. Bible teaching should be preventative. 'Better a fence at the top of the cliff, than an ambulance station at the bottom!'

iii) It was distressing to Paul
"For many walk, of whom I have told you often, and now tell you even **weeping**

(klaio)...". It has been said that children 'cry', but men 'weep' The Lord Jesus "wept" (*klaio*: to sob, or 'a loud expression of grief', W.E. Vine) over Jerusalem (Luke 19.41). He "wept" (*dakruo*, to shed tears: silent weeping) at the tomb of Lazarus (John 11.35). Paul wept in view of the spiritual peril which confronted the Philippians. His tears disclosed his deep affection for them. He was deeply concerned about the spiritual welfare of God's people. Notice his tears in Acts 20.19 ("Serving the Lord with all humility of mind, and with many tears"); Acts 20.31 ("By the space of three years I ceased not to warn every one night and day with tears"); 2 Corinthians 2.4 ("For out of much affliction and anguish of heart I wrote unto you with many tears"). It is one thing to stridently denounce error and bang the platform (!), but quite another to denounce error, and weep with "godly sorrow" (2 Cor. 7.10). How much are we really concerned about each other? When things go wrong, we are quick to condemn, but not quite so quick to weep.

iv) It involved denial of the cross
"They are enemies of the cross of Christ". While these people undoubtedly professed to be Christians, and used His Name, their conduct effectively denied the meaning of His cross. They acknowledged Christ, but not the implications of salvation through His death. Rightly understood, the cross spells the end of our old and sinful life: "They that are Christ's have crucified the flesh with the affections and lusts" (Gal. 5.24). The same people are evidently described in Titus 1.16, "They profess that they know God; but in works they deny him, being abominable, and disobedient, and unto every good work reprobate", and in 2 Peter 2.1, "Denying the Lord that bought them". It is worth noting in connection with the second reference that the word "bought" does not mean 'to redeem': it refers rather to the price paid with a view to redemption.

W.E. Vine is worth quoting in full here: "They were not enemies merely by their unbelief, they denied Him actually, while outwardly professing allegiance to Him. They entertained and promulgated the appalling doctrine that the atoning sacrifice of the cross, the divinely-appointed basis and means of holiness, was designed to make room for licentiousness, thus turning the grace of God into lasciviousness".

We should note that "the cross of Jesus" (John 19.25) stresses its **historical** aspect; that "the cross of our Lord Jesus Christ" (Gal. 6.14) stresses its **moral** aspect: Paul's use of the Lord's full title emphasises his passionate devotion to Him; that "the cross of Christ" (here and 1 Cor. 1.17) stresses its **doctrinal** aspect: it proclaims man's ruin, and God's remedy for his ruin.

v) It brought destruction to its adherents
"Whose end is destruction" The word "destruction" *(apoleia)* means 'loss of well-being, not of being' (W.E. Vine). It is rendered "perdition" in 1.28. The wicked will not be annihilated.

vi) It involved depravity of life
"Whose God is their belly, and whose glory is in their shame, who mind earthly things".

- **"Whose God is their belly"**. This emphasises their total sensuality and self-indulgence. It is the very antithesis of self-restraint and purity. The words, "whose **god**, RV, is the belly", strongly suggests religious profession. They used God's name, but they actually worshipped at the altar of self-gratification. Compare Romans 16.17-18, "Now I beseech you, brethren, mark them which cause divisions and offences contrary to the doctrine which ye have learned; and avoid them. For they that are such serve not our Lord Jesus Christ, but their own belly; and by good words and fair speeches deceive the hearts of the simple".

- **"Whose glory is in their shame"**. This emphasises that they not only practised sensuality and self-indulgence, but actually boasted in their supposed liberty. The words, "their shame", is Paul's evaluation of their conduct. The people concerned obviously did not think for one moment that it was shameful.

- **"Who mind earthly things"**. This emphasises that they had no appreciation of things "not seen" and "eternal". They are concerned solely with "things which are seen" and "temporal" (2 Cor. 4.18). James calls it "this wisdom" which "descendeth not from above, but is earthly, sensual, devilish" (James 3.15). As W.E. Vine observes, "These persons find their great representative in Bunyan's muckrake". (Now you've got to read *Pilgrim's Progress!*).

But if these people "mind (*phroneo*; see our comments at 2.1) earthly things", the believer sets his "affection (*phroneo*) on things above, not on things on the earth" (Col. 3.2). This follows:

c) The expectation of Christ's return, vv.20-21
"For our conversation (citizenship) is in heaven; from whence also we look for the Saviour, the Lord Jesus Christ: who shall change our vile body, that it may be fashioned like unto his glorious body, according to the working whereby he is able to subdue all things unto himself". The previous verses describe people who

Chapter 3C

"mind earthly things" (see Psalm 17.9, 11, 14), but these two verses describe the heavenly hopes and aspirations of people whose 'citizenship' *(politeuma)* is in heaven. Faith in Christ makes every believer a 'citizen' of heaven. A kindred word *(politeia)* is used in 1.27 ("only let your conversation be as it becometh the gospel of Christ"). Paul was a Roman citizen: "And the chief captain answered, With a great sum obtained I this freedom *(politeia)*. And Paul said, But I was free born" (Acts 22.28).

It is very appropriate that Paul should refer to the heavenly citizenship of believers in this epistle. Philippi was given the status of a Roman colony in 42BC, following the victory of Antony and Octavius over Brutus and Cassius. See Acts 16.12. Philippi was therefore a replica in miniature of Rome. Its inhabitants valued the privilege of Roman citizenship. See Acts 16.21; 37-39. "Being Romans" was something to be proud of at Philippi. Its citizens had their names enrolled at Rome, and owed allegiance to Caesar. However, the Christians at Philippi, together with all Christians, were a colony of heavenly citizens located on earth. Their names were enrolled in the register of heaven (4.3), and they owed allegiance to Christ as Lord. This does not mean, of course, that Christians oppose civil order. They are "subject unto the higher powers" (Rom. 13.1). They render "to Caesar the things that are Caesar's, and to God the things that are God's" (Mark 12.17). Problems only arise when 'Caesar' demands "the things that are God's", in which case "we ought to obey God rather than men" (Acts 5.29), and take the consequences. As 'heavenly citizens', we have a heavenly hope, and this follows. We will take note of the following: the place, the prospect, the Person, the perfection, and the power.

i) The place

"For our conversation is in **heaven;** from whence also we look for the Saviour, the Lord Jesus Christ" The word "heaven" is plural in the original text, and signifies "the region in its fulness, in contrast to earth" (W.E. Vine). The Christian's hope is not vested in this world. We "wait for his Son from **heaven**" (1 Thess. 1.10). The Lord Jesus will "descend from **heaven** with a shout" (1 Thess. 4.16). He will fulfil His own promise, "I will come again, and receive you unto myself; that where I am, there ye may be also" (John 14.3).

ii) The prospect

"For our conversation is in heaven; from whence also we **look** for the Saviour, the Lord Jesus Christ". But this isn't a casual "look". The word *apekdechomai* means "to await or expect eagerly" (W.E. Vine). It is used of creation in Romans 8.19 ("For the earnest expectation of the creature **waiteth** for the manifestation

105

of the sons of God"), as well as Christians (Rom. 8.23, 25; 1 Cor. 1.7). How eagerly are **we** waiting for the Lord's coming?

iii) The Person
"For our conversation is in heaven; from whence also we look for **the Saviour, the Lord Jesus Christ**". The title "Saviour" is emphasised here. (He was not the Saviour of the people who minded "earthly things"). He **is** our Saviour, and He will come to **complete** the work of salvation. See Romans 13.11, "It is high time to awake out of sleep: for now is our **salvation** nearer than when we believed". We must all take time to ponder His Name, "the Lord Jesus Christ". Time spent in this way will deepen and enrich our appreciation and worship. We are exhorted to "put...on the Lord Jesus Christ" (Rom. 13.14). What will this mean for us? Something important to ponder here.

iv) The perfection
"Who shall change our vile body, that it may be fashioned like unto his glorious body". The word "change" *(metaschematizo)* means 'to fashion anew'. The word is used three times of Satan and his "ministers" in 2 Corinthians 11.13-15, from which we conclude that it refers to outward change. We will not have a new body, but we will have a changed body. This verse, therefore, does not mean that the person will be changed, but that the mode of his existence will be changed. It is not deliverance *from* the body, but the deliverance *of* the body.

This "vile body" ('body of our humiliation', JND/RV) will be "fashioned like unto his glorious body (the body of his glory, JND/RV)". Paul describes the present state of our body as "the body of our humiliation", not because, in itself, it is worthless and to be despised (contra 1 Thessalonians 5.23), but because it is subject to "sufferings and indignities and all the effects of sin" (W.E. Vine). "When our Lord was here in the days of His flesh, He suffered every kind of humiliation at the hands of men. It was the body of His humiliation. His is now a body of glory" (W. Sanderson).

But the transformation of our bodies will not be only external. The word "fashioned" ("that it may be fashioned like unto his own glorious body") means 'conformed' *(summorphos),* and emphasises the reality of an inward change. It will be a body 'conformed' to the Lord Jesus Christ's 'body of glory'. His 'body of glory' is, of course, His body in resurrection and ascension, through which He displays His divine personality and attributes. Our bodies are going to be conformed, not only externally, but in nature and reality, to His 'body of glory'. "We know that, when he shall appear, we shall be like him; for we shall see him as he is" (1 John 3.2). We have been called "to the obtaining of the glory of our Lord Jesus Christ" (2 Thess. 2.14).

v) The power
This will be accomplished "according to the working whereby he is able even to subdue (subject) all things unto himself". So there is no doubt about the reality of the great prospect which lies before us. "He is able!" This phrase makes a very interesting study. For example, "Now to him that ***is able*** to establish you" (Rom.16.25. JND); "Now unto him that ***is able*** to do exceeding abundantly above all that we ask or think" (Eph.3.20); "Now unto him that ***is able*** to keep you from falling" (Jude 24).

It is usually suggested that Chapter 4.1 is part of Chapter 3. The connecting word "therefore" ("so that", JND), gives weight to the suggestion. We know that chapter divisions are not inspired! However, we will leave this verse where it is, and deal with it in our next study, God willing.

READ CHAPTER 4.1-7

"Help those women"

Philippians Chapter 3 ends with the happy prospect of the Lord's return. "For our conversation is in heaven; from whence also we look for the Saviour, the Lord Jesus Christ; who shall change our vile body ('our body of humiliation'), that it may be fashioned like unto his glorious body '(his body of glory'), according to the working whereby he is able even to subdue all things unto himself".

It is very important to notice that the Lord's coming is never taught in a vacuum. It is intended to produce practical results in our lives. The Old Testament prophets addressed the present in the light of the future, and that is equally true in the New Testament. His coming should produce **activity** (1 Cor.15.58), **tranquility** (1 Thess. 4.18), and **purity** (1 John 3.3). Rightly understood, the Lord's coming should also produce **stability,** and this is emphasised here. "Therefore (so what follows is based on the preceding verses), my brethren dearly beloved and longed for, my joy and crown, so **stand fast** in the Lord, my dearly beloved" (v.1). In this case, it is "stand fast" because danger threatened. See 3.2. Do remember that the section commences with "rejoice in the Lord", and concludes with "stand fast in the Lord". We must be like Shammah. See 2 Samuel 23.11-12.

Our appreciation of the new position, the new purpose, and the new prospect which we have in Christ, will give us stability and preserve us from error. It is not just 'Stand fast', but "Stand fast **in the Lord**". This means that all our resources are in Him, and we must be subject to His authority. He is "Lord". Nothing must interrupt our fellowship and communion with Him.

At the same time, and this is most important, this verse sets the atmosphere for what follows: "I beseech Euodias, and beseech Syntyche, that they be of the same mind in the Lord". Bearing this in mind, we can divide the chapter into two main sections: **(1)** peace in the assembly (vv.1-9); **(2)** provision by the assembly (vv.10-23). The headings should be self-explanatory, as long as you read the passage!

Chapter 4A

1) PEACE IN THE ASSEMBLY, vv.1-9

In this paragraph, Paul addresses two named sisters (v.2), an unnamed brother (v.3), and the assembly at large (vv.4-9). We can look at the section as follows, borrowing the first two titles from elsewhere: *(a)* "Be at peace among yourselves" (vv.1-2); *(b)* "Blessed are the peacemakers" (vv.3-5); *(c)* "The peace of God" (vv.6-7); *(d)* "The God of peace" (vv.8-9).

a) "Be at peace among yourselves", vv.1-2

The sub-title is taken from 1 Thessalonians 5: 13. These verses emphasise two aspects of this very necessary subject: *(i)* the right atmosphere is needed (v.1); *(ii)* the right action is needed (v.2).

i) The right atmosphere, v.1

"Therefore, my brethren dearly beloved and longed for, my joy and crown, so stand fast in the Lord my dearly beloved." Whilst, as we have seen, this is a fitting conclusion to Chapter 3, which begins with a warning against false teaching, it also provides the right atmosphere for Paul's appeal to Euodias and Syntyche. His appeal to the two warring sisters is permeated with his deep love for them. Remember his introduction: "For God is my record, how greatly I long after you *all* in the bowels of Jesus Christ" (1.8) They were all "dearly beloved and longed for", including Euodias and Syntyche. Paul's deep love for them is emphasised by the expressions, "*my* brethren...*my* joy and crown". We must notice how he describes them:

- *"Brethren beloved"*. We cannot doubt Paul's deep affection for the assembly. He loved them dearly. The Lord Jesus taught that "love one to another" was to be the outstanding characteristic of His disciples. "By this shall all men know that ye are my disciples, if ye have love one to another" (John 13.34-35). It is a mark of the new birth. See 1 Peter 1.22-23, 1 John 3.14. The capacity to love one another lies in the indwelling Holy Spirit. See Romans 5: 5. It is the essential atmosphere of assembly life, without which the various gifts bestowed by the Holy Spirit will be ineffective. See 1 Corinthians 12.14, where Paul discusses the way in which gifts have been **provided** (Chapter 12), the atmosphere by which they must be **permeated** (Chapter 13), and the principles on which they must be **practised** (Chapter 14). We can now see why Chapter 13 comes between Chapters 12 & 14! See also Romans 12.10.

Our love for the Lord Jesus will promote our love for each other. See 1 John 5.1. We will be in the right condition to "consider one another" (Heb. 10.24), when we first "consider him" (Heb. 3.1).

- **"Longed for"**. Love for one another will promote the desire for fellowship with one another. We have already noted the way in which Paul emphasises this in introducing the epistle: "For God is my record, how greatly *I long after you* all in the bowels of Jesus Christ" (1.8). Compare Romans 1.11 ("For *I long* to see you"); 2 Timothy 1.4 ("greatly *desiring* to see thee"). Let's say it again, love for one another ("brethren beloved") will promote the desire for fellowship with one another ("longed for").

- **"My joy"**. This too is emphasised in Paul's introduction: "Always in every prayer of mine for you all making request with joy" (1.4). Paul rejoiced as he remembered their excellent spiritual qualities. He remembered their "fellowship in the gospel from the first day until now" (1.5). Assembly elders should be able to serve with joy: "Obey them that have the rule over you, and submit yourselves: for they watch for your souls, as they that must give account, that they may do it with joy, and not with grief; for that is unprofitable for you" (Heb. 13.17). (The words, "that they may do it with joy", refer to the work itself, not to the account of the work). Are **we** making the work of the elders difficult? The assembly at Philippi brought Paul great joy. It is possible, of course, to love the saints, but have very little reason to rejoice in them!

- **"My "crown"**. Paul refers here to the victor's crown of reward *(stephanos)*. See also 1 Thessalonians 2.19-20, "For what is our hope, or joy, or **crown** of rejoicing? Are not even ye in the presence of our Lord Jesus Christ at his coming? For ye are our glory and joy".

This is a superb introduction to what follows, where Paul refers to the one reserve in his joy (see 1.26-27; 2.2), but not at the expense of his deep affection for the responsible people. He evidently esteemed them highly. See v.3.

ii) The right action, v.2
"I beseech Euodias (meaning 'fragrant'), and beseech Syntyche (meaning 'affableness'), that they be of the same mind in the Lord". Compare 1 Corinthians 1.10-11. The word "beseech" *(parakaleo)* means to exhort, or call to a person, and is a stronger word than 'ask'. We must notice that he appeals to them equally. The word "beseech" is used in both cases, and by doing this, Paul carefully avoids apportioning blame. He is not concerned with who is right and who is wrong. As already noted, he urges them, not just 'to be of the same mind', but to "be of the same mind *in the Lord*". This takes us back to 2.1-5. Paul wanted them to have the 'mind of Christ', which is expressed in 2.4-5, "Look not every man on his own things, but every man also on the things of others. Let this mind be

in you, which was also in Christ Jesus". The Lord Jesus did not pursue His own personal interests: He was, rather, deeply concerned with "the things of others". We do not know what had fractured the fellowship of these two sisters, but we **do** know that the best way to spoil fellowship is to give priority to our own position and our own interests. That is **not** Christlike. To "be of the same mind in the Lord", is far more than 'agreeing to differ', or 'making our apologies', or even 'deferring to one another'. It is, positively, acting in each others best interests. Compare Romans 12.16.

b) "Blessed are the peacemakers", vv.3-5
The sub-title is taken from Matthew 5.9. Paul now enlists the help of a local brother (that's important: local brethren should remember their responsibilities) in settling the problem that had arisen between the two sisters: "And I intreat thee also, true yokefellow, help those women ('these women', RV) which laboured with me in the gospel, with Clement also, and with other my fellow-labourers whose names are in the book of life". These are most interesting and challenging verses.

i) The "true yokefellow"
His actual name is withheld. It could have been "Synzygus", a Greek name meaning 'yokefellow'. In other words, Paul appealed to a brother who was worthy of his own name. He was a "**true** yokefellow". However, this does seem a little unlikely. The word "true" (*gnesios,* meaning sincerely, genuinely, truly) is used of Timothy in 2.20, "I have no man likeminded, who will naturally *(gnesios)* care for your state", and this has led some to the conclusion that Timothy was the "true yokefellow". However, it seems more likely that Paul was appealing to Epaphroditus. He was from Philippi, with Paul at the time, and about to return. He was Paul's "companion in labour" (2.25). Paul appeals to him by using the word *erotao*, meaning 'to beseech' ("intreat", AV). It was used when making a request to an equal.

Very clearly, Paul and the unnamed brother worked well together. Why not investigate the references to "yoke" in Scripture? See, for example, Deuteronomy 22.10, "Thou shalt not plough with an ox and an ass together". The two animals walk differently, reminding us that if we are going to enjoy fellowship in service (ploughing), we have got to walk in harmony together. Paul refers to an 'unequal yoke': "Be ye not unequally yoked together with unbelievers" (2 Cor. 6.14). While we can certainly apply this to marriage, it is applicable in many other ways as well. Now here's something quite different: "Take my yoke upon you, and learn of me; for I am meek and lowly in heart: and ye shall find rest unto your souls. For my yoke is easy, and my burden is light" (Matt. 11.29-30).

The "true yokefellow" was more than a local man: he was a most suitable local man! He was not the sort of man to treat God's people as if they belonged to him (1 Peter 5.3, JND margin). On the contrary, He knew what it was to labour with others. Who better to "help those women" which laboured with Paul in the Gospel?

ii) "Those women"

Euodias and Syntyche had evidently once laboured with Paul, but had subsequently fallen out of fellowship with each other. It is rather significant that Paul refers to Epaphroditus and himself as 'yokefellows', when dealing with two people who were once 'yokefellows!' Whilst there was evidently no doctrinal issues at stake, two discordant saints can cause mayhem! Some important lessons emerge:

- **The need to recognise the importance of harmony.** When Joseph sent his brothers back to his father in Canaan, he said "See that ye fall not out by the way" (Gen. 45.24). This is a timely word for us all! Christians sometimes fall out with each other for the most petty reasons. It often happens because we put our own interests before the Lord's interests, and the interests of our fellow-believers. We should avoid giving offence, and we should avoid taking offence.

- **The need to recognise the role of sisters in gospel work.** Euodias and Syntyche "laboured" with Paul "in the gospel". This does not mean that they preached publicly! But it does not mean either that they just made the tea and washed the dishes! Some Christians, men of course, seem to think that this is the limit of sisters' service! But is it really confined to the most important work of bringing up children (2 Tim. 3.15), and "teaching (training) the young women"? (Titus 2.4).

- **The need to recognise the nature of service.** It is not an 'armchair' work. Paul uses the word, "laboured", meaning 'to contend together' *(sunathleo)* as in 1.27, "Striving together for the faith of the gospel". We are not to contend with one another, but to contend for the Gospel! The Greek word *athleo* (hence our English word 'athletics') means 'to contend in the games'. "Strive for masteries" (2 Tim. 2.5) means "contend in the games" (RV). The work of God requires effort!

iii) "Other my fellowlabourers"

"With Clement also, and with other my fellowlabourers *(sunergos)*, whose names are in the book of life". The word "fellowlabourers" is used elsewhere in the New Testament. See Philemon 1.24; Philippians 2.25 ("companion in labour"); 1 Corinthians 3.9 ("labourers together"); 3 John 8 ("fellowhelpers to the truth").

It is rather interesting that reference is made to Clement by name, and to "other my fellowlabourers, whose names are in the book of life". **We** do not know their names, but that is not particularly important. They are all known to **God!** Their names are "in the book of life". So we needn't worry too much if nobody seems to recognise us on earth. God knows! Like Job, we can say, "my witness is in heaven, and my record is on high" (Job 16.19). Paul could say with confidence, "I know whom I have believed, and am persuaded that he is able to keep that which I have committed unto him against that day" (2 Tim. 1.12). On earth, people are soon forgotten, but not in heaven: it is the "book of **life**". Names can fade on headstones, and records can be defaced, but no name will ever be 'blotted out' of "the book of life" (Rev. 3.5).

iv) The assembly at Philippi

Paul now refers to the assembly at large. Quite suddenly, it seems, he exclaims, "Rejoice in the Lord alway: and again I say, rejoice". There is a wonderful spontaneity about this. He has just referred to names "in the book of life", and his heart is filled with praise. We should all "rejoice in **the Lord**", because it is through **His grace** that our names are there! Perhaps Paul was recalling the words of the Lord Jesus to His disciples: "Notwithstanding in this rejoice not, that the spirits are subject unto you; but rather rejoice, because your names are written in heaven" (Luke 10.20). We may not always be able to rejoice in our circumstances, but we can always "rejoice in the Lord!" Paul himself did this in adverse circumstances, (1.18).

At the same time, the exhortation to "rejoice in the Lord", is vital if we are to enjoy harmony in the assembly. Quarrels between believers inevitably rob them of joy, and we can visualise the tension between Euodias and Syntyche. Paul therefore urges the whole assembly to 'set their feet on higher ground'. He urges them to share his passion for Christ. To "rejoice in the Lord" will certainly enable us to "be of the same mind in the Lord". We should notice the expressions "Stand fast *in the Lord*" (v.1), "Be of the same mind *in the Lord*" (v.2), and "Rejoice *in the Lord*" (v.4).

To "rejoice in the Lord" is not an end in itself. It has a result in our lives. This follows: "Let your moderation be known unto all men (so non-believers are amongst the observers). The Lord is at hand". We should notice:

- *"Your moderation".* The RV margin has 'gentleness'. The word *(epieikes)* is translated "gentle" in Titus 3.2 ("to be no brawlers, but **gentle**"), in James 3.17 ("the wisdom that is from above is first pure, then peaceable, **gentle**...."), and in 1 Peter 2.18 ("not only to the good and **gentle,** but also to the forward"). It is translated "patient" in 1 Timothy 3.3 ("not given to wine, no striker, not greedy of filthy lucre: but **patient,** not a brawler, not covetous"). It means "equitable, fair, moderate, forbearing, not insisting on the letter of the law" (W.E. Vine). Other translations are "forbearance...yieldingness... moderation" (JND). Matthew Henry has "sweet reasonableness". A person whose "moderation" is "known unto all men", will be someone who does not insist on their rights, and who does not stand on their dignity. They will be selfless. They will be people with 'the mind of Christ'. We cannot fail to see the connection with the previous verses. Euodias and Syntyche needed such "moderation".

When it comes to doctrine, we must "stand fast in the Lord" (v.1). But we must be ready to yield in the interests and welfare of our brothers and sisters in Christ: "In lowliness of mind let each esteem other better than themselves" (2.3).

- *"The Lord is at hand".* According to W.E. Vine, the expression "at hand" *(engus)* is a Greek translation of the Aramaic *maranatha* (1 Cor. 16.22). It is used with reference to **time** in Revelation. 1.3; 22.10 ("for the time is at hand"), and in Romans 13.12 ("the day is at hand"). It is also used with reference to **place.** See John 19.42 ("for the sepulchre was nigh at hand"). It is not easy to determine whether Paul refers here to time or to place. His reference to the Lord's coming in 3.20-21 could suggest the former. Compare James 5.8-9. But it could refer to His near presence **now.** We often hear it rendered, 'The Lord is at your elbow'! But whether Paul is referring to the Lord's soon return, or to His presence with us now, makes no difference. Both should have the same result in our lives.

c) *"The peace of God", vv.6-7*
No need to look elsewhere for the sub-title here! If "moderation" before "all **men**" was essential for peace and harmony in the assembly, then prayer to **God** was also essential. "Be careful for nothing; but in every thing by prayer and supplication with thanksgiving let your requests be made known unto God. And the peace of God, which passeth all understanding, shall keep your hearts and minds through Christ Jesus". We should notice *(i)* the request, and *(ii)* the result.

i) The request
In this connection, we should notice the words "nothing" and "everything". "Be careful for **nothing**; but in **everything** by prayer..."

- *"Nothing"*. The words, "Be careful for **nothing**", are elsewhere translated, "In nothing be anxious" (RV). That is, 'do not bear the burden yourself'. See Matthew 6.25-32, where the words, "Take no thought" *(merimnao)* mean, "Be not anxious" (RV). See also 1 Peter 5.7, "Casting all your care *(merima)* upon him, for he careth for you". Paul himself had learned to do this: see 4.11-12, "I have learnt in those circumstances in which I am, to be satisfied in myself" (v.11, JND). If you prefer the AV, substitute 'therein' for the italicised "therewith"). Remember that Paul was in prison at the time! (The word "care" is used in a good sense in 2.20). In the words of W.E. Vine, "Anxiety harasses the soul; it enfeebles, irritates, ruffles the temper, is a sign of mistrust and of failing obedience, and distracts the mind from communion with God".

- *"Everything"*. That is exactly what it means! But do we cover "everything" in our prayers? This verse includes four of the seven words used in the New Testament for prayer. *"Prayer" (proseuchomai)*: this is the usual word for prayer in general. *"Supplication" (deesis)*: this refers to petitions in cases of special need. See, for example, Luke 1.13 in connection with Zacharias, and Romans 10.1 where Paul refers to Israel. *"Thanksgiving" (eucharistia). "Requests" (aitemata)*, meaning 'petitions'. See 1 John 5.15. The other words are *erotao, euchomai,* and *enteuxis*. See W.E. Vine's Expository Dictionary.

ii) The result
"And the peace of God, which passeth all understanding, shall keep your hearts and minds through Christ Jesus". We do not know **how** it "passeth understanding" (meaning 'above, or better, than understanding'), but we know that it **does** happen! As a result of prayer, the Saviour says, "Peace be still", and there is "a great calm", causing us to say, "What manner of man is this?" Paul uses a military term here: "the peace of God...shall **keep** *(phroureo)* your hearts and minds through Christ Jesus". See 2 Corinthians 11.32, "In Damascus the governor under Aretas the king **kept** the city with a garrison"; 1 Peter 1.5, "who are **kept** (guarded) by the power of God through faith unto salvation ready to be revealed in the last time".

The "peace of God" will be in our **hearts** ("the secret spring of all activity, as can be seen from its many references in Old and New Testaments", Sydney Maxwell) and in our **minds**. The word, *noema,* denotes "'what is thought out; hence a purpose, device: it is translated 'devices' in 2 Corinthians 2.11" (W.E. Vine). It refers to mental activity. As W.E. Vine points out, it is "all 'in Christ Jesus', for peace can be enjoyed only in realised communion with him, the Living One, on the ground of His death". The order of the words, "Christ Jesus", emphasises that He is risen and ascended to glory. The teaching of these verses is applicable to ourselves as individuals, and, bearing in mind the context, most applicable to assembly life.

d) *"The God of peace", vv.8-9*

Again, no need to look elsewhere for the sub-title here. See v.9. We will deal with this at the beginning of our next study, God willing.

READ CHAPTER 4.8-14

"Think on these things"

In our previous study, we suggested that this chapter can be divided into two major sections: **(1)** peace in the assembly (vv.1-9); **(2)** provision by the assembly, (vv.10-23). This study therefore straddles the division between the two sections!

1) PEACE IN THE ASSEMBLY, vv.1-9
In this section of the chapter, Paul deals with the problem which robbed him of unqualified joy in the assembly at Philippi. See 2.1-2. After gently alluding to the subject in the earlier part of the epistle, he addresses it directly here: "I beseech Euodias, and beseech Syntyche, that they be of the same mind in the Lord" (v.2). We have noticed that the subject of peace in the assembly pervades the entire section.

a) *"Be at peace among yourselves", vv.1-2*
We have noticed that there was nothing harsh or abrasive about Paul's appeal to the two sisters. He appeals to them out of his deep love for **all** the believers at Philippi (v.1). There was no question of 'banging their silly heads together'. Yes, **we** do feel like that sometimes, don't we?!

b) *"Blessed are the peacemakers", vv.3-5*
A local man (we suggested Epaphroditus) was enlisted to "help those women which laboured with me in the gospel". The greatest antidote to strife is occupation with Christ. To "rejoice in the Lord" will enable us to be "of the same mind in the Lord".

c) *"The peace of God", vv.6-7*
It doesn't 'just happen'. It is through "prayer and supplication with thanksgiving". Then, and only then, will "the peace of God, which passeth all understanding" keep our "hearts and minds through Christ Jesus". Remember, Paul is writing to an assembly. Just think of the effect this will have on our fellowship! This brings us to:

d) "The God of peace", vv.8-9

The words, "Finally, brethren", introduce Paul's last point in connection with the problem at Philippi. We can easily see its relevance to the situation described in v.2, but, at the same time, he is addressing the whole assembly. Paul is constantly raising his expectations for the assembly at Philippi. In the first place, it was "the peace of God which passeth all understanding", but now it is the presence in the assembly of "the God of peace!" But certain conditions must be fulfilled, and these can be described as follows. *(i) consideration:* "think on these things" (v.8); *(ii) application:* "those things, which ye have both learned and received, and heard, and seen in me, do" (v.9). This reminds us of James 3.17-18, "But the wisdom that is from above is first pure, then **peaceable,** gentle, and easy to be intreated, full of mercy and good fruits, without partiality, and without hypocrisy. And the fruit of righteousness is sown in **peace** of them that make **peace**".

i) Consideration, v.8

Having excluded anxious thoughts (v.6), Paul is concerned that their minds should be occupied with the right things. After all, a vacuum only sucks in dirt! "He begs them to give their minds, thus 'safeguarded' by 'the peace of God', all possible pure and healthy material to work upon" (H.C.G. Moule). So, "think on these things". Remember, "As he thinketh in his heart, so is he" (Prov. 23.7). Do notice the context of this quotation: do **we** just maintain outward appearances? Let's remember as well, that every one of "these things" resides perfectly in the Lord Jesus. So think about Him, as you think about "these things". Notice that Paul uses the word "whatsoever" in each case. This emphasises that the six things which follow are important in their own right.

- *"Whatsover things are TRUE".* The word "true" *(alethes)* means, "primarily, unconcealed, manifest...hence, actual, true to fact" (W.E. Vine). The noun (here it is, of course, an adjective) is used in John 17.17, "Sanctify them through thy **truth:** thy word is truth"; in John 14.6, "I am the way, the **truth,** and the life"; in Ephesians 4.20-21, "But ye have not so learned Christ; if so be that ye have heard him, and have been taught by him, as (the) **truth** is in Jesus".

We are to think, not about what is false, or hearsay, or rumour, or talebearer's gossip, but about **truth.** This excludes things with a double meaning, and 'hidden agendas'. We are not to think about false doctrine either!

- *"Whatsoever things are HONEST".* The word "honest" *(semnos)* means honourable or venerable. The meaning, 'nobly serious', has been suggested. The RV margin has 'reverent'. We are to think about things 'which claim respect'. The noun is used in 1 Timothy 3.4, "having his (the overseer) children in subjection with all **gravity**"; 1 Timothy 2.2, "In all godliness and **honesty**" ('gravity', RV); Titus 2.2, "That the aged men be... **grave**"; 1 Timothy 3.8, "Likewise must the deacons be **grave**"; 1 Timothy 3.11, "Even so must their wives be **grave**" or "Women in like manner must be grave" (RV). Here, however, it is used of "things", so we are not to give our minds to things which are 'flippant', but to things that inspire reverence and awe.

- *"Whatsoever things are JUST".* The word occurs in 1.7, "Even as it is **meet** for me to think this of you all". It is often rendered 'righteous'. It is used of God, "O **righteous** Father (John 17.25). It is used of the Lord Jesus, "the Holy One and the **Just**" (Acts 3.14); "they have slain them which shewed before the coming of the **Just** One" (Acts 7.52); "The God of our fathers hath chosen thee, that thou shouldest know his will, and see that **Just** One" (Acts 22.14). We are therefore to give our minds to what is right and righteous.

- *"Whatsoever things are PURE".* The word "pure" *(hagnos)* signifies "pure from defilement" or "pure from admixture of evil", and comes from the same root as 'holy'. It means uncontaminated, or chaste. See 1 Timothy 5.22, "Keep thyself **pure**". It is used of the Lord Jesus in 1 John 3.3, "Even as he is **pure**". As W.E. Vine observes, "Unchastity and all sins of the flesh are excluded". H.C.G. Moule explains it as "holy chastity in thought and act".

- *"Whatsoever things are LOVELY".* The word "lovely" *(prosphilos)* comes from *pros,* meaning towards, and *phileo,* meaning to love. It carries the meaning of pleasing or agreeable. "Saul and Jonathan were lovely and pleasant in their lives" (2 Sam. 1.23).

- *"Whatsoever things are of GOOD REPORT".* The words "good report" translate *euphemos,* from *eu,* meaning well, and *pheme,* a saying or report. It "denotes, firstly, well-sounding, then well-speaking...attractive, winning" (W.E. Vine). We must therefore avoid everything scandalous and dubious.

Paul concludes: "If there be any **virtue** (moral goodness or excellence), and if there be any **praise** (*epainos*, whatever is praiseworthy), think on these things". The word "think" *(logizomai)* means, literally, 'to reckon', or 'to take account', and in this passage, "make those things the subjects of your thoughtful consideration" (W.E. Vine). The world bombards us with the very opposite of these six things, and we need to 'gird up the loins of our mind' (1 Pet. 1.13) and 'be transformed by the renewing of our mind' (Rom. 12.2).

ii) Application, v.9

"Those things, which ye have both learned, and received, and heard, and seen in me, do: and the God of peace shall be with you". We can look at it like this:

- **Exposition.** "Those things, which ye have both **learned,** and **received**". They had "learned" those things by example (the word *manthano* frequently means to learn by enquiry or observation, W.E. Vine), and "received" them orally. But Paul's teaching was backed by:

- **Example.** "Those things, which ye have...**heard** and **seen** in me". It is often said that 'example is better than precept'. But 'example with precept' makes a very powerful combination! Paul reminded the Ephesian elders of this: "Ye know, from the first day that I came into Asia, after what manner I have been with you at all seasons" (Acts 20.18). The church at Thessalonica was equally aware of Paul's consistency: "Ye are witnesses, and God also, how holily and justly and unblameably we behaved ourselves among you that believe: as ye know how we exhorted and comforted and charged every one of you, as a father doth his children" (1 Thess. 2.10-11). See also 1 Timothy 4.16; 2 Timothy 3.10. There was no discrepancy between the teaching and the life of the Lord Jesus. See Acts 1.1.

- **Exhortation.** "Those things, which ye have...heard and seen in me, **do**", meaning 'go on doing'. As Sydney Maxwell observes, "The balance of teaching and practice is to be noted in this verse. The order is most important. There must be instruction in the doctrine, then the working it out in the life, and Paul had no hesitation, setting himself forth as a pattern for them".

- **Encouragement.** "And the God of peace shall be with you". Compare 1 Thessalonians 5.23, "And the very **God of peace** sanctify you wholly"; Hebrews 13.20, "Now the **God of peace,** that brought again from the dead our Lord Jesus Christ". "The peace of God" (v.7) denotes His **provision**, and "the God of peace" (v.9), denotes His **presence.** It has been nicely said that as "the God of peace", He cannot be disturbed: He is above every crisis.

2) PROVISION BY THE ASSEMBLY, vv.10-23

This section describes the fellowship of the Philippians in three ways: **(a)** in relation to Paul (vv.10-14); **(b)** in relation to themselves (vv.15-17); **(c)** in relation to God (vv.18-19). The chapter concludes with a doxology and greetings (v.20-23).

a) Their fellowship in relation to Paul, vv.10-14

We should notice that Paul speaks about *(i)* their care (v.10); *(ii)* his contentment (vv.11-13); *(iii)* their communication (v.14).

i) Their care, v.10

"But I rejoiced in the Lord greatly, that now at the last your **care** of me hath flourished again; wherein ye were also careful, but ye lacked opportunity". We must notice that the Lord was glorified through their fellowship: "I rejoiced in **the Lord** greatly". As noted, joy is a characteristic of the epistle. The word "care" *(phroneo)* means 'to take thought' leading to the translation, "Ye have revived your thinking of me" (JND) with the footnote, "But I do not mean that ye did not think of me, but that ye had no good occasion to show it". The gift sent by Epaphroditus was evidence of their thought for him. We must notice Paul's courtesy here. He did not want them to think that he was complaining in any way. Circumstances precluded the opportunity to show fellowship with him. It is always helpful to explain ourselves, and avoid ambiguity! The words, "flourished again", remind us of a tree that leaves behind its winter dormancy, and breaks into life once favourable conditions return. Compare Ezekiel 17.24.

To emphasise that he was not complaining, and that it was not his need that made him speak in this way, Paul speaks of his sufficiency through Christ. The believer who is Christ-centred will not complain!

ii) His contentment, vv.11-13

Attention is drawn to the fact of his contentment (v.11), to the conditions of his contentment (v.12), and to the secret of his contentment (v.13)

- **The fact of his contentment, v.11.** "Not that I speak in respect of want (*husteresis,* meaning need, poverty, privation): for I have learned, in whatsoever state I am, (omit *therewith*) to be content". He was content *in* his circumstances, rather than *with* his circumstances.

The word "*learned*" *(manthano:* see also v.9) means to 'learn as a disciple', that is, by use and practice. It was not automatic. It was learned by experience. Perhaps Paul refers here to the period during which he was obliged to wait for the gift to arrive. (Even Paul had to learn!) The word occurs in 1 Timothy 5.4, "Let them *learn* first to shew piety at home"; 1 Timothy 5.13, "And withal they *learn* to be idle"; Titus 3.14, "And let ours also *learn* to maintain good works". The words, *"to be content"*, mean 'sufficient in oneself' or 'self-sufficient'. But this does not mean, as we shall see, that Paul was self-reliant, and it does not mean that he was 'resigned' to his circumstances! Paul was not crushed by external conditions. He did not depend on his circumstances for satisfaction. He was quite unlike the man who prayed: "Give me neither poverty nor riches; feed me with food convenient for me: lest I be full and deny thee, and say, Who is the Lord? Or lest I be poor, and steal, and take the name of my God in vain" (Prov. 30.8-9).

- *The conditions of his contentment, v.12.* Having said that he was not crushed by external conditions, he now describes them. "I know both how to be abased, and I know how to abound: every where and in all things I am instructed both to be full and to be hungry, both to abound and to suffer need".

"I *know* (meaning, 'I have perceived') both how to be **abased** (meaning, 'to be brought low': often rendered 'humbled' as in 2.8: used in classical Greek of a river running low), and I know how to **abound** '(to be over and abound', as in 1.9; 1.26; 4.18)". Paul is evidently referring here to material comforts.

He continues: "Every where ('in everything', RV, JND), and in all things *I am instructed* both to be full and to be hungry, both to abound and to suffer need". The words, "I am instructed" translate the verb *mueo*, meaning "to initiate into the mysteries" (W.E. Vine). Hence, "I have learned the secret" (RV). We shall discover what "the secret" is in the next verse.

The remaining part of v.12 needs no explanation. The words "both to be **full** (*chortazo*, 'to be fed full') and to be **hungry**" remind us of 2 Corinthians 11.27, "in hunger and thirst". The Lord Jesus experienced hunger (Matt. 4.2). He knew "both to be full and to be hungry, both to abound and to suffer need". We have already noticed the meaning of "**abound**" in the earlier part of the verse, and "**want**" in v.11. But how could Paul possibly withstand such extremes?

- *The secret of his contentment, v.13.* "I can do all things through Christ which strengtheneth me" or "I have strength for all things *in Him* who gives me power" (JND). So Paul was 'self-sufficient' in **Christ!** We must notice that Paul is speaking personally here: "*I* can do all things through Christ which strengtheneth me". The words, "which **strengtheneth** me", have been variously translated: for example, "which makes me strong"; "which enables me"; "Who pours His strength into me".' The word *(endunamoo)* is used in 2 Timothy 4.17 ("Notwithstanding the Lord stood with me and **strengthened** me"); 1 Timothy 1.12 ("I thank Christ Jesus our Lord, who hath **enabled** me").

But we must not think for one moment that Paul was ungrateful to the Philippians for their fellowship. Whilst he was dependent on the Lord for strength in changing circumstances, he was deeply grateful to them for their care.

iii) Their communication, v.14

"Notwithstanding ye have **well done,** that ye did communicate with my affliction". The word "communicate" *(sunkoinoneo)* means 'to have fellowship with'. It conveys the idea of sharing what one has with others, in order to meet their needs. The Philippians took a share in his affliction. The word "affliction" *(thlipsis)* means 'pressure', and in the context means pressure from want or deprivation.

Here is a fitting commentary on the above: "For the administration of this service not only supplieth the want of the saints, but is abundant also by many thanksgivings unto God; Whiles by the experiment of this ministration they glorify God for your professed subjection unto the gospel of Christ, and for your liberal distribution unto them, and unto all men; And by their prayer for you, which long after you for the exceeding grace of God in you" (2 Cor. 9.12-14).

Having considered their fellowship in relation to Paul (vv.10-14), we will devote our final study to their fellowship in relation to themselves (vv.15-17), and their fellowship in relation to God (vv.18-19).

But in the meantime it is appropriate to ask ourselves the question, "Will **we** receive the Lord's "well done", because of our good stewardship?

READ CHAPTER 4.15-23

"An odour of a sweet smell"

For the purpose of our studies, we have divided this chapter into two major sections: *(1)* peace in the assembly (vv.1-9; *(2)* provision by the assembly (vv.10-23). We have also noted that the second section describes the fellowship of the Philippians in three ways: *(a)* in relation to Paul (vv.10-14); *(b)* in relation to themselves (vv.15-17); *(c)* in relation to God (vv.18-19). We can put it like this: through our giving, God's people are helped, we are enriched, and God is glorified. The chapter closes with a doxology and greetings (vv.20-23).

a) Their fellowship in relation to Paul, vv.10-14
In our last study we noticed that Paul speaks about *(i)* their care (v.10); *(ii)* his contentment (vv.11-13); *(iii)* their communication (v.14). This brings us to:

b) Their fellowship in relation to themselves, vv.15-17
"Now ye Philippians know also, that in the beginning of the gospel, when I departed from Macedonia, no church communicated with me as concerning giving and receiving, but ye only. For even in Thessalonica ye sent once and again unto my necessity. Not because I desire a gift: but I desire fruit that may abound to your account". The Philippians were people who cared (v.10), who communicated (v.14) and who continued (vv.15-16). We must notice the following: *(i)* the promptness of their giving (v.15); *(ii)* the spontaneity of their giving (v.16); *(iii)* the frequency of their giving (v.16); *(iv)* the reward for their giving (v.17).

i) The promptness of their giving, v.15
"And know also, O Philippians..." (JND). We can catch the depth of Paul's appreciation here. He was deeply moved by their fellowship. Now compare 2 Corinthians 6.11, "O ye Corinthians", and Galatians 3.1, "O foolish Galatians". Paul was deeply moved here as well, but not in the same way. He was deeply grieved when he thought about the assembly at Corinth and the assemblies in Galatia. Sydney Maxwell (*What the Bible Teaches – Philippians*) contrasts the **narrowness** of the Corinthians and the **foolishness** of the Galatians, with the **devotedness** of the Philippians.

Chapter 4C

The assembly at Philippi gave practical help to Paul at the earliest possible date. It took place during his visit to Thessalonica ("even in Thessalonica"), immediately after leaving Philippi (Acts 17.1), and before he actually left the province of Macedonia. Paul identifies the time as "the beginning of the gospel", which must refer to Acts 16 when the gospel was first preached at Philippi. He calls it "your fellowship in the gospel from the **first day** until now" (1.5). We have already noted that word "communication" (*sunkoinoneo*), means 'to have fellowship with' (see v.14). It has been defined as 'sharing what we have with others in order to meet their needs'. The Philippians soon recognised their responsibility to help the man who had preached the gospel to them. "Even so hath the Lord ordained that they which preach the gospel should live of the gospel" (1 Cor. 9.14). The Philippians recognised their responsibilities. Do **we?** Unlike so many so-called 'Christian' organisations today, the early gospel preachers "went forth, taking nothing of the Gentiles". Our practical fellowship with them makes us "fellowhelpers to the truth" (3 John 7-8).

ii) The spontaneity of their giving, v.16

"For even in Thessalonica **ye sent** once and again unto my necessity". It was voluntary. Paul certainly did not command their support. He did not even ask for it! He certainly used his apostolic authority in asking for support for other Christians (see, for example, 1 Corinthians 16.1), but never for himself. He deliberately declined the right to ask for support. See 1 Corinthians 9.15. Paul did not send out 'begging letters!'

There should be a similar spontaneity about **our** giving. See 2 Corinthians 9.7, "Every man according as he purposeth in his heart, so let him give; not grudgingly, or of necessity: for God loveth a cheerful giver".

iii) The frequency of their giving, v.16

"For even in Thessaionica ye sent **once and again** unto my necessity". This indicates their ongoing concern for him. It was not a case of 'out of sight, out of mind'.

As we have already noticed, the words, "even at Thessalonica", indicate the promptness with which the Philippians sent gifts to Paul. But they also remind us that whilst Paul worked at Thessalonica "night and day" (1 Thess, 2.9; 2 Thess. 3.8), this was not sufficient to meet his needs. "Ye sent once and again unto **my necessity**". This is worth remembering. We should not withhold support for a missionary or an evangelist because he takes a job to help him meet expenses. It is highly unlikely that the Christians at Philippi sat down and attempted to calculate Paul's expenditure! They gave, as constrained by God Himself. It is also worth noticing that Paul took a job, not only to help himself, but those with him! See Acts 20.34: "Yea, ye yourselves know, that these hands have ministered to my necessities, and to **them that were with me**".

A similar situation arose at Corinth, but for different reasons. At **Thessalonica,** Paul supported himself, "because we would not be chargeable to any of you". See, again, the two references above. Thessalonica and Philippi, both located in Macedonia, were poor assemblies in financial terms, and Paul did not wish to put additional strain on their slender resources. Notwithstanding, they went "beyond their power (ability)" to help the needy Christians in Judaea. See 2 Corinthians 8.1-4. At **Corinth,** Paul supported himself by following his trade as a tent-maker (Acts 18.3), not because of their poverty (Corinth was evidently a wealthier church), but because he wished to make it absolutely clear that, unlike others, financial gain was not his motive in preaching the gospel. Read 2 Corinthians 11.7-12; 12.11-18. Notice, again, that although Paul took a job to help pay his expenses, this did not meet his expenditure. "I robbed other churches (sounds bad, doesn't it?!), taking wages of them, to do you service. And when I was present with you, and **wanted**, I was chargeable to no man: for that which was **lacking** to me the brethren which came from Macedonia supplied".

iv) The reward for their giving, v.17
This is quite delightful. Once again, Paul displays 'the mind of Christ'. As we know, the Lord Jesus looked not "on his own things, but on the things of others" (2.4). Paul rejoiced, not so much in the benefit **he** derived from their gift, but in the benefit **they** derived! "Not 'because I desire *(epizeteo,* to seek earnestly) a gift; but I desire fruit that may abound to **your** account". According to W.E. Vine, the word "account" *(logos)* is used in a commercial sense. He describes it as "a financial metaphor, suggestive of interest". We must not think that Paul was ungrateful. He has already expressed his deep gratitude and appreciation. But their reward was more important than his comfort! Compare 2 Corinthians 12.14, "I seek not yours, but **you**". Paul was certainly devoid of covetousness. See Acts 20.33: "I have coveted no man's silver, or gold, or apparel".

The words, "fruit that may abound to your account", point us heavenward: "Lay not up for yourselves treasures upon earth, where moth and rust doth corrupt, and where thieves break through and steal: but lay up for yourselves treasures in heaven" (Matt. 6.19-20); "For God is not unrighteous to forget your work and labour of love, which ye have shewed towards his name, in that ye have ministered to the saints, and do minister" (Heb. 6.10). Paul's desire for "fruit that may abound" to their account recalls his prayer in 2 Corinthians 9.10, "Now he that ministereth seed to the sower both minister bread for your food, and multiply your seed sown, and increase the fruits of your righteousness".

c) Their fellowship in relation to God, vv.18-19
"But I have all, and abound; I am full, having received of Epaphroditus the things which were sent from you, an odour of a sweet smell, a sacrifice acceptable, wellpleasing to God. But my God shall supply all your need according to his riches in glory by Christ Jesus". There are two very lovely statements here: *(i)* God's appreciation of their fellowship with Paul (v.18) and *(ii)* God's ability to completely meet their need (v.19).

i) God's appreciation of their fellowship with Paul, v.18
Having said that their reward was more important than his comfort, Paul quickly assures the Philippians that he appreciated their fellowship, but of even more importance, **God** appreciated their fellowship.

- **Paul's appreciation.** "But I have all things in full supply and abound; I am full, having received of Epaphroditus the things (sent) from you" (JND). We must remember that the man who wrote these words was in prison at the time! W.E. Vine points out that the verb 'to have' *(apecho)* means 'to have in full'. It is used in Matthew 6.2, 5, 16; "They have their reward". W.E. Vine continues, "Here it means, 'you have paid me in full in all respects'". The word "abound" *(perisseuo)* means 'to be abundantly furnished'. It occurs in Philippians 1.26. He was not only full, but overflowing! The word "full" *(pleroo)* is used in 1.11 ("filled with the fruits of righteousness") and 2.2 ("fulfil ye my joy"). Paul therefore uses the most telling words possible to express his appreciation of their fellowship. There is not the slightest hint of a murmur or complaint at his circumstances. He rejoices in their care.

- **God's appreciation.** This is even greater, and Paul now uses two words whose significance can be ascertained from the two other places in which they occur together in the New Testament. He describes their gift as "an odour *(osme)* of a sweet smell *(euodia)*, a sacrifice acceptable, wellpleasing to God". Now read Ephesians 5.2, "And walk in love, as Christ also hath loved us, and hath given himself for us an offering and a sacrifice to God for a sweetsmelling *(osme)* savour *(euodia)*" or an "odour of a sweet smell" (RV). Follow this with 2 Corinthians 2.14-16, "Now thanks be unto God, which always causeth us to triumph in Christ, and maketh manifest the savour *(osme)* of his knowledge by us in every place. For we are unto God a sweet savour *(euodia)* of Christ, in them that are saved, and in them that perish: To the one we are the savour *(osme)* of death unto death; and to the other the savour *(osme)* of life unto life". (In the Septuagint, the Greek version of the Hebrew Old Testament, commonly written as LXX in Bible commentaries etc, the phrase is used of Noah's offering: see Genesis 8.21). The word *osme* is used of Mary's box of ointment in John 12.3. We should also remember that *euodia* was a lady's name! But you couldn't say that Euodias was very sweet-smelling (speaking metaphorically, of course) when it came to Syntyche! In this case she was, it seems, distinctly 'odious!'.

This is far from a technical study. The gift sent to Paul by the Philippians was permeated with the sweetness of Christ Himself! God saw something of His Son in "the things which were sent". This puts practical fellowship on the highest possible level. Remember too, that the Macedonian assemblies were poor. They gave "to their power (ability) and beyond their power (ability)". The Lord Jesus gave Himself.

Paul concludes his description of the gift with the words, "a sacrifice acceptable, wellpleasing to God". This is not the first time in the epistle that Paul describes their fellowship as a "sacrifice (*thusia*)". See 2.17. Now read Ephesians 5.2 again: "Christ also hath loved us, and hath given himself for us an offering and a sacrifice (*thusia*) to God for a sweetsmelling savour". It is rather striking that the Holy Spirit, through Paul, should use three words *(osme, euodia* and *thusia)* in one verse to describe the gift of the Philippians which are used in another verse to describe the death of the Lord Jesus. Like the death of the Lord Jesus, the gift sent to Paul was a "sacrifice". It was not easily given. Unlike the majority of people who "did cast in of their abundance", the Philippians, like the widow (Mark 12.41-44), had given 'all their living'. Or, to put it in Paul's words, out of "their deep poverty" (2 Cor. 8.2). No wonder it was "a sacrifice **acceptable**". Peter uses the same word in 1 Peter 2.5, "An holy priesthood, to offer up spiritual sacrifices, **acceptable** to God by Jesus Christ". This reminds us that the death of the Lord Jesus (Ephesians 5.2) and the giving of the Philippians, were 'worshipful sacrifices'. Notice too, that Peter uses a strengthened form of Paul's word "acceptable." It is *dextos* in Philippians and *'euprosdextos'* (a very favourable acceptance) in 1 Peter 2.5.

The words, "wellpleasing to God" remind us that in addition to our giving, every part of our lives should be "wellpleasing" *(euarestos)* to Him. See, for example, Romans 12.1-2: "Present your bodies a living sacrifice (yes, *thusia),* holy, acceptable (well-pleasing, *euarestos*) unto God...that ye may prove what is that good, and acceptable (well-pleasing, *euarestos*), and perfect, will of God"; 2 Corinthians 5.9, "Wherefore we labour (make it our aim), that, whether present or absent, we may be accepted (well-pleasing, *euarestos*) of him". See also Romans 14.18; Ephesians 5.10; Colossians 3.20; Hebrews 13.21.

ii) God's ability to completely meet their need, v.19
This verse could easily be the subject of a separate study! It is full of precious lessons, and the following should whet your appetite!

- **The background to the promise.** It is conditional on v.18. The Philippians had supplied the needs of Paul. They had 'communicated with his affliction'. But 'God is no man's debtor': He would meet all **their** need. "My God shall supply *(pleroo,* to fulfil) all **your** need".

- **The assurance of the promise.** Paul knew from his own experience that God was faithful. "**My** God shall supply all your need". He says, in effect, 'He will be to you all that He has been to me'. Thus far, the Philippians might not have had the same experience as Paul. He assures them that they would! Hence the personal note here, "**My** God".

- **The certainty of the promise.** "My God **shall** supply all your need". Perhaps we should remember more often the words of the Lord Jesus in Matthew 6.25-34. "Wherefore, if God so clothe the grass of the field, which today is, and tomorrow is cast into the oven, shall he not much more clothe you, O ye of little faith? Therefore take no thought (anxious thought), saying, What shall we eat? or, What shall we drink? or, Wherewithal shall we be clothed?...for your heavenly Father knoweth that ye have need of all these things".

- **The scope of the promise.** "My God shall supply **all your need**". Not 'all your wants!' The same word is rendered "necessity" in v.16. Our materialistic Western world is more concerned with 'wants' than 'needs'. See 1 Timothy 6.6-8, "Having food and raiment let us be therewith content"; Hebrews 13.5, "Be content with such things as ye have: for he hath said, I will never leave thee, nor forsake thee".

- **The resources of the promise.** "According to **his riches in glory by Christ Jesus**". Paul does **not** say, 'Out of his riches in glory by Christ Jesus'. A millionaire might donate a pound to some charitable cause. In this case, he gives 'out of his riches'. But if he gave 'according to his riches', he would give a vast sum of money! Need we say more? God can meet our need "**according** to his riches in glory by Christ Jesus!" There is no scant measure here. The grace available to us is infinite. There is no recession in heaven!

- **The security of the promise.** "According to his riches **in glory by (in) Christ Jesus**". The resources available to us cannot be reached by our adversaries, whether human or satanic. They are located in the glorified Lord Jesus Christ. Hence the title "Christ Jesus". God makes everything available to us in Him.

Doxology and greetings, vv.20-23

"Now unto God and our Father ('our God and Father', JND) be glory for ever and ever Amen". According to J.N. Darby's footnote there is an emphatic article here, 'the glory', which refers to "the due divine glory which cannot be given in English". It means more than giving God glory for what has just been said: it is recognition of God's excellence and attributes. Notice that Paul does not now say '*my* God and Father' (see v.19), but "*our* God and Father" (JND).

"Salute every saint in Christ Jesus. The brethren which are with me greet you. All the saints salute you, chiefly they that are of Caesar's household". "Salute" and "greet" translate the same word (*aspazomai*). We discussed the word "saint" in connection with 1.1. See Study 2. "The brethren which are with me" would include Timothy (1.1). "All the saints salute you" is evidently a greeting from the Christians at Rome. There is a wholeheartedness about these greetings: "Salute *every* saint...*all* the saints salute you". The words, "chiefly they that are of Caesar's household", does seem to refer to people reached through Paul's imprisonment at Rome. See 1.13. The Gospel had penetrated the palace.

"The grace of our Lord Jesus Christ be with you all" or "The grace of the Lord Jesus Christ (be) with your spirit" (JND).' It has been pointed out that the word "your" is in the plural, but the word "spirit" is in the singular, indicating Paul's desire that the assembly should be completely united in love and fellowship.

The epistle therefore commences with "grace from the Lord Jesus Christ", (1.2), and concludes with the "grace of our Lord Jesus Christ." Every divine benefit is in Him.

While, we are told, some manuscripts omit "Amen", there can hardly be a better word on which to end the epistle!

Chapter 4C

COLOSSIANS

by
John M Riddle

COLOSSIANS

INTRODUCTION

Read Chapter 1:1-8 & 2:9-19

"Paul, an apostle of Jesus Christ by the will of God, and Timotheus our brother, to the saints and faithful brethren in Christ which are at Colosse: Grace be unto you, and peace, from God our Father and the Lord Jesus Christ". Paul commences the epistle, as he does in Philippians, with reference to their **spiritual** location and their **geographical** location. They were "in Christ", and they were "at Colosse". The first emphasises the source of our blessings: the second emphasises the sphere of our service.

It is rather striking to notice that whilst Paul had visited Philippi, and was acquainted with the Christians there, he had evidently not been to Colosse (see 2:1). But he was equally interested in them, and deeply concerned about them. Paul did not have his 'favourites'. All God's people were precious to him, whether he knew them or not. There is something Christ-like about this. The Lord Jesus prayed, not only for "the men which thou gavest me out of the world", but "for them also which shall believe on me through their word" (John 17:6, 20). We must remember of course, that whilst Paul was deeply interested in the welfare of fellow-believers he had never met, the Lord Jesus is personally acquainted with every one of us!

In our introductory study, we will attempt to cover the following: **(1)** the circumstances of Paul; **(2)** the city of Colosse; **(3)** the conversion of the Colossians; **(4)** the confusion at Colosse; **(5)** the contents of the epistle.

1) THE CIRCUMSTANCES OF PAUL

Colossians is one of Paul's 'prison epistles', and was written during the time of his first imprisonment at Rome. Three others were written during this period: Ephesians, Philippians and Philemon. (Compare Colossians with Ephesians: there are many similarities in structure and content). It has been suggested that since

Introduction

the apostle was evidently expecting an early release (see Philippians 1:25 and Philemon 22), these letters were written late in his imprisonment, perhaps in AD 62 or 63 (T. Bentley, *What the Bible Teaches - Colossians*). Paul describes himself in this epistle as "in bonds" (4:3), and refers to Aristarchus as "my fellowprisoner" (4:10). But he was not cowed by his imprisonment. To the contrary, he rejoiced in prison ("who now rejoice in my sufferings for you", 1: 24), and looked for every opportunity to "speak the mystery of Christ" (4:3). There is a little 'jingle' that says

> Two men looked through prison bars:
> One saw mud; the other - stars!

Well, Paul certainly looked higher than even the stars. He had his eyes fixed on the Creator of the stars: "Who is the image of the invisible God, the firstborn of every creature: for by him were all things created, that are in heaven, and that are in earth, visible and invisible, whether they be thrones, or dominions, or principalities, or powers: all things were created by him, and for him: and he is before all things, and by him all things consist" (1:15-17).

2) THE CITY OF COLOSSE

Colosse, in the Roman province of Asia (now part of modern Turkey), was one of a triangle of cities situated approximately one hundred miles east of Ephesus in the valley of the river Lycus. The other two cities were Laodicea and Hierapolis, which are mentioned together in the epistle (4:13), and Laodicea by itself (2:1; 4:15-16). The region is volcanic, and subject to severe earthquakes. "The fine sheep, and the chemical qualities of the streams which made the waters valuable for dyeing purposes, fostered a lively trade in dyed woollen goods. All three cities were renowned for the brilliancy of their dyes" (M.R. Vincent, *Word Studies in the New Testament*). Colosse was once a prosperous city, but was in decline by the time Paul wrote this epistle. Its former glory had been eclipsed by Laodicea and Hierapolis, and it had become little more than a country town. However, Colosse occupied an influential position "on the great highway between Ephesus and the Euphrates, and was, therefore, a place where new ideas and new thoughts were always likely to flourish" (T. Bentley). Not many generations after the epistle was written, the site was completely lost. It was rediscovered in the Nineteenth Century. Its ruins are insignificant.

3) THE CONVERSION OF THE COLOSSIANS

One of the delightful facets of Paul's character was his genuine joy over God's blessing on the labours of fellow-servants. There was no 'professional jealousy' about Paul! The man used by God to evangelise the Lycus valley was Epaphras.

See 1:5-8. He is described as "our dear fellowservant, who is for you a faithful minister of Christ; who also declared unto us your love in the Spirit". It was through him that they "knew the grace of God in truth". In due course, we shall notice that Epaphras was the man who **preached** the gospel to them (see above), who bestowed **pastoral** care on them (2:7; "as ye have been taught"), and who **prayed** for them (4:12-13).

Paul evidently intended to evangelise in Asia during his second missionary journey (see Acts 16:6). He made a brief visit to its principal city, Ephesus, on the way home from Corinth (Acts 18:19-20), and returned for a much longer visit during his third missionary journey (Acts 19), but does not appear to have moved inland at all. Hence we read, "For I would that ye knew what great conflict I have for you, and for them at Laodicea, and for as many as have **not seen my face in the flesh**" (2:1). At some point, possibly for the first time at Rome, Paul had met Epaphras, who was his "fellowprisoner in Christ Jesus" (Philemon 23), and "who also declared unto us your love in the Spirit" (1:8). We also know that Philemon, who was a citizen of Colosse, was saved through Paul (Philemon v.19), and so, later, was his runaway slave Onesimus (Philemon v.10). The church at Colosse met in the house of Philemon (Philemon v.2), and the church at Laodicea met in the house of Nymphas (Col. 4:15).

4) THE CONFUSION AT COLOSSE
New Testament churches were often troubled places. We have only to think of the numerous problems at Corinth, and the way in which the churches in Galatia were attacked by false teachers who "would pervert the gospel of Christ" (Gal. 1:7). At first glance, this seems a little unfair. After all, God could have preserved these young churches from spiritual harm, until they had become sufficiently mature to withstand the 'shock of battle'. Let us suppose that this actually happened. In the process of time, the apostles, with their unique knowledge and authority, would have 'finished their course'. This would mean that when the problems and difficulties did arise, there would have been no men of sufficient weight and authority to deal with them, and the churches would have been left floundering down to this very day, that is, if they survived at all. After all, in principle, if not in detail, we face precisely the same problems as the early church. But God providentially allowed these difficulties to arise whilst the apostles were alive, so that both the early churches and ourselves could be guided and strengthened by authoritative teaching in the ongoing battle against wrong doctrine and practice.

There has been great discussion on the precise nature of the heresy confronting

Introduction

the church at Colosse, and whilst Paul does not formally state the errors he opposes, it does seem that these took two forms. The first was the error of **gnosticism**, or mysticism (C.I. Scofield), and the second was the error of **Judaism**. This requires some explanation.

a) Gnosticism

The word 'gnostic' comes from the Greek word *gnosis*, meaning knowledge, and refers to teachers who prided themselves in their knowledge, particularly mystical knowledge. Needless to say, their philosophy took them beyond the boundaries of Scripture, and therefore from the certainty of God's word to the uncertainty and speculation of their own imagination. Hence Paul writes, "Beware lest any man spoil you through philosophy and vain deceit, after the tradition of men, after the rudiments of the world, and not after Christ" (2:8). The dangers of 'gnosticism' are clearly stated by the apostle: "Let no man beguile you of your reward in a voluntary humility and worshipping of angels, intruding into those things which he hath not seen, vainly puffed up by his fleshly mind" (2:18). This is a warning to us all. False teaching, whatever its form, inevitably demeans Christ. It either excludes Christ, or diminishes His identity and glory. In this case, angels received the worship due to Him alone.

It is deeply significant that Paul uses the word *epignosis* five times in this epistle (1:6, 9, 10, 2:2, 3:10). It "denotes exact or full knowledge, discernment, recognition, and is a strengthened form of *gnosis*, expressing a fuller or full knowledge, a greater participation in the object known, thus more powerfully influencing him" (W.E. Vine). The 'gnostics' prided themselves in their *gnosis*, but Christians enjoy *epignosis!* This is not because they are academically brilliant, but because they know Christ, "in whom are hid all the treasures of wisdom and knowledge" (2:3). We must never forget that the knowledge imparted by the Holy Spirit in the Word God cannot be exceeded or excelled, for the simple reason that it is not the product of human research, but **divine revelation.**

As we have noted above, Paul describes the false teaching of the 'gnostics' as "philosophy and vain deceit". For the purposes of this introductory study, we will confine ourselves, as simply as possible, to two aspects of 'gnostic' teaching These people taught *(i)* that God is incomprehensible, and *(ii)* that matter is evil.

i) God is incomprehensible

The 'gnostics' taught that God is not personally involved in creation, and has expressed Himself through layers of spiritual beings in the form of a hierarchy. Howard A Barnes (writing in the *Believer's Magazine*) states that "these various layers of spiritual beings were given names such as 'thrones (at the top)...dominions...principalities...powers' (see 1:16)". Since, according to the 'gnostics', these spiritual beings were expressions of God himself, they were to be worshipped. Hence the reference to angel-worship (2:18).

Paul combats this teaching by emphasising that God is not incomprehensible, and has revealed Himself, not through lesser spirit beings, but in His Son, the Lord Jesus Christ. He is "the image of the invisible God" (1:15). Furthermore, God did not create the world through spirit beings, as taught by the 'gnostics', but through His Son: "For by him were all things created, that are in heaven, and that are in earth, visible and invisible" (1:16). His creation therefore includes all spirit beings. He is both Creator and Head of "all principality and power" (2:10), which are inferior to Him and subject to Him. He is "pre-eminent" in every sphere 1:18). But this is not all. The very spirit beings worshipped by the 'gnostics', had been defeated by Christ at Calvary. He "spoiled principalities and powers" making "a shew of them openly, triumphing over them in it (the cross)" (2:15). His death on the cross was a decisive triumph over all the demonic powers of evil. He turned apparent defeat into conquest, disarming Satan's hosts of their power to retain dominion over men and women. See Luke 11:22; Hebrews 2:14-15

(ii) Matter is evil
The 'gnostics' taught that because God was holy, and matter (they said) was evil, He could have no direct contact with creation. In fact, He could not have created the universe in the first place! Hence the need for a range of intermediate spirits. The 'gnostics' therefore maintained, amongst other things, that men could only bring pleasure to God by acting like Him, and disassociating themselves from anything material. This must lead to a rigid ascetic life. See 2:20-23, which end with the words, "Which things have indeed a shew of wisdom in will worship, and humility, and neglecting of the body ('harsh treatment of the body', JND); not in any honour to the satisfying of the flesh". The 'gnostics' failed to realise that it is not matter that is evil, but human nature! We are not required to "mortify" (put to death) our bodies, but the things done through the body: "fornication, uncleanness, inordinate affection, evil concupiscence, and covetousness, which is idolatry" (3:5).

But the ultimate proof that matter, and therefore the human body, is not evil in itself, lies in the incarnation of the Lord Jesus: "For in him dwelleth all the fulness of the Godhead **bodily**" (2:9). We "that were sometime alienated and enemies in...mind by wicked works, yet now hath he reconciled in the **body** of his

Introduction

flesh through death, to present you holy and unblameable and unreproveable in his sight" (1:21-22)

The apostle John was obliged to confront the same error. The 'gnostics' argued that since matter was evil, God could not have become man, and therefore rejected the incarnation. Hence John's insistence on "Jesus Christ come in flesh" (1 John 4:1-13; 2 John 7). We must beware of all teaching based either on human logic, or on human speculation. This brings us to the second error which confronted the church at Colosse:

b) Judaism
The 'Judaisers' were the 'pests' of apostolic times. We meet them throughout the New Testament. Their teaching can be summed up in the words of Acts 15:1, "And certain men which came down from Judaea taught the brethren, and said, Except ye be circumcised after the manner of Moses, ye cannot be saved". Paul calls this teaching "weak and beggarly", and continues "ye observe days, and months, and times, and years" (Gal.4:9-10). These teachers endeavoured to foist Jewish ordinances on Gentile believers.

Paul clearly refers to this in Colossians 2:11-17. He points out that whereas circumcision was physical, Christians are "circumcised with the circumcision made without hands, in putting off", not a small part of the body, but "the body of the sins of the flesh by the circumcision of Christ". Furthermore, the 'meat...drink... holydays...new moons... sabbath days' connected with Judaism, were "a shadow of things to come, but the body (the substance of the shadows) is of Christ" (2:16-17). We are saved and sanctified, through the death of the Lord Jesus.

One thing should now be very clear indeed, whether it is 'gnosticism' or Judaism, or for that matter, any other brand of false teaching, the answer is Christ and His triumph in death and resurrection! All false teaching attacks Christ, and therefore we must hold fast to "the things concerning himself". It is worth pointing out that the 'gnostics', with their claim to be the repositories of superior knowledge, have their counterparts today. For example, the Roman Catholic church asserts that it has sole ability and authority to interpret the Scriptures. The 'Judaisers' also have their counterparts today. They asserted, effectively, that salvation was based on faith plus works, which is precisely the message of Christendom. We now come to the final part of our introduction:

5) THE CONTENTS OF THE EPISTLE
Any attempt to summarise the epistle with a set of chapter headings must be

inadequate. The following headings therefore reflect a prominent theme in the four chapters of the epistle, and must not be regarded as comprehensive.

a) Chapter 1: The pre-eminence of Christ
This is the central theme of Chapter 1. The Lord Jesus is pre-eminent in the sphere of **creation** (vv.15-17), and in the sphere of the **church** (v.18). It is through Him that both creation and the church exist, and through Him that both will be perfected. See vv.19-23. Both will be perfected on the basis of His death.

If Christ is pre-eminent in creation and the church, then He is to be pre-eminent in every part of our lives. This is stressed throughout the chapter. He is to be pre-eminent in our **preaching** (vv.1-8); Epaphras was "a faithful minister of Christ" (v.7). He is to be pre-eminent in our **progress** (vv.9-11); Paul prayed that they "might walk worthy of the Lord unto all pleasing" (v.10). He is to be pre-eminent in our **praise** (vv.12-14); "Giving thanks unto the Father…who hath translated us into the kingdom of his dear Son: in whom we have redemption through his blood, even the forgiveness of sins" (vv.13-14). He is to be pre-eminent in our **purpose** (vv.24-29); "Christ in you, the hope of glory: whom we preach, warning every man, and teaching every man in all wisdom; that we may present every man perfect in Christ Jesus" (vv.28-29).

b) Chapter 2: Complete in Christ
As we have already noticed, it is in this chapter that Paul confronts the false teaching at Colosse. Believers need nothing more but Christ: "Ye are complete **in him**, which is the head of all principality and power: **in whom** also ye are circumcised with the circumcision made without hands, in putting off the body of the sins of the flesh by the circumcision of Christ". Notice the surrounding warnings. "And this I say, lest **any man** should beguile you with enticing words" (v.4): "Beware lest **any man** spoil you through philosophy and vain deceit" (v.8): "**Let no man** therefore judge you in meat…drink…holyday… new moon…sabbath days" (v.16): "**Let no man** beguile you of your reward in a voluntary humility and worshipping of angels" (v.18). They must not be swayed **by Judaism,** because it only offered "a shadow of things to come", while "the body (the substance of those shadows) is of Christ" (v.17). They must not be swayed **by gnosticism,** because it was at the best speculative, and at the worst, blasphemous. The teachings of gnosticism were absorbing but empty, and must not be allowed to divert attention away from Christ. In Paul's own words, "Not holding the Head, from which all the body by joints and bands having nourishment ministered, and knit together, increaseth with the increase of God" (v.19). If we fail to hold Christ fast, we expose ourselves

Introduction

to every kind of diversion and error. Notice, again, that the answer to both errors, is **Christ and His finished work!**

c) Chapter 3: Risen with Christ
The chapter commences with the second of two complimentary statements. "If ye be dead with Christ" (2:20), and here, "If ye be risen with Christ" (3:1). The opening verses of the chapter teach us *(i)* that the new life is to be nourished (vv.1-4) and *(ii)* that the old life is to be put to death (v.5). The new life is nourished as we "seek those things which are above, where Christ sitteth on the right hand of God" (v.1). The old life is put to death (the meaning of "mortify") when we deal ruthlessly with our "members which are upon the earth; fornication, uncleanness, inordinate affection, evil concupiscence, and covetousness, which is idolatry" (v.5).

Paul then considers the effect of the new life in four areas: *(i)* in our **personal** lives (vv.5-7); *(ii)* in our **social** lives (vv.8-17); notice the expression, "one to another", (vv.9, 13, 16); *(iii)* In our **marital** lives (vv.18-21), where he refers to wives, husbands, children and fathers; *(d)* in our **commercial** lives (3:22 - 4:1), where he refers to servants and masters. "Risen with Christ" is far more than a theological statement: it is a rule of life.

d) Chapter 4: Fellowship in Christ
Having urged the Colossian Christians to "continue in prayer" (notice the emphasis on prayer at the beginning and end of the epistle (1:3; 4:2), to "walk in wisdom", and to speak "with grace, seasoned with salt" (vv.2-6), Paul paints ten miniature portraits. Some of them seem almost microscopic, but they are all of absorbing interest. There are eight portraits of Paul's companions and fellow-labourers at Rome: Tychicus, Onesimus, Aristarchus, Marcus, Jesus which is called Justus, Epaphras, Luke and Demas. There are two portraits of local Christians: Nymphas at Laodicea, and Archippus, who was evidently the son of Philemon (see Philemon 2), at Colosse. As ever, there are valuable lessons to be learned, even from "Jesus which is called Justus", of whom we know nothing!

This section of the epistle illustrates that people from totally different backgrounds, and with totally different personalities, can enjoy fellowship and harmony in Christ. Like Epaphras (v.12), we must "labour fervently...in prayers" for each other, that we "may stand perfect and complete in all the will of God".

READ CHAPTER 1.1-11

"We give thanks...praying always for you"

Why are we studying Colossians? Let's never forget that the New Testament epistles addressed 'real life' situations, and that they have been preserved, not merely to provide a picture of early church life, but to give us guidance and help in similar circumstances. The Scriptures are always relevant, and 'more up to date than tomorrow morning's newspaper'. Let's study this epistle because, amongst other things, we might need to use its teaching at any time. One illustration will suffice. In one of their tracts, the Jehovah's Witnesses appeal to Colossians 1:15 ("Who is the image of the invisible God, the firstborn of every creature") in support of their teaching that 'God's first creation was His Son'. How would *you* deal with that? We must therefore look carefully at this verse in due course. It stresses the need to be "nourished up in the words of faith and of good doctrine" (1 Tim. 4:6).

Colossians 1 may be divided into six sections as follows: *(1)* thanksgiving for faith in Christ (vv.1-8); *(2)* praying for progress in Christ (vv.9-11); *(3)* describing our position in Christ (vv.12-14); *(4)* describing the preeminence of Christ (vv.15-19); *(5)* describing the purpose of Christ (vv.20-23); *(6)* working towards perfection in Christ (vv.24-29).

1) THANKSGIVING FOR FAITH IN CHRIST, vv.1-8
"We *give thanks* to God and the Father of our Lord Jesus Christ, praying always for you, since we heard of your faith in Christ Jesus, and of the love which ye have to all the saints". Paul *refers* to his prayers for them in v.3, and tells us *how* he prayed for them in vv.9-11. He deals with three related subjects in this section: *(a)* the character of the believers (vv.1-5a); *(b)* the character of the gospel (vv.5b-6); *(c)* the character of the messenger (vv.7-8).

a) The character of the believers, vv.1-5a
i) **The writer.** "Paul, an apostle of Jesus Christ ('Christ Jesus', RV) by the

144

will of God, and Timotheus our brother" (v.1). While the letter was written by Paul ("the salutation by the hand of me Paul", 4:18: notice the occurrences of "I" and "my" throughout the epistle), he includes Timothy in the opening greeting, and elsewhere. Hence the occurrences of "we" and "us". It is always delightful to see these two men happily serving God together. On one hand we have "Paul the **aged**" (Philemon v9), and on the other Timothy, of whom Paul wrote, "Let no man despise thy **youth**" (1 Tim. 4:12). So the 'age gap' did not hinder their fellowship and service. Their differing backgrounds did not hinder their fellowship either. Paul was "of the stock of Israel" (Phil. 3:5). He was of pure blood. But whilst Timothy's mother was a Jewess, his father was a Greek (Acts 16:1).

The fact that Paul was "an apostle by the will of God" emphasises that God hath "set the members every one of them in the body, as it hath pleased him": the fact that Timothy is described as "our brother" emphasises the relationship common to all believers. It is reassuring to know that we serve according to "the will of God"; it is equally reassuring to know that we serve in fellowship with our brethren in Christ.

ii) **The readers.** "To the saints and faithful brethren in Christ which are at Colosse: Grace be unto you, and peace, from God our Father and the Lord Jesus Christ" (v.2). Paul describes them as "saints". That is what they were **positionally.** All Christians are "saints". Some of the Christians at Corinth were not behaving in a 'saintly' way, but Paul describes them as "sanctified in Christ Jesus, called (omit 'to be') saints, with all that in every place call upon the name of Jesus Christ our Lord, both theirs and ours" (1 Cor.1:2). We are all 'set apart' (the meaning of "sanctified" and "saint") for God, and by God. Compare 1 Corinthians 14:33. We should notice that Paul places his readers in the same category as Timothy. He calls Timothy "our brother" ('the brother', JND) and the Colossians "faithful brethren in Christ". In describing the Colossian believers in this way, Paul tells us what they were **practically.** They were trustworthy, steadfast and unswerving, particularly in view of erroneous teaching at Colosse. See 2:5.

We have already noticed their spiritual location ("in Christ") and their geographical location ("at Colosse"). The first emphasises the **source** of their blessings: the second emphasises the **sphere** of their service. While Paul himself was unable to impart "grace" and "peace" to them, he prayed that they would enjoy these rich blessings from "God our Father and the Lord Jesus Christ".

F.F. Bruce observes that the regular Greek greeting was "Rejoice!" *(chaire)*, and the regular Hebrew greeting was "Peace!" *(shalom)*. Paul commonly combines the two, but replaces *chaire* by the similarly sounding but richer greeting, *charis* ("grace"). We should also note the order. It is "grace...and peace", not 'peace... and grace'. Peace is the result of grace! We could not enjoy either "peace **with** God" (Rom. 5:1), or "the peace **of** God" (Phil. 4:7), apart from His grace. "Grace" is what Christ **brought** (see Titus 2:11): "peace" is what He **left** (see John 14:27). We must also notice that it is, "Grace be unto you, and peace, from **God our Father, and the Lord Jesus Christ**". By naming the Lord Jesus with the Father as the joint source of grace and peace, Paul emphasises His deity, and discloses the place given to Him in the confession and worship of early Christians. We must notice an important distinction between "God our Father, and the Lord Jesus Christ" (v.2), and "God and the Father of our Lord Jesus Christ" (v.3). The first emphasises our relationship **with** God and Christ, the second emphasises the relationship **between** God and Christ. See John 20:17, "I ascend unto **my** Father, and **your** Father; and to **my** God, and **your** God". The Lord Jesus did not say 'our Father' and 'our God'.

For Paul, news of God's people meant prayer for God's people. "We give thanks to God (Paul refers to thanksgiving six times in this epistle) and the Father of our Lord Jesus Christ, praying always for you, **since we heard** of your faith in Christ Jesus, and of the love which ye have to all the saints, for ('on account of' JND) the hope which is laid up for you in heaven". Christians share a common hope, and this should promote mutual love. Does news about God's people lift up **our** voices in thanksgiving, and bow **our** knees in prayer? What have we done with all those reports of the Lord's work? What have we done with the news we receive from one another, and about one another? Paul was so thankful, and so prayerful, when he heard about their salvation and progress. He was an example of his own ministry. See 4:2. Daniel was a man who prayed and gave thanks. See Daniel 2:18-23; 6:10.

Paul mentions their "faith...love...hope". He elsewhere calls them "these three" (1 Cor. 13:13) See also 1 Thessalonians 1:3; 5:8. Do notice that it is "faith in **Christ Jesus**", and "love...to **all** the saints". Paul knew the Lord Jesus as "Christ Jesus", while Peter knew Him as "Jesus Christ". Paul came to know Him after His return to heaven. God "hath made him both Lord and Christ". Peter came to know Him on earth. The evidence of their initial and ongoing "faith in Christ Jesus" lay in their "love...to all the saints". There was nothing selective about this: they loved "all the saints". Do we? Or are we guilty of partiality and favouritism? There is nothing uncertain about the Christian's hope. As T. Bentley points out, the verb translated "laid up" occurs in only three other New Testament passages (Luke 19:20, 2 Timothy 4:8, Hebrews 9:27). It conveys the reservation and security of the hope. It is "laid up....in *heaven*". No one can touch it there! Compare 1 Peter 1:3-4.

But how did the Colossians come to have "faith in Christ Jesus", and "love...to all saints", and "the hope which is laid up...in heaven"? The answer follows: all three became theirs through the gospel. This brings us to:

b) The character of the gospel, vv.5b-6
These verses emphasise three things about the gospel: *(i)* it is trustworthy; *(ii)* it is effective; *(iii)* it is of grace.

i) **The gospel is trustworthy.** "Whereof ye heard before (that is, "before" the false teachers got busy: it hadn't changed since then!) in the word of the truth of the gospel". The total reliability of the gospel is emphasised by the words, "word" and "truth". In connection with the former, which translates the Greek word *logos*, we immediately think of such expressions as "the word of the Lord". It has been pointed out that *logos* is the opposite of *mythos,* and this speaks for itself! There is nothing speculative about the gospel. It is the "word of the **truth** of the Gospel". This emphasises its complete integrity, as opposed to the "philosophy and vain deceit...after the tradition of men". Compare 1 Timothy 1:15, "This is a faithful saying, and worthy of all acceptation"; Titus 1:9, "Holding fast the faithful word".

ii) **The gospel is effective.** "Which is come unto you, as it is in all the world; and bringeth forth fruit ('bearing fruit and growing', JND), as it doth also in you, since the day ye heard of it". Paul does not, of course, infer, that the entire world had heard the gospel. He is emphasising the universal scope of the gospel. The message preached at Colosse was the message preached everywhere. The gospel message does not have to be altered and amended to meet different circumstances and cultures. The veracity of the gospel is demonstrated by its results. It changes the lives of those who believe. See, for example, 1 Corinthians 6:9, where Paul states that "the unrighteous shall not inherit the kingdom of God", and proceeds to define unrighteousness ("fornicators... idolaters... adulterers...effeminate...abusers of themselves with mankind... thieves...covetous... drunkards...revilers...extortioners"), adding "and such were some of you: but ye are washed, but ye are sanctified, but ye are justified in the name of the Lord Jesus, and by the Spirit of our God" (vv.9-11). We should also note that there was an immediate change. It took place "since the day ye heard" (Colossians 1:6). Newly saved people (call them 'young believers' if you like) were exhibiting new life. If there is no evidence of faith in Christ, we have legitimate grounds to question whether it exists at all.

iii) The gospel is of grace. Paul describes their conversion as knowing "the grace of God in truth". The word "knew" is understood by some to mean 'full knowledge', by others to mean 'thorough appreciation', and by yet others to mean 'acknowledge'. Hence, in the words of W. Hendriksen *(Colossians),* "to come to acknowledge the grace of God". One thing is perfectly clear: the grace of God takes no account of "works". See Ephesians 2:8-9, "For by grace are ye saved through faith...not of works, lest any man should boast". See also Romans 4:1-4.

Through whom did they hear "the word of the truth of the gospel" and "the grace of God in truth"? We now meet the preacher:

c) The character of the messenger, vv. 7-8
"As ye also learned of Epaphras our dear fellowservant, who is for you a faithful minister of Christ; who also declared unto us your love in the Spirit". As we noted in our introduction, Epaphras had a threefold connection with the church at Colosse. He **preached** the gospel to them (1:7), he bestowed **pastoral** care on them (2:7, "as ye have been taught"), and he **prayed** for them (4:12-13). We should notice at least three things about him:

i) He was a "dear (or 'beloved') fellowservant". Paul really loved his colleagues. Tychicus was "a beloved brother" (4:7), Onesimus was a "beloved brother" (4:9), and Luke was the "beloved physician" (4:14). The word "fellowservant" *(sundoulos)* is, literally, 'fellow-bondman'. A slave has no will of his own, and servants of God are wholly subject to their Lord's will. It is delightful to note the cordial relationship between servants of God, even though they laboured in different areas. Paul does not 'pull rank' on Epaphras by stating his apostleship.

ii) He was a "faithful minister of Christ". The Colossians "heard" nothing but "the word of the truth of the gospel" (v.5), and they "heard" nothing but the "grace of God in truth" (v.6). The term "minister of Christ" *(diakonos tou christou)* "denotes the servant in relation to his Lord" (T. Bentley). We should notice the present tense. Not '**was** for you a faithful minister of Christ, but "**is** for you a faithful minister of Christ". Perhaps Paul had in mind the ongoing ministry of Epaphras on behalf of the Colossians. He was no longer able to preach in the area, but he could **pray!** See 4:12-13.

Do notice that the Colossian believers were not disadvantaged because they had not heard Paul's voice. They had heard the right message!

iii) He was the bearer of good news. "Who also declared unto us your love in the Spirit". (This is the only reference to the Holy Spirit in the epistle). We can imagine how much this delighted Epaphras, and how much it delighted Paul and Timothy! It is always satisfying to speak well of other Christians! We should always endeavour to do this. Remember that the "words of a talebearer are as wounds" (Prov. 26:22). If we cannot say anything good about a fellow-Christian, it is generally better to say nothing. The Colossians were evidently enjoying the ministry of the Holy Spirit amongst them, for "the fruit of the Spirit is *love*…", which reminds us that

> Every virtue we possess,
> And every victory won,
> And every thought of holiness,
> Are His alone.

2) PRAYER FOR PROGRESS IN CHRIST, vv.9-11

The first thing we should notice is that there is no 'half-heartedness' and no 'half-measures' in Paul's prayer.

There is no **half-heartedness.** "Praying always for you" (v.3). "For this cause we also, since the day we heard it, do not cease to pray for you ('do not cease praying and asking for you', JND)" (v.9). He was persistent. J.N. Darby's translation emphasises Paul's definite requests. Compare 1 Thessalonians 3:10, "Night and day praying exceedingly".

There are no **half-measures.** Paul prayed that they might be "***filled*** with the knowledge of his will in *all* wisdom and spiritual understanding; that ye might walk worthy of the Lord unto *all* pleasing, being fruitful in *every* good work, and increasing in the knowledge of God; strengthened with *all* might, according to his glorious power, unto *all* patience and longsuffering with joyfulness". Epaphras prayed similarly. See 4:12.

There are three paragraphs in Paul's prayer. He desires *(a)* that they might enjoy God's provision (v.9); *(b)* that they might achieve God's purpose (v.10); *(c)* that they might experience God's power (v.11).

a) God's provision, v.9
"That ye might be filled with the knowledge of his will in all wisdom and spiritual understanding". As we have often noticed, every word counts in Scripture.

i) "That ye might be **filled** with the knowledge of his will". Compare Psalm 40:8; 143:10. It is one thing to recognise the will of God theoretically. It is something entirely different to make the will of God the supreme desire of our lives. Paul speaks about the "***knowledge***" of God's will here. He speaks about "***understanding***" His will in Ephesians 5:17, and "***doing***" His will in Ephesians 6:6.

ii) "That ye might be filled with the ***knowledge*** of his will". As we noticed in our introduction, Paul employs the word *epignosis* here. Let's go over it again. It "denotes exact or full knowledge, discernment, recognition, and is a strengthened form of *gnosis,* expressing a fuller or full knowledge, a greater participation in the object known, thus more powerfully influencing him" (W.E. Vine). The 'gnostics' prided themselves in their *gnosis,* but Christians at Colosse enjoyed *epignosis!* Paul wanted the very best for his brethren at Colosse!

iii) "That ye might be filled with the knowledge of ***his*** will". Nothing can be more important. The philosophers at Colosse endeavoured to divert the church from pursuing the "knowledge of his will". See 2:8, 18. The Judaisers endeavoured to do the same. See 2:20-23. Rightly understood, "the knowledge of his will" will preserve us from all error. However, it is more than mere acquaintance with the facts of God's will. This follows:

iv) "That ye might be filled with the knowledge of his will in **all wisdom and spiritual understanding**" or "spiritual wisdom and understanding" (RV). This describes an intelligent grasp of God's will. It has been suggested that "wisdom" will save us from foolish conduct, and "spiritual understanding" will save us from false teaching. "Wisdom" is the **application** of God's will, and "spiritual understanding" is the **appreciation** of God's will.

"Wisdom" is spiritual skill. It is the acquired skill of Christian maturity. It is the ability to implement the will of God, both amongst believers (see 3:16) and unbelievers (4:5). It involves meeting "enticing words", with the "treasures of wisdom and knowledge" found in Christ (2:3-4). It involves meeting "a show of wisdom ('an appearance of wisdom', JND) in will (voluntary) worship" with sound teaching (2:20-23). The very way in which Paul deals with the problems at Colosse, demonstrates "spiritual wisdom and understanding" (RV). Instead of launching an immediate attack on the false teachers, he first sets out the unique glories of Christ, and the immense blessings of all who belong to Him. ***"Spiritual understanding"*** describes the way in which we discern God's will.

Read 1 Corinthians 2:12-16 in this connection. "Spiritual understanding is **not** acquired by listening to "the words which man's wisdom teacheth, **but** which the Holy Ghost teacheth".

We should add that the Judaisers and 'gnostics' (the philosophers) doubtless claimed wisdom, but it was certainly not "***spiritual*** wisdom".

b) God's purpose, v.10

"That ye might walk worthy of the Lord unto all pleasing, being fruitful in every good work, and increasing in the knowledge of God". Compare 1 Thessalonians 2:12. This emphasises the practical results which flow from v.9. While "wisdom and spiritual understanding" are not tangible things, they certainly produce tangible results! Once again, every word counts:

i) "That ye might walk worthy of the Lord unto all pleasing. Like Enoch! 1 Thessalonians 4 has been called the 'Enoch chapter'. (The clue is found in Hebrews 11:5). It commences with Paul's urgent request that "as ye have received of us how ye ought to walk and to please God, so ye would abound more and more". Compare 3 John 6: "Whom if thou bring forward on their journey after a godly sort (JND 'worthily of God', JND), thou shalt do well". Our great business in life is not to please ourselves, or to please others, but to please the Lord. This should be our spiritual ambition. See 2 Corinthians 5:9 RV. We must make it our aim to be well-pleasing to Him in ***walk*** (here), in ***worship*** (Heb. 13:15-16), in ***warfare*** (2 Tim. 2:4), and in ***witness*** (1 Thess. 2:4).

ii) "Being fruitful in every good work". This is the ***result*** of the gospel (see v.6), the ***evidence*** of salvation (see Acts 9:36: Dorcas was "full of good works"), and the ***purpose*** of God (see Ephesians 2:10 and Titus 2:14). Such fruit in our lives can only be produced as we 'abide in him'. See John 15:4-5.

iii) "And increasing in (or 'by', JND) the knowledge of God". Once again it is *epignosis*. Do notice a very distinct progress in these verses. Paul refers to the knowledge of God's grace in v.6, the knowledge of God's will in v.9 and, now, the knowledge of God Himself v.10. Spiritual development can only be nurtured and sustained through personal communion with God.

c) God's power, v.11

"Strengthened with all might, according to his glorious power, unto all patience and longsuffering with joyfulness". (Not 'according to ***our*** need', but "according to ***his*** glorious power"!). Paul concludes his prayer for the Colossians by asking that they may be continually strengthened with all power "'according to the might of his glory" (JND). This expression is probably best understood with reference to the Lord's resurrection. See Romans 6:4, "Christ was raised up from the dead by the glory of the Father". Compare Eph. 1:19. Hence Paul prays that they may be empowered with the same might by which Christ was raised from the dead. However, we should also notice Ephesians 3:16 in this connection, where the expression "strengthened with might", is connected with the power of the Holy Spirit.

The purpose of this power follows: not spectacular miracles and brilliant oratory, but "unto all patience and longsuffering with joyfulness". "**Patience**" (*hupomone*) is the "quality that does not surrender to circumstances, or succumb under trial". "**Longsuffering**" *(makrothumia)* is self-restraint in the face of provocation. The former is used in connection with circumstances: the latter is used in connection with people. But neither are to be exercised with stoicism and gloom. Paul adds, "with joyfulness". He had the moral right to say this. See Acts 16:25. James also had the moral right to say "count it all joy when ye fall into divers temptations" (1:2) since he was one of the apostles who, having been beaten, "departed from the presence of the council, rejoicing that they were counted worthy to suffer shame for his name" (Acts 5:40-41). It can be nicely summarised as follows: no 'giving up' ("patience"); no 'giving back' ("longsuffering"); no 'giving in' ("joyfulness").

READ CHAPTER 1.12-19

"That in all things he might have the preeminence"

We have noticed that Colossians 1 may be divided into six sections as follows: *(1)* thanksgiving for faith in Christ (vv.1-8); *(2)* praying for progress in Christ (vv.9-11); *(3)* describing our position in Christ (vv.12-14); *(4)* describing the preeminence of Christ (vv.15-19); *(5)* describing the purpose of Christ (vv.20-23); *(6)* working towards perfection in Christ vv.24-29). The chapter may also be divided in the following way: the saints (vv.1-13); the Saviour (v.14-23); the servants (vv.24-29).

1) PAUL'S THANKSGIVING FOR THEIR FAITH IN CHRIST, vv.1-8
In our previous study, we noticed Paul's thanksgiving for the "fruit"of the gospel in the lives of the Colossians. As a result of hearing "the grace of God in truth" through Epaphras, they had become "saints and faithful brethren in Christ", with "faith in Christ Jesus", "love...to all the saints", and enjoyment of the "hope...laid up...in heaven".

2) PAUL'S PRAYER FOR THEIR PROGRESS IN CHRIST, vv.9-11
We also noticed Paul's ongoing prayer for them. "We also, since the day we heard it, do not cease to pray for you". He prayed that they might *(i)* "be filled with the knowledge of his will"; *(ii)* "walk worthy of the Lord unto all pleasing"; *(iii)* be "strengthened with all might, according to his glorious power". This brings us to:

3) PAUL'S DESCRIPTION OF OUR POSITION IN CHRIST, vv.12-14
Towards the end of the epistle, Paul urges us to "continue in prayer, and watch in the same with thanksgiving" (4:2). He is certainly an example of his own ministry! Having prayed in vv.9-11, Paul now gives thanks in v.12: "Giving thanks unto the Father". Unregenerate people are unthankful. See Romans 1: 21 and 2 Timothy 3:2. But not Paul! He points out that in the Lord Jesus we have a new quality (v.12), a new authority (v.13), and a new liberty (v.14).

a) A new quality, v.12

"Giving thanks unto the Father, which hath made us meet (fit) to be partakers of the inheritance of the saints *in light*". We were once in "darkness" (v.13), and totally unworthy of divine blessing. What we could never accomplish by personal merit, God has accomplished for us. He has made us fit for His presence, both now and in eternity. The words "in light" refer to the location of our inheritance. "God is light". Our inheritance is in the presence of God. It is "reserved in heaven" (1 Pet. 1:4).

b) A new authority, v.13

"Who hath delivered us from the power (*exousia*, meaning 'authority') of darkness, and hath translated us into the kingdom of his dear Son ('the Son of his love', JND)". The word "delivered" *(rhuomai)* means 'to rescue', and the word "translate" means to 'transfer to another place'. (The word used of Enoch is very similar: see Hebrews 11:5). There has been a change of authority in our lives. We were once subject to the 'authority of darkness' (compare Ephesians 2:2), but now we are subjects of the 'kingdom of God's dear Son'. The very word "kingdom", implies reign and authority. People should, of course, see the change of authority in our lives. Do they?

But what a difference! There was no love for us under the previous authority, but there is now! We enjoy the love of God in Christ. In connection with the lovely words, "the kingdom of his **dear Son *('the Son of his love')***", we should read the following: John 3:35 ("The Father ***loveth*** the Son, and hath given all things into his hand"); John 5:20 ("For the Father ***loveth*** the Son, and sheweth him all things that himself doeth"); John 10:17 ("Therefore doth my Father ***love*** me, because I lay down my life, that I might take it again"); John 15:9 ("As the Father hath ***loved*** me, so have I loved you"); John 17:24 ("Thou ***lovedst*** me before the foundation of the world").

c) A new liberty, v.14

"In whom we have redemption *(apolutrosis)* through his blood, even the forgiveness of sins" Compare Galatians 3:13, "Christ hath redeemed (*exagorazo*) us from the curse of the law"; Titus 2:14, "Who gave himself for us, that he might redeem *(lutroo)* us from all iniquity"; 1 Peter 1:18, "Ye were not redeemed *(lutroo)* with corruptible things, as silver and gold". The word "redemption" *(apolutrosis)* means 'to release on payment of a ransom'. Once we were in bondage to sin, but now we are free. The price has been paid. It was "his blood", and this provides for the removal of all our sins. But who stands behind this? The answer follows:

4) PAUL'S DESCRIPTION OF THE PREEMINENCE OF CHRIST, vv.15-19

The Lord Jesus is preeminent *(a)* in relation to creation (vv.16-17), and *(b)* in relation to the church (v.18). Such preeminence can only belong to God Himself, and the section therefore commences and concludes with reference to the deity of the Lord Jesus: "Who is the image of the invisible God, the firstborn of all creation" (v.15 JND); "For it pleased the Father that in him should all fulness dwell" (v.19), or "For in him all the fulness (of the Godhead) was pleased to dwell" (JND). Since v.15 refers particularly to the relationship of the Lord Jesus to creation, we will consider vv.15-17 as a unit.

a) His preeminence in relation to creation, vv.15-17

We must notice *(i)* the Person of Christ, v.15a, *(ii)* the precedence of Christ (v.15b), and *(iii)* the power of Christ (vv.16-17). All in relation to creation.

i) The Person of Christ, v.15a. "Who is the image of the invisible God". The word "Who" emphasises His uniqueness. The word "is" emphasises that He is unchanging. He is the essential embodiment of deity. In the New Testament, the Holy Spirit uses two Greek words when describing the Lord Jesus as the "image of God".

- *'Eikon'.* This is used here and in 2 Corinthians 4:4, "Lest the light of the glorious gospel of Christ, who is the *image* of God, should shine unto them". There, He is described as "the image of God" while here, He is described as "the image of the *invisible* God". As the "image of God", Christ is "essentially and absolutely the perfect expression and representation of God". As "the image of the invisible God", Christ is "the visible representation and manifestation of God to created beings" (W.E. Vine). Compare Hebrews 10:1, "For the law having a shadow of good things to come, and not the very image of those things".

The word *eikon* is used in Matthew 22:20 ("whose is this *image* and superscription?"), in 1 Corinthians 11:7 ("For a man indeed ought not to cover his head, forasmuch as he is the *image* and glory of God"), and in Revelation 13:15 ("And he had power to give life unto the *image* of the beast"). In each case, the "image" is not the reality: it represents and manifests the reality. In the case of a coin, the image will change as a reign proceeds, but not Christ. He does not age or deteriorate! But the Lord Jesus does not represent the reality: He *is* the "image of God" absolutely and essentially. He is not the *likeness* of the invisible God, but the "*image*" of the invisible God". He alone has manifested God. See John 1:18 ("No man hath seen God at any time; the only begotten Son, which is in the bosom of the Father, he hath declared him"), and John 14:9 ("He that hath seen me hath seen the Father"). He displays the very nature and attributes of God by His power, omniscience, holiness and love. In this respect we must distinguish between Adam and Christ. Adam was **made** in the "image of God" (Gen. 1:26-27), and "men...are **made** after the similitude of God" (James 3:9). But the Lord Jesus was not **made** in "the image of God". He **is** God.

- *'Charakter'.* This is used in Hebrew 1:3, "Who being the brightness of his glory, and the express image of his person..." The word *charakter*, from a verb meaning 'to engrave or 'cut into', originally denoted the instrument used in engraving, which we call a 'stamp' or 'die', but it came to signify the impression made by the instrument. Just as all the features of the impression correspond exactly with the instrument which makes it, so Christ bears the exact impress of the divine nature and character. (M.R. Vincent/W.E. Vine)

ii) The precedence of Christ, v.15b. "The firstborn of every creature" or "The firstborn of all creation" (JND). This statement is used by the Jehovah's Witnesses to support their assertion that "God's first creation was His Son". The Lord Jesus is described as "the firstborn" on five occasions in the New Testament: Romans 8:29; Colossians 1:15, 18; Hebrews 1:6; Revelation 1:5. The word is used in the plural in Hebrews 12:23 ("the church of the firstborn, which are written in heaven"). In the Old Testament, the title "firstborn" was not synonymous with the 'first to be born'. See, for example, 1 Chronicles 26:10-11, "Also Hosah, of the children of Merari, had sons; Simri the chief (for though he was not the firstborn, yet his father made him the chief), Hilkiah the second...Tebaliah... Zechariah". The position of Joseph illustrates the point. See 1 Chronicles 5:1-2, "Now the sons of Reuben the firstborn of Israel, (for he was the firstborn; but, forasmuch as he defiled his father's bed, his birthright was given unto the sons of Joseph the son of Israel: and the genealogy is not to be reckoned after the birthright. For Judah prevailed above his brethren, and of him came the chief ruler; but the birthright was Joseph's)". We can add the cases of Jacob and Esau, and Ephraim and Manasseh (Genesis 48:5-20), and it is clear from events in the patriarchal families that the word "firstborn" referred to the head or principal son in the family. It described the unique relationship between the father and the son designated in this way. In Psalm 89:27, David is described as "my firstborn, higher than the kings of the earth". He is supreme amongst earthly monarchs. It is even more applicable to the Lord Jesus, who is of "the house and lineage of David"!. See Luke 2:4.

The Jehovah's Witnesses also use Revelation 3:14 ("The beginning of the creation of God") to bolster their blasphemous doctrine that Christ is a created being. However, the word "beginning" (arche) means 'originator'. He is not, as they suggest, the "first to be created" but the Creator! He is the 'originator' of creation. The 'active cause' (W.E. Vine) of creation.

As 'the firstborn of all creation', the Lord Jesus has both precedence and preeminence over creation. The reasons follow: "**For** by him were all things created..." He is the Creator and sustainer of "all things". This brings us to

iii) The power of Christ, vv.16-17. The universe is Christ-centred! His preeminence in relation to creation is explained in five ways. (We are indebted to Mr. F. Epps, Canterbury, for the following headings).

- *He is the Architect of creation, v.16a.* "For by *(en)* him were all things created, that are in *(en)* heaven, and that are in (*epi*, meaning upon) earth, visible and invisible, whether they be thrones, or dominions, or principalities, or powers..." The preposition *en* leads to the translation, "For **in** him were all things created". He designed every part of creation! Quite obviously, therefore, He is outside of creation, distinct from, creation, and greater than creation. The words, "thrones... dominions...principalities...powers" evidently refer, not to human authorities, but to unseen authorities. This is clear from the fact that they are mentioned in connection with creation. See also Ephesians 6:12, where "principalities and powers" certainly refer to the spirit world.

> At His voice creation sprang at once to sight:
> All the angel-faces, all the hosts of light,
> Thrones and dominations, stars upon their way,
> All the heavenly orders, in their great array.

- *He is the Agent of creation, v.16b.* "All things were created by him". The preposition here is *dia,* meaning 'through'. He is "the instrumental power" (JND margin). He not only designed the universe, He built it! "All things were made by him: and without him was not any thing made that was made" (John 1:3); "And, Thou, Lord, in the beginning hast laid the foundation of the earth; and the heavens are the works of thine hands" (Heb. 1:10).

- *He is the Aim of creation, v.16c.* "All things were created by him, and **for** him". See also Hebrews 2:10. Compare Revelation 4:11, "Thou art worthy, O Lord, to receive glory and honour and power: for thou hast created all things, and for thy pleasure they are and were created". We can therefore be absolutely certain that "the whole creation" which "groaneth and travaileth in pain together until now" (Rom. 8:22), will ultimately fulfil its purpose, and bring joy and pleasure to its Creator.

- **He is Antecedent to creation, v.17a.** "And he is before *(pro)* all things". He precedes creation. He precedes creation because, unlike creation, He is unoriginated and underived. Unlike Melchisedec, He has actually "neither beginning of days, nor end of life" (Heb. 7:3).

- **He is the Administrator of creation, v.17b.** "And by him all things consist" or "All things subsist together by him" (JND). Creation 'adheres' by His power. The Lord Jesus upholds "all things by the word of his power" (Heb. 1:3). He has created "all things", and He maintains "all things". The law of gravity, and every other 'law' in creation, are His laws. Nothing moves or functions without Him! Christ is "the unifying power of creation, or else the cosmos would be in chaos" (T. Bentley).

We can add, of course, that He will succeed creation. See Hebrews 1:10-12. He is therefore preeminent in creation. But this is not all.

b) His preeminence in relation to the church, v.18
This is His 'new creation'. "And he is the head of the body, the church: who is the beginning, the firstborn from the dead; that in all things (whether in creation or the church) he might have the preeminence". The connection with the previous verses is clear. The Lord Jesus, Who has originated and Who maintains creation, originated and maintains the church. We must therefore notice the following:

i) **He is "the head of the body, the church".** This is emphatic. "***He*** is the head of the body". There is no reference to the "body" until the "head" is in heaven. See Ephesians 1:22-23. This emphasises the intimate connection between Christ and His church. A body without a head would be a corpse. There could be no church at all apart from a risen Christ. We must also remember that Christ is head of the **whole** body. The New Testament does not use such expressions as 'the church on earth', or 'the church in heaven!'

The expression, "head of the body", conveys at least two aspects of His ministry in relation to the church. It emphasises His **control,** or authority: "For the husband is head of the wife, even as Christ is **head** of the church...Therefore as the church is **subject unto Christ,** "so let the wives be to their own husbands in every thing" (Eph. 5:23-24). The authority of the Lord Jesus over the church is conveyed by His word. The church, comprising every true believer in the Lord Jesus, should therefore display its subjection to Him by obedience to His word. It also expresses His *care* for the church: "For no man ever yet hated his own flesh; but nourisheth and cherisheth it, even as the Lord the church (Eph. 5:29). The Lord Jesus 'nourishes' and 'cherishes' the church by bestowing the gifts necessary for the maintenance and development of its life. See, for example, Ephesians 4:11-13.

ii) He is "the beginning". The word "beginning" *(arche)* means, as already noted, "'the source, the originating power, and the active cause" (W.E. Vine). At creation, God "breathed into his (Adam's) nostrils the breath of life; and man became a living soul" (Gen. 2:7). On the day of Pentecost, the Lord Jesus "breathed"on His disciples (as He did symbolically in John 20:22), and they became a living church. In both cases, He breathed creatively. Peter explained this to the crowds at Jerusalem: "Therefore, being at the right hand of God exalted, and having received of the Father the promise of the Holy Ghost, he hath shed forth this, which ye now see and hear" (Acts 2:33). This brings us to:

iii) He is "the firstborn from the dead". The word "firstborn" *(prototokos)* means, as we have already noted in connection with its occurrence in v.15 ("the firstborn of every creature"), first in rank, or priority. The Lord Jesus is "the firstborn from the dead", because "being raised from the dead", He "dieth no more; death hath no more dominion over him" (Rom. 6:9). Various people in Old and New Testaments were raised from the dead prior to Christ's resurrection, but it could not be said of them that they "dieth no more". The Lord Jesus is Lord of all creation, and "head of all principality and power" (2:10) by divine right. He is "the firstborn of all creation". But He is Lord and Head of the church by death and resurrection. He is "the firstborn from the dead". He is responsible for the commencement of the church, the continuance of the church, and for the consummation of the church. He will "present it to himself a glorious church, not having spot, or wrinkle, or any such thing: but that it should be holy and without blemish" (Eph. 5:27).

When we think of creation, and when we think of the church, Christ has preeminence. Both creation and the church are Christ-centred. He is not just prominent, or predominant, He is preeminent. It therefore follows that He should have preeminence in our lives, both as Creator, and as Redeemer. If this is so, it goes without saying that He will have preeminence in our assembly life. The assembly should not be the place where we love "to have the preeminence" (3 John 9), but the place where we love to give Christ the preeminence.

Chapter 1A

The preeminence of the Lord Jesus in creation and the church rests, not only on what He has done, but on His identity. "*For* it pleased the Father that in him should all fulness dwell". However, the competent authorities are agreed that there is nothing in the original text answering to the words "the Father". As W.E. Vine points out: "The original reads, 'it was the good pleasure that in him should all the fulness dwell'". Or, according to the New Translation (JND), "For in him all the fulness [of the Godhead] was pleased to dwell". Compare 2:9. "For in him dwelleth all the fulness of the Godhead bodily". The word "fulness" *(pleroma)*, from the verb 'to fill full' *(pleroo)*, describes here the divine nature and divine attributes in all their completeness. The 'gnostics' taught that the 'fulness' of God was vested in the unseen world of "principalities and powers". Paul counters this "notion in this glorious affirmation that 'all the fulness' dwells permanently in Christ". The word "dwell" means "to abide, or to be at home", and "all the attributes of deity...are at home in Christ" (T. Bentley). Only God could create the universe and only God could form the church. Hence we sing of the Lord Jesus:

> True image of the Infinite,
> Whose essence is concealed:
> Brightness of uncreated light,
> The heart of God revealed.

But this is not all. The Lord Jesus is not only the Creator of the universe, and the Head of the church. He will perfect creation, and will perfect the church. This brings us to:

5) PAUL'S DESCRIPTION OF THE PURPOSE OF CHRIST, vv.20-23

On the basis of his work at Calvary, "the blood of his cross", the Lord Jesus **will** reconcile creation (v.20). He has **already** reconciled His people, and will present them "holy and unblameable and unreproveable in his sight" (vv.21-22).

We will consider this, God willing, in our next study.

READ CHAPTER 1.20-29

"Christ in you, the hope of glory"

We have noticed that Colossians 1 may be divided into six sections as follows: *(1)* thanksgiving for faith in Christ (vv.1-8); *(2)* praying for progress in Christ (vv.9-11); *(3)* describing our position in Christ (vv.12-14); *(4)* describing the preeminence of Christ (vv.15-19); *(5)* describing the purpose of Christ (vv.20-23); *(6)* working towards perfection in Christ vv.24-29). A little revision will not go amiss!

1) PAUL'S THANKSGIVING FOR THEIR FAITH IN CHRIST, vv.1-8
As a result of hearing "the grace of God in truth" through Epaphras, the believers at Colosse had become "saints and faithful brethren in Christ", with "faith in Christ Jesus", "love...to all the saints", and enjoyment of the "hope...laid up... in heaven".

2) PAUL'S PRAYER FOR THEIR PROGRESS IN CHRIST, vv.9-11
Thanksgiving leads to prayer. "For this cause we also, since the day we heard it, do not cease to pray for you". He prayed that they might: *(i)* "be filled with the knowledge of his will"; *(ii)* "walk worthy of the Lord unto all pleasing"; *(iii)* be "strengthened with all might, according to his glorious power". This leads to more thanksgiving as Paul reflects on our position in Christ. He is certainly an example of his own ministry! See 4.2. Unregenerate people are unthankful. See Romans 1.21 and 2 Timothy 3.2.

3) PAUL'S DESCRIPTION OF OUR POSITION IN CHRIST, vv.12-14
In the Lord Jesus we have a new **quality:** we are "meet to be partakers of the inheritance of the saints in light" (v.12); we are under a new **authority**: once it was "the power of darkness": now we are citizens of the "kingdom of his dear Son" (v.13); we have a new **liberty**: "we have redemption through his blood" (v.14). These blessings all flow from Christ and are guaranteed by Him.

4) PAUL'S DESCRIPTION OF THE PREEMINENCE OF CHRIST, vv.15-19
"That in all things he might have the preeminence". The Lord Jesus is preeminent

in the sphere of creation of which He is the Creator and Sustainer. "For by him were all things created...all things were created by him, and for him: and he is before all things, and by him all things consist" (vv.15-17). The Lord Jesus is preeminent in the new creation, the church, of which He is Creator and Head, "And he is the head of the body, the church: who is the beginning, the firstborn from the dead" (v.18). But this is not all. The Lord Jesus is not only the Creator of the universe, and Head of the church. He will perfect creation, and will perfect the church. This brings us to:

5) PAUL'S DESCRIPTION OF THE PURPOSE OF CHRIST, vv.20-23
On the basis of His work at Calvary, "the blood of his cross", the Lord Jesus will reconcile creation (v.20). He has already reconciled His people, and will present them "holy and unblameable and unreproveable in his sight" (vv.21-22). Justification is God's remedy for man's unrighteousness, and reconciliation is God's remedy for man's emnity towards Him. We can look at these verses as follows:

a) The source of reconciliation
It is totally divine. God will reconcile creation through Christ. He will harmonise creation. In the same way, God takes the initiative in reconciling man. Man does not make peace with God. God provides peace for man. The very God, Whose "fulness" dwells perfectly in Christ, has made reconciliation available through the death of the Lord Jesus. This is staggering! Just look at the passage again. On the one hand, 'all the fulness (of the Godhead) was pleased to dwell' in Him: on the other, "the blood of his cross". Only the love of God could bring statements like this together.

b) The basis of reconciliation
"Having made peace through the blood of his cross, by him to reconcile all things unto himself". Peace and reconciliation with God rest upon a righteous basis. Through the death of the Lord Jesus, provision has been made to deal with the sin that has both invaded creation, and alienated men and women from God. Peace has been procured "by the blood of his cross".

c) The scope of reconciliation
This includes both creation ("whether they be things in earth, or things in heaven", v.20) and Christians ("you, that were sometime alienated...yet now hath he reconciled in the body of his flesh through death", vv.21-22).

i) Creation. Through the Lord Jesus, God will "reconcile all things unto himself;

by him, I say, whether they be things in earth, or things in heaven" (v.20). At present, creation is 'red in tooth and claw'. It "groaneth and travaileth in pain together until now" (Rom. 8:22). But not for ever. Just think about the glowing pictures of peace and productivity described in such passages as Psalm 72, Isaiah 11-12, Isaiah 35 and Amos 9:13-15. These will be "days of heaven upon the earth" (Deut. 11:21). The reconciliation of creation will take place, not through human resources or scientific progress, but as a result of "the blood of his cross". Creation itself will benefit from the death of the Lord Jesus. It will be purged from every trace of misery and decay. "The creature (creation) itself also shall be delivered from the bondage of corruption" (Rom. 8:21).

ii) Christians. "And you, that were sometime alienated and enemies in your mind by wicked works, yet now hath he reconciled in the body of his flesh through death, to present you holy and unblameable and unreproveable in his sight" (vv.21-22). The reconciliation of creation is still future. The reconciliation of Christians is already accomplished: "yet now hath he reconciled". W.Kelly puts it like this: "I do not doubt there is an intended contrast. The reconciliation of all things is not yet accomplished. The foundation for *all* is laid, but it is not applied. But meanwhile it is applied to *us* who believe". In this connection, we must notice:

- *The necessity for our reconciliation.* We were "alienated (estranged) and enemies in...mind by wicked works" (v.21). Compare Ephesians 2:1-3.

- *The provision for our reconciliation.* We have been reconciled "in the body of his flesh through death". Reconciliation was not accomplished by the incarnation of the Lord Jesus, but by the *death* of the incarnate Son of God. His incarnation could not save us. His perfect life could not save us. We are saved by His sacrificial death. It was with this in mind that He became incarnate. His perfect life enabled Him to offer "himself without spot to God" (Heb. 9:14). Compare Hebrews 10:4-5. The reality of Christ's humanity is stressed in both passages. It is stressed in order to counter the 'gnostic' teaching that Christ was not a real man.

- *The result of our reconciliation.* "To present you holy and unblameable and unreproveable in his sight". The ultimate purpose of God is to have a people "free from every trace and taint of sin" (T. Bentley). "*Holy*" means 'separated' or 'sanctified'. Separated from sin and consecrated to God. "According as he hath chosen us in Him before the foundation of the world, that we should be holy" (Eph. 1:4). "*Unblameable*" *(amomos)* means "without blemish" (RV). The word occurs, for example, in 1 Peter 1:19 ("without blemish"), Hebrews 9:14 ("without spot"), and Jude v.24 ("faultless"). *"**Unreproveable**" (anenkletos)* means 'blameless...cannot be called into account'. It means the absence of even a charge or accusation. The word is rendered "blameless" in connection with elders (1 Tim. 3:10; Titus 1:6-7. William Lincoln *(Lectures on the Epistle to the Colossians)* suggests that it is "holy" before God, "blameless" before others, and "unreproveable" by Satan. On the other hand, it could be "holy" Godward, "unblameable" selfward, and "unreproveable" manward. One thing is clear, we will be the exact opposite to what we were by nature!

He will look upon us with divine satisfaction **then**, but what about our spiritual condition **now?** We must "make it our aim" ('labour', AV) that "whether at home or absent, to be well-pleasing unto him" (2 Cor. 5:9, RV). Not 'well-pleasing' to the brethren, but 'well-pleasing to **Him**".

- **The proof of our reconciliation.** "If ye continue in the faith grounded and settled, and be not moved away from the hope of the gospel, which ye have heard..." (v.23). At first glance, this is alarming! Does our presentation, "holy and unblameable and unreproveable in his sight", depend on an impeccable track-record? If so, where will any of us stand? We must look at the context carefully. Paul does not speak here about the judgment seat of Christ, before which we must all appear "that every one may receive the things done in his body... whether it be good or bad" (2 Cor 5.10). He is speaking about the outcome of reconciliation. All who are reconciled will be presented "holy and unblameable and unreproveable in his sight". This rests on divine grace, not on our flawless character and service. Continuity proves the reality of reconciliation. Paul is therefore warning against departure from "**the** faith": it is "if ye continue in **the** faith grounded and settled". Departure from the faith is apostasy. Continuity proves the reality of salvation. "The passage does not refer to someone being overtaken, or even having committed some serious sin, but of apostasy; hence it reads, 'if ye continue in **the** faith'" (J.M. Davies).

The words used here fully support this interpretation. They emphasise the need to remain firm under pressure to renounce the doctrines of salvation. The word "continue" *(epimeno)* means 'to remain' or 'abide'. See, for example, 1 Timothy 4:16, "take heed unto thyself, and unto the doctrine; continue in them..." The word "grounded" *(themelioo)* means 'founded' as in 'foundation'. "Settled" *(hedraios)* means, literally, 'seated', and means 'steadfast or firm'. It occurs in 1 Timothy 3:15 ("pillar and **ground** of the truth"). The danger facing these believers is particularly emphasised by the words, "Be not moved away from the hope of the gospel". Powerful influences were at work If they succumbed to false teaching, particularly the philosophical speculations of the 'gnostics', there was no hope for the future. False teaching does not give hope. To be moved away from the "hope of the gospel" is to substitute something for that hope. While the danger was present, Paul is happy to note that they had not capitulated to false teaching: "Am I with you in spirit, joying and beholding your order, and the steadfastness of your faith in Christ" (2:5). Notice that Paul uses the word "hope" three times in this chapter: "the **hope** which is laid up for you in heaven" (v.5); "the **hope** of the gospel, which ye have heard" (v.23); "Christ in you, the **hope** of glory" (v.27). As W. Kelly observes, "It (the hope) is in a heavenly Christ Who died for us, giving us the assurance of being with Himself there".

The preeminence of Christ in every sphere therefore rests on the fact that both creation and the church owe their existence to Him (vv.15-19), and that He died to secure the perfecting of creation, and the perfecting of His people (vv.20-23).

We must notice that Paul alludes to the universality of the gospel here, and his part in its proclamation. "The gospel, which ye have heard (through Ephaphras: see 1:5-7), and which was preached to every creature ('the whole creation', JND) which is under heaven (compare 1:5-6: 'the truth of the gospel; which is come unto you, as it is in all the world'); whereof I Paul am made a minister". The gospel preached at Colosse was consistent with the gospel preached everywhere. The word "minister" *(diakonos)* occurs in vv.7, 25. It means 'a servant', and is used widely in the New Testament. For further occurrences of the word in connection with Paul's ministry, see, for example, 1 Corinthians 3:5; Ephesians 3:7.

6) *PAUL'S WORK TOWARDS THEIR PERFECTION IN CHRIST, vv.24-29*
The apostle tells us about his objective in vv.28-29, "Whom we preach, warning every man, and teaching every man in all wisdom; that we may **present every man perfect in Christ Jesus:** whereunto I also labour, striving according to his working, which worketh in me mightily". Compare Ephesians 4:14-15, "That we henceforth be no more children, tossed to and fro, and carried about with every wind of doctrine...but speaking the truth in love, may grow up into him in all things". The attainment of this objective, involved **(a)** suffering (v.24); **(b)** stewardship (vv.25-27); **(c)** striving (vv.28-29). Paul was both "a minister" of the gospel (v.23) and a "minister" of the church: "who now rejoice in my sufferings for you, and fill up that which is behind ('is lacking', RV) of the afflictions of Christ in my flesh for his body's sake, which is the church: whereof I am made a minister." (vv.24-25).

Chapter 1B

a) Paul's suffering, v.24

We now learn that, like the Lord Jesus, Paul was a suffering servant. The details of his sufferings are given in 2 Corinthians chs. 4 and 11. They were very real: "***my*** sufferings". In 2 Corinthians ch.11, he refers to things that happened ***once***: "once was I stoned...a night and a day I have been in the deep" (v.25); to things that happened ***three times***: "thrice was I beaten with rods...thrice I suffered shipwreck" (v.25); to things that happened ***five times***: "of the Jews five times received I forty stripes save one" (v.24); to things that happened "***oft***": "in prisons more frequent, in deaths oft" (v.23). These were sufferings that could be seen by men, but there were sufferings which could not be seen by men: "who now rejoice in my sufferings for you, and fill up that which is behind of the afflictions of Christ in my flesh for his body's sake, which is the church". So Paul describes his sufferings in two ways:

i) "My sufferings". But he does not emphasise them. He emphasises his ***joy*** in suffering. "Who now ***rejoice*** in my sufferings for you". Compare v.11, "strengthened...unto all patience and longsuffering with ***joyfulness***". Paul rejoiced in his sufferings, including his present imprisonment, because of the benefit others received through them: "who now rejoice in my sufferings ***for you***". He was prepared to suffer in order to secure the spiritual benefit of the Gentiles. This is evidently the meaning of "for you". See v.27, "to whom God would make known what is the riches of the glory of this mystery among the Gentiles". Paul therefore rejoiced in his sufferings, because they were contracted in connection with the glorious ministry of bringing the gospel to the Gentiles, and giving help to Gentile believers. (The apostles rejoiced in their sufferings for a different reason in Acts 5:41. See also James 1:2). Are ***we*** prepared to suffer in order that others might be helped? The joy of bringing God's word to others, whether saints or sinners, will more than adequately compensate for any suffering involved.

ii) "The afflictions of Christ". Paul recognised that they were not his sufferings alone. He has called them "***my*** sufferings": now he calls them "the afflictions of ***Christ*** in my flesh". We learn then that the Lord Jesus continues to suffer. Not for sin, of course! The word rendered "afflictions" *(thlipsis)* is only used of Christ here, and does not refer to His sufferings for sin. But the sufferings of the Lord Jesus were not completed at Calvary. See, for example Acts 9:4, "Saul, Saul, why persecutest thou me?", and 2 Corinthians 1:5, "For as the sufferings of Christ abound in us, so our consolation also aboundeth by Christ". (Compare Isaiah 63:9). Paul rejoiced that he was able to enter into the completion of Christ's suffering for the church. This is the meaning of "fill up that which is behind ('completing that which is lacking' or 'remaining') of the afflictions of Christ in my flesh for his body's sake, which is the church". It has particular reference to God's purpose that Gentiles and Jews should be blessed together in one body. What an amazing way to view suffering! We must emphasise again that this has nothing at all to do with Christ's suffering for sin. He alone suffered for sin. Paul is concerned with the welfare of the church in this passage.

We must add that this passage emphasises the relationship between Christ and His church. The church is His body. Paul therefore suffered for "his body's sake" (v.24). He did not suffer simply on behalf of others, or on behalf of fellow-believers, but on behalf of something precious to Christ: "his body's sake, which is the church". This view of his sufferings enabled Paul to rejoice in them. His ministry in this way brings us to

b) Paul's stewardship, vv.25-27
"The church: whereof I am made a minister (as we have seen, *diakonos*), according to the dispensation of God which is given to me, to fulfil the word of God". Paul now defines his particular role in connection with the church. The words "dispensation of God" refers to Paul's divinely-given stewardship. The word "dispensation" *(oikonomia)* signifies "the management of a household or of household affairs...and so a stewardship" (W.E. Vine). It occurs, for example, in Ephesians 3:2 ("the dispensation of the grace of God") and 1 Corinthians 4:1-2 ("stewards of the mysteries of God. Moreover it is required in stewards, that a man be found faithful"). We should notice that Paul says "whereof I am **made** a minister, according to the dispensation of God which is **given to me** for you". See, for example, 1 Corinthians 3:5; Romans 12:3. Paul describes his stewardship in two ways:

- **Generally.** "To fulfil the word of God" or "to complete the word of God" (JND). This does not mean to complete the word of God in the sense of 'conclude the word of God'. Paul is not referring here to the completion of the canon of Scripture. John wrote after Paul. Paul completed the word of God in the sense of completing the **doctrine** of the word of God. The church is God's crowning revelation. The Lord Jesus said, "I have yet many things to say unto you, but ye cannot bear them now" (John 16:12).

- **Specifically.** The doctrine of the word of God was completed, as we have seen, by the revelation of "the mystery which hath been hid from ages and from generations, but now is made manifest to his saints" (v.26). Compare Ephesians 3:3-9. In the New Testament, the word "mystery" does not refer to something

Chapter 1B

concealed, but something ***revealed.*** Not to something ***withheld,*** but something ***imparted.*** Here, of course, it refers to the doctrine and character of the church: the union between the Head and the body (v.24), involving Gentiles as well as Jews (v.27). We must notice the "mystery" as to time (v.26), and the "mystery" as to character (v.27).

- **As to time.** In connection with the past, we read, "which hath been ***hid***". In connection with the present we read, "but ***now*** is made manifest to his saints (not to all men)". Compare Ephesians 3:1-9: "How that by revelation he made known unto me the mystery...which in other ages was not made known unto the sons of men, as it is now revealed unto his holy apostles and prophets by the Spirit; that the Gentiles should be fellowheirs, and of the same body, and partakers of his promise in Christ by the gospel...and to make all men see what is the fellowship of the mystery, which from the beginning of the world hath been hid in God, who created all things by Jesus Christ". Paul was, of course, "the apostle of the Gentiles": see Romans 11:13; Ephesians 3:8; 1 Timothy 2:7.

- **As to character.** "To whom God would make known what is the riches of the glory of this mystery among the Gentiles; which is Christ in you, the hope of glory". So God wants all the saints to know about this "mystery". He graciously acquaints us with His purposes, reminding us of the words of the Lord Jesus, "Henceforth I call you not servants; for the servant knoweth not what his lord doeth: but I have called you friends" (John 15:15). The "mystery" of Jew and Gentile brought together in one body is no second rate thing! God is not miserly! Judaism was "beggarly" (Gal. 4:9). It had no power to enrich. But Paul speaks here about the "***riches*** of the ***glory*** of this mystery". Everything about God's dealings is 'glorious'. See, for example, the superior glory of the new covenant (2 Cor. 3:6-11).

The "riches of the glory of this mystery" lie particularly in the blessing of the Gentiles. This is the outstanding feature of the church. While the future blessing of Gentile nations ***was*** clearly predicted in the Old Testament, the eternal purpose of God to unite believing Jews and Gentiles ***in one body*** was ***not*** revealed in the Old Testament. The RSV puts it like this: "To them (the saints) God chose to make known how great among the Gentiles are the riches of this mystery". The Amplified Version reads, 'To whom God was pleased to make known how great for the Gentiles are the riches of this mystery". How wonderful that God should bless the Gentiles in this way! But the outstanding feature of the church is more than uniting Jew and Gentile in one body: it is Christ dwelling in them! Here, particularly, Christ dwelling in believing Gentiles. Hence, "the riches of the glory of this mystery among the Gentiles; which is Christ in *you* (Paul is referring to the Colossians themselves here), the hope of glory". Gentiles are not only united to Jews in Christ (Ephesians), but indwelt by Him (Colossians). His indwelling is the pledge of future glory. Gentile believers, who had no previous expectation of glory, can now anticipate the time when the Lord Jesus will "be glorified in his saints, and...admired in all them that believe" (2 Thess. 1:10).

c) *Paul's striving, vv.28-29*
Paul now tells us how he discharged his stewardship. He tells us *(i)* what he did, *(ii)* why he did it, and *(iii)* how he did it.

i) What he did. "Whom we preach (*katangello*, to proclaim), warning (*noutheteo*, to admonish) every man, and teaching *(didasko)* every man in all wisdom". His ministry involved **proclamation.** He preached Christ. Not philosophy, but a Person. It involved **admonition.** Warning based on instruction. See Acts 20:31. Warning against error. It involved **edification.** Paul taught the truth as well as warning against error. We must notice that he warned and taught "every man...in all wisdom". Compare Colossians 3:16. (The 'gnostics' were a 'select' group, and prided themselves in *their* wisdom!). This is a good example for every assembly teacher and elder. None should be excluded from the scope of the ministry.

(ii) Why he did it. "That we may present (*paristemi*, as in v.22) every man perfect *(teleios)* in Christ Jesus". This is why none should be excluded from the scope of the ministry. The desire of every teacher and elder should be the maturity of the Lord's people. The word "perfect" does not mean sinless perfection! It refers to spiritual maturity, which, in a word, is Christ-likeness. See Ephesians 4:12-15. We should notice that Paul had a firm goal in his ministry. He was focussed in his service for God. It has been said that 'he that aims at nothing usually hits it!' What goals do *we* have in our Christian service?

(iii) How he did it. "Whereunto I also labour, striving according to his working, which worketh in me mightily". This statement is charged with energy! "Labour" *(kopiao)* means 'toil resulting in weariness, laborious toil' (W.E. Vine). "Striving" (*agonizomai*) means to 'contend' and takes us into the arena. See also 4:12. But look at his resources! "Striving according to *his* working *(energeia)*, which worketh *(energeia)* in me mightily (v.29) (*en dunamei* from *dunamis*)". *Energeia* conveys the power of God, and *dunamis* conveys the ability of God. Paul therefore acknowledges that the effectiveness of his labour is entirely due to divine power and ability. Compare 1 Corinthians 15:10; 2 Corinthians 3:5; Ephesians 3:20.

READ CHAPTER 2.1-7

"In whom are hid all the treasures of wisdom and knowledge"

If Chapter 1 concludes with Paul's general objective for all believers, then Chapter 2 commences with his particular concern for the believers at Colosse. In this connection, we should notice;

i) Paul's general objective for all believers, 1:28-29. This involved *"every man"*: "whom (Christ) we preach, warning every man, and teaching every man in all wisdom; that we may present every man **perfect** in Christ Jesus" (1:28). Paul refers to this 'presentation' earlier: "to present you holy and unblameable and unreproveable *in his sight*" (1:22). As we have already noted, this involved

- **Suffering for Paul.** "Who now rejoice in my sufferings for you, and fill up that which is behind of the afflictions of Christ in my flesh for his body's sake, which is the church" (1:24). He rejoiced in his sufferings, because they were incurred in such a worthy purpose. As we noticed in our previous study, whilst they were Paul's sufferings, they were also the sufferings of Christ.

- **Stewardship for Paul.** "Whereof I am made a minister, according to the dispensation (meaning 'stewardship') of God which is given to me for you, to fulfil (or 'complete") the word of God" (1:25). Paul was a 'steward' of divinely-revealed teaching about the church, with its unique inclusion of Jew and Gentile in one body. This is the "mystery which hath been hid from ages and from generations, but now is made manifest to his saints" (1:26-27). Compare Ephesians 3:8-11. Whilst Paul's writings did not complete the **canon** of the Scripture, they did complete the **doctrine** of Scripture. The church is God's crowning revelation.

- **Striving for Paul.** "Whereunto I also labour, striving according to his working, which worketh in me mightily". Paul was not left to his own devices. Divine resources were both available and adequate for the task. Compare 1 Corinthians 15:10, and Ephesians 3:20.

Chapter 2

ii) Paul's particular concern for the Colossian believers, 2:1. Paul now turns to the Colossian believers in particular. Notice the connection: *"For* I would that ye knew what great conflict I have *for you,* and for them at Laodicea, and for as many as have not seen my face in the flesh". Paul's deep concern for *all* believers (1:28) was expressed in his concern for believers at Colosse and Laodicea. We should notice the following:

- "For I would that ye knew what **great conflict** I have for you", literally 'how great a conflict I have for you'. The noun *(agon)* takes us to the athletics contest. Hence the translations, "what combat I have for you" (JND), and "how greatly I strive for you" (RV). The verb occurs in 1:29 ("striving"), and in 4:12 ("labouring fervently for you in prayers"). Paul was deeply affected by the problems and dangers confronting the Colossians. How much are **we** concerned about the welfare of fellow-believers?

- "What great conflict I have for you, and for them at **Laodicea**". No reference is made to Hierapolis, but Laodicea is specifically mentioned. Perhaps, and this is as far as we can go, Paul saw the beginning of the decline described by the Lord Jesus: "Thou sayest, I am rich, and increased with goods, and have need of nothing; and knowest not that thou art wretched, and miserable, and *poor*, and blind, and naked" (Rev 3:17). The church at Laodicea was rich materially, but poor spiritually. Perhaps Paul knew that they were failing to possess "all *riches* of the full assurance of understanding", and failing to appreciate that in Christ are hid "all the *treasures* of wisdom and knowledge" (2:2-3).

- "What great conflict I have for you, and for them at Laodicea, and for *as many as have not seen my face in the flesh"*. This is usually understood to mean that Paul had not been to the area, and could therefore include Hierapolis. It could, of course, be a general statement, but the verses that follow strongly suggest that he refers to the local area.

Having noted the connection between Chapters 1 and 2, we can now proceed with three studies in Chapter 2. The chapter may be divided into four paragraphs as follows: *(1)* our progress in Christ (vv.1-7); *(2)* our completeness in Christ (vv.8-15); *(3)* our superior position in Christ (vv.16-19); *(4)* our identification with Christ (vv.20-23).

It has been nicely said that this chapter emphasises the Lordship of Christ (see v.6), so we need no other **authority**, the Deity of Christ (see v.9), so we need no other **addition,** and the Headship of Christ (see v.19), so we need no other **arrangement.**

1) OUR PROGRESS IN CHRIST, vv.1-7

Paul was concerned for these believers in two ways. He was concerned for progress in their understanding of Christ (vv.2-3), and for progress in their experience of Christ (vv.6-7). He gives the reasons for his concern in the intervening verses. "**And this I say**, lest any man should beguile you with enticing words. For though I be absent in the flesh, yet am I with you in the spirit, joying and beholding your order, and the stedfastness of your faith in Christ" (vv.4-5). We should therefore note the following.

a) Progress in their understanding of Christ, vv.2-3

The object of spiritual progress is clearly set out in these verses. Paul desires that these believers (and us) should possess "all riches of the full assurance of understanding, to the acknowledgement **(to the full knowledge)** of the mystery of God, and of the Father, and of Christ; in whom are hid all the treasures of wisdom and knowledge". T. Bentley *(What the Bible Teaches - Colossians)* points out that "readings based on various manuscripts differ, as do the consequent interpretations", and continues, "the Revised Version accepts the simplest reading, 'the mystery of God, even Christ', which meets the general requirements of the context". W.E. Vine follows the RV reading in his commentary. Christ is the "mystery of God". He has fully manifested God.

As throughout the Scriptures, every word counts in these verses! Paul was deeply concerned that:

i) "Their hearts might be **comforted**". In this setting, the word "comforted" *(parakaleo)* means 'encouraged'. If the Colossians listened to 'gnostic' teaching, they would be discouraged from making spiritual progress! But they had every reason to be encouraged in view of Paul's teaching about the Lord Jesus in Chapter 1!

Paul was certainly not like the ten spies whose report resulted in the cry, "our brethren have discouraged our heart" (Deut. 1:28). It is all too easy to be 'wet blankets!' We all need encouragement, and we all need to encourage each other. The first three occurrences of the word "heart" in Scripture (Genesis 6:5-6, and 8:21) help us to define its meaning. It covers our entire inner life.

ii) "Being **knit together** in love". We now learn that fellowship is vital to spiritual progress. Quite clearly, Paul is writing about their corporate progress. An assembly cannot make spiritual growth without fellowship. "Being knit together in love" is more than 'coming to meetings'. It emphasises the true quality of fellowship. There is something terribly wrong with a person who has little or no desire for the company and fellowship of fellow-believers, and who takes every opportuntiy **not** to be with them.

iii) "Being knit together in **love**". It is impossible to make progress in the atmosphere of bitterness and strife. Hence the necessity to "put off all these; **anger** (ill-will suppressed), **wrath** (ill-will expressed)" (3:8)." Compare Ephesians 4:15, "But speaking the truth in love, may grow up into him in all things, which is the head, even Christ".

iv) "Unto **all riches** of the full assurance of understanding". Not just 'unto the riches of the full assurance of understanding', but "unto **all** riches of the full assurance of understanding". Here is true wealth! The relentless pursuit of material prosperity will rob us of spiritual prosperity. The parable of the 'rich fool' is not without lessons for Christians! Are **we** "rich toward God?" This was evidently true of Gaius: "Beloved, I wish above all things that thou mayest prosper and be in health, even as **thy soul prospereth**" (3 John 2). For other references to true prosperity, see Joshua 1:8; Psalm 1:1-3.

v) "Unto all riches of the **full assurance of understanding**". This was so important for the Colossian believers in view of 'gnostic' teaching. The word rendered "full assurance" *(plerophoria)* means 'a fulness, abundance' (W.E. Vine). There is no 'gnosticism' here! The word occurs in 1 Thessalonians 1:5 ("much assurance"), and in Hebrews 6:11 and 10:22 ("full assurance"). We need to be assured of divine truth. We all begin, like the man born blind, and say, "One thing I know". But assurance should keep pace with increasing knowledge, enabling us to "be ready always to give an answer to every man that asketh you a reason of the hope that is in you" (1 Pet. 3:15). If we lose our assurance and confidence in the Word of God, we become vulnerable to error.

This is very important. Ability to use the right language (jargon) is not sufficient. It is all too easy to trot out stock phrases, which may be perfectly correct in themselves, without knowing what they really mean. It's all very impressive until someone starts asking questions! Big bold words can mask shallow thinking. (Hence the scribbled instructions in the margin of the preacher's notes, 'Argument weak here - shout!').

But Paul has something particularly in mind when he speaks about the "full assurance of understanding". So:

vi) "To the acknowledgement of the **mystery of God,** and of the Father, and of Christ". We have already noted the RV rendering here, "That they may know the mystery of God, even Christ". The word rendered "acknowledgement" *(epignosis)* means 'full knowledge', as opposed to the boasted knowledge of the 'gnostics'. They had their own ideas about God, but Paul states that God can only be fully known in Christ. **He** is the "mystery of God". We must remember that a "mystery", in the New Testament sense, is something previously withheld, but now revealed. This is confirmed by the previous reference to the word: "Even the mystery which hath been **hid** from ages and from generations, but now is **made manifest** to his saints" (1:26). For confirmation, we can do no better than quote the apostle John; "No man hath seen God at any time; the only begotten Son, which is in the bosom of the Father, he hath declared him" (John 1:18). We sing:

> True image of the infinite,
> Whose essence is concealed:
> Brightness of uncreated light,
> The heart of God revealed.

It is worth noting that expression, "mystery of God", also occurs in Revelation 10:7, "But in the days of the voice of the seventh angel, when he shall begin to sound, the mystery of God should be finished, as he hath declared to his servants the prophets". The context here is quite different, and "the mystery of God" refers, in this case, to the completion of God's prophetic programme.

vii) "In whom are **hid all the treasures of wisdom and knowledge**". If this was rendered literally, it would look like this: 'In whom are all the treasures of wisdom and knowledge kept secret, or hidden away, from'. This doesn't read very well in English, but it does convey the meaning of the verse. "The treasures of wisdom and knowledge *(epignosis)*" are all located in Christ. They are not generally apparent, or generally known. They are known only to **believers.** "The treasures of wisdom" are hid, not **from** us, but **for** us in Christ (Matthew Henry). The Lord Jesus put it very beautifully when He said, "I thank thee, O Father, Lord of heaven and earth, because thou hast hid these things from the wise and prudent, and hast revealed them unto babes" (Matt. 11:25). The **'gnostics'** thought that they were the repositories of wisdom and knowledge. Paul answers with a resounding, 'No!', and proceeds to warn the Colossians about the dangers of gnosticism.

When the Jews listened to the teaching of the Lord Jesus, "in whom are hid all the treasures of wisdom and knowledge", they "marvelled, saying, How knoweth this man letters, having never learned?" (John 7:15). Paul sat at the feet of Gamaliel, a renowned doctor of the law (Acts 22:3), but who taught the Lord

Jesus? Paul himself exclaims, "O the depth of the riches both of the wisdom and knowledge of God! How unsearchable are his judgments, and his ways past finding out! For who hath known the mind of the Lord? or who hath been his counsellor?" (Romans 11:33-34). The Jews had been listening (John 7:15 above) to God manifest in flesh. But, wonder of wonders, at the same time, He took the place of a Servant and exclaimed, "The Lord GOD hath given me the tongue of the learned, that I should know how to speak a word in season to him that is weary: he wakeneth morning by morning, he wakeneth mine ear to hear as the learned" (Isa. 50:4).

b) Progress can be halted by false teaching, vv.4-5
Paul now explains why he is so concerned about them (v.1), and why he desires their progress in understanding "the mystery of God, even Christ" (v.2). "And this I say…"

i) "Lest any man should **beguile** you with **enticing words**" (v.4). The word "beguile" *(paralogizomai)* means, literally, 'to deceive by false reasoning'. (A different word is used in 2:18). It occurs in James 1:22, "But be ye doers of the word, and not hearers only, deceiving your own selves". "Enticing words" *(pithanologia)* comes from an adjective meaning 'specious, plausible, persuasive'. "The terminology used here is practically equivalent to our English expression, 'to talk someone into something'" *(Linguistic Key to the Greek New Testament).* There can be no doubt that Paul is referring here to the "philosophy and vain deceit" of the 'gnostics' (vv.8, 18). It is worth saying here, that false teaching often has a curiosity value. Unless we are careful, we can be swept away by attractive new ideas.

We should notice that Paul saw the danger, and dealt with it beforehand. Compare 1 Thessalonians 3:4: "For verily, when we were with you, we told you **before** that we should suffer tribulation; even as it came to pass, and ye know". Assembly elders and Bible teachers must be aware of what is happening, and what is likely to happen, in secular society and in so-called Christian society, and give appropriate teaching. This is followed by encouragement.

ii) "For though I be absent in the flesh, yet am I with you in (the) spirit, joying and beholding your order, and the stedfastness of your faith in Christ" (v.5). Paul noted their excellent qualities, and desired that these should be maintained (v.6). He did not want to see their "order" *(taxis)* and "stedfastness" *(stereoma)* spoilt. The word "order", which could have a military connection, signifies order as opposed to confusion. Compare 1 Corinthians 14:40, where it is used in connection with assembly gatherings. Paul knew that if the Colossians succumbed to false teaching, their order would give place to chaos, and their steadfastness would give place to deviation. False teaching ruins godly conduct. It brings disruption and discord. This brings us to:

c) Progress in their experience of Christ, vv.6-7

The great bulwark against error is not only correct understanding, but submission to Christ, and enjoyment of Christ. These two verses have been summed up as follows: *(i)* "walk ye in him": that is, **step forward**; *(ii)* "rooted...in him": that is, **strike down**; *(iii)* "built up in him": that is, **spring up**; *(iv)* "stablished in the faith": that is, **stand firm;** *(v)* "abounding therein with thanksgiving": that is, **spread out.**

The sequence begins with, "As ye have therefore received Christ Jesus **the Lord**". This takes us back to our conversion. "As many as received him, to them gave he power to become the sons of God ('children of God)', even to them that believe on his name" (John 1:12). Quite obviously, Epaphras had followed the example of the apostles, who proclaimed "let all the house of Israel know assuredly, that God hath made that same Jesus, whom ye have crucified, both **Lord** and Christ" (Acts 2:36). See also Acts 10:36, "The word which God sent unto the children of Israel, preaching peace by Jesus Christ: (he is **Lord** of all)". The Colossians received Him as "Christ...Jesus...the Lord". They were now to:

i) **Step forward.** "So walk ye in him". Their Christian life began by receiving "Christ Jesus the Lord": their Christian lives were now to proceed on the **same basis.** They were to be subject to "Christ Jesus the Lord". This applies to every aspect of life. Read 3:17-24, and notice the references to "the Lord". The passage covers family relationships, and the attitude of employees to employers. The word "walk" refers to the whole round of life. Compare Ephesians 4:1, 17; 5:2, 8, 15.

ii) **Strike down.** "Rooted...in him". This is in the perfect tense: 'having been rooted', 'an act having been once accomplished with permanent results'. This happened at conversion. "God rooted them in Christ, as a plant is firmly rooted in the soil" (T. Bentley). The believer cannot be uprooted. However, this is a good opportunity to discuss the nature and function of **roots.** They are unseen (at least, in most cases) and link supply with need. We do need to ensure that our spiritual roots of unseen fellowship and communion with God are functioning as they should. Problems at the root of a plant usually mean the death or deterioration of the plant. The lesson is clear. Look at the relationship between roots and branches in Hosea 14:5-6, and between roots and fruit-bearing in

Isaiah 37:31. See also Matthew 13:21: "Yet hath he no root in himself, but dureth for a while: for when tribulation or persecution ariseth because of the word, by and by he is offended". Read Psalm 1:3; 92:13-14.

iii) **Spring up.** "Built up in him". This is in the present tense, and refers to a continuing process. "The present tense of the verb suggests the attitude of a believer toward Christ which enables him to be constantly and consistently growing, as a building rises progressively towards its completion" (T. Bentley). Hence, literally, "*In Him* walk ye, rooted and built up *in Him*".

iv) **Stand firm.** "And stablished in the faith, as ye have been taught". The word "stablished"" means 'being made firm'. Bearing in mind the pattern of New Testament evangelism, there can be little doubt that they had been taught by Epaphras. As G.B. Wilson *(Colossians and Philemon)* observes, "Far from interfering with the work of an honoured colleague, Paul places the whole weight of apostolic authority behind it". Compare 1:23.

v) **Spread out.** "Abounding therein with thanksgiving". This is the hallmark of spiritual life. See 1:12; 3:15; 3:17; 4:2. As Paul says elsewhere, "In every thing give thanks; for this is the will of God in Christ Jesus concerning you" (1 Thess. 5:18). Unregenerate men and women are unthankful. See Romans 1:21. Religious profession ("having a form of godliness, but denying the power thereof") is unthankful. See 2 Timothy 3:2.

While we gladly recognise that "every good gift and every perfect gift is from above, and cometh down from the Father of lights, with whom is no variableness, neither shadow of turning" (James 1:17), we must add, above every thing else, "Thanks be unto God for his unspeakable gift" (2 Cor. 9:15).

READ CHAPTER 2.8-15

"Ye are complete in him"

In our last study, we suggested that Colossians 2 may be divided into four paragraphs: **(1)** our progress in Christ (vv.1-7); **(2)** our completeness in Christ (vv.8-15); **(3)** our superior position in Christ (vv.16-19); **(3)** our identification with Christ (vv.20-23).

1) OUR PROGRESS IN CHRIST, vv.1-7
We have already noticed that Paul was concerned for progress in their understanding of Christ (vv.2-3), and for progress in their experience of Christ (vv.6-7). He gives the reason for his concern in the intervening verses (vv.5-6). If we are not making spiritual progress, we are probably slipping back! Standing still is **not** an option.

2) OUR COMPLETENESS IN CHRIST, vv.8-15
Paul meets the suggestions and demands of the false teachers by emphasising the total sufficiency of the Person and work of the Lord Jesus. The Colossians had to contend with:

i) The philosophers (the 'gnostics'), whose wares are described as "philosophy and vain deceit" (v.8). But Christians have something infinitely better in Christ: "in him dwelleth all the fulness of the Godhead bodily. And ye are complete ***in him,*** which is the head of all principality and power" (vv.9-10).

ii) The Jewish teachers, who endeavoured to impose circumcision (hence the reference to this rite in vv.11, 13) and other Judaistic ordinances (see v.16) on these Gentile believers. But once again, Christians had something infinitely better in Christ, and Paul therefore continues: "***in whom*** (Christ) also ye are circumcised with the circumcision made without hands, in putting off the body of the sins of the flesh by the circumcision of Christ" (v.11). In Christ, God had dealt, not with part of our bodies, but with our sinful nature.

We may therefore divide these verses as follows **(a)** complete in Christ (vv.8-10): Paul's answer to gnosticism; **(b)** circumcised in Christ (vv.11-15): Paul's answer to Judaism.

a) Complete in Christ, vv.8-10

The section begins with a warning: "Beware lest any man spoil you through philosophy and vain deceit, after the tradition of men, after the rudiments of the world, and not after Christ". This explains the phrase "enticing words" (v.4): "And this I say, lest any man should beguile you with **enticing words**". Paul evidently believed that to be 'forewarned was to be forearmed'! He saw the potential danger, and warned them accordingly. Prevention is certainly better than cure!

We should notice Paul's strategy in dealing with false teaching. He does not launch an immediate 'all out' attack. The best way to preserve God's people from error is to ensure that they know and enjoy the truth! Paul therefore, first of all, sets out the glories of Christ as Creator of the universe and Head of the church. He is supreme in both: "that in all things he might have the pre-eminence". We really ought to read Chapter 1 again! The epistle commences by reminding the Colossians of the identity and work of their Saviour, and continues by urging progress in their understanding and experience of Him (2:1-7). Having given positive teaching, Paul **then** combats erroneous teaching by emphasising the total sufficiency of the Person of Christ and the work of Christ.

These three verses contrast human reasoning (v.8) with divine revelation (vv.9-10), and emphasise the utter superiority of the latter over the former.

i) Human reasoning, v.8. "Beware ('take heed' or 'be on your guard') lest any man spoil you through philosophy and vain deceit, after the tradition of men, after the rudiments of the world, and not after Christ". The word "philosophy" *(philosophia)* "denotes the love and pursuit of wisdom" (W.E. Vine). The philosophers (the noun only occurs in Acts 17:18) claimed superior knowledge. Hence, as we have previously noted, the term 'gnostic' from *gnosis,* meaning knowledge. They were very proud of their alleged superior knowledge. Paul describes it as "vainly puffed up by his fleshly mind" (2:18).

The word "**spoil**" means 'to carry off as spoil', or 'despoil'. It could refer either to bondage imposed on the believers themselves, or to robbing them of the enjoyment of their treasures in Christ. Both are true. We must not forget that truth brings liberty, but error brings bondage. Given the opportunity, the 'philosophers' would have diverted the attention of the Colossians from the certainty and clarity of divine revelation, to the uncertainty and speculation of human wisdom. As we shall see, one of the elements of their "philosophy and vain deceit" was to elevate angels to the level of deity (v.18), and that turns their 'philosophy' into blasphemy.

"**Philosophy**" and "**vain deceit**" both refer to the same thing. "Philosophy" is **their** term. "Vain deceit" is **Paul's** term. He is certainly not very complimentary about them! Compare 1 Timothy 6:20-21, where the word "science" *(gnosis)* means 'knowledge'. Paul describes their "philosophy" in four ways.

- It is "**vain**" *(kenos)*, meaning 'empty, valueless'. "Vain deceit" suggests that the deceit is void of anything profitable (W.E. Vine).

- It is "**after the tradition of men**": it consists of men's ideas. Note the references to "man" and "men" in this chapter (vv.8, 16, 18, 22). In the final analysis, it is men versus Christ.

- It is "**after the rudiments of the world**". Paul is evidently referring here to the religious world: the word translated "rudiments" *(stoicheion)* is used in this connection elsewhere in the New Testament. See Galatians 4:3, 9 ("the *elements* of the world...weak and beggarly *elements*": they have no power to strengthen or enrich), and Hebrews 5:12 ("first principles"). It occurs again in this chapter (v.20). The word means "first things from which others in a series, or a composite whole, 'take their rise' it was used of the letters of the alphabet, as elements of speech" (W.E. Vine). We could define its meaning as 'elementary principles'. It could be said that Adam and Eve introduced the "rudiments of the world" when, in their own wisdom, they "sewed fig leaves together, and **made themselves** aprons" (Gen. 3:7). Human religion follows this pattern, and attempting to gain favour with God by "the works of the law" (Gal. 2:16) is an outstanding example of the principle. The "philosophy" confronting the Christians at Colosse followed the usual pattern of worldly religion. Gnosticism involved asceticism (v.23).

- It is "**not after Christ**". This is its crowning error. It disregards the glory of Christ. After all:

> 'What think ye of Christ?' is the test,
> To try both your state and your scheme:
> You cannot be right in the rest
> Unless you think rightly of Him.

ii) Divine revelation, vv.9-10. In these two wonderful verses, we have, firstly, the fulness of God which resides in Christ (v.9), and, secondly, the fulness that the believer has in Christ (v.10). In the first case, Paul uses the noun *pleroma*, meaning "that of which a thing is full" (W.E. Vine). In the second case, he uses the verb *pleroo*, meaning "to be made full".

- The fulness of God which resides in Christ, v.9. We must notice the connection with the previous verse: "Beware lest any man spoil you through philosophy and vain deceit, after the tradition of men, after the rudiments of the world, and not after Christ. **For** in him dwelleth all the fulness of the Godhead bodily". On the one hand we have the emptiness of philosophy, and on the other we have the perfect revelation of God in Christ. In the first case, it is speculation, and in the second it is revelation. "In Christ dwells all the fulness (completeness) of the absolute Godhead, essentially and perfectly: the very Personality of God. The fulness of the Godhead never dwelt in the Father **bodily,** or in the Holy Ghost, but only in Christ" (Wm. Kelly). God is known because of incarnation: hence, "in him dwelleth all the fulness of the Godhead **bodily**". (Do note the present tense here: the fulness of the Godhead dwelt in Him perfectly while on earth, and dwells perfectly in Him now in heaven). There is nothing speculative here. The Lord Jesus is "God manifest in the flesh", of Whom John wrote: "That which was from the beginning, which we have heard, which we have seen with our eyes, which we have looked upon, and our hands have handled, of the Word of life" (1 John 1:1). This is one of the great truths about Christ which we confess at the Lord's Supper: "Take, eat: this is my body, which is broken for you: this do in remembrance of me".

We have already noticed the meaning of the word "***fulness***" *(pleroma)*. It also occurs in Colossians 1:19; Ephesians 1:23, 3:19; John 1:16. The word "***Godhead***" *(theotes)* here differs from its occurrence in Romans 1: 20 *(theiotes)* and Acts 17:29 *(theios)*. The word *theotes* refers to the state of being God. "Paul is declaring that in the Son there dwells all the fulness of absolute Godhead; they were no mere rays of Divine glory which gilded Him, lighting up His Person for a season and with a splendour not His own; but He was, and is, absolute and perfect God" (W.E. Vine quoting Trench). In Romans 1:20, *theiotes* refers to what belongs to God, that is, His power and attributes revealed in nature.

- The fulness that the believer has in Christ, v.10. "And ye are complete (made full) in Him". This contrasts vividly with human philosophy, which is nothing else than "vain deceit". But in Christ **we have all that we can ever need.** We do not, therefore, need to look elsewhere. "The believer needs no supplement.

He requires no help from any subordinate whether he is high or low, angelic or demonic, for Christ is all" (T. Bentley, *What the Bible Teaches - Colossians*). God has not "spoiled" us (v.8): He has blessed us in Christ beyond imagination! It is important to notice the plural here. "And **ye** are complete in him". **All** believers are "complete in him". This does not apply to a favoured few or a limited circle. Unlike the philosophers whose wisdom was exclusive to themselves and their devotees, every believer is 'made full' in Christ.

As G.B. Wilson observes, the words, "who is the head of all principality and power", are "added to convince them of the futility of invoking angelic powers when these are all subject to the supreme lordship of Christ". He adds, "but though Christ is described as their 'head'', it should be noted that they (the angelic powers) are not called his 'body', for the special intimacy of that relationship is reserved for Christ's people (1:18)". Christ is the Creator of "principalities and powers" (1:16), the Controller ("head") of "all principality and power" (2:10), and the Conqueror of "principalities and powers" (2:15).

b) Circumcised in Christ, vv.11-15
Having dealt, for the time being, with gnosticism, Paul now deals with Judaism. "In whom also ye are circumcised with the circumcision made without hands, in putting off the body of the sins of the flesh by the circumcision of Christ". Our relationship with Christ excludes the need to explore the unseen world, because He is "the head of all principality and power". In the same way, our relationship with the Lord Jesus excludes the need for religious rites and ceremonies, because He has dealt with our sinful nature. It might be helpful to compare physical circumcision with "the circumcision of Christ."

i) Physical circumcision dealt with the vehicle of sin.
The vehicle of sin is the human body. It is through the body that sin is expressed. Physical circumcision involved part of the body, an external rite, and human participation: it was made 'with hands'. While circumcision was "a seal of the righteousness of the faith which he (Abraham) had yet being uncircumcised" (Romans 4:11), and should have been the outward sign of faith in God on the part of every Israelite, it became an outward rite and nothing more. Hence the solemn charge levelled at Israel, "Ye stiffnecked and uncircumcised in heart and ears, ye do always resist the Holy Ghost: as your fathers did, so do ye" (Acts 7:51). Compare Exodus 6:12-30; Deuteronomy 30:6; Jeremiah 4:4, 6:10. Note Romans 2:28-29, "For he is not a Jew, which is one **outwardly:** neither is that circumcision, which is **outward** in the flesh: But he is a Jew, which is one **inwardly;** and circumcision is that of the heart, in the spirit, and not in the letter".

It is worth remembering that we too can be so occupied with outward correctness that we forget the need for inward reality. It is sadly possible for even Christians to have "a form of godliness", but deny "the power thereof" (2 Tim. 3:5).

ii) The circumcision of Christ dealt with the root of sin. That is, sinful human nature. The "circumcision of Christ" involved, not part of the physical body, but "the body of...the flesh", which describes our sinful fallen nature; not an external physical operation, but an internal spiritual work; not a rite performed by physical hands, but something made "without hands": it was divinely accomplished. Hence, "In whom also ye are circumcised with the circumcision made without hands, in putting off the body (of the sins) of the flesh by the circumcision of Christ". We should note that the words "*of the sins* of the flesh" are omitted by RV/JND. The "circumcision of Christ" therefore describes the way in which God has dealt with our corrupt human nature. It no longer controls us. God has annulled its activity and power. We once lived "after the flesh", but now we are no longer "in the flesh" (Rom. 8:5-9). This is how Paul sets it out in Philippians 3:2, "Beware of dogs, beware of evil workers, beware of the concision, For we are the circumcision, which worship God in the spirit, and rejoice in Christ Jesus, and have no confidence in the flesh".

It is called the "circumcision of Christ" because it became effective in our lives at conversion, when two things took place. First of all, God dealt with **us,** and Paul deals with this with reference to baptism (vv.12-13a). Secondly, God dealt with **our sins,** and Paul deals with this with reference to the cross, where God's claims against us were fully met and discharged (vv.13b-14).

- God dealt with us, vv.12-13b. What happened at conversion, was displayed at baptism. So, "Buried with him in baptism ('having been buried', aorist tense), wherein also ye are risen with him through the faith of ('in', RV) the operation (working) of God, who hath raised him from the dead. And you, being dead in your sins and the uncircumcision of your flesh, hath he quickened together with him". Only dead people are buried, and they are only buried after they are dead! When we were baptised, we testified to the fact that when we trusted Christ, our old life came to an end. Whilst Christ alone bore the divine judgment we deserved, God deemed that this very sentence was carried out on us as well. But more than that, when Christ rose from the dead, God deemed that we rose with Him. This is not something that can be proved scientifically. We accept this **by faith.** We believe that this is what happened at conversion in exactly the same way that we believe in His resurrection. We accept the word of God. Hence Paul's words, "wherein also ye are risen with him **through...faith** of (in) the operation (working) of God, who hath raised him from the dead".

Our resurrection with Christ is stressed from a slightly different angle in v.13. In v.12, we were buried with Christ and raised with Him. In v.13, we were dead, and have been made alive. In fact, we were dead in two ways. We were dead because of what we **had done**: "dead in your sins *(paraptoma*, meaning 'offence' or 'trespass') or "dead in offences" (JND). We were also dead because of what we **were**: "dead...in the uncircumcision of your flesh", referring, as we have seen, to our fallen human nature. But on what basis can God possibly associate us with Christ in resurrection? The answer follows.

- *God has dealt with our sins, vv.13b-14.* "And you, being dead in your sins *(paraptoma)* and the uncircumcision of your flesh, hath he quickened together with him, *having forgiven you all trespasses (paraptoma)*; blotting out the handwriting of ordinances that was against us, which was contrary to us, and took it out of the way, nailing it to his cross". Baptism is not a mere ceremony: it signifies something that really has taken place. The word rendered "forgiven" *(charizomai)* stresses the grace in forgiveness, as opposed to the usual word *aphiemi*, meaning 'to send away'. But how could God forgive our trespasses, which by their very nature implies contravention of the divine law? The answer follows:

"Blotting out the handwriting of ordinances that was against us, which was contrary to us, and took it out of the way, nailing it to his cross". This is yet another wonderful statement.

- "*Blotting out* the handwriting of ordinances that was against us, which was contrary to us". The words "blotting out" are, literally 'having blotted out', denoting a decisive act. The phrase was used for wiping out a memory of an experience, or for cancelling a vote, or annulling a law, or cancelling a charge or debt, or washing out writing on a papyrus. See Isaiah 44:22.

- "Blotting out *the handwriting of ordinances that was against us, which was contrary to us*". While some commentators refer this to a signed statement of indebtedness, a written acknowledgement of debt, it seems more likely that Paul is referring to the demands of the law which find "all mankind hopelessly in debt and totally guilty before God" (T. Bentley). Compare Ephesians 2:15. The law was against us. It was hostile towards us by making it clear that we could not meet its claims.

- "*And took it out of the way, nailing it to his cross*". The words, "took it out of the way" are in the perfect tense, which emphasises the abiding significance of what happened at the cross. His work has permanent value. Christ has completely removed the "handwriting of ordinances that was against us, which was contrary to us". He has taken it "out of the way": it does not stand between us and God. He has done this by the Lord's death on the cross, which publicly demonstrated that the required sentence had been carried out.

The Lord's death on the cross was a tremendous victory over sin. But it was also a tremendous victory over the **unseen** hostile forces which opposed Him in accomplishing this work. "And having spoiled principalities and powers, he made a show of them openly, triumphing over them in it" (v.15). There can be little doubt that this refers to the powers of darkness, acting under Satan (Eph. 6:12), which gathered against Christ at Calvary. In various ways, Satan had endeavoured to prevent the death of the Lord Jesus on the cross. In the wilderness, he offered Him glory without death (Matt. 4:8-9). When Peter rebuked the Lord Jesus, "saying, Be it far from thee, Lord: this shall not be unto thee", the Saviour replied, "Get thee behind me, Satan" (Matt. 16:22-23). With the cross immediately before Him, the Lord said, "This is your hour, and the power of darkness" (Luke 22:53). When the Saviour was on the cross, "they that passed by" cried, "If thou be the Son of God, **come down** from the cross". The chief priests, scribes and elders said the same: "If he be the King of Israel, let him now **come down** from the cross, and we will believe him". The thieves added their voices: they "cast the same in his teeth" (Matt. 27:39-44).

But what would have happened if the Lord Jesus had "come down" from the cross? Satan and his hosts would have won a devastating victory, and we would all be eternally lost. But the Lord Jesus was totally victorious. Satan's 'last ditch' attempt to thwart God's intention to secure our eternal salvation was defeated. He "spoiled principalities and powers".

Once again, every word counts! "And having **spoiled** principalities and powers". The word *apekduo* also occurs in Colossians 3:9 ("*put off* the old man with his deeds"), and the noun *apekdusis* is found in 2:11 ("*putting off* the body of the sins of the flesh"). The Lord 'put off' or 'stripped off' from Himself the "**principalities and powers**" which attacked Him. He "**made a shew of them openly** (it was a decisive victory) **triumphing over them in it**". This refers to the cross or, better, to the work accomplished on the cross. He cried, "It is finished". The cross was His consummating triumph. What seemed to human eyes a mighty defeat, was in fact a mighty triumph. "Through death", He destroyed "him that had the power of death, that is, the devil"; and delivered "them who through fear of death were all their lifetime subject to bondage" (Heb. 2:14-15). Through the death of the Lord Jesus, Satan no longer has the power to retain the "spoils (Luke 11:22), and **we** can be "more than conquerors".

Through Christ we can be "more than conquerors" over our three enemies. In these verses, reference is made to our external enemy ("rudiments of the **world**", v.8), our internal enemy ("body of the sins of the **flesh**", v.11), and our infernal enemy (the hosts of Satanic "principalities and powers", v.15).

READ CHAPTER 2.16-23

"Let no man therefore judge you"

In introducing the chapter, we suggested that the passage may be divided as follows: *(1)* our progress in Christ (vv.1-7); *(2)* our completeness in Christ (vv.8-15); *(3)* our superiority in Christ (vv.16-19); *(4)* our identification with Christ (vv.20-23).

1) OUR PROGRESS IN CHRIST, vv.1-7
We noticed that this section of the chapter Paul is concerned for progress in their understanding of Christ (vv.2-3) and for progress in their experience of Christ (vv.6-7). He gives the reason for his concern in the intervening verses (vv.5-6).

2) OUR COMPLETENESS IN CHRIST, vv.8-15
We noticed here that Paul meets the suggestions and demands of the false teachers by emphasising the total sufficiency of the Person and work of the Lord Jesus. See particularly vv.10-11: "And ye are complete *in him* (Paul's answer to philosophy, or gnosticism), which is the head of all principality and power; *in whom* (Paul's answer to Judaism) also ye are circumcised with the circumcision made without hands, in putting off the body of the sins of the flesh by the circumcision of Christ". This brings us to:

3) OUR SUPERIORITY IN CHRIST, vv.16-19
Bearing in mind that our relationship with Christ excludes the need for both "philosophy" (which Paul calls "vain deceit") and Judaism, with its various rites and ceremonies of which circumcision was the most prominent, Paul makes it clear that Christians are to disregard both claims. In Christ, we have infinitely superior blessings. We should notice that although, unlike the Galatians (see, for example, Gal. 3:1), the Colossians had not succumbed to false teaching (see 1:5), Paul was obliged to warn them of the danger.

i) They were to disregard the claims of Judaism, vv.16-17: "*Let no man therefore judge you* in meat, or in drink, or in respect of an holy day, or of the new moon, or of the sabbath days". The reason follows: "which are a shadow of things to come, but the body (the substance of the shadows) is of Christ". There is an implied warning that Judaism would alienate them from Christ. It failed to recognise that He has fulfilled the shadows of the Old Testament.

ii) They were to disregard the claims of the philosophers, vv.18-19: *"Let no man beguile you* of your reward in a voluntary humility and worshipping of angels, intruding into those things which he hath not seen, vainly puffed up by his fleshly mind". There is an implied warning that this 'gnostic' teaching would alienate them from Christ. It would turn them away from dependence on Him as "the Head" of the body, the church. They would no longer benefit from the spiritual nourishment He bestowed upon the church.

Both exhortations therefore carry warnings, and this serves to remind us that if we heed **any** false teaching, it will alienate us from Christ. We must now look at these two exhortations in more detail.

a) Our superiority over Judaism, vv.16-17
"Let no man therefore judge you in meat, or in drink, or in respect of an holy day, or of the new moon (the beginning of the month), or of the sabbath days". G.B. Wilson deals with this most helpfully: "They must let no one take them to task in the matter of eating and drinking". Paul refers here to the Mosaic ordinances. They were not to capitulate to criticism for their refusal to recognise the regulations and ordinances of Judaism. Paul had occasion to remonstrate with the Galatians on this same subject: "But now, after that ye have known God, or rather are known of God, how turn ye again to the weak and beggarly element, whereunto ye desire again to be in bondage? Ye observe days, and months, and times and years" (Gal. 4:9-10).

The reason follows. "But the body (as opposed to the shadow, which has no independent existence) is of Christ". He is the great object of all the types and shadows. This is why He describes Himself as "the **true** vine" (John 15:1) and "the **true** bread" (John 6:32). The Lord Jesus was not distinguishing between the false and the true, but between the **shadow** and the **substance.** Compare Hebrews 9:8-12, which, after referring to the tabernacle, continues: "which was a **figure** for the time then present, in which were offered both gifts and sacrifices, that could not make him that did the service perfect, as pertaining to the conscience; which stood **only** in meats and drinks, and divers washings, and carnal ordinances, imposed on them **until** the time of reformation. **But Christ being come** an high priest of good things to come, by a greater and more perfect tabernacle, not made with hands, that is to say, not of this building; neither by the blood of goats and calves, but by his own blood he entered in once into the holy place, having obtained eternal redemption for us". You couldn't have a better explanation than this of the words, "but the body is of Christ!" Sadly, the Jewish teachers (the Judaisers) failed to see that their religious ordinances were the "shadow of things to come", and that in Christ, the shadows had given place to the substance.

This does not mean that we should not study the tabernacle, or the Levitical sacrifices, or the "feasts of the Lord". They contain beautiful pictures of Christ and his work. The Old Testament is so rich in its teaching about Him, and "whatsoever things were written aforetime were written for our learning". Paul is making the point here that Christians have no need to **keep** and **observe** the requirements of the Old Testament, because we have their fulfilment in Christ! The attempts of the Judaisers to turn Gentile Christians into good Jews had serious implications:

- It was adding works to faith for salvation. Human religion is built on that foundation. But salvation is "not of works, lest any man should boast".

- It was implying that the Old Testament scriptures had not yet been fulfilled. To go back to the "shadow of things to come" was saying that Christ had not yet come!

b) *Our superiority over gnosticism, vv.18-19*
"Let no man beguile you of your reward in a voluntary humility and worshipping of angels, intruding into those things which he hath not seen, vainly puffed up by his fleshly mind" or "Let no man fraudulently deprive you of your prize" (JND) or "Let no man rob you of your prize" (RV). This looks perfectly clear to the layman! But the verb *katabrabeuo*, meaning 'to give judgment against', or 'condemn', may not refer to a prize. Hence W.E. Vine's observation: "Another rendering closer to the proper meaning...is 'let no man decide for or against you' (i.e. without any notion of a prize); this suitably follows the word 'judge' in v.16, that is, 'do not give yourselves up to the judgment and decision of any man'". If this is correct, then Paul is saying that they must 'let no one take them to task' for their refusal to become involved in the teaching of the philosophers at Colosse. He now describes their "philosophy" in four ways:

i) It was "voluntary humility" or "doing his own will in humility" (JND). This was evidently one plank in their argument when they condemned the Christians at Colosse for refusing to bow to their "philosophy". They said, in effect, 'we are such humble people: we prostrate ourselves before the angels. Why don't you follow our example, and humble yourselves in the same way'. They took great pleasure in their humility! As T. Bentley observes, "Were these errorists not hoping to gain advantage over the Colossians by a spurious humility in which they took great pride?" Incidentally, it is only in this chapter (see vv.18, 23) that humility means something quite different to its usual New Testament usage. "When men become proud of their humility, it ceases to be a virtue; rather it is a vice" (T. Bentley).

ii) It was "intruding into those things which he hath not seen" or "dwelling in the things that he hath seen" (RV). The word "intruding" means 'to step in and on', and so, 'to dwell, enter'. J.N. Darby's footnote here is interesting: "Many omit 'not' here (see RV)...if 'not' is omitted, the passage speaks of what the visionaries *allege*". If left in, **Paul is denying that they actually saw anything at all!** (In Darby's exact words, "it is the apostle's own denial of their having really seen the angelic choirs"). In other words, it was all speculation and supposition.

iii) It was to be "vainly puffed up by his fleshly mind". The word "vainly" *(eike)* means 'without cause'. The words "puffed up" *(phusioo)* come from a word meaning 'bellows' *(phusa)*. The words, "fleshly mind" emphasise the nature of philosophic speculation. It is simply food for the old nature. So the "voluntary humility" to which Paul refers (v.18) was nothing less than "vainly puffed up in his fleshly mind!"

iv) It was "not holding ('holding fast', JND) the Head from which all the body by joints and bands having nourishment ministered, and knit together, increaseth with the increase of God". This is the crowning condemnation of the philosophers, or gnostics. They had no vital link with Christ. He meant nothing to them. They were not part of the church, "the body", of which Christ is "Head", and therefore did not enjoy the nourishment, maintenance and growth which flows from Him.

Now let's turn the negative into a positive, and notice how the church is nourished, maintained and grows. We must notice the vivid contrast between "puffed up in his fleshly mind", and "increasing with the increase of God!" The first is **insubstantial:** the second **substantial.** There was no spiritual nourishment in "philosophy and vain deceit", but every nourishment through "holding fast the Head".

i) The Source of maintenance for the body. "Holding fast the **head**" (JND). There can be no growth apart from this. There must be a sustained personal relationship with Him. "Holding fast" *(krateo)* means 'to be strong, mighty, to prevail'. Nothing must be allowed to interrupt our communion and fellowship with Him. Nothing must be allowed to divert our attention from Him. We must "seek those things which are above, where Christ sitteth on the right hand of God" (3:1).

*ii) **The means of maintenance for the body.*** "From which all the body by joints and bands having nourishment ministered, and knit together, increaseth with the increase of God" or "From whom (the word is masculine) all the body, ministered to and united together by the joints and bands, increases with the increase of God" (JND). We must notice the development of the verse.

- It begins with Christ. He is the source of every blessing enjoyed by the church.

- He is concerned with the welfare and organic unity of the church. The words "having nourishment ministered" translate *epichoregeo*, meaning to 'supply fully, abundantly' (W.E. Vine). There is nothing miserly about the Head of the church! The words "knit together" or "united together" (JND) emphasise the unity of the body in its vital connection with the Head.

- The welfare and unity of the church is achieved by "joints and bands". The church is united by "joints and bands" in the same way as the physical body. It has been suggested that "joints" convey the strength and rigidity of the body, and "bands" (ligaments) convey the flexibility of the body, but perhaps this should not be taken too far! T. Bentley makes the sensible suggestion that the "joints and bands" could "speak of the inter-relationship of the members of the body, showing their mutual dependence one upon another". Compare Ephesians 4:16, "from whom the whole body fitly joined together and compacted (connected) by that which every joint supplieth, according to the effectual working in the measure of every part, maketh increase of the body unto the edifying of itself in love".

*iii) **The result of the maintenance of the body.*** It "increaseth (*auxano*, 'to grow or increase') with the increase of God". This is divinely empowered growth, "the increase which comes from God" (W.E. Vine). This can only take place when we hold fast to the Lord Jesus, "the Head".

4) IDENTIFICATION WITH CHRIST, vv. 20-23
Quite clearly, the four final verses of the chapter are part of a section which extends to the four opening verses of the following chapter. "Wherefore **if ye be dead with Christ** from the rudiments of the world, why, as though living in the world, are ye subject to ordinances...**If ye then be risen with Christ,** seek

those things which are above, where Christ sitteth on the right hand of God". It is equally clear that Paul is appealing here to his previous teaching. The statements, "if ye be dead with Christ…if ye then be risen with Christ" are based on "buried with him in baptism, wherein also ye are risen with him through (the) faith of (in) the operation of God, who hath raised him from the dead" (2:12). Paul now emphasises the practical implications of our identification with Christ in baptism. We are to recognise *(a)* the implications of being **dead** with Christ, and *(b)* the implications of being **risen** with Christ. The false teachers at Colosse would encourage the believers to find their life in **this world** (v.20), but Paul encourages them to find their life in the world **above** (3:1).

a) "If ye be dead with Christ", 2:20-23

When Paul refers to our death and resurrection with Christ in v.12, it is with particular reference to the demands of the **Judaisers,** who demanded compliance with the law of Moses, and in particular, circumcision. This is clear from vv.11-14. But here, Paul is evidently referring to our identification with Christ in death and resurrection with reference to the teaching of the **philosophers** at Colosse. They taught that matter is essentially evil, and therefore the body should be treated harshly. This is called 'asceticism', and involved a life of severe self-denial and disipline. T. Wilson (New Zealand), writing in *Precious Seed*, helpfully analyses vv.11-23 as follows: *(i)* legalism (vv.11-17); *(ii)* mysticism (vv.18-19); *(iii)* asceticism (vv.20-23). While some commentators suggest that vv.20-23 refer, again, to the requirements, dietary and otherwise, of the Mosaic law (see Mark 7:1-23), the language of these verses does seem to point in another direction. See, for example, "ordinances…after the commandments and doctrines of men" (vv.20-22); "which things have indeed a shew of wisdom in will worship, and humility, and neglecting of the body; not in any honour to the satisfying of the flesh" (v.23). This does not sound like Judaism!

Paul sets out our position in connection with asceticism (v.20) and with the practice of asceticism (vv.21-23)

i) Our position in connection with asceticism, v.20.

Paul's argument against asceticism, by which, it was alleged, the sinful body could be controlled, rests upon the fact that Christians have passed beyond the influence of worldly religion. The religious practices of the world can exert no power over a dead man! We are "dead with Christ from the rudiments of the world". As we saw earlier in connection with v.8, the word "rudiments" refers to elementary principles and, in this case, to worldly religion which consists mainly of external rites and ceremonies. When we trusted in the Lord Jesus, we severed our connection with worldly religion.

Hence the question, "Why, as though living in the world (*kosmos:* the world-system), are ye subject to ordinances?" or "If ye have died with Christ from the elements of the world, why **as if alive in the world,** do ye subject yourselves to ordinances" (JND). The word "ordinances" (it comes from *dogma)* is very strong. (It occurs in v.14: "blotting out the handwriting of ordinances that was against us"). Quite obviously, the proponents of this teaching invested their views with compelling importance! But however much importance they attached to their views, the fact remains that it was quite inconsistent to be "dead with Christ" and 'alive in the world'. How can people who are "dead with Christ" accept the notion that sin can be controlled by worldly principles?

ii) Our connection with the practice of asceticism, vv.21-23. Having made the believer's **position** clear, Paul makes two main points in connection with the **practice** of asceticism.

- Asceticism had no moral value, because its demands, "touch not; taste not; handle not", "all are to perish with the using". The words, "all to perish with the using", mean "all to perish as they are 'used up'". It has been suggested that these prohibitions are in "an ascending order of stringency - Do not take it, do not even taste it, do not so much as touch it!" (J. Agar Beet quoted by G.B. Wilson). The argument is simple: 'what is the point in seeking greater holiness by abstaining from material things, since those very things perish as you use them, and have no moral or spiritual effect?' This is precisely the point made by the Lord Jesus when dealing with the criticism levelled at his disciples by the Pharisees ("thy disciples...eat bread with unwashen hands"): "Do ye not perceive, that whatsoever thing from without entereth into the man, it cannot defile him; because it entereth not into his heart, but into the belly...that which cometh out of the man, that defileth the man" (Mark 7:17-23).

- Asceticism had no moral value, because while it was a **useful** tool in enhancing human reputation, it was a **useless** tool in controlling sin: "These have indeed an appearance of wisdom in promoting rigour of devotion and self-abasement and severity to the body, but they are of no value in checking the indulgence of the flesh" (v.23, RSV). Asceticism had an effect on the body, but that was all. It did not touch the root of sin which lies in sinful human nature.

b) "If ye then be risen with Christ", 3:1-4
These wonderful words should whet our appetite for the next study!

READ CHAPTER 3.1-4

"Set your affection on things above"

We have already noticed that the first four verses of this chapter complement the last four verses of the previous chapter. The eight verses (2:20-3:4) are a unit. "Wherefore **if ye be dead with Christ** from the rudiments of the world, why, as though living in the world, are ye subject to ordinances...**If ye then be risen with Christ,** seek those things which are above, where Christ sitteth on the right hand of God". Quite clearly, Paul is appealing here to his previous teaching. The statements, "if ye be dead with Christ...if ye be risen with Christ" remind us that we were "buried with him in baptism, wherein also ye are risen with him through (the) faith of (in) the operation of God, who hath raised him from the dead" (2:12). The section emphasises the practical implications of our identification with Christ in baptism. We are to recognise the implications of being **dead** with Christ, and the implications of being **risen** with Christ. We must carefully review these implications.

i) "Dead with Christ", 2:20-23. When we trusted in the Lord Jesus, God annulled the power of sin in our lives, not by dealing with our bodies, which exhibit the **fruit** of sin in our lives, but with our nature, which is the **root** of sin in our lives. Paul calls this "the circumcision made without hands, in putting off the body of (the sins of) the flesh by the circumcision of Christ" (2:11) It is called "the circumcision made **without hands**", as opposed to physical circumcision, to emphasise its inward and spiritual power. Compare Romans 2:29, "But he is a Jew, which is one inwardly; and circumcision is that of the heart, in the spirit, and not in the letter; whose praise is not of men, but of God". Christians are no longer subject to the mastery and power of the old nature, which Paul calls the "body...of the flesh". Baptism is a public statement that this took place when we became Christians.

Bearing this in mind, Paul argues that it would be quite inconsistent for Christians to think that holiness can be achieved by physical means. "These ('touch not; taste not; handle not') have indeed an appearance of wisdom in promoting rigour of devotion and self-abasement and severity to the body, but they are of no value in checking the indulgence of the flesh" (RSV). Paul calls this 'living in the world': "If ye have died with Christ from the elements of the world, why as if alive in the world do ye subject yourselves to ordinances?" (v.20, JND).

But how **can** holiness be achieved? The answer follows. It is not by acting as though we find our life in the religious practices of this world (2:20), but by recognising that our lives are now centred on the world above (3:1). In other words, our spiritual life is not sustained by physical means, but by spiritual means. This brings us to:

ii) "Risen with Christ", 3:1-4. If it is **inconsistent** with our relationship with the Lord Jesus to live as if we belong to this world, then it is **consistent** with our relationship with Him to live as people who belong to another world. "If ye then be risen with Christ, seek those things which are above, where Christ sitteth on the right hand of God. Set your affection on things above, not on things on the earth". **Now** we know how spiritual life **is** nourished and enriched! Not by afflicting our bodies, but by occupation with Christ!

With the passage in its proper context, we can now give further consideration to the implications of being "risen with Christ". Chapter 3:1-4:1 tell us two important things: **(1)** how we are to maintain our new life (3:1-4), and **(2)** how we are to manifest our new life (3:5-4:1).

1) THE MAINTENANCE OF OUR NEW LIFE, vv.1-4
The new life is to be nourished by recognising **(a)** that we are raised with Christ (vv.1-2); **(b)** that we are hidden with Christ (v.3); **(c)** that we will be manifested with Christ (v.4).

a) "Risen with Christ", vv.1-2
Christians do not belong to this world. Faith in Christ places us in a totally new sphere. We are "risen with Christ". Natural life is sustained by its environment, and so is spiritual life. Our life in Christ cannot be sustained by the "rudiments of the world": it can only be sustained by "those things which are above, where Christ sitteth on the right hand of God". With this in mind, we are to "seek those things which are above" (v.1), and to set our "affection on things above" (v.2). We are told that the words "seek" and "set" are in the imperative mood.

i) "Seek those things which are above", v.1. The word "seek" *(zeteo)* is used here, "not to search for, but to desire earnestly and to strive after...It implies a greater effort than *epithumeo*, to desire" (W.E. Vine). It can rightly be translated, 'keep seeking'. Compare Matthew 6:33. How earnestly do **we** seek God's interests? The "things which are above" are qualified by the words, "where Christ sitteth on the right hand of God" or "seek those things that are above, where Christ is, seated on the right hand of God" (RV). We are to "seek those things which are above" because Christ is there "in the position of supreme authority and power" (W.E. Vine). In this connection, we should note the following:

- **His place.** He is at the centre of the "things which are above". (He said, "I am from above", John 8:23). The philosophers were also interested in "things which are above", but not these things! They were involved in "worshipping...angels, intruding into those things which he hath not seen" (2:18). As we have already noticed, this was nothing more than "vain deceit". The philosophers had not actually seen anything! But we rise above their speculation and supposition, to the highest place in the universe (inadequate language), "where Christ is, seated on the right hand of God" (RV). There can be no higher place than that! He is at God's "own right hand in the heavenly places, far above all principality and power, and might, and dominion, and every name that is named, not only in this world, but also in that which is to come" (Eph. 1:20-21).

- **His posture.** He is seated. "Christ **sitteth** on the right hand of God". Compare Hebrews 1:3; 8:1; 10:12; 12:2. All these verses cite Psalm 110:1, "The LORD *(Jehovah)* said unto my Lord *(Adon,* meaning 'Sovereign Lord, Master, Possessor, or Proprietor')*,* Sit thou at my right hand, until I make thine enemies thy footstool". Peter drew attention to the same passage: "For David is not ascended into the heavens: but he saith himself, the LORD said unto my Lord, Sit thou on my right hand, until I make thy foes thy footstool. Therefore let all the house of Israel know assuredly, that God hath made that same Jesus, whom ye have crucified, both Lord and Christ" (Acts 2:34-36). See also Mark 12:35-37.

The Lord Jesus is seated "on the right hand of God" because His saving work is complete: "And every priest standeth daily ministering and offering oftentimes the same sacrifices, which can never take away sins: but this man, after he had offered one sacrifice for sins for ever, sat down on the right hand of God" (Heb. 10:11-12). This passage is often rendered: "But this man, after he had offered one sacrifice for sins, for ever sat down on the right hand of God", emphasising the point that the priests continued to stand because their work was **never** complete, but the Lord Jesus is seated, and seated for ever, because His work in relation to sin is **eternally** complete.

The finality of Christ's work answers those who, in G.B. Wilson's words, 'took them to task in the...matter of eating and drinking' (2:16). Those things were "a shadow of things to come; but the body (the substance of the shadow) is Christ". Christ, seated "at the right hand of God" spells the end of Judaism.

- **His position.** He is seated "on the **right hand** of God". For the significance of "right hand"", see Genesis 48:13 (privilege), Exodus 15:6 (power), and Psalm 16:11 (pleasure). The Lord Jesus is in the place of supreme power and authority. He is totally able to meet the needs of His people. Seeking "those things which are above" means "holding the Head, from which all the body by joints and bands having nourishment ministered, and knit together, increaseth with the increase of God" (2:19). This brings us to the second injunction:

ii) "Set your affection on things above", v.2. "Set your mind (*phroneo*, 'to think, to set the mind on') on the things that are above" (RV). This is "an advance of expression" from "seek those things which are above", and refers to "the set purpose of the mind" W.E. Vine), or, in the words of J.B. Lightfoot, "You must not only *seek* heaven, you must also *think* heaven". Compare Romans 8:5, "For they that are after the flesh do **mind** *(phroneo)* the things of the flesh". What governs **our** thinking? We are obliged to live in the world. We must engage in its lawful activities, and discharge our responsibilities. But that does not mean that we 'set our mind...on things on the earth'. Nothing must be allowed to distract us from putting God's glory and interests first in our lives. The Lord Jesus urged His disciples to "lay up for yourselves treasures in heaven, where neither moth nor rust doth corrupt, and where thieves do not break through nor steal: for where your treasure is, there will your heart be also" (Matt. 6:19-21). This does not mean that it is possible to be 'so heavenly minded that you are no earthly use!' If we want to be of 'earthly use', we **must** be 'heavenly minded!' Do remember that "no man can serve two masters" (Matt. 6:24).

In the Old Testament, the children of Israel were to "make them fringes in the borders of their garments...and...put upon the fringe of the borders a ribband ('lace', JND) of blue" (Num.15:37-40). The "ribband of blue" was a constant reminder to them of "all the commandments of the LORD", under whose feet was "as it were a paved work of a sapphire stone, and as it were the body of heaven in his clearness" (Exod. 24:10) We may not wear "a ribband of blue", but we must never forget that we are a heavenly people.

This brings us to the second way in which our new life is to be nourished and maintained. We must recognise that our lives are

b) Hidden with Christ, v.3

The connection with the previous two verses is clear: "Set your affection on things above, not on things on the earth. For ye are dead, and your life is hid with Christ in God". We are to 'set our minds on things above, not on things on the earth', because we are dead to the latter, and alive to the former. Notice the apparent contradiction: "Ye are **dead,** and your **life** is hid with Christ in God".

But what is the significance of the expression, "your life is hid with Christ in God?" The word "hid" *(apokruphos)* means "concealed" or "hidden away from". Christian life does not subsist in tangible or visible religious practices. It is "associated with Christ and bound up with Him, and for that reason it is invisible" (W.E. Vine). Quite obviously, Paul is **not** saying that Christian life cannot be seen: he **is** saying that the source and nature of Christian life cannot be seen. We have this life through union with Christ. The world just 'hasn't a clue' about this: it is completely outside human comprehension.

Adam hid **from** God (Gen. 3:8), but as opposed to external religion (2:20-23), our lives are "hid with Christ **in** God" (3:3). This "denotes the security and safety of that life. It is beyond the reach of any alien force, neither can it be defiled by any evil thing" (T. Bentley). It also means that although "the new life is hidden from the world...his union with Christ means that he partakes of all the fulness of God (see 2:9)" (G.B. Wilson). The 'gnostics' were proud of their alleged superior knowledge, but because our lives "are hid with Christ in God", we can enjoy "all the treasures of wisdom and knowledge" (2:3). As we have noted previously, the 'gnostics' were proud of their *gnosis* (knowledge), but in Christ we have *epignosis* (fulness of knowledge)!

But this concealment from the world is not permanent. The third way in which the new life is nourished is by recognising that we will be:

c) Manifested with Christ, v.4

"When Christ, who is our life, shall appear, then shall ye also appear with him in glory". This is an advance on the previous statement. In v.3, our life is "hid with Christ in God". In v.4, Christ is our life. Compare 1 John 5:11-12, "And this is the record, that God hath given to us eternal life, and this life is in his Son. He that hath the Son hath life; and he that hath not the Son of God hath not life".

W.E. Vine has a helpful piece on the word "appear" (or 'manifested', *phaneroo*, from *phaino* meaning 'to shine'): "To be manifested, in the Scriptural sense of the word, is more than to appear. A person may appear in a false guise, or without a disclosure of what he truly is; to be manifested is to be revealed in one's true character".

We should notice the certainty in this statement: "**When** Christ, who is our life, shall appear, **then** shall ye also appear with him in glory". This refers to 2 Thessalonians 1:10, "When he shall come to be glorified in his saints, and to be admired in all them that believe...in that day". The believer has **died** with Christ, been **buried** with Christ, been **raised** with Christ, his life is **hid** with Christ, and he will be **manifested** with Christ in glory.

We cannot miss that contrast between "hid" and "appear" (manifested). At the moment, the world cannot see or appreciate the nature of our relationship with the Lord Jesus. But this will all change "when the Lord Jesus shall be revealed from heaven" (2 Thess. 1:7). Compare Romans 8:18-21. At the moment, "the world knoweth us not, because it knew him not". But "when he shall appear, we shall be like him; for we shall see him as he is" (1 John 3:1-20). At present, we are identified with Christ in His rejection by the world. But we **will** be identified with Him in His manifestation to the world.

This brings us to the second major paragraph in the present section of the Epistle. We have noticed how the new life is to be maintained. We must now notice how it is to be manifested, and this involves putting the old life to death. So:

2) THE MANIFESTATION OF OUR NEW LIFE, 3:5-4:1
We will consider this in our next two studies.

READ CHAPTER 3.5-11

"Put on...put off"

As we have already noticed, the teaching in this chapter flows out of the statements, "Wherefore if ye be dead with Christ" (2:20) and "If ye then be risen with Christ" (3:1). These, in turn, flow from the statement, "buried with him in baptism, wherein also ye are risen with him through the faith of the operation of God, who hath raised him from the dead" (2:12).

Colossians 3:1-4:1 therefore tell us two important things; *(1)* how we are to **maintain** our new life (3:1-4); *(2)* how we are to **manifest** our new life (3:5-4:1). This involves the mortification of the old life.

1) THE MAINTENANCE OF OUR NEW LIFE, 3:1-4
The new life will be nourished by recognising *(a)* that we are raised with Christ: "If ye then be risen with Christ, seek those things which are above, where Christ sitteth on the right hand of God. Set your affection on things above, not on things on the earth" (vv.1-2); *(b)* that our lives are hidden with Christ: "For ye are dead, and your life is hid with Christ in God" (v.3); *(c)* that we will be manifested with Christ: "When Christ, who is our life, shall appear, then shall ye also appear with him in glory" (v.4).

2) THE MANIFESTATION OF OUR NEW LIFE, 3:12-4:1
It will be manifested in the following ways. *(a)* In our personal lives (3:5-7). Paul deals here with our appetites and desires. *(b)* In our assembly lives (3:8-17): notice "one to another" (vv.9, 13, 16). He deals here with our attitudes and disposition. *(c)* In our family lives (3:18-21). He refers here to wives, husbands, children and fathers. *(d)* In our business lives (3:22-4:1). He refers here to servants and masters.

a) In our personal lives, 3:5-7
This section commences with "therefore", which indicates that Paul is drawing a conclusion from teaching in the previous verses. The conclusion is simple:

the new life and the old life cannot co-exist. If we are going to 'set our mind on things ***above***' (v.2, RV), we must do something about our "members which are upon the ***earth***" (v.5). As we have noticed, this cannot be achieved by religious ordinances, which "have no value in checking the indulgence of the flesh" (2:23, RSV) In fact, we are required to do something quite drastic: "Mortify ***therefore*** your members which are upon the earth". We must endeavour to answer four questions which arise in connection with these verses.

i) What are our "members? "Mortify therefore your ***members*** which are upon the earth; fornication, uncleanness, inordinate affection, evil concupiscence, and covetousness, which is idolatry". W. Hendriksen (*Colossians and Philemon*, in the Geneva Series of commentaries) asks the obvious question, "But how can members (i.e. the members of our body) be vices?" Hendrikson quotes several commentators, including F.F. Bruce *(Commentary on the Epistle to the Colossians)*: "But what he is really thinking of is the practices and attitudes to which his readers' bodily activity and strength had been devoted in the old life". This must be right since it is the explanation given by Paul himself: "For when we were in the flesh, the motions of sins, which were by the law, did ***work in our members*** to bring forth fruit unto death" (Rom. 7:5); "For if ye live after the flesh, ye shall die: but if ye through the Spirit do mortify the ***deeds of the body***, ye shall live" (Rom. 8:13). Compare Matthew 18:8-9, which evidently refers to the sinful desires behind the offending hand or foot, and the offending eye, rather than the members themselves. "Ensure that it (hand, foot, or eye) is inoperative as an instrument of the flesh" (J. Heading).

The "members" are now specified. The list begins with actions, continues with motives, and ends with idolatry. "Fornication": this is specific, and refers to an illicit sexual act. "Uncleanness": this refers to general impurity, "uncleanness in any form" (W.E. Vine). "Inordinate affection" or "vile passions" (JND): "ungovernable desire" (W.E. Vine). "Evil concupiscence" or "evil lust" (JND). "Covetousness, which is idolatry" or "unbridled desire which is idolatry" (JND). The context here, together with the context of Ephesians 5:5, which refers to a "covetous man, who is an idolator", suggests sensuality, as opposed to covetousness in its normal meaning. The desire of David for Bath-sheba is a sad example of transgressing the tenth commandment: "Thou shalt not covet... thy neighbour's wife" (Exod. 20:17). Sensual things can become the be-all and end-all, and therefore constitute idolatry.

ii) What should we do with our "members"? "***Mortify*** therefore your members which are upon the earth". The word "mortify" means 'to make dead' (*nekroo* from *nekros*, meaning 'dead'). The children of Israel were to totally eliminate the 'old life' in Canaan, and Joshua "left none remaining, but utterly destroyed all that breathed, as the LORD God of Israel commanded" (Joshua 10:40). We are to do exactly the same with our 'old life'. Having described its features (v.5), Paul continues, "in the which ye also walked some time, when ye **lived in them**" (v.7). But no longer. They are to be put to death. Compare Romans 8:13, "If ye through the Spirit do mortify *(thanatoo)* the deeds of the body, ye shall live".There is no contradiction between v.3 ("For ye are dead) and v.5 ("Mortify therefore your members which are upon the earth"). The first refers to our **position:** the second refers to our **practice.**

We "mortify" the 'old life' by taking steps to ensure that it receives no encouragement and no help whatsoever. Our inward and outward lives must be pure. The new life is nourished and enriched by seeking "those things which are above, where Christ sitteth on the right hand of God" (v.1). The old life must be starved to death: "put ye on the Lord Jesus Christ, and **make not provision** for the flesh, to fulfil the lusts thereof" (Rom. 13:14). Do remember that "he that soweth to his flesh shall of the flesh reap corruption; but he that soweth to the Spirit shall of the Spirit reap life everlasting" (Gal. 6:8) and that when we "walk in the Spirit" we will "not fulfil the lusts of the flesh" (Gal. 5:16).

iii) What does God think about our "members?". "For which things' sake the wrath of God cometh on the children of disobedience". The tense ("cometh", or 'is coming') emphasises the certainty of divine judgment. For other examples of what is often called the 'prophetic present tense', see John 4:21; 14:3. Note the parallel passage in Ephesians 5:3-7, which concludes with the words, "Let no man deceive you with vain words: for because of these things cometh the wrath of God upon the children of disobedience. Be not ye therefore partakers with them". See also Romans 1:18. "Calvin very appropriately observes that the real purpose of this prophecy about the inevitability of God's wrath being visited upon confirmed evildoers is 'that we may be deterred from sinning'. Accordingly, even such a wrath-statement is filled with mercy!" (W. Hendrikson).

We were once "children (sons) of disobedience" and "children of wrath". We "walked according to the course of this world, according to the prince of the power of the air, the spirit that now worketh in the children of disobedience: among whom also we all had our conversation in times past in the lusts of our flesh, fulfilling the desires of the flesh and of the mind; and were by nature the children of wrath, even as others" (Eph. 2:2-3). Now, by divine grace, we are "children of God" and "sons of God" (Rom. 8:16, 19).

iv) What about the past influence of our "members?". "In the which ye also walked some time, when ye lived in them". The word "walked" refers to behaviour and conduct: the word "lived" refers to disposition or character. The Colossians were once absorbed by these vices. It was not a case of immorality, but of amorality, that is, no morals at all, and no thought of them. Things are to be so different now: "If we live in the Spirit, let us also walk in the Spirit" (Gal. 5:25). Paul compares pre-conversion and post-conversion life as follows: "For when ye were the servants of sin, ye were free from righteousness. What fruit had ye then in those things whereof ye are now ashamed? for the end of those things is death. But now being made free from sin, and become servants to God, ye have your fruit unto holiness, and the end everlasting life" (Rom. 6:20-22).

b) In our assembly lives, 3:8-17

In these verses, there is a particular emphasis on relationships between believers. Hence the expressions "one to another" (v.9) and "one another" (vv.13, 16). Notice that we must make our practice correspond with our position, or, to put it another way, we are to make our state correspond with our standing. We are, therefore, to "put off all these", because we **have** "put off the old man with his deeds". Moreover, because we **have** "put on the new man", we are to "put on...bowels of mercies, kindness, humbleness of mind, meekness, longsuffering". Verses 8-11 are complemented by verses 12-14.

These verses (vv.8-17) contain two injuctions: *(i)* "put off all these" (vv.8-9): *(ii)* "Put on therefore..." (vv.10-17).

i) "Put off all these, vv.8-9. Paul refers here, first of all to our **practice** ("But now ye also put off all these...", v8-9a), and then to our **position** ("ye have put off the old man with his deeds", v.9b).

- **Our practice, vv.8-9a.** "But *now* (as opposed to the past, "some time", v.7) ye also put off all these..." We expect "anger, wrath" and their companions in the lives of unsaved people, but they should be absent in our lives. Notice that Paul does not say 'put off some of these', but "*all* these". Bearing in mind the tense, the literal translation is ''cast aside from yourselves once and for all... anger, wrath, malice'. The words "put off" *(apotithemi)* occur in their literal sense in Acts 7:58, where "the witnesses *laid down* their clothes at a young man's feet, whose name was Saul". The expressions "put off" and "put on" strongly suggest the removal of clothing and replacement of clothing. Character and clothing are linked in the Bible on several occasions. See, for example, Psalm 132:9; Isaiah 11:5, 61:10.

The list follows. *"Anger"*. Human anger and divine anger are quite different. So far as the former is concerned, as here, it is hidden hostility. It is the feeling of ill-will suppressed. A refusal to 'get over it'. The attitude that doesn't want to forgive. *"Wrath"*. Once again, human wrath and divine wrath are not the same thing. Here, it is anger out of control. It is the feeling of ill-will expressed. "Anger" *(orge)* indicates a feeling of hatred; "wrath" *(thumos)* indicates an outburst of passion (W.E. Vine). Note Ephesians 4:26, "Be ye angry, and sin not; let not the sun go down upon your wrath". Quite obviously, we must distinguish between anger and sinful anger! In this verse, the word "wrath" is *parorgismos*, a strengthened form of *orge* ("anger"). If we allow our sinful anger to smoulder all night, it is likely to turn into a blazing fire in the morning! *"Malice"*. This is a determination to inflict evil on others. The attitude that says, 'I'll get you for this'. *"Blasphemy"*. This is railing, evil-speaking, slandering. *"Filthy conversation"*. This is 'base speech, and includes filthy talk and any kind of foul-mouthed speech' (W.E. Vine). Compare Ephesians 5:4. It was said of the Lord Jesus that they "all bear him witness, and wondered at the gracious words which proceeded out of his mouth" (Luke 4:22).

To these five things is added, "**Lie not one to another,** seeing that ye have put off the old man with his deeds". Fellowship is founded on truth. It has been said that 'falsehood violates brotherhood'. The solemn judgment of Ananias and Sapphira reminds us that lying is not necessarily verbal. T. Bentley points out that "Joseph's brethren unsympathetically allowed their father to believe that his son was dead by presenting the blood-stained coat". Ananias was told that he had "lied to the Holy Ghost", and "unto God" (Acts 5:3-4).

- Our position, v.9b. We are to "put off all these" (vv.8-9a), because we have already "put off the old man with his deeds". We must do in practice what we have already done in principle. When we trusted in Christ, our former lives came to an end. The expression "old man" is not synonymous with the old nature. It means, 'the man that I once was': that is, what we once were in Adam. The "new man" describes what we have become in Christ. (Someone has said that converted Roman Catholics have 'put off the old man with his **beads!**'). W.E. Vine points out that the word *palaios* ("old") "suggests that which belongs to a past period and is worn out". He continues, this "is a fitting description of that which should not be worn by those who have been born of God". When we trusted in Christ, we threw away our old clothes!

ii) "Put on the new man", vv.10-17. In this case, Paul reverses the order. He places our position first, "and **have put on** the new man, which is renewed in knowledge after the image of him that created him", and then refers to our practice: "**Put on** therefore, as the elect of God, holy and beloved, bowels of mercies, kindness, humbleness of mind, meekness, longsuffering".

- **Our position, vv.10-11.** We have "put on the new man, which is renewed in knowledge after the image of him that created him" (v.10). Preachers today speak about 'unpacking' a verse, which is all very well as long as they don't tip the verse upside down on the floor! All we will say is that there is plenty to 'unpack' here!

We "have **put on the new man**". Paul uses the word *neos* ("new") here, which means "'new in time, new in contrast to that which was of long duration" (W.E. Vine). The other word translated "new" *(kainos)* means new "in quality and character". So when we trusted in Christ we put on new clothes! The word *kainos* is used in the Ephesians 4:24 (a corresponding passage), emphasing "a new character of manhood, spiritual and moral, after the pattern of Christ" (W.E. Vine). But it does not end there. This "new man" is "**renewed**" or, since Paul uses the present continuous tense, is 'being renewed'. It is "maintained continually in vigour and growth" (W.E. Vine). So the "new man", unlike the "old man" will never wear out! It is "renewed" with an objective in view: "renewed **in ('unto') knowledge**". But not any old knowledge, but the knowledge of God! It is not *gnosis*, but *epignosis*, that is, fulness of knowledge. That is the knowledge, not only of God's will and purpose (1:9), but of God Himself (2:2, where the word translated "acknowledgement" is actually *epignosis*, fulness of knowledge*)*. But it is not 'knowledge for the sake of knowledge'. The object of this knowledge is conformity to the character of God Himself. So "renewed in knowledge **after the image of him that created him**". While this alludes to Genesis 1:26-27 ("Let us make man in our image, after our likeness"), it refers to the new creation: "If any man is in Christ, there is a new creation" (2 Cor. 5:17 RV margin). The purpose for which we have "put on the new man" is that we might reflect the character of God. "The aim of the renewal is God's image, the likeness of the very One who created this new man in the hearts and lives of believers, just as He once created the first Adam in His own image" (W. Hendrikson).

It follows, of course, that this overall purpose transcends all human divisions: "Where there is neither Greek nor Jew, circumcision nor uncircumcision, Barbarian, Scythian, bond nor free: but Christ is all, and in all". It has been observed that "the inclusion of the Greeks and the uncircumcised counters the Jewish element in the Colossian heresy, as 'barbarian' serves to dismiss its stress on superior knowledge, while the case of Onesimus would make the reference to slave and freeman especially relevant." G.B. Wilson.

The "old man" recognised and promoted division, but the "new man" recognises that in Christ, there are no boundaries of any sort. There are:

No national divisions	-	"Greek nor Jew"
No religious divisions	-	"Circumcision nor uncircumcision"
No cultural divisions	-	"Barbarian, Scythian"
No social divisions	-	"Bond nor free"

With regard to "Greek nor Jew", see, for example Romans 10:12. With regard to "circumcision nor uncircumcision", see, for example, Galatians 6:15. With regard to "Barbarian, Scythian", see, for example, Romans 1:14. According to W.E. Vine, "the Scythian was simply the lowest type of Barbarian". In the eyes of the Greeks, a barbarian was someone who was ignorant of Greek language and culture (help!). "Bond nor free" speaks for itself! Compare Galatians 3:27-28, which refers particularly to the great blessing of justification by faith. This is available to all without any distinction.

"Grace bridges all chasms" (W. Hendrikson). Standing in Christ is the only thing that matters! Christ is the common centre, and the common life, of all His people. "Christ is all", that is, "He is everything to true believers. They see Him in all the circumstances of their life. He it is who supplies their need and satisfies their desires, and is the One who fills their vision and is acknowledged by them. He occupies their whole sphere of life" (W.E. Vine). "Christ is....in all", that is, "Christ, indwelling all those who are His, is the great Personal means of their spiritual unity. This could not exist apart from Him" (W.E. Vine).

- *Our practice, vv.12-17.* This will be the starting point in our final study in this section of the epistle.

Addendum

Colossians 3:10-11

Additional note on Colossians 3:10-11

The features listed in Colossians 3:5-9 are connected with the fallen first creation: "mortify therefore your members which are upon **the earth**" (v.5). The features listed thereafter are connected with the new creation: "the image of him that **created** him" (v.10).

Of the first creation, it is written, "So God created man in his own image, in the image of God created he him" (Gen. 1:27). The "new man" bears "the image of him that created him".

The first creation was corrupted by sin. Not so the second, for we are indwelt by Christ Himself, and that new creation depends on Him! It is His life, and we have been made partakers of the divine nature.

The intrusion of sin divided the first creation, the deepest cleavage of which came to be that of Jew and Gentile - circumcision and uncircumcision. In the new creation, national barriers are removed, particularly that between Jew and Gentile, including the prejudices and practices of the former, and all find a common relationship in Christ, who is "all in all".

The old creation speedily deteriorated with the introduction of sin. The new creation is in constant process of renewing and remoulding towards the image of its Creator. This is expressed in Ephesians 4:11-13, where the existence of gifts in the church from its risen Head are said to be for "the perfecting of the saints, for the work of the ministry, for the edifying of the body of Christ: till we all come in the unity of the faith, and of the knowledge of the Son of God, unto a perfect man, unto the measure of the stature of the fulness of Christ".

READ CHAPTER 3.12-4.1

"Do all in the name of the Lord Jesus"

As we have noticed, Colossians 3:1-4:1 tell us two important things. **(1)** how we are to **maintain** our new life (3:1-4); **(2)** how we are to **manifest** our new life, (3:5-4:1).

1) THE MAINTENANCE OF OUR NEW LIFE, 3:1-4
The new life will be nourished by recognising **(a)** That we are raised with Christ (vv.1-2); **(b)** that our lives are hidden with Christ (v.3); **(c)** that we will be manifested with Christ (v.4).

2) THE MANIFESTATION OF OUR NEW LIFE, 3:5-4:1
It will be manifested **(a)** in our personal lives (3: 5-7); **(b)** in our assembly lives (3:8-17); **(c)** in our family lives (3:18-21); **(d)** in our business lives (3:22-4:1).

a) In our personal lives, 3: 5-7
The nourishment of our new life in Christ must be accompanied by the death of the old life: "Mortify (put to death) therefore your members which are upon the earth". We must deal ruthlessly with "the motions of sins...in our members" (Rom. 7:5).

b) In our assembly lives, 3:8-17
We have already noticed that in these verses, there is a particular emphasis on relationships between believers. Hence the expressions "one to another" (v.9) and "one another" (vv.13, 16). We are to make our practice correspond with our position. We are, therefore, to "put off all these" (the things mentioned in vv.8-9) because we **have** "put off the old man with his deeds" (v.9), and because we **have** "put on the new man" (v.10), we are to "put on...bowels of mercies, kindness, humbleness of mind, meekness, longsuffering" (v.12). Verses 8-11 are complemented by verses 12-14. In our last study, we considered the injunctions "put off", in relation to our *practice* and our *position* (vv.8-11), and "put on", in relation to our *position* (vv.10-11). We must now consider this in relation to our *practice* (vv.12-17).

Since we have "put on the new man, which is renewed in knowledge after the image of him that created him", it follows that "the new man" will display the character of Christ Himself. We can therefore divide vv.12-17 as follows: *(i)* His character reflecting in our lives (vv.12-14); *(ii)* His peace ruling in our hearts (v.15); *(iii)* His word dwelling in us richly (v.16); *(iv)* His name controlling our service (v.17).

i) His character reflecting in our lives, vv.12-14. "Put on therefore, as the elect of God, holy and beloved...." Similar language is used of the Lord Jesus: "Behold my servant, whom I have chosen; my beloved, in whom my soul is well pleased" (Matt. 12:18). This quotes, Isaiah 42:1, "Behold my servant, whom I uphold; mine elect, in whom my soul delighteth". As "the **elect** of God", we are to "put on bowels of mercies, kindness, humbleness of mind, meekness, longsuffering; forebearing one another, and forgiving one another". The Lord Jesus, "mine **elect**", displayed these qualities perfectly. They are summed up in the description of His ministry: "He shall not strive, nor cry; neither shall any man hear his voice in the streets. A bruised reed shall he not break, and smoking flax shall he not quench" (Matt. 12:19-20).

The words "elect of God, holy and beloved", remind us that the doctrine of election is never taught in a vacuum. **Election has practical results!** As "the elect of God", we **are** "holy", set apart for God, and we are to **be** holy in life and conduct. God has "chosen us in him (Christ) before the foundation of the world, that we should be **holy** and without blame before him" (Eph. 1:4). Peter reminds us that "as he which hath called you is holy, so **be ye holy** in all manner of conversation; because it is written, Be ye holy; for I am holy" (1 Pet. 1:15-16). Having enumerated the features which we are to display in our lives, Peter urges us to 'give diligence to make our calling and election sure' (2 Pet. 1:10). That is, we are to see to it that the practical purpose of our election is achieved. See also Ephesians 2:10. **Election also displays the love of God.** As "the elect of God" we are "beloved". See also 1 Thessalonians 1:4, JND: "Knowing, brethren **beloved by God,** your election".

As "the elect of God, holy and beloved", we are to "put on" seven items of new clothing. "**Bowels of mercies**". The word "bowels" *(splanchna)* is rendered "inward affection" (2 Cor. 7:15); "bowels and mercies" (Phil. 2:1) or "tender mercies" (RV). "In the New Testament, it always has reference to feelings of kindness, goodwill and pity" (W.E. Vine). Christians should have a compassionate heart and display tender affection. We should notice the "compassion" *(splanchnizomai)* of the Lord Jesus. See, for example, Mark

1:41. "**Kindness**". The word *(chrestotes)* denotes 'goodness'. It occurs here as a noun, and as an adjective in Ephesians 4:32, "And be ye *kind* one to another, tenderhearted (*eusplanchnos*, akin to 'bowels of mercies')". It means 'pleasant': showing 'goodness of heart'. It has been defined as 'the friendly and helpful spirit which seeks to meet the needs of others by kind deeds'. "**Humility**". This speaks for itself. Humility is an acknowledgement of complete dependence on God. "**Meekness**". This denotes total absence of self-assertiveness and self-interest. It has been defined as 'power under control', and is therefore definitely not weakness! Moses was "very meek, above all the men which were upon the face of the earth" (Num. 12:3). The Lord Jesus was "meek and lowly in heart". "**Longsuffering**". W.E. Vine defines "longsuffering" *(makrothumia)* as "the quality of self-restraint in the face of provocation, which forbears to retaliate and is not prompt to punish; it is the opposite of anger". The Lord Jesus displayed this perfectly: "Who, when he was reviled, reviled not again; when he suffered, he threatened not" (1 Pet. 2:23). "**Forbearing one another**". The verb, *anecho*, literally means 'to hold up', and signifies 'to bear with', or 'endure'. It is used in 2 Thess. 1:4 of enduring "persecutions and tribulations", and in 2 Timothy 4:3 of not enduring "sound doctrine". So we have to bear with people who try our patience. Not easy! The forbearance of God is mentioned in Romans 2:4; 3:25. "**Forgiving one another,** if any man have a quarrel against any: even as Christ forgave you, so also do ye". Compare Ephesians 4:32. See Matthew 18:21-35, where note v.27: "Then the lord of that servant was moved with compassion, and loosed him, and forgave him the debt". The word "quarrel" *(momphe)* denotes "blame...an occasion of complaint" (W.E. Vine). It has been said that:

> He little knows of God and heaven
> Who never breathes the word 'Forgiven'.

"And above all these things put on charity (love), which is the bond of perfectness (completeness)". "Love is the outer garment, which had a binding effect upon the others, keeping them in their places" (W.E. Vine). It has been said that love is 'like the cement which binds the bricks together, and like the egg in a cake-mix!'. It holds all the other virtues together, and gives them completeness. They would be incomplete without love. Now read 1 Corinthians 13, and compare the features of love there with this passage.

*ii) **His peace ruling in our hearts, v.15.*** "And let the peace of God ('the peace of Christ', RV/JND) rule in your hearts, to the which also ye are called in one body; and be ye thankful". "The peace of God" should be displayed in three ways:

- ***It should arbitrate when facing problems.*** The word "rule" means to arbitrate or act as an umpire. The context decides the meaning. Our relationships with fellow-believers should be governed by "the peace of God". This is the test. Does our attitude towards brothers and sisters in Christ bring us peace, or does it leave us agitated and disturbed?' Do we look at them with 'bowels of mercies, kindness, humbleness of mind, meekness, longsuffering, forbearance and forgiveness?' If not, our attitude is wrong. But if we can look at each other, and relate to each other, with peace in our hearts, our attitude is right. The peace of God cannot possibly be in our hearts if all we do is complain about each other, and take every opportunity to criticise each other. The use of the plural here, "your hearts", reminds us that our personal relationships have a direct effect on the assembly.

- ***It is the purpose for which God has brought us together.*** "To the which also ye are called in one body" reminding us that "Behold, how good and how pleasant it is for brethren to dwell together in unity!" (Psalm 133:1). We are not, therefore, to be agitators and critics, sniping from the sidelines.

- ***It will result in thankfulness***. "And be ye thankful". The enjoyment of peace in our hearts, and amongst us, will inevitably result in thanksgiving to God who has made such blessings possible through the death of His Son.

iii) His word dwelling in us richly, v.16. "Let the word of Christ dwell in you richly in all wisdom; teaching and admonishing one another in psalms and hymns and spiritual songs, singing with grace in your hearts to the Lord". This verse may be rendered as follows: "Let the word of Christ dwell in you richly: in all wisdom teaching and admonishing one another: in psalms and hymns and spiritual songs singing with grace in your hearts unto the Lord". We should notice at least three things in this gigantic verse:

- ***The word of Christ and ourselves.*** "Let the word of Christ dwell in you richly". While this could refer to teaching **about** the Lord Jesus, it evidently refers to teaching given **by** the Lord Jesus. The "word of Christ" is evidently not confined to His teaching whilst on earth. T. Bentley defines it as "the ministry which comes from the risen Head". It is to dwell in us "richly" which has "the twofold meaning of quantity and degree" (W.E. Vine). It is to dwell in us "richly" in terms of its amount, and in terms of the value we place upon it. The word "dwell" means far more than mental comprehension. It means that the word of Christ finds a home in our hearts and lives. It means that we enjoy it. It means that we give it liberty at all times and in all circumstances of life.

- **The ministry of the word to others.** "In all wisdom; teaching and admonishing one another". (Paul was an example of his own ministry: see 1:28). This is mutual: "teaching and admonishing **one another**". Quite obviously, we cannot help each other if the "word of Christ"does not dwell in us richly! We would have nothing worthwhile to say if that was the case. Social chit chat does not edify God's people. There is no substitute for the word of God wisely taught and wisely applied! Teaching is positive imparting of truth. Admonition "has mainly in view the things that are wrong and call for warning" (W.E. Vine). See, for example, Acts 20:31, "By the space of three years I ceased not to warn ('admonish', JND) every one night and day with tears".

- **The accompanying praise to God.** If "the word of Christ" dwells in us "richly" then our audible praise will flow from grateful hearts. "In psalms and hymns and spiritual songs, singing with grace in your **hearts**, to the Lord". So while the New Testament does not provide for trained singers or choir pieces, it does have something to say about singing! See also 1 Corinthians 14:15, "I will sing with the spirit, and I will sing with the **understanding** also". While enjoying good tunes, we must give attention to the words of our hymns and choruses. (Remember that hymn and chorus writers are not always good theologians!). It has been suggested that the word "**psalms**" may have a wider connotation than the book of Psalms, and refers to expressions of praise, like the Psalms themselves, arising from experience with God. This may or may not be so. We **do** sing Psalm 23, to name but one! The word "**hymns**" meaning songs of praise, could well refer to New Testament compositions. "**Spiritual songs**" means a composition which expresses "some spiritual truth" (A. Leckie). For example, our hymn, "Thou art the everlasting Word", certainly falls within that category. We should notice that it is "**spiritual** songs", not just "songs!".

Compare Ephesans 5:18-19, where there is a different emphasis: "And be not drunk with wine, wherein is excess; but be filled with the Spirit; speaking to yourselves *(heautois)* in psalms and hymns and spiritual songs, singing and making melody in your heart to the Lord". While the word *heautois* could signify 'one to another', it is more often rendered "to yourselves". As A. Leckie *(What The Bible Teaches - Ephesians)* observes, "personal not public worship is the subject". While the expression, "making melody", means to sing with a stringed instrument accompaniment, here it is the heart that is the instrument!

iv) His name controlling our service, v.17. "And whatsoever ye do in word or deed, do all in the name of the Lord Jesus, giving thanks unto God and the

Father by him". The expression "in word" embraces "teaching...admonishing... singing". The injunction, "do all in the name of the Lord Jesus", is far more than a verbal formula. It means speaking and acting in accordance with His will, and therefore for His glory. This is the test we should apply to every situation in life. If, on reflection, we cannot claim His authority and blessing on what we are doing, or what we are saying, or where we are going, or what we are reading, or what we are watching, then we must simply not do it! But it is rather more than even that. It is not a case of 'Do I have His approval?', but 'Is He leading me in this direction?' It is not a case of, 'Can I take the Lord Jesus with me to the cinema?', but, 'Is He leading me to the cinema?' The answer is obvious, isn't it? After all, could you really "give thanks to God the Father by him" in those circumstances? This brings us to the third area in which our new life will be manifested. It will be seen:

c) In our family lives, 3:18-21
This section covers "wives...husbands...children...fathers". So our new life in Christ must be displayed in our natural relationships as well as in our spiritual relationships. Notice the reciprocal nature of the teaching: Paul addresses wives and husbands, children and fathers, and then servants and masters.

i) "Wives", v.18. "Wives, submit yourselves unto your own husbands, as it is fit in the Lord". See also Ephesians 5:22-24. This is the consistent teaching of Scripture. See, for example, Genesis 3:16; 1 Peter 3:1-6. It is "fit in the Lord", because it is in harmony with His will as revealed in the Scriptures. God has ordained that it is for the husband to lead, and for the wife to follow. This does not, for one moment, imply that wives are inferior to their husbands. Whilst the roles of husbands and wives differ, they enjoy equality in their standing before God (see Galatians 3:28), and equality in importance. As W. Hendrikson observes, "It is when a wife recognises this basic distinction (the creatorial order) and acts accordingly, that she can be a blessing to her husband, can exert a gracious, very powerful, and beneficial influence upon him, can promote not only his but also her own happiness".

ii) "Husbands", v.19. "Husbands, love your wives, and be not bitter against them". The best commentator on this passage is Paul himself. Read Ephesians 5:25-33. The husband's love for his wife must reflect the deep, sacrificial love of Christ for the church. It will, therefore, be marked by absence of "harshness and provocation". The husband will not be given to anger and severity. He will "lovingly seek the best interests of the wife under all circumstances" (W.E. Vine). The word "bitter" also contains the idea of 'irritation'.

iii)   "Children", v.20. "Children, obey your parents in all things: for this is wellpleasing unto the Lord". Compare Ephesians 6:1-3. The Lord Jesus "went down with them (Mary and Joseph), and was subject unto them" (Luke 2:51). God expresses His displeasure over disobedience to parents Rom. 1:30; 2 Tim 3:2). While Paul evidently has in mind a Christian home where Christian principles prevail, Christian children in non-Christian homes could face a crisis of conscience if parents require their children to do something contrary to Bible teaching. If it becomes necessary to invoke Acts 5:29, this must be done with courtesy and respect.

iv) "Fathers", v.21. "Fathers, provoke not your children to anger, lest they be discouraged". Compare Ephesians 6:4. W.E. Vine suggests that the change from "parents" in the previous verse to "fathers" here, suggests that fathers are more likely than mothers to provoke their children! He continues: "the word *erethizo*, rendered 'provoke', here implies an irritation which, by reason of its exacting character, would produce moroseness or despondency". T. Bentley adds that "when a child feels that he can never do anything right, he gives up trying".

d) In our business lives, 3:22-4:1
Well, not quite! Strictly speaking, 'business lives' is a misnomer! Paul is actually referring to slaves *(doulos)* and masters, and he **may** have a particular case in mind. See his letter to Philemon. This section certainly balances Paul's earlier statement that in Christ there is "neither...bond nor free" (3:11). We must recognise that while all believers have equal standing before God, they do not have equal standing in the world. Without forgetting the immediate circumstances, this passage contains abiding guidance to employees and employers. These verses should be read in conjunction with Ephesians 6:5-9.

i) "Servants", 3:22-25. We should notice how they were to serve (v.22), who they were to serve (v.23), and what they would receive (vv.24-25).

- ***How they were to serve, v.22.*** "Servants, obey in all things (which must, surely, be regulated by Acts 5:29) your masters according to the flesh; not with eyeservice, as menpleasers; but in singlenesss of heart, fearing God". The words "not with eyeservice, as menpleasers" mean, not serving only when the earthly master is watching. This is complemented by the words, "but in singleness of heart, fearing God". In other words, serving in view of the fact that the heavenly Master is watching all the time! "Singleness of heart" means without duplicity. Compare Titus 2:9-10.

- **Who they were to serve, v.23.** "And whatsoever ye do, do it heartily, as to the Lord, and not unto men". The word "heartily" *(ek pusche)* is, literally, 'from the soul'. Service, however humdrum and menial, must be undertaken cheerfully. W.Hendrikson renders this: "Whatever you do, put your soul into the work, as for the Lord and not for men". This was a totally new way to look at slave-service! Imagine its impact on society. It was 'adorning the doctrine of God our Saviour' (Titus 2:10). The "little maid" who waited on Naaman's wife is a splendid example (2 Kings 5:2-4).

- **What they would receive, vv.24-25.** "Knowing that of the Lord ye shall receive the reward of the inheritance: for ye serve the Lord Christ". A slave received no pay. He certainly did not have an inheritance on earth! But he would "receive the reward (recompence) of the inheritance" from his heavenly Master. The divine Employer would reward His faithful servants. Remember that Paul is speaking here about 'secular' service. God will reward those who honour Him in the discharge of their daily responsibilities.

But bad work will also be rewarded. "But he that doeth wrong shall receive for the wrong which he hath done: and there is no respect of persons" (v.25). Bearing in mind the previous verse, this evidently refers to requital for bad work from the Lord, rather than from an earthly employer. This does not mean, of course, loss of salvation, but loss of the reward. Bearing in mind the words, "and there is no respect of persons", it has been suggested that this verse applies not only to slaves, but to masters.

ii) "Masters", 4:1. "Masters, give unto your servants that which is just and equal; knowing that ye also have a Master in heaven". As W. Hendrikson observes, "Let the masters realise that just as their slaves are accountable to them, so they, in turn, will have to answer to the Master in heaven. If they understand this, they will not treat their slaves harshly". This does not mean that they were to treat their slaves as social equals, but with proper consideration for their welfare. The word "equal" here carries the idea of fairness, rather than equality.

READ CHAPTER 4.2-18

"Continue in prayer"

Colossians 4 comprises *(1)* final exhortations (vv.2-6) and *(2)* final greetings (vv.7-18). In connection with the former, Paul refers to the prayers, walk and speech of God's people. In connection with the latter, Paul mentions ten brethren, and concludes with his own greetings. Of the ten brethren, two were *en route* to Colosse from Rome, six were at Rome, one was at Laodicea and one at Colosse. The references, however brief, are all most illuminating, and prove, yet again, that we can expect the Holy Spirit to instruct us from every part of God's word. "All scripture is given by inspiration of God".

1) FINAL EXHORTATONS, vv.2-6
The three exhortations are: *(a)* "Continue in prayer" (vv.2-4); *(b)* "Walk in wisdom" (v.5); *(c)* "Let your speech be alway with grace" (v.6).

a) "Continue in prayer", vv.2-4
In this connection, Paul refers to *(i)* general prayer: "Continue in prayer, and watch in the same with thanksgiving" (v.2), and to *(ii)* specific prayer: "Withal praying also for us" (vv.3-4).

i) General prayer, v.2
We should notice three things in this connection: continuance, watchfulness, and thanksgiving.

- *"Continue in prayer"*. Paul certainly put his own ministry into practice. See 1:3, 9. The word rendered "continue" (*proskartereo*) is derived from two Greek words meaning 'towards', used intensively, and 'to be strong' (W.E. Vine)' It has therefore been translated, more exactly, 'persevere'. Prayer is not therefore limited to times of crisis. The word 'persevere' implies habitual earnestness and diligent application. We pray during encouragements and discouragements. We "pray without ceasing" (1 Thess. 5:17). It has been said that the "maintenance of spiritual life depends on intercourse with God".

Persevering in prayer is beautifully illustrated by the uplifted hands of Moses during the conflict between Israel and Amalek: "But Moses' hands were heavy; and they took a stone, and put it under him, and he sat thereon; and Aaron and Hur stayed up his hands, the one on the one side, and the other on the other side: and his hands were **steady** until the going down of the sun" (Exod. 17:12). Compare 1 Timothy 2:8, "I will therefore that (the) men pray everywhere, lifting up holy hands, without wrath and doubting". We tend to be people of fluctuating enthusiasm. The picture before us emphasises the necessity for regularity and consistency in prayer, without which the work of God will suffer reverse: "When Moses held up his hand...Israel prevailed: and when he let down his hand, Amalek prevailed". Although so disappointed with Israel, Samuel determined to persevere in prayer: "Moreover as for me, God forbid that I should sin against the LORD in ceasing to pray for you" (1 Sam. 12:23). We must display greater diligence in our personal prayers, and in our attendance, and participation, in the assembly prayer meeting.

- **"And watch in the same".** This suggests spiritual vigilance to ensure that nothing weakens our effectiveness in prayer. The word "watch" *(gregoreo)* occurs in Acts 20:31, "Therefore **watch** and remember". The elders from Ephesus were to "watch" in view of the "grievous wolves" and "men...speaking perverse things". It also occurs in 1 Thessalonians 5:6, "Let us **watch** and be sober", that is, in view of the Lord's coming. See also Revelation 3:2, "Be **watchful**, and strengthen the things which remain". The Lord Jesus urged His disciples to "watch and pray" (Matt. 26:41).

But it also suggests alertness in bringing occasions of difficulty and blessing, joy and sorrow, anything, everything, to God in prayer. There should never be any lack in our petitions: every aspect of our lives and work for God should be included. How often we allow a situation to develop - or find ourselves carried away with some new venture - or endeavour to order the details of our complex lives, without recourse to God in prayer. The believer who is spiritually alert will sing wholeheartedly

> What a privilege to carry
> Everything to God in prayer

- **"With thanksgiving".** Our prayers should be permeated, not with the spirit of murmuring anxiety, but with grateful acknowledgement of God's goodness, and with confidence in Him. Alertness in bringing everything to God in prayer, must be matched by alertness in thanksgiving for His response to our prayers.

In this case, it is thanksgiving in advance, rather like Jehoshaphat's "singers" who praised "the beauty of holiness" as "they went out before the army" against "the children of Ammon, Moab, and mount Seir" (2 Chron. 20:21-22).

ii) Specific prayer, vv.3-4
"Withal (at the same time) praying also for **us**". Once again, every word is weighty. We should notice that Paul refers to the following in his 'prayer request':

- **The opportunity for preaching.** "That God would open unto us a door of utterance" or "a door of the word" (JND). Paul was primarily concerned, not for himself, but for the progress of the word of God. He did not pray for deliverance *from* his circumstances, but for effectiveness *in* his circumstances. Compare Ephesians 6:19: "And for me, that utterance may be given unto me, that I may open my mouth boldly, to make known the mystery of the gospel". In Ephesians 6, Paul refers to the **ability** to speak, whereas here, he refers to the **opportunity** to speak. Notice the same priority in 2 Thessalonians 3:1-2, "Finally, brethren, pray for us, that the word of the Lord may have free course, and be glorified... and that we may be delivered from unreasonable and wicked men". God places His people where *He* wants them to be. That is *His* prerogative, and we can safely leave the matter with Him. Our business is to speak worthily of Christ in our circumstances, as God gives us opportunity.

- **The subject of the preaching.** "To speak *(laleo:* the usual word for speaking or talking) the mystery of Christ, for which I am also in bonds". The "mystery of Christ" is the inclusion of Jew and Gentile in one body, the church. See Colossians 1:26-27; Ephesians 3:3-6. Paul was in prison because he proclaimed that, through the gospel, God saved and blessed Jews and Gentiles without distinction. This was deeply offensive to the Jews. See 1 Thessalonians 2:15-16 ("Forbidding us to speak to the Gentiles"); Acts 22:21-22 ("And he said unto me, Depart: for I will send thee far hence unto the Gentiles. And they gave him audience unto this word, and then lifted up their voices, and said, Away with such a fellow from the earth: for it is not fit that he should live").

- **The clarity of the preaching.** "That I may make it ('the mystery of Christ') manifest, as I ought to speak". See, again, Ephesians 6:19-20. The words "make it manifest" mean 'state it clearly'. The word "ought" *(dei)* means 'it is necessary' or 'one must. (W.E. Vine). Compare Luke 18:1.

b) "Walk in wisdom", v.5
"Walk in wisdom toward them that are without, redeeming the time". Another

verse "full of matter" (Job 32:18). We should notice the references to "wisdom" in the epistle: 1:9; 2:3; 3:16; 4:5.

- *"Walk in wisdom".* The word "walk" is, literally, 'walk about', and signifies our conduct and behaviour. This involves the knowledge of God's will. See 1:9-10: "that ye might be filled with the knowledge of his will in all wisdom and spiritual understanding; that ye might walk worthy of the Lord unto all pleasing". Compare Ephesians 5:17.

- *"Toward them that are without".* For "them that are without", see 1 Corinthians 5:12-13; 1 Thessalonians 4:12; 1 Timothy 3:7. The last of these refers to an elder's testimony in the world, but we must all ensure that we maintain a good witness before non-Christians: "Give none occasion to the adversary to speak reproachfully" (1 Tim. 5:14). In Titus 2:4-5, Paul describes the way in which "young women" are to behave, so that "the word of God be not blasphemed". Young men do not escape either! "Young men (including Titus himself) likewise exhort to be sober minded...that he that is of the contrary part may be ashamed, having no evil thing to say of you" (Titus 2:6,8). It would be tragic if our conduct deterred someone from becoming a Christian.

- *"Redeeming the time",* or "seizing every good and favourable opportunity" (JND margin). The Amplified Version puts it like this: "make the very most of the time, and seizing (buying up) the opportunity". So alertness in prayer (v.2) is to be matched by alertness in witnessing for Christ. But it is not a lot of good making use of every opportunity to witness for Christ if we are not walking "in wisdom toward them that are without".

c) *"Let your speech be alway with grace", v.6*
"Let your speech be alway with grace, seasoned with salt, that ye may know how ye ought to answer every man".

- *"Let your speech be alway with grace".* Not 'sometimes with grace', or 'occasionally with grace', or even 'nearly always with grace', but *"**alway** with grace!"* It speaks for itself, doesn't it?! This means avoidance of sarcasm and bitterness. It means that we must be "swift to hear, slow to speak, slow to wrath" (James 1:19). Notice the gracious way in which the Lord Jesus, aged twelve, handled the situation when Mary said, "Thy **father** and I have sought thee sorrowing" (Luke 2:48-49). The Lord Jesus was known for His gracious speech. See Luke 4:22; John 7:46. In describing the character of the "virtuous woman", with her perpetual motion, the writer only mentions her mouth once, but what a testimony! "She openeth her mouth with wisdom; and in her tongue is the law of kindness" (Prov. 31:26). If our speech is "alway with grace", we will avoid talebearing. See Proverbs 26:17-28. We must remember that "love covers a multitude of sins" (1 Pet. 4:8 JND). Love does not shout about the imperfections in other people. Remember that even if something is true, that does not mean that we can broadcast it for all to hear.

- *"Seasoned with salt"*. (Notice that it is "seasoned with salt" not 'seasoned with pepper!'). The word "seasoned" means 'to arrange...make ready...fitly prepared'. "Seasoned with salt" emphasises the **purifying** and **antiseptic** qualities that should mark our speech. Hence, "Let no corrupt communication proceed out of your mouth, but that which is good to the use of edifying, that it may minister grace unto the hearers" (Eph. 4:29). "Corrupt communication" includes, "foolish talking" and "jesting" which are "not convenient", as opposed to "giving of thanks" (Eph. 5:4).

The whole statement, "Let your speech be alway with grace, seasoned with salt", is illustrated perfectly in the life of the Lord Jesus. He was "full of grace and truth". See, for example, John 4:14-16, "Whosoever drinketh of the water that I shall give him shall never thirst (grace)...Go, call thy husband, and come hither (salt)"; John 8:11, "Neither do I condemn thee (grace): go, and sin no more (salt)".

Salt was required in the meal offering: "And every oblation of thy meat offering (or, meal offering) shalt thou season with **salt;** neither shalt thou suffer the salt of the covenant of thy God to be lacking from thy meat offering: with all thine offerings thou shalt offer **salt**" (Lev. 2:13). This reminded God's people of His absolute righteousness and purity, but it also reminds us that such purity was seen perfectly in the life of the Lord Jesus, of whom the sacrifices speak so eloquently. See also Numbers 18:19, "It (the heave offering for the priests) is a **covenant of salt** for ever before the LORD unto thee and to thy seed with thee". Compare 2 Chronicles 13:5, where Abijah is addressing Jeroboam: "Ought ye not to know that the LORD God of Israel gave the kingdom over Israel to David for ever...by a **covenant of salt**". So salt is also a symbol of **reliability.**

In this connection, we should notice Mark 9:49-50: "For every one shall be **salted** with fire (that is, tested by God's righteousness and purity), and every sacrifice shall be **salted with salt**". We are, therefore, to "have **salt** in yourselves" (that is, we must be people marked by purity and faithfulness), and it must never decline, for "if the **salt** have lost his saltness, wherewith will ye **season** it?".

Chapter 4

- *"That ye may know how ye ought to answer every man"*. Paul is emphasising here, not so much **what** we are to say, but **how** we are to say it: "speech...alway with grace, seasoned with salt", will enable us to effectively "answer every man". Grace does not permit a brow-beating and argumentative spirit! Peter puts it as follows: "But sanctify the Lord God in your hearts: and be ready always to give an answer to every man that asketh you a reason of the hope that is in you with **meekness and fear**" (1 Pet. 3:15). 'Walking in wisdom' will also influence how we "answer every man". Do notice the different ways in which Daniel and his friends answered the authorities. See Daniel 1:11-13; 2:14; 3:16-18. We come now to:

2) FINAL GREETINGS, vv.7-18

In actual fact, these verses cover more than greetings. Paul gives us a little 'snapshot' of ten people.

a) Tychicus, vv.7-8

Tychicus is mentioned in four other places in the New Testament, but without comment apart from the parallel passage in Ephesians 6:21. He is described as "a beloved brother, and a faithful minister and fellowservant in the Lord". This speaks volumes. Tychicus was not only respected for his loyalty to the truth: he was 'esteemed very highly in love' (1 Thess. 5:13). His faithful ministry had not made him a hard dogmatist who stood alone and aloof. There was a warmth and attractiveness in his character which drew the love and affection of those who knew him.

Tychicus too must have been a tonic to other Christians: "whom I have sent unto you...that he might know your estate, and comfort your hearts", or "that ye might know **our** estate" (RV), which seems better in context. The sense of "comfort" is 'encourage'. Tychicus was evidently an inspiration and encouragement to his brethren in Christ. The Colossians, faced with false teaching, would benefit from his visit, and be better equipped to combat error as a result. How much of a tonic are we to each other: or are we more like 'wet blankets? Do remember what happened at Kadesh-barnea (Deut. 1:28).

b) Onesimus, v.9

He is described as "a faithful and beloved brother". He was from Colosse ("one of you"). Tychicus and Onesimus were travelling together. This was wise: Tychicus could vouch for Onesimus. It is an interesting, but significant, combination! In view of his past record, we could hardly expect a runaway slave to be called "a faithful and beloved brother!" (Notice that Tychicus was "beloved" and "faithful", whereas Onesimus was "faithful" and "beloved": this emphasises the tremendous change in his life). Onesimus means 'profitable', and this appears to have been in Paul's mind when he wrote to Philemon: "Which in time past was to thee unprofitable, but now profitable to thee and to me". Onesimus illustrates 2 Corinthians 5:17, "Therefore if any man be in Christ, he is a new creature: old things are passed away; behold all things are become new". Having come to Christ through Paul at Rome, there had been a 'sea change' in Onesimus, and this should be true of us all. No doubt Paul was returning him to his master at the first opportunity, from which we can deduce that he was probably a fairly new convert. But he was obviously shaping well, and displaying excellent spiritual qualities. An effective Christian life is not the prerogative of older believers!

c) Aristarchus, v.10
Aristarchus was a Thessalonian (Acts 20:4) who, with Gaius, had been seized at Ephesus and conveyed to the theatre where for two hours the populace shouted "Great is Diana of the Ephesians". Now at Rome, he is again suffering the reproach of Christ as Paul's fellowprisoner. Loyalty to Christ and His word, are not likely to earn us the applause of our fellow men. We must expect opposition, antagonism and misunderstanding. "Yea, and all that will live godly in Christ Jesus shall suffer persecution" (2 Tim. 3:12).

d) Marcus, v.10
In earlier days, Mark had proved a big disappointment to the apostle Paul. His return to Jerusalem from Asia Minor during the first missionary journey weighed very heavily against him in Paul's judgment when Barnabas suggested his company on the second journey. See Acts 15:36-41. Notice that Mark was a relative of Barnabas. Did Barnabas allow family connections to influence his judgment? We do not know the answer, but it is worth remembering that family considerations should never override spiritual considerations. Sometimes, the shortcomings of family members are conveniently overlooked, and the work of God suffers in consequence.

But John Mark did not suffer Paul's permanent disapproval. His commendation here by Paul, plus Paul's desire to see him during the second imprisonment at Rome ("Take Mark, and bring him with thee: for he is profitable to me for the ministry", 2 Tim. 4:11), makes it clear that an earlier disappointment did not prejudice the apostle in later years. There are two important lessons here: firstly, that we must not 'write off' people because of their past misjudgments or lapses in conduct, and secondly, we must ensure that we learn lessons from our **own** mistakes.

e) Jesus which is called Justus, v.11

It seems unlikely that "Jesus which is called Justus" is the same man mentioned in Acts 18:7. Titus Justus (RV) was evidently a Gentile. We therefore know nothing about the man mentioned here. We can assume that he was not particularly conspicuous in any way, but like Job, his "record is on high" (Job 16:19). The inclusion of his name here reminds us that although we may not be conspicuous amongst our brothers and sisters, our quiet inconspicuous work is fully recognised by God. There is no fear of being overlooked by heaven!

Aristarchus, Marcus, and Jesus which is called Justus, all of whom sent greetings ("saluteth you") were evidently of Jewish descent, and they alone, presumably amongst Jewish believers at Rome, had been a "comfort" to Paul. The word "comfort" *(paregoria)* means, literally a soothing, or solace. It is a medical term. In English, a 'paregoric' is a medicine which allays irritation. It is always good to be in the company of brethren who do that! The list of names in the chapter evidently includes both Jews and Gentiles, which illustrates "the mystery of Christ" which Paul proclaimed (see v.3).

f) Epaphras, vv.12-13

Epaphras was a Colossian. It was Epaphras who first evangelised Colosse, and Paul refers to his preaching at the beginning of the epistle, describing him as a "faithful minister of Christ" (1:7). He was now in prison (see Philemon v.23), but his energy remained unabated! "Always labouring fervently for you in prayers, that ye may stand perfect and complete in all the will of God. For I bear him record, that he hath a great zeal *(ponos*, meaning labour) for you, and for them that are in Laodicea, and them in Hierapolis". The words "labouring fervently" are represent one Greek word *(agonizomai)* which is elsewhere rendered "'fight" or "labour", and conveys the idea of striving, wrestling and toiling in prayer. The prayers of Epaphras were not dead repetitions or sweeping generalisations. The welfare of the Colossians was a matter of intense personal concern to him, and brought urgency and vitality to his prayers. His prayer was focussed. Knowing the false teaching which confronted them, he prayed that they may "stand *(stathete,* from *histemi,* 'to be made to stand') perfect *(teleios,* 'mature') and complete *(plerophoreo,* 'fully assured') in all the will of God". He knew only too well that false teaching would destroy their stability, maturity and assurance.

g) Luke, v.14

At a later date Paul wrote, "Only Luke is with me" (2 Tim. 4:11). Faithful Luke! The Lord never removed Paul's "thorn in the flesh", but He gave him a "beloved physician". The shadow of death loomed large over the prison cell, but Luke remained.

h) Demas, v.14

Demas was at Rome along with Aristarchus, Marcus, Jesus which is called Justus, Epaphras and Luke. He was one of Paul's "fellow-labourers" at the time. See Philemon 24. But possibly only two years later, he had gone: "Demas hath forsaken me, having loved this present world" (2 Tim. 4:10). We are not told that Demas had 'denied the faith', rather he "hath forsaken *me*". He evidently found the reproach of Christ, for which Paul was shortly to die, too much to bear. Unlike Onesiphorus (2 Tim. 1:16), he became ashamed of the man in chains. Life in the outside world was far more tolerable without the stigma of fellowship with a man who had been imprisoned for his faith. James 4:4 and 1 John 2:15-17 now become compulsory reading. But do notice how quickly backsliding can take place, and we are *all* vulnerable. From a 'fellow-labourer' with the apostle Paul to a 'lover of the world' in two years. But it doesn't always take as long as that, does it?

i) Nymphas, v.15

Nymphas evidently lived in Laodicea. The Lord Jesus addressed a letter to the assembly there some thirty years later. See Revelation 3:14-22. That is all we can say at the moment. The phrase, "the church which is in his house", is variously translated 'her house' (see RV margin) and 'their house' (see JND margin). Perhaps we do well to leave the AV as it is! The church at Colosse evidently met in the house of Philemon (v.2). These references remind us that our homes should be available for the Lord's use.

There is some ground for suggesting that the epistle mentioned in v.16 may have been the Epistle to the Ephesians. Some of the earliest authorities for the text of Ephesians 1:1, omit the words "at Ephesus", and this, according to F.F. Bruce, has led to the view, together with the fact that no personal references are contained in the epistle, that the letter was intended to be read not only by the Christians at Ephesus, but by those in other cities of the province of Asia as well. Perhaps, again, we do well to leave the AV as it is!

j) Archippus, v.17

"And say to Archippus, Take heed to the ministry which thou hast received of the Lord, that thou fulfil it". It appears that Archippus was the son of Philemon and Apphia. See Philemon 1-2. He was evidently "growing slack in his vigilance, and neglecting his service in the Lord" (T. Bentley). He certainly wasn't the last man to do that. What about *us?* The injunctions, "Neglect not the gift that is in thee" (1 Tim. 4:14) and "Stir up the gift of God, which is in thee" (2 Tim. 1:6), are timely exhortations to us all. Caleb "wholly followed the LORD", right into old age (Joshua 14:6-15).

Paul concludes the epistle with his own greetings, and request for prayer: "The salutation by the hand of me Paul. Remember my bonds. Grace be with you. Amen".

1 THESSALONIANS

by
John M Riddle

1 THESSALONIANS

INTRODUCTION: THE CHURCH AT THESSALONICA

READ ACTS 17:1-10 AND 1 THESSALONIANS

Whilst all believers were close to the heart of Paul, he regarded the church at Thessalonica as parents regard their children. When they were new converts, he tended them "even as a nurse cherisheth her (own) children", and "exhorted and comforted and charged every one of you, as a father doth his children." When he was obliged to leave the city, it was like being bereaved. "But we, brethren, being taken from you ('being bereaved of you') for a short time in presence, not in heart, endeavoured the more abundantly to see your face with great desire." He looked forward with joy to seeing them again. "For what is our hope, or joy, or crown of rejoicing? Are not even ye in the presence of our Lord Jesus Christ at his coming? For ye are our glory and joy." The word "ye" is in a place of emphasis. Paul regarded them with deep interest and affection.

In this introduction, we will briefly cover the following: **(1)** The city of Thessalonica; **(2)** The contact with Thessalonica; **(3)** The church at Thessalonica; **(4)** The confidence over Thessalonica; **(5)** The contents of this epistle to Thessalonica.

1) THE CITY OF THESSALONICA

Thessalonica was an old maritime city. Originally named Therma, it was refounded by Cassander in BC315. He renamed it Thessalonica after his wife, who was the sister of Alexander the Great. Perhaps he wanted to keep on the right side of the great conqueror! Macedonia was conquered by the Romans in BC168, and Thessalonica became a naval station, complete with docks. It was a port, and a nodal point for communication and trade. Under Roman rule, it had a population of approximately 200,000, and was situated on the Egnatian Road, the great military highway linking Rome with the Orient. It is still a thriving port, now called Salonica, and stands at the head of the Gulf of Salonica.

Thessalonica was a free city. It was self-governing and not garrisoned by the

Romans. It was a city democracy (from *demos*, meaning 'the people'), and governed by a board of magistrates called *politarchs*, which simply means 'a ruler of a city.' This accounts for the popular assembly described in Acts 17:6-8, "And they troubled the people and the rulers of the city, when they heard these things." There was a Jewish synagogue in Thessalonica (Acts 17:1), which served the area, and as usual, it was from there that opposition arose. The Lord Jesus called the synagogue at Smyrna, "the synagogue of Satan" (Revelation 2:9), and this description certainly fits other synagogues as well.

2) THE CONTACT WITH THESSALONICA

Paul first visited Thessalonica, probably towards the end of AD50, on his second missionary journey. Having arrived at Troas, Paul received a vision in which "there stood a man of Macedonia, and prayed him, saying, Come over into Macedonia, and help us." In response, "assuredly gathering that the Lord had called us for to preach the gospel unto them", Paul crossed the Aegean Sea, disembarked at Neapolis (now called Kavala), and struck inland to Philippi. Read Acts 16:6-40. After leaving Philippi, at the request of the magistrates, Paul and his colleagues travelled south-west, via Amphipolis and Appolonia, to Thessalonica. Now read Acts 17:1-9. As a result of his visit, a strong active church was planted there, enabling Paul to write "And ye became followers of us, and of the Lord, having received the word in much affliction, with joy of the Holy Ghost: so that ye were ensamples to all that believe in Macedonia and Achaia" (1 Thess.1:6-7). The word "ensamples" *(tupos)* means 'an example to be followed.' Preachers have therefore called Thessalonica, 'a model church.' No doubt the believers at Thessalonica would have strongly protested at this appellative, but they certainly exhibited some desirable features!

We do not know how long Paul remained at Thessalonica, but it does seem that it was longer than three weeks. Whilst he was there, for example, he received at least two gifts from the assembly at Philippi (Phil. 4:15-16). Three Sabbath days are mentioned in Acts 17:2, but this could refer to the duration of his teaching in the synagogue. After leaving Thessalonica, he went to Berea, where he left Silas and Timothy (Acts 17:10-14), and then to Athens, from which he sent a message for Silas and Timothy to rejoin him (Acts 17:15-16). Once Timothy arrived at Athens, he was sent back to Thessalonica (1 Thess. 3:1-2), and Paul moved on to Corinth (Acts 18:1). Timothy returned from Thessalonica to Paul at Corinth with good news (1 Thess. 3:6; Acts 18:5), and Paul then wrote the First Epistle to the Thessalonians from Corinth. The Second Epistle followed shortly after. He paid a second visit to Macedonia during his third missionary journey. See Acts 20:1-6. Thessalonica is not specifically mentioned, but Luke does tell us "when he had **gone over those parts**, and had given them much exhortation, he came into Greece, and there abode three months. And when the Jews laid wait for him, as he was about to sail into Syria, he purposed to return through Macedonia...and we sailed away from Philippi after the days of unleavened bread."

3) THE CONFIDENCE OF PAUL
Paul had no regrets as he reviewed his ministry at Thessalonica. He could refer to his visit without embarrassment: "ye are witnesses, and God also, how holily and justly and unblameably we behaved ourselves among you that believe" (2:10). He could appeal to witnesses on earth and in heaven. Notice the occurrence of the expression "ye know":

i) **He was undaunted by persecution.** See 2:2, "But even after that we had suffered before, and were shamefully entreated, as **ye know,** at Philippi, we were bold in our God to speak unto you the gospel of God with much contention."

ii) **He was untainted by selfishness.** See 2:5, "Neither at any time used we flattering words, as **ye know**, nor a cloke of covetousness; God is witness."

iii) **He was unstinted in devotion.** See 2:11, "As **ye know** how we exhorted and comforted and charged every one of you, as a father doth his children."

iv) **He was uncompromising in teaching.** See 4:2, "For **ye know** what commandments we gave you by the Lord Jesus."

4) THE CHURCH AT THESSALONICA
Amongst other things, we should notice the following: *(a)* its constitution; *(b)* its education; *(c)* its evangelism; *(d)* its characteristics.

a) The constitution of the church
As a result of Paul's evangelism in the synagogue over three successive "sabbath days", various classes of people were saved. "And some of them (Jews in the synagogue) believed, and consorted with Paul and Silas; and of the devout Greeks a great multitude, and of the chief women not a few" (Acts 17:2-4). However, when Paul and his fellow-preachers were obliged to make a hasty exit, it was "the brethren" who sent them away to Berea. Paul uses the word "brethren" twenty-four times in 1 & 2 Thessalonians. It is used by the Lord Jesus to describe all who trust in Him. See John 20:17 and Hebrews 2:11-12. We are

His "brethren." Not 'Christian Brethren', and certainly not 'Plymouth Brethren!' When believers meet together, they do so as "brethren" (including brothers and sisters) without any further distinction.

b) The education of the church
The believers at Thessalonica were certainly well taught during Paul's stay in the city. In the two epistles, we have a number of references to teaching given by Paul at that time. For example, in the First Epistle, Paul refers to the way in which he "exhorted and comforted and charged every one of you" (2:11). More specifically, he had warned them about coming persecution: "when we were with you, we told you before that we should suffer tribulation" (3:4). He had taught them "how ... to walk and to please God" (4:1-2). In the Second Epistle, Paul refers to teaching given about the advent of the "man of sin", and associated events: "Remember ye not, that, when I was yet with you, I told you these things?" (2:5). (Yes, newly-saved people were told about coming events!). Paul had also told them to be industrious: "For even when we were with you, this we commanded you, that if any would not work, neither should he eat" (3:10). The teaching was balanced, wasn't it? Then they were urged not to depart from teaching given: "Stand fast, and hold the traditions which ye have been taught, whether by **word,** or our epistle" (2 Thess. 2:15). Very clearly, Paul did not 'harp on one string': there was a good 'mix' in his ministry. In the Old Testament, a man belonging to the family of Aaron was disqualified from the priesthood if, among other things, he had scurvy. See Leviticus 21:20. Scurvy is an ailment resulting from a lack of a balanced diet, including fresh fruit and vegetables. The believers at Thessalonica did not suffer from spiritual 'scurvy'! Remember that God's word contains all the spiritual vitamins we need. Read the scriptures widely and regularly.

c) The evangelism by the church
The excellent balanced teaching given by Paul did not turn them into walking Bible dictionaries, and little else. Some churches have become, we are told, a 'holy huddle.' But not Thessalonica! "From you sounded out the word of the Lord not only in Macedonia and Achaia, but also in every place your faith to God-ward is spread abroad." Remember that these believers did not distribute tracts, they did not drive cars, and they did not use radio. They didn't even have Email! But through them, without any modern 'aids', the gospel message reached an area approximating to modern Greece! It makes ***us*** look rather pathetic, doesn't it? Do we really care about lost men and women? The assembly at Thessalonica exemplified the exhortation in 1 Corinthians 15:58, "Be ye stedfast, unmoveable, **always abounding in the work of the Lord**..."

d) The characteristics of the church

Paul remembered "without ceasing" their "work of faith, and labour of love, and patience (endurance) of hope in our Lord Jesus Christ" (1:3). These three features are expanded in the same chapter: "For they themselves shew of us what manner of entering in we had unto you, and how ye turned to God from idols (their "work of faith") to serve the living and true God (their "labour of love"); and to wait for his Son from heaven (their "patience of hope"), whom he raised from the dead, even Jesus, which delivered us from the wrath to come" (1:9-10).

Of the three, their "patience of hope" needed strengthening. When Timothy returned from Thessalonica, he brought "good tidings of your faith and charity" (3:6), but no reference is made to hope. When Paul wrote the Second Epistle, he gave thanks that "your faith groweth exceedingly, and the charity of every one of you all toward each other aboundeth" (1:3), but hope is not mentioned. Their "brotherly love" was outstanding, but Paul still urges them to "increase more and more!" (4:9-10). Their "hope" needed strengthening for two reasons:

i) In the First Epistle, we learn that the Christians at Thessalonica were deeply concerned about fellow-believers who were "asleep" (4:13). This is the way in which the Bible describes "the dead in Christ" (4:16). Stephen was "stoned", but he "fell asleep" (Acts 7:59-60). He was amongst those that "sleep in Jesus" (4:14). Paul therefore points out that these believers would not be disadvantaged in any way, for at the return of the Lord Jesus, "the dead in Christ shall rise first: then we which are alive and remain shall be caught up together with them in the clouds, to meet the Lord in the air: and so shall we ever be with the Lord." In view of this Paul adds, "Wherefore comfort (encourage) one another with these words."

ii) In the Second Epistle, we learn that the persecuted Christians at Thessalonica were reeling under teaching that the dreadful events of the 'day of the Lord' (AV "day of Christ") had burst upon them. Paul therefore reminded them that this could not be the case, because the 'day of the Lord' would be preceded by the Lord's coming for the church: see 2:1, and, secondly, by certain recognisable events on earth: see 2:3-4. In view of this Paul prays, "Now our Lord Jesus Christ himself, and God, even our Father, which hath loved us, and hath given us everlasting consolation and good *hope* though grace, comfort (encourage) your hearts, and stablish you in every good word and work" (2:16-17)).

5) *THE CONTENTS OF THE EPISTLE*
This can be the most difficult part of any introduction! Yards of headings and

Introduction

subheadings induce that terrible disease called 'mego' (my eyes glaze over). It is particularly deadly when listening to preaching, and can be quite devastating when reading! So simplicity and brevity are now desperately needed!

The epistle can be divided into four sections as follows *(a)* the historical section (1:1 - 3:13); *(b)* the practical section (4:1-12); *(c)* the prophetical section (4:13 - 5:11); *(d)* the ecclesiastical section (5:12-28). We will take a very brief look at each section.

a) The historical section, 1:1 - 3:13
In this section, Paul looks back, and recalls *(i)* their conversion (1:1-10); *(ii)* his conduct at Thessalonica (2:1-12); *(iii)* their persecution (2:13-20); *(iv)* Timothy's visit (3:1-13).

b) The practical section, 4:1-12
In this section, Paul discusses two very important subjects: *(i)* purity of life (vv.1-8); *(ii)* brotherly love (vv.9-12).

c) The prophetical section, 4:13 - 5:11
In this section, Paul turns his attention to the future, and carefully distinguishes between two future events: *(i)* an event that will bring unending joy (4:13-18); *(ii)* an event that will bring inescapable travail (5:1-11). The first deals with people destined for blessing: the second with people subject to judgment. The first deals with people taken out of the world: the second with people resident on earth. The first deals with a welcome event: the second with an unwelcome event.

d) The ecclesiastical section, 5:12 - 28
In this section, Paul deals with conduct and behaviour in the local church. The section closes with final requests and Paul's customary benediction.

Each of the five chapters in this epistle concludes with a reference to the Lord's coming.

Chapter 1 ends with **salvation** at the Lord's coming: "And to wait for his Son from heaven, whom he raised from the dead, even Jesus, which delivered us from the wrath to come."

Chapter 2 ends with **exultation** at the Lord's coming: "For what is our hope, or joy, or crown of rejoicing? Are not even ye in the presence of our Lord Jesus Christ at his coming? For ye are our glory and joy."

Chapter 3 ends with ***sanctification*** at the Lord's coming: "To the end he may stablish your hearts unblameable in holiness before God, even our Father, at the coming of our Lord Jesus Christ with all his saints."

Chapter 4 ends with ***consolation*** in view of the Lord's coming: "Then we which are alive and remain shall be caught up together with them in the clouds, to meet the Lord in the air: and so shall we ever be with the Lord. Wherefore comfort one another with these words."

Chapter 5 ends with ***preservation*** until the Lord's coming. "And the very God of peace sanctify you wholly; and I pray God your whole spirit and soul and body be preserved blameless unto the coming of our Lord Jesus Christ."

PAUL AT THESSALONICA

Read Acts 17:1-10

Before we commence our studies in 1 Thessalonians itself, we must accompany Paul to Thessalonica. His visit is described in Acts 17:1-10, and we can divide the passage as follows: *(1)* the reasoning (vv.1-3); *(2)* the response (v.4); *(3)* the riot (vv.5-10).

1) THE REASONING, vv.1-3
As we will see, it wasn't 'preaching' in the usually accepted sense of the word! It was more like a debate! We should notice the following:

a) The place
"Now when they had passed through Amphipolis and Apollonia, they came to Thessalonica, where was a synagogue of the Jews: and Paul, as his manner was, went in unto them." Compare Acts 9:20, 13:5,14. Bearing in mind that opposition almost inevitably sprang from the synagogue, he displayed remarkable zeal and conviction in making for the synagogue at Thessalonica!

Although he was the apostle to the Gentiles (Rom. 11:13; Gal. 2:7-9), Paul had a deep love for his fellow-Jews. See Romans 9:1-3; 10:1. We know, of course, that the gospel is "the power of God unto salvation to every one that believeth; to the Jew first, and also to the Greek" (Rom. 1:16). While this could refer to the historical order in which the gospel has progressed ("Jerusalem...Judaea...Samaria...the uttermost part of the earth"), there is no doubt that it was Paul's policy to preach "to the Jew first" (hence, "Paul, *as his manner was*, went in unto them") and when he reached Rome, where he was chained to a Roman soldier, the first people he contacted were Jews. See Acts 28:16-31.

There are two important lessons here. *(i)* Paul went where he knew people would congregate, and *(ii)* Paul used existing contacts. As a Jew, he could capitalise on his connections, and use them effectively in preaching the gospel. We live in a different society and a different culture. Our contacts with men and women are quite different, but like Paul, we should 'redeem the time' or 'buy up the opportunities' (Eph. 5:16; Col. 4:5).

b) The method
"And Paul, as his manner was, went in unto them, and three Sabbath days reasoned with them out of the scriptures, opening and alleging, that Christ must needs have suffered, and risen ... from the dead." There are some interesting words here!

i) Reasoning. He "reasoned *(dialegomai)* with them out of the scriptures." You can see our English word dialogue there! It's the same word in Acts 17:17 ("disputed"), 18:19 ("reasoned"), 19:8-9 ("disputing"), and 24:25 ("reasoned"). It doesn't need much imagination to see the 'cut and thrust' of debate, with the two sides arguing and counter-arguing. That would liven up our gospel meetings!

But Paul's argument was based on a solid foundation. He argued his case from the scriptures, and whether we are talking **with** people, or talking **to** people, we have absolutely nothing to say apart from the word of God. Quite obviously, Paul's 'reasoning' was based on the Old Testament scriptures, and his familiarity with them enabled him to argue with confidence. Let's make it very clear that service for God demands a good working knowledge of His word. We all begin with the man in John 9, "One thing I know, that, whereas I was blind, now I see", but we mustn't stay there. "Be ready always to give an answer to every man that asketh you a reason of the hope that is in you" (1 Pet. 3:15). Paul calls this, "the defence and confirmation of the gospel" (Phil. 1:7). Preaching, whatever form it takes, must always be thoroughly based on the scriptures, and must, therefore, always lead to Christ.

Notice, too, that Paul always bore in mind the background of his audience. With a Jewish audience, he could appeal to the scriptures and argue from them. Both preacher and hearer were on the same ground. When Paul got to Athens, he had to change his approach. He certainly went to the synagogue (Acts 17:17), but he had a totally different audience on Mars Hill, comprising "certain philosophers of the Epicureans, and of the Stoicks." He therefore referred them to creation, and to their own poetry. His address was as scriptural as anything he said in the synagogues, but the approach was quite different! Do notice, however, that in both cases, Paul got to the same destination. He preached Christ! There are important lessons for us here. We cannot assume that people know **anything** about the Bible. Past generations were at least familiar with some 'stock in trade' Bible stories, but that is not the case today.

ii) Opening. "Opening and alleging, that Christ must needs have suffered." This carries the idea of explanation. The word (*dianoigo)* means 'to open up completely' (W.E. Vine). We have a wonderful illustration of this in Luke 24:31-32, "And their eyes were **opened**, and they knew him; and he vanished out of their sight. And they said one to another, Did not our heart burn within us, while he talked with us by the way, and while he **opened** to us the scriptures?"

iii) Alleging. The word *(paratithemi)* means 'to place beside or to set before'. It is used here of 'setting subjects before one's hearers by way of argument and proof' (W.E. Vine). The three words ("reasoned...opening...alleging") emphasise that the scriptures are capable of intelligent and logical application.

c) The subject
"Opening and alleging, that Christ must needs have suffered, and risen ... from the dead; and that this Jesus, whom I preach unto you, is Christ." Paul set out to prove two things:

i) That the Old Testament required the death and resurrection of the Messiah. The title, "Messiah", as in Daniel 9:25-26, means 'the anointed' (*mashiach),* as in Psalm 2:2. The New Testament equivalent is "Christ". Paul was obliged to demonstrate that the Old Testament scriptures demanded the death and resurrection of the Messiah for the simple reason that the Jews did not expect this to happen. The two disciples *en route* to Emmaus are a case in point. "The chief priests and our rulers delivered him to be condemned to death, and have crucified him. But we trusted that it had been he which should have redeemed Israel...Then he said unto them, O fools, and slow of heart to believe all that the prophets have spoken: Ought not Christ to have suffered these things, and to enter into his glory?" (Luke 24:21-26). We can visualise the Saviour taking them through the scriptures: Psalm 22, Isaiah 50, Isaiah 53. In fact, "he expounded unto them in all the scriptures the things concerning himself." When Paul wrote to the Corinthians, he said, "Christ died for our sins according to the scriptures (the Old Testament scriptures); and that he was buried, and that he rose again the third day according to the scriptures (the Old Testament scriptures)" (1 Cor. 15:3-4). This was offensive to the Jewish mind: "We preach Christ crucified, unto the Jews a stumblingblock, and unto the Greeks foolishness" (1 Cor.1:23).

We must notice that Paul stated that "Christ **must needs** have suffered, and risen ... from the dead." This was not only because it was predicted, but because it was essential to salvation. The necessity for the death and resurrection of Christ was emphasised. In New Testament language, "And as Moses lifted up the serpent in the wilderness, even so **must** the Son of man be lifted up: that whosoever believeth in him should not perish, but have eternal life" (John 3:14-15).

ii) That Jesus was none other than the Messiah. This was Paul's final point. The long-awaited Christ of Old Testament prophecy **had** come; He **had** died; He **had** risen from the dead. Who was He? "This **Jesus,** whom I preach unto you, is Christ." Having proved from the Old Testament that Christ must suffer and rise again, Paul identifies Him. He is "this Jesus!" Luke does not give us the details of Paul's arguments here, but we can imagine that he pointed out that, in accordance with the prophecies, He was born at Bethlehem (Micah 5:2): He was of the tribe of Judah (Genesis 49:10): He was descended from Jesse, and of the royal line of David (Isaiah 11:1, 10): He came at the time predicted (Daniel 9:24-27): His appearance, character and work corresponded, for example, with the predictions in Isaiah 53: His miracles proved that He was the Messiah.

When Paul said, "that this Jesus, whom I preach unto you, is Christ", he was also speaking out of his own experience: "Who art thou, Lord? And the Lord said, I am **Jesus** whom thou persecutest" (Acts 9:5). It would have been bad enough for Paul if the Lord had said, 'I am Christ whom thou persecutest', but His words, "I am Jesus", must have devastated him. The despised and hated Jesus was speaking to him from the glory of heaven!

2) THE RESPONSE, v.4
"And some of them believed, and consorted with Paul and Silas; and of the devout Greeks a great multitude, and of the chief women not a few." Additional information is given in 1 Thessalonians. They "received the word in much affliction, with joy of the Holy Ghost" (1:6). They received the gospel "not as the word of men, but, as it is in truth, the word of God, which effectually worketh also in you that believe" (2:13). Three classes of people are named here, including Jews and Gentiles, men and women:

a) Jews in the synagogue
"And some of them believed, and consorted with Paul and Silas." We must notice the words used to describe their conversion:

i) They "believed." The word means 'persuaded' *(peitho)*. W.E. Vine explains as follows: 'to apply persuasion, to prevail upon or win over, to persuade, bringing about a change of mind by the influence of reason or moral considerations.' It occurs elsewhere in the New Testament. See, for example, Matthew 27: 20 ("But the chief priests and elders **persuaded** the multitude"); Matthew 28:14 ("And if this come to the governor's ears, we will **persuade** him"); Acts 13:43) ("Paul and Barnabas... **persuaded** them to continue in the grace of God"); Acts 19:8 ("He went into the synagogue...disputing and **persuading** the things concerning the kingdom of God"). These people were not carried away by their emotions. They were convinced and convicted by the strength of Paul's arguments. It involved their will.

ii) They "consorted with Paul and Silas." The word "consorted" *(proskleroo)* means 'to assign by lot.' Translation is, we gather, rather difficult, but it evidently has the meaning, 'they joined themselves to Paul and Silas', or, 'they threw in their lot with Paul and Silas.' We must remember that there was no assembly as yet at Thessalonica, so they identified themselves with the preachers. (The word 'consorted' is a very appropriate translation. Prince Philip is consort to H. M. The Queen. The word therefore implies loyalty, support, close association, affection and fellowship. (The AV translators are to be congratulated!)

b) "The devout Greeks"
"And of the devout Greeks a great multitude." The word "devout" *(sebomai)* means 'to feel awe', to be 'full of awe.' We are told that these were people attached to the synagogue, but as yet uncircumcised, and therefore not fully proselytised. The same word is used of Lydia in Acts 16:14 ("which worshipped God"), and Justus in Acts 18:7 ("that worshipped God"). See also Acts 13:43, "Now when the congregation was broken up, many of the Jews and religious *(sebomai)* proselytes followed Paul and Barnabas."

c) "The chief women"
"And of the chief women not a few." The word "chief" *(protos)* means 'first.' Compare Acts 17:12, "Therefore many of them believed; also of honourable women which were Greeks, and of men, not a few." The word "honourable" *(euschemon)* means 'of honourable estate', and refers to the upper classes. See also Acts 13:50: "but the Jews stirred up the devout and honourable women."

But this was not the only response to the proclamation of the gospel. As usual there were "many adversaries" (1 Cor. 16:9).

Paul's Visit

3) THE RIOT, vv.5-10

Having been told that "some of them believed" (v.4), we are now told about those that "believed not" (v.5). The gospel divides people very sharply. There is no middle course. The Lord Jesus taught that "he that is not for us, is against us." Men either accept Christ, or reject Him. We should notice three things here: *(a)* the agitators (v.5); *(b)* the accusation (vv.6-8); *(c)* the action (vv.9-10).

a) The agitators, v.5

"But the Jews which believed not, moved with envy (*zeloo*: 'jealousy'), took unto them certain lewd fellows of the baser sort, and gathered a company, and set all the city on an uproar, and assaulted the house of Jason, and sought to bring them out to the people." The Jews, having lost the argument in the synagogue, turned hostile, and went for the man. This is exactly what happened in the case of Stephen. The Jewish leaders were unable to "resist the wisdom and the spirit by which he spake", so they turned to violence and false accusation. Read Acts 6:10-12. But this is exactly what happened in the case of the Lord Jesus. Pilate "knew that for envy *(phthonos)* they had delivered him" (Matt. 27:18). W.E. Vine differentiates between envy and jealousy as follows: "envy desires to deprive another of what he has: jealousy desires to have the same or the same sort of thing for itself". In this case, Jewish jealousy was engendered by the results of Paul's preaching. Suffering and persecution are the norm in Christian experience. See Philippians 1:29-30.

The greatest opposition to the gospel has always come from institutionalised religion. In the case of the Jews, Paul observes, they "both killed the Lord Jesus, and their own prophets, and have persecuted us; and they please not God, and are contrary to all men: forbidding us to speak to the Gentiles that they might be saved" (1 Thess. 2:15-16). We have only to think of the dreadful persecutions initiated by Rome to illustrate religious hostility to the gospel over many centuries.

The Jews did not do 'the dirty work' themselves. They hired the local 'Rentamob' to do the job for them. They "took unto them certain lewd fellows of the baser sort." The RV has, 'vile fellows of the rabble.' The word "lewd" *(poneros)* means 'evil in influence and effect.' The words, "baser sort", are literally, 'of the market place.' So they were 'idle persons of the market place.' But 'Rentamob' says it all!

b The accusation, vv.6-8

"And when they found them not, they drew Jason and certain brethren unto the rulers *(politarchs*: the elected leaders or magistrates) of the city, crying, These

245

that have turned the world upside down are come hither also; whom Jason hath received: and these all do contrary to the decrees of Caesar, saying that there is another king, one Jesus. And they troubled the people and the rulers of the city, when they heard these things." It has been conjectured that Jason was a kinsman of Paul (see Romans 16:21). Quite clearly, he was a courageous man. He willingly identified himself with the unpopular preachers. People at Thessalonica had a price to pay when they 'threw in their lot with Paul and Silas.' There were two charges:

i) That the preachers had caused trouble. The oft-quoted words, "these that have turned the world upside down", mean, 'these that have set the world in tumult' (JND). The words "turned...upside down" translate *'anastatoo'*, which means 'to stir up, excite, unsettle' (W.E. Vine). In actual fact, the tumults were caused, not by the gospel preachers, but by the people that opposed them. It was the "lewd fellows of the baser sort", incited by the Jews, who "set all the city on an uproar." It happened again at Berea. See v.13. The gospel requires believers to be good citizens. See 1 Peter 2:11-17.

ii) That the preachers had incited rebellion. "These all do contrary to the decrees of Caesar, saying that there is another king, one Jesus." The Jews had done this before: see Luke 23:2, "And they began to accuse him, saying, We found this fellow perverting the nation, and forbidding to give tribute to Caesar, saying that he himself is Christ a King." See also John 19:12-15. Compare Matthew 2:1-3. Paul and his colleagues were therefore following the footsteps of the Lord Himself. Both the Lord Jesus and His servants were accused of a political crime. It seems extremely likely that the charge arose out of preaching about the kingdom of God. The message had been deliberately misquoted and misrepresented in order to fabricate a false charge. The strategy certainly had the desired effect at Thessalonica: "they troubled the people and the rulers of the city, when they heard these things". The Jews used this strategy against Stephen, "This man ceaseth not to speak blasphemous words against this holy place, and the law: for we have heard him say, that this Jesus of Nazareth shall destroy this place, and shall change the customs which Moses delivered us" (Acts 6:8-15). As noted above, they did it again at Berea (v.13).

c) The action, vv.9-10
"And when they had taken security of Jason, and of the other, they let them go. And the brethren immediately sent away Paul and Silas by night unto Berea." The "security" was probably a bond as part of an undertaking that Paul would not return to the city. Paul possibly refers to this in 1 Thessalonians 2:18.

The fact that "the brethren immediately sent away Paul and Silas", may well imply that the new converts had made good spiritual progress, and were able to maintain the testimony themselves. We know from 1 & 2 Thessalonians that they had received good balanced teaching, and that they continued steadfastly under pressure. The expression, "the **brethren**...sent away Paul and Silas", is most significant. Not now believing Jews, or "devout Greeks", or "chief women", but "the brethren!" Old divisions are done away. The term "brethren" includes "the chief women." Paul refers to his readers as "brethren" twenty-four times in his two letters to them.

As we have already noted, the word "brethren" is used by the Lord Jesus to describe all who trust in Him. See John 20:17 and Hebrews 2:11-12. We are *His* "brethren." When believers meet together, they do so as "brethren" (including brothers and sisters) without any further distinction. Titles, status, culture, colour, etc, divide men and women in the world, but they must never cause division in the assembly.

> Oft we forget that we are one
> With every saint that loves His Name –
> To Him united on the throne,
> Our life, our hope, our Lord the same.

READ CHAPTER 1:1-4

"We give thanks to God"

As we noticed in our introduction, preachers frequently refer to the assembly at Thessalonica as 'a model church.' This description is based on the words, "Ye were ensamples *(tupos)* to all that believe in Macedonia and Achaia" (1:7). Paul certainly didn't have a church 'league table', but he spoke highly of this assembly in both epistles. Compare 2 Thessalonians 1:3-4: "we ourselves glory in you in the churches of God for your patience and faith in all your persecutions and tribulations that ye endure." We do not have to read far in either epistle before meeting the excellent spiritual qualities of these believers.

1 Thessalonians 1 can be divided into three paragraphs: *(1)* the reasons for thanksgiving (vv.1-4): "We give thanks to God always for you all... remembering"; *(2)* their response to the gospel (vv.5-7): "Ye...received the word in much affliction, with joy of the Holy Ghost"; *(3)* the reality of their faith (vv.8-10): "They themselves shew of us...how ye turned to God from idols."

1) THE REASONS FOR THANKSGIVING, vv.1-4
There are at least four important things to notice in these opening verses. They can be summarised as follows: *(a)* the position of the church (v.1); *(b)* the prayer for the church (v.2); *(c)* the progress of the church (v.3); *(d)* the people in the church (v.4).

a) The position of the church, v.1
"Paul, and Silvanus, and Timotheus, unto the church of the Thessalonians which is in God the Father and in the Lord Jesus Christ: Grace be unto you, and peace, from God our Father, and the Lord Jesus Christ."

Paul, Silas and Timothy had all laboured and suffered at Thessalonica (Acts 17:10-14), and it was therefore appropriate that all three should greet the assembly there. Solomon tells us that "a threefold cord is not quickly broken" (Eccl. 4:12). The composition of the trio is significant. Paul was an apostle, Silas was one of the "chief men among the brethren" (Acts 15:22), and Timothy was a younger man (1 Tim. 4:12). A good balance! Older and younger believers should always be willing to work together. Younger believers should value the help and experience of older believers, and older believers should give every encouragement to younger believers.

Notice that Paul does not mention his apostleship. This is significant. It was unnecessary for him to assert his authority. See also Philippians and Philemon. Compare Galatians 1:1, where he strongly emphasises his apostleship. Grave doctrinal error had infected the believers in Galatia, and this must be dealt with by an authoritative man. But Paul had every reason to rejoice over the assembly at Thessalonica. Additionally, the believers there were under severe pressure, and Paul wrote to encourage them. He did not adopt a standard introduction when he wrote his epistles, but 'tailored' his approach to suit the circumstances at the time.

The epistle is addressed, not to 'the church at Thessalonica' (compare "the church of God which is at Corinth": "the churches of Galatia"), but to "the church of the Thessalonians." (For the meaning of "church", see addendum). This possibly reflects Paul's special interest in every believer. They were his spiritual children. He had tended them as "a nurse (nursing mother) cherisheth her (own) children", and had "exhorted and comforted and charged" every one of them, "as a father doth his children" (2:7, 11).

The "church of the Thessalonians" was located in two places. It was, obviously, at Thessalonica, but it was, equally, in "God our Father and in the Lord Jesus Christ." See also 2 Thessalonians 1:1.

i) It was on earth, and in time
It was "the church of the Thessalonians." This reminded them of their earthly and local responsibilities. With this in mind, they were urged to "study to be quiet, and to do your own business, and to work with your own hands, as we commanded you; that ye may walk honestly toward them that are without, and that ye may have lack of nothing." See also 2 Thessalonians 3:10-12.

ii) It was in heaven, and in eternity
The church was "in God our Father and in the Lord Jesus Christ." As believers at Thessalonica, they were subject to harm and danger. As believers "in God our Father and in the Lord Jesus Christ", they were beyond harm and danger. Their spiritual life was secure. They were shielded and protected from "every evil work."

The words, "*In* God our Father and in the Lord Jesus Christ", emphasise the impossibility of separation from them. The title, "God our **Father**", emphasises His love. The title, "**Lord** Jesus Christ", emphasises His authority.

The well-known words, "grace be unto you, and peace", remind us that the Lord Jesus brought us grace (Titus 2:11), and left us peace (John 14:27). The order is important. It is "grace...and peace", not 'peace...and grace!' There could not be peace apart from grace. Peace is the result of grace!

The greeting comes jointly from "God our Father" and "the Lord Jesus Christ", emphasising the Saviour's deity. The characteristic greeting amongst Greeks was 'Rejoice!' (*chairete*), but Paul uses "grace" *(charis)*. The characteristic greeting amongst Jews was 'Peace!' (*shalom*). See Matthew 10:12-13, Luke 10:5. Notice that on the resurrection morning, the Saviour greeted the women with, "All hail" (literally, 'O joy': from *chairo,* to rejoice), and in the evening, He greeted the disciples with, "Peace be unto you", John 20:19. See also John 20:26.

b) The prayer for the church, v.2
"We (Paul, Silas and Timothy) give thanks to God always for you all, making mention (translated 'remembrance' elsewhere) of you in our prayers." We must notice: *(i)* The order. Thanksgiving is placed first, followed by petition: "making mention of you in our prayers"; *(ii)* The occasion. 'We constantly give thanks.' The word "always" *(pantote)* means 'on all occasions' (W.E. Vine). *(iii)* The occupation. "Making mention of you in our prayers *(proseuche)*" or "making mention of you at our prayers' (JND). Paul's thanksgiving and prayers were consistent ("always") and comprehensive ("for you all"). His thanksgiving and prayer were based on what they had displayed (v.3), and on what God had displayed (v.4). This brings us to:

c) The progress of the church, v.3
"Remembering without ceasing your work of faith, and labour of love, and patience of hope in our Lord Jesus Christ, in the sight of God and our Father." W.E.Vine has an interesting and illuminating piece here: "An old papyrus letter, lately discovered in Egypt but written as far back as the Apostles' days, speaks of an "incessant cough." Thus, not uninterrupted prayer, but constantly recurring prayer, is the thought here". The three things mentioned by the apostle embrace past, present and future.

i) "Your work of faith"
This is expanded in v.9: "ye turned to God from idols".The Lord Jesus defined

the "work of faith" as follows: "this is the work of God, that ye **believe** on him whom he hath sent" (John 6:29).

ii) "Your…labour of love"
This is expanded in v.9: "to serve the living and true God." The word "labour" *(kopos)* signifies 'toil resulting in weariness.' (See also 5:12, "know them which labour among you"). It was a "labour of **love.**" This translates the Greek word *'agape.'* God's service will become a chore, and ultimately dry up altogether, if it does not flow from love for God and Christ. The Lord Jesus emphasised this when speaking to Peter about his future service. "Simon, son of Jonas, lovest *(agape)* thou me more than these…Simon, son of Jonas, lovest *(agape)* thou me?" (John 21:15-16).

iii) "Your…patience of hope"
This is expanded in v.10: "to wait for his Son from heaven, whom he raised from the dead, even Jesus, which delivered us from the wrath to come." The word "patience" *(hupomone)* is better translated 'endurance.' Their anticipation of the Lord's return enabled them to endure under trial. Hence, Paul writes: "Your…patience of hope **in our Lord Jesus Christ**". We should notice that "hope" is connected with the unseen and with the future (Rom. 8:24-25).

It has often been pointed out that the Lord Jesus referred to the same three characteristics at Ephesus: "I know thy works, and thy labour, and thy patience" (Rev. 2:2). But faith, love, and hope are omitted. Works, labour and patience are all praiseworthy in themselves, but it will be a case of 'going through the motions', if they are not empowered by a vital and ongoing relationship with God. God saw the inward reality of the believers at Thessalonica: "Remembering without ceasing your work of faith, and labour of love, and patience of hope in our Lord Jesus Christ, in **the sight of God and our Father.**" It was a question of cause and effect: Paul could discern the **cause** of the great change in their lives ("faith…love…hope, v.3). People in Macedonia and Achaia could see the **effect** (vv.9-10).

The words, "in the sight of God and our Father" ('before our God and Father', JND), also remind us that He was thoroughly aware of their difficult and trying circumstances.

d) The people in the church, v.4
"Knowing, brethren beloved, your election of God" or "Knowing, brethren beloved of God, your election" (JND). He describes the believers at Thessalonica in three ways:

i) "Brethren"

As we have noted previously, and if our addition is correct, the word occurs twenty-four times in 1 & 2 Thessalonians. The once proud Pharisee addresses the once despised Gentiles as "brethren!" The Lord Jesus made the relationship clear in Mark 3:31-35, "For whosoever shall do the will of God, the same is **my brother**, and my sister, and my mother."

Earthly relationships end with death, but not spiritual relationships. This relationship commences with the new birth when, in the case of Thessalonica, believing Jews, devout Greeks and honourable women (Acts 17:4), became "brethren" (Acts 17:10). At the end of this epistle, Paul refers to "all the holy brethren" (5:27). This does not refer to a particular class of believers at Thessalonica, but to every one of them. We are all "holy brethren, partakers of the heavenly calling" (Heb. 3:1). This is explained in Hebrews 2:11-12, "For both he that sanctifieth and they who are sanctified are all of one: for which cause he is not ashamed to call them brethren, Saying, I will declare thy name unto my brethren, in the midst of the church will I sing praise unto thee."

ii) "Beloved"

The linguists tell us that this is in the perfect tense, meaning the abiding result of a past act. Compare Revelation 1:5, "Unto him that loveth us" (R.V.). The love that He displayed toward us at Calvary, continues to embrace us. We are not only "brethren", we are "brethren beloved."

iii) 'Elect'

In Ephesians 1, the subject of election is related to eternity, "He hath chosen us in him before the foundation of the world", and to time, "that we should be holy and without blame before him in love" Eph. 1:4). Here, the second is emphasised. This is clear from the words, **"knowing,** brethren beloved, your election of God." Paul knew that they were God's elect by observation. The verb '*oida*' (to know) "intimates that this knowledge came, not by revelation, nor by intuition, but from observation; hence the rest of the chapter recounts what led Paul to conclude that these Thessalonians were among the elect of God" (W.E. Vine).

Election is not an abstract doctrine. It is never taught in a vacuum. The New Testament always emphasises its practical results. See, for example, Ephesians 2:10; 2 Peter 1:10. Rightly understood, the doctrine of election glorifies the love and grace of God. It should never become the 'bench mark' of spirituality, and lead to boasting and pride. As A.C. Gooding once observed, "Some people argue over election: I like to sit down and enjoy it!"

Chapter 1

It has been rightly said that 'truth, taken to its logical conclusion, becomes error.' While believers can say, "God...hath saved us, and called us with an holy calling, not according to our works, but according to his own purpose and grace, which was given us in Christ Jesus before the world began" (2 Tim. 1:9), this does not mean that He has selected others for judgement. When Paul and Barnabas preached at Antioch, "as many as were ordained to eternal life believed" (Acts 13:48), but that does not infer that the rest were 'ordained to eternal damnation.' This is human inference, not Biblical teaching. God "will have all men to be saved, and to come unto the knowledge of the truth" (1 Tim. 2:4).

The doctrines of God's sovereignty and human responsibility are both taught in Scripture. We have an example in John 6:37, "All that the Father giveth me shall come to me; and him that cometh to me I will in no wise cast out." Notice God's sovereignty, and man's responsibility, in Acts 2:23: "Him, being delivered by the determinate counsel and foreknowledge of **God, ye** have taken, and by wicked hands have crucified and slain."

Paul links election with gospel preaching as follows: "But we are bound to give thanks alway to God for you, brethren beloved of the Lord, because God hath from the beginning chosen you to salvation through sanctification of the Spirit and belief of the truth: whereunto he called you by our gospel, to the obtaining of the glory of our Lord Jesus Christ" (2 Thess. 2:13-14).

Paul now discusses his preaching at Thessalonica, and we will consider this in our next study.

Addendum

In our New Testament, the word "church" comes from the Greek word *ekklesia* (hence our English, *ecclesiastic*) which has two simple parts: *ek,* meaning 'out of', and *klesis,* meaning 'a calling.' We therefore learn, immediately, that in the New Testament, the word "church" cannot refer to the building in which people meet, but to the people themselves. This should be obvious to all who read the New Testament, which refers to "the church in thy house" (Philemon v.2). After all, you can't get a church, in the usually accepted sense, into a house!

In fact *ekklesia* is more accurately rendered 'assembly' or 'congregation', and it is worth pointing out that this is not a denominational title (we sometimes hear people say, 'churches and assemblies'), but a good Bible word. Don't be ashamed of it! So, in simple terms, it describes people who have been gathered or called out **from** something, and gathered or called **to** something. The word was used generally in New Testament times, e.g. Acts 19.32 ("the **assembly** was confused; and the more part knew not wherefore they were come together); Acts 19:39 ("If ye enquire any thing concerning other matters, it shall be determined in a lawful **assembly**"); Acts 19:41, ("And when he had thus spoken, he dismissed the **assembly**"). While, quite obviously, there is no allusion here to "the church" in the technical sense, these references do clearly illustrate the meaning of the word. But if the people in Acts 19 had been called out of their homes and from their workshops to attend a meeting in the theatre, in what way is the word *ekklesia* usually employed in the New Testament?

Let's answer this by citing 1 Corinthians 1:2, which refers to one of "the churches": "the church of God which is at Corinth...them that are sanctified in Christ Jesus." Corinth was a vile place (6.9-11), but there was a body of people in the city who were totally different. The "church of God...at Corinth" describes men and women who had severed their association with the immorality and depravity of Corinth, and who had been brought into fellowship with God. In short, the church is a body of people **called out of the world** with its sin and immorality, with its pleasures and pursuits, and with its politics and religion, and **called into sacred fellowship with God** through His Son, the Lord Jesus Christ.

Remember, "the church is the people, not the steeple!"

The following report by Eric Browning and Anton Stier, in connection with the work of the Society for the Distribution of Hebrew Scriptures, shows that history has a habit of repeating itself. There is a striking similarity between AD54 and AD 1997!

Visit to Thessalonica with the Gospel – November 1997

"These were more noble than those in Thessalonica, in that they received the word with all readiness of mind" (Acts 17:11). We left Istanbul on the 20th November for Thessalonica in Greece. After finding a hotel and a night's rest, we went to the Jewish Community Centre, where we met with a Rabbi, whom we learned was a leader of the community. On hearing our purpose, he flatly refused any Scriptures for himself and the other members of the large office. It was disappointing, but we always remember that when rejection occurs, this is the Lord's work, and that He knows the end from the beginning. We have since prayed that the Lord will present another opportunity for him to receive the Written Word and the Living Word. Next we went to a Jewish museum, where the attendant gladly received two boxes from us, one for the museum library and the other for the Curator. In Acts 17, the Jews of Thessalonica made it so difficult for Paul and Silas that they had to leave. Nearly two thousand years later, we did not have to leave, but the Word was rejected again on behalf of those who need it as we do. Let us remember the Jews of Thessalonica in our prayer times.

READ CHAPTER 1:5-10

"Ye were ensamples to all that believe"

In introducing this chapter, we suggested that it can be divided into three paragraphs: *(1)* the reasons for thanksgiving (vv.1-4): "We give thanks to God always for you all...remembering"; *(2)* their response to the gospel (vv.5-7): "Ye...received the word in much affliction, with joy of the Holy Ghost"; *(3)* the reality of their faith (vv.8-10): "They themselves shew of us...how ye turned to God from idols."

1) THE REASONS FOR THANKSGIVING, vv.1-4
In the opening verses of the chapter, Paul deals with the following: *(a)* the position of the church (v.1); *(b* the prayer for the church (v.2); *(c)* the progress of the church (v.3); *(d)* the people in the church (v.4). This brings us to:

2) THEIR RESPONSE TO THE GOSPEL, vv.5-7
In this paragraph, we must notice *(a)* the preaching (v.5); *(b)* the preachers (v.5); *(c)* the product (vv.6-7).

a) The preaching, v.5
"For our gospel came not unto you in word only, but also in power, and in the Holy Ghost, and in much assurance." Paul refers to the gospel in various ways. For example, in this epistle, "the gospel of God" (2:2, 8, 9), which emphasises its source and authority; "the gospel of Christ" (3:2), which emphasises its subject. Elsewhere he describes it as the "glorious gospel of Christ" (2 Cor. 4:4) or, "the gospel of the glory of Christ" (RV), and as the "glorious gospel of the blessed God" (1 Tim. 1:11) or "the gospel of the glory of the blessed God" (RV). But here, the apostle calls it "our gospel", and elsewhere "my gospel" (Rom. 2:16; 2 Tim. 2:8). This emphasises the deep personal interest in the gospel on the part of the preachers. It was precious to them. They felt its weight. They did not preach dispassionately.

Their preaching was more than a statement of faith. It was not "in word *(logos)* only", but "also in power, and in the Holy Ghost, and in much assurance." We must notice, however, that while the gospel preaching was more than "in word only", it was certainly "in word!" Gospel preaching must have a doctrinal content. It must be scriptural. Paul "reasoned with them out of the scriptures, opening and alleging, that Christ must needs have suffered, and risen again from the dead; and that this Jesus, whom I preach unto you, is Christ" (Acts 17:2-3). The use of *logos* here (not *rhema*, the spoken word) refers to the message preached, rather than the actual preaching.

But the "word" was accompanied by divine power. This does not mean that they were marvellous orators! A man can be an orator, and have nothing to say of spiritual value! Changed lives proved the power of the preaching. "Ye turned to God from idols." The words, "in power *(en dunamei)*, and in the Holy Ghost", mean, 'even in the power of the Holy Ghost.' If the gospel is to be effective, it must be preached through the enabling of the Spirit of God. See 1 Peter 4:11, "If any man speak, let him speak as the oracles of God." (Peter is evidently referring here to Bible teaching as opposed to gospel preaching, but the principle remains the same). The Old Testament prophets spoke as the mouthpiece of God. See, for example, 2 Chronicles 36:22. It was through Isaiah, speaking as God's mouthpiece, that God said, "So shall my word be that goeth forth out of my mouth" (Isa. 55:11). Paul and his colleagues did not preach with self-assurance. Their "much assurance" was rooted in their consciousness of the help and power of the Holy Spirit. They had every confidence in the message they preached. They did not preach apologetically. They knew that the gospel was "the power of God unto salvation to every one that believeth" (Rom. 1:16). Notice too, that there were no miraculous signs.

Jude urges us to pray "in the Holy Ghost" (v.20), that is, in accordance with the will of the Holy Spirit, and Paul preached "in the Holy Ghost", that is, in the power of the Holy Spirit.

b) The preachers, v.5
"As ye know what manner of men we were among you for your sake." There was no inconsistency between the message and the messengers. Paul develops this in Chapter 2:1-6, where the expression, "as ye know", is repeated. The demeanour of the preachers commended their preaching. The lives of Paul and his colleagues commended the gospel, and therefore contributed to the eternal blessing of the Thessalonians. Their lives, as well as their preaching, was "for your sake." Now that's worth remembering! What we **say** may be right, but are **we** right? We could endanger the effectiveness of the message by bad behaviour.

c) The product, vv.6-7

"And ye became followers of us, and of the Lord, having received the word *(logos)* in much affliction (it was preached with "much assurance", and received with "much affliction"), with joy of the Holy Ghost. So that ye were ensamples to all that believe in Macedonia and Achaia." The Thessalonians became "followers (imitators)" (v.6), "ensamples" (v.7), and heralds (v.8).

i) "Followers", v.6

They became "followers" of Paul and his colleagues, not by becoming their disciples, but in their changed manner of life. They then became examples to others (v.7)! However, the context suggests that the Thessalonians 'became imitators of us, and of the Lord' in suffering and persecution. See also 2:14, "For ye, brethren, became followers (imitators) of the churches of God which in Judaea are in Christ Jesus: for ye also have suffered like things of your own countrymen, even as they have of the Jews." The word, "followers" (imitators), is used in another context in 1 Corinthians 4:16; 11:1, Ephesians 5:1. The word "became" is in the aorist tense, indicating a decisive act. The same tense is used in v.9: "Ye turned to God from idols". Two things become immediately clear:

- **The animosity they experienced**. The gospel was not generally attractive. Those who "received the word" did so "in much affliction."

- **The reality they displayed**. The gospel produced abiding results. In the 'parable of the sower', men received the word with joy, but affliction followed, with disastrous results. See Matthew 13:20-21. But that is reversed here! The word was received "in much affliction", and joy followed! Compare Romans 5:1-5. These believers also rejoiced amidst persecution. Notice, too, that Paul himself rejoiced in his afflictions. See 3:7-9.

In this connection, we should notice the **outward circumstances** in which they "received the word: it was "in much affliction", and **the inward condition**: it was "with joy of the Holy Ghost." The former could not touch the latter! Notice too that there is no hint of the so-called 'second blessing' here: they "received the word" in much affliction, **with** joy of the Holy Ghost." (Notice the ministry of the Holy Spirit in the preachers, v.5; and in the hearers, v.6). But the affliction they experienced did not hinder their spiritual development. They became:

ii) "Ensamples", v.7

"So that ye were ensamples ('models', JND) to all that believe in Macedonia and

Achaia." (The word *'tupos'*, rendered "ensamples" here, is translated "print" in John 20:25, "Except I shall see in his hands the print of the nails..."). In v.6, they received the gospel individually: in v.7, they were an example collectively: "so that ye became an ensample to all that believe in Macedonia and Achaia" (RV), although JND is not so sure: see his marginal note. The believers at Thessalonica were a fitting pattern for others to follow in two ways: by their **conduct** (v.6): they "received the word in much affliction, with joy of the Holy Ghost" and by their **confession** (v.8). The order is important. Their good confession was rooted in their good conduct. As we have noted, they also became *(iii)* heralds, and Paul now turns to this in describing:

3) THE REALITY OF THEIR FAITH, vv.8-10
This was demonstrated *(a)* in their testimony **to** others (v.8), and *(b)* in the testimony **of** others (vv.9-10).

a) Their testimony to others, v.8
"For from you sounded out the word of the Lord not only in Macedonia and Achaia, but also in every place your faith to God-ward is spread abroad; so that we need not to speak any thing." Our contributor Justin Waldron draws attention to the three occurrences of the expression, "the word of the Lord", in the Thessalonian Epistles: here it stresses the **authority** of the word: in 4:15, it stresses the **assurance** of the word, and in 2 Thessalonians 3:1 it stresses the **activity** of the word. The word "you" ("For from you") is plural. So they **all** 'rolled up their sleeves' and got involved in this great work of evangelising the area. It wasn't left to a few. We should all ask ourselves, 'How can **I** be engaged in gospel work?' In what capacity can **I** serve God? The practical change in their lives was unmistakeable: "in **every place** your **faith to God-ward** is spread abroad". We should notice at least three things here:

i) The centre of their witness
"From **you** sounded out the word of the Lord." The assembly at Thessalonica was the base from which the believers launched out with the gospel. We must remember that in the New Testament, an evangelist was a pioneer. He went to places where the gospel had not been preached before. He didn't go from assembly to assembly, holding gospel campaigns! See Acts 8:5; Romans 15:20-21. Paul was certainly not 'higgledy-piggledy;' in his approach. He majored on centres of population. He preached in places which had a commanding position in the country, from which the gospel could spread to the surrounding areas. Once established, local churches were responsible for evangelising their own districts. Hence, at Thessalonica, "from **you** sounded out the word of the Lord."

This reminds us that assemblies should have specific aims in their evangelism. All too often, gospel work is conducted on a 'hit and miss' basis.

ii) The clarity of their witness
"From you **sounded out** the word of the Lord." The words, 'sounded out', mean "to sound forth as a trumpet or thunder" (W.E. Vine). The English word 'echo' is derived from the Greek word here *(execheo)*. W.E. Vine observes that the expression "commonly refers to the sounding of a herald's trumpet". A similar word *(echos)* occurs in Acts 2:2 ("And suddenly there came a **sound** from heaven"), and Hebrews 12:19 ("the **sound** of a trumpet"). A different word *(phone)* is used in 1 Corinthians 14:8.

This emphasises the need for clarity and simplicity. Ezra and the Levites "read in the book in the law of God distinctly, and gave the sense, and caused them to understand the reading" (Neh. 8: 8). Gospel preachers should never forget that their business is to make people understand their need to be saved, and how they can be saved. Make it clear! Keep it simple! A trumpet emits a clear note! On a practical note, it is important to speak up! Preachers should put a sufficient gap between their upper and lower teeth (or dentures). Don't mumble, preacher, and don't drop your voice. Remember, your message must be clear, and so must your voice!

iii) The content of their witness
"From you sounded out the **word of the Lord**." Once again, Paul uses *'logos'*, meaning, as we have seen, the message preached, rather than the actual preaching. This statement can be understood in various ways, all of which are mutually complementary:

- It is *"the word of the Lord"* as to its **origin**. It is His word. Hence the expressions, "the gospel of God", and "the gospel of Christ." It is not our property, and therefore we must not tamper with it. Jeremiah said, *"**Thy** words were found, and I did eat them; and **thy** word was unto me the joy and rejoicing of mine heart"* (Jer. 15:16).

- It is the *"word of the Lord"* as to its **subject.** Hence Paul wrote, "We preach not ourselves, but Christ Jesus the Lord; and ourselves your servants for Jesus' sake" (2 Cor. 4:5); "Preaching peace by Jesus Christ: (he is Lord of all)" (Acts 10:36).

- It is the *"word of the Lord"* as to its **authority**. This applies to the preachers. They have a duty to proclaim "the whole counsel of God." See, for example,

Matthew 28:19-20, "Go ye therefore, and teach (make disciples) all nations, baptizing them in the name of the Father, and of the Son, and of the Holy Ghost; teaching them to observe all things whatsoever I have commanded you." This applies to the hearers. They have a responsibility to obey.

Very clearly, we have a duty to emulate the Thessalonians. They not only preached "the word of the Lord", but they preached **nothing else** but "the word of the Lord." This was recognised by everybody: "not only in Macedonia and Achaia, but also in every place your faith to God-ward is spread abroad; so that we need not to speak any thing." It was not just a case of enthusiastic preaching. The preachers were known for the change in their lives.

b) The testimony of others, vv.9-10

"For they themselves shew of us what manner of entering in we had unto you, and how ye turned to God from idols to serve the living and true God; and to wait for his Son from heaven, whom he raised from the dead, even Jesus, which delivered us from the wrath to come." We must notice what they said about the preachers, and what they said about the converts:

i) About the preachers

"For they themselves shew of us what manner of entering in we had unto you." This refers to v.5, "For our gospel came not unto you in word only, but also in power, and in the Holy Ghost, and in much assurance." See also 2:1, "For yourselves, brethren, know our entrance in unto you, that it was not in vain."

ii) About the converts

People noticed three great changes in the converts, and we could call this 'the consistency of their witness.' We must notice their **salvation** ("ye turned to God from idols"), their **occupation** ("to serve the living and true God"), and their **anticipation** ("to wait for his Son from heaven"). They were:

- **Distinctive people.** "Ye turned to God from idols." They had a new **object.** They were known for the change in their lives. The word "turned" *(epistrepho)* signifies a deliberate act. It is sometimes translated 'converted.' The change in their lives followed a deliberate choice. See Psalm 51:13, "Then will I teach transgressors thy ways; and sinners shall be converted unto thee." This was their "work of faith" (v.3).

Paul does not say, 'Ye turned from idols to God', but "Ye turned to God from idols". W.E. Vine puts it like this: "The order is significant; the motive in this conversion was not that they were repelled by the grossness of their idols, but that they were attracted by the character of God". We need to remember that this should be ongoing in our lives. See 1 John 5:21. Is God still overwhelmingly attractive to **us?**

- **Devoted people.** "To serve the living and true God." They had a new **occupation.** They served as bondslaves. Once "the servants (bondslaves, *doulos*) of sin", they had become "the servants of righteousness", Romans 6:17-18. This was their "labour of love", v.3.

They were occupied in the service of the "living and true God." The word "living" means rather more than the opposite of 'dead.' It conveys the idea of activity. See Acts 14:15, "We also are men of like passions with you, and preach unto you that ye should turn from these vanities unto the living God, which made heaven, and earth, and the sea, and all things that are therein." The word "true" means rather more than the opposite of 'false.' It conveys the idea of reality and genuineness. Paul refers here to Jeremiah 10:10, "But the Lord is the true God, he is the living God, and an everlasting King."

- **Durable people.** "To wait for his Son from heaven, whom he raised from the dead, even Jesus, which delivered us from the wrath to come." They had a new **outlook.** The word translated "wait" *(anameno)* occurs only here in the New Testament. (In the Septuagint Version, '*anameno*' occurs in Job 7:2). It "carries with it the suggestion of waiting with patience and confident expectancy" (W.E. Vine). It is active, rather than passive. (A different word is used in 1 Corinthians 1:7, "waiting for the coming of our Lord Jesus Christ"). This was their "patience of hope" (v.3). They lived in the light of the Lord's return. Compare Genesis 49:18, Isaiah 25:9. We can analyse v.10 as follows.

- **The Person:** "His **Son.**" This emphasises His greatness. "The Son of God, who loved me, and gave himself for me." He will come for us!

- **The place:** "His Son **from heaven.**" The preposition, "from" *(ek:* out of), means that He will come out from heaven.

- **The pledge:** "His Son from heaven, whom he **raised from the dead**." Paul uses the same preposition again, "from" *(ek),* with the same meaning. He came out of death. The Lord's resurrection is the guarantee of His coming. The name "Jesus" emphasises His humanity. As man, He went into death, and came out of death, thereby assuring us that every believer who dies will rise again. See

4:14, "If we believe that Jesus died and rose again, even so them also which sleep in Jesus will God bring with him."

- **The prospect:** "which delivered us from the wrath to come" or "our deliverer from the coming wrath" (JND).' In this case, the preposition, "from", translates *'apo'* ('away from') in the Received Text, but *'ek'* elsewhere. For a technical discussion, see *The Epistles to the Thessalonians*, Hogg and Vine. While the word "wrath" *(orge)* is used of eternal judgment, it is more frequently used of wrath on earth. T.E. Wilson *(What the Bible Teaches – 1 Thessalonians)* points out that the word *orge* is used five times of the Great Tribulation in Revelation 6-19. (6:16, 17; 11:18; 16:19; 19:15). In this case, the 'coming wrath', is the wrath connected with the "day of the Lord" (5:2, 9). The church will not pass through this period of unparalleled judgment on earth. Notice that the word "wrath" occurs three times in the epistle: See 1:10, 2:16 and 5:9.

> The wrath of God that was our due
> Upon the Lamb was laid;
> And by the shedding of His blood
> The debt for us was paid.

In the Old Testament, **Ruth** "turned to God from idols", served "the living and true God", and waited for the kinsman-redeemer! **Abraham** "turned to God from idols", served "the living and true God", and "looked for a city which hath foundations, whose builder and maker is God." (D.Buckeridge).

READ CHAPTER 2:1-12

"Our entrance...was not in vain"

1 Thessalonians 2 can be divided into two major sections: *(1)* Paul's presence at Thessalonica (vv.1-16); *(2)* Paul's absence from Thessalonica (vv.17-20). However, we will divide the chapter into three sections as follows: *(1)* the responsibilities of the preachers (vv.1-12): how gospel of God was conveyed to them; *(2)* the response of the hearers (vv.13-16): how the word of God was received by them; *(3)* the renewal of fellowship (vv.17-20): how the servants of God desired to be with them.

The chapter expands Paul's statement in 1:9, "For they themselves shew of us what manner of entering in *(eisodos)* we had unto you, and how ye turned to God from idols to serve the living and true God." The words, "what manner of entering in we had unto you", are expanded in vv.1-12, and the words, "and how ye turned to God from idols", are expanded in vv.13-16.

1) THE RESPONSIBILITIES OF THE PREACHERS, vv.1-12
In this section, Paul refers to his ministry at Thessalonica. (Strictly speaking, 'their ministry at Thessalonica'!). He describes *(a)* his gospel preaching (vv.1-6) and *(b)* his pastoral care (vv.7-12). It is important to notice that Paul and his colleagues were not 'hit and run' preachers. Having preached the gospel, they spent time caring for the converts and planting new assemblies. In the case of the Thessalonians, Paul was obliged to leave very quickly, but he remained at Corinth for at least eighteen months (Acts 18:11, 18), and at Ephesus for three years (Acts 20:31).

"For yourselves, brethren, know our entrance in unto you, that it was not in vain." (The word "vain", *kenos*, means 'empty': see also 1 Cor. 15:10, 58). The very existence of the assembly, at Thessalonica was adequate proof of this statement! Paul could address them as "brethren." There could be no better witnesses to the triumphs of the Gospel at Thessalonica than the Thessalonians themselves! This is why the word, "yourselves", is in a position of emphasis in the sentence.

The expression, "our entrance in unto you" (see also 1:9), refers, not to their initial arrival at Thessalonica, but to the whole period of their stay. Paul looked back with a clear conscience. Notice the following: "for yourselves, brethren, know" (v.1); "as ye know" (vv.2, 5); "ye remember" (v.9); "ye are witnesses" (v.10); "as ye know" (v.11). Compare Acts 20:18, "Ye know, from the first day that I came into Asia, after what manner I have been with you at all seasons." More important still, God was witness: see vv.5, 10. Paul had no regrets as he reviewed his ministry at Thessalonica. He could refer to his visit without embarrassment. Not many of us can look back on our service for God like that! But we ought to make it our aim.

Perhaps we should add that other people don't always see our conduct in quite the same way. It was at Thessalonica that Paul's words were twisted, and he was accused of treason. See Acts 17:7. His enemies attempted to discredit him by attacking his character and motives. We must now consider:

a) Their gospel preaching, vv.1-6
Paul deals with **(i)** the manner in which they preached (vv.1-2), and **(ii)** the motives of their preaching (vv.3-6).

i) The manner in which they preached, vv.1-2
"For yourselves, brethren, know our entrance in unto you, that it was not in vain: but even after that we had suffered before, and were shamefully entreated, as ye know, at Philippi, we were **bold** in our God to speak unto you the gospel of God with **much contention**." We must notice at least two things here:

- **Paul was undeterred by opposition**. Their experiences at Philippi, before reaching Thessalonica (Acts 17:1), did not deter them. Paul and his companions left "brethren" in Philippi (Acts 16:40), but these converts had not been won with ease. The preachers had "suffered", and been "shamefully entreated." But they didn't 'throw in the towel', and go home! After all, men who could sing in prison were not likely to be easily deterred! They pressed on with new resolve. We must notice, however, that it was more than dogged determination. So:

- **Paul was undiminished in enthusiasm**. "We were bold in our God to speak unto you the gospel of God with much contention" or "we were bold in our God to speak unto you the glad tidings of God with much earnest striving" (JND). This does not directly refer to the opposition at Thessalonica, but to the determination of Paul and his colleagues to preach the gospel. *The Linguistic Key to the New Testament* (Fritz Rienecker/Cleon Rogers) puts it like this: "the word *(agon)* implies the intense effort and strenuous exertion with which Paul preached the gospel, especially in the face of hostility and conflict which he had with the Jews at Thessalonica". The same word is rendered "conflict" in Philippians 1:30. Notice: "much assurance" (1:5), "much affliction" (1:6), and "much contention" (2:2).

We mustn't attribute all this to Paul's personal determination. His "intense effort and strenuous exertion", was not a natural attribute. See, for example, 1 Corinthians 2:3. In his own words, "we were bold in our God to speak unto you the gospel of God." He was undeterred by opposition, and undiminished in enthusiasm, because he enjoyed divine help ("bold in our God"), and was inspired by the message ("the gospel of God"). Notice that Paul does not say, 'bold in God', but "bold in **our** God." (Compare Philippians 4:19). Paul knew from personal experience that he could completely rely on God's strength and help. His confidence was rooted in his fellowship with God. Like the Psalmist, he could say, "God, even our own God, shall bless us" (Psalm 67:6). Like David, he could 'encourage himself in the Lord his God' (1 Sam. 30:6). Paul's determination and enthusiasm was also attributable to his confidence in the message. It was the "gospel of God" (see also vv.8, 9) This emphasises its divine origin. It is not ours to alter or amend! It is, equally, the "gospel of Christ" (3:2). God is its source: Christ is its centre. Paul also calls it "our gospel" (1:5), even "my gospel" (Rom. 2:16). These expressions stress the personal interest in the message on the part of the preachers. It was precious to them!

ii) The motives of their preaching, vv.3-6
Since Paul and his colleagues preached the "gospel of God", it was important that their motives should be pure. We must therefore notice:

- The absence of false motives, v.3. "For our exhortation *(paraklesis)* was not of deceit, nor of uncleanness, nor in guile." The word "exhortation" means 'appeal.' Paul refers here to his gospel preaching, in which men and women were urged to put away sin. Compare Acts 2:40. It was not a cold appeal: it had the character of an exhortation: it was calculated to stir them up, and touch their conscience. The "exhortation" was:

"Not of deceit." This refers to the material of his preaching. The word "deceit" *(plane)*, means 'wandering', that is, "wandering from the right path" (W.E. Vine). It doesn't take much education to see that our word 'planet' comes from this Greek word! We speak about a 'wandering planet.' So Paul did not preach error. He did not wander from the truth. The word also occurs in Eph. 4:14, where the expression, "lie in wait to deceive" (*planos*), is elsewhere rendered 'wiles of error' (RV).

"Nor of uncleanness." This refers to the motive of his preaching. Paul had no impure motive. He did not preach for personal gain. See 2 Corinthians 2:17, "For we are not as many, which corrupt ('make a trade of') the word of God."

"Nor in guile." This refers to the method of his preaching. The word "guile" *(dolos)* means a bait or snare. It is borrowed from fishing. There was no craft, deceit or subtlety in Paul's preaching. His preaching was open and straightforward. See 2 Corinthians 4:2, "But have renounced the hidden things of dishonesty, not walking in craftiness, nor handling the word of God deceitfully *(doloo);* but by manifestation of the truth commending ourselves to every man's conscience in the sight of God."

The "gospel of God" demands purity of material, purity of motive, and purity of method.

- The presence of true motives, vv.4-6. "But as we were allowed of God to be put in trust with the gospel, even so we speak; not as pleasing men, but God, which trieth our hearts." We should notice three things here:

The ministry. The words, "as we were allowed of God" are actually, 'as we have been approved *(dokimazo)* of God' (JND). Paul and his colleagues were trusted and proved servants. They had been approved after trial. The word '*dokimazo*' was used for proving metals. As proved servants they had been "put in trust with the gospel." See also 1 Timothy 1:11. The fact that they had been entrusted with the gospel emphasises that it did not belong to them. Compare 1 Corinthians 4:1-2, "Let a man so account of us, as of the ministers of Christ, and stewards, of the mysteries of God. Moreover, it is required in stewards that a man be found faithful." While this is generally true, the apostles were "put in trust with the gospel" in a unique sense. They were the channels through which the doctrines of the gospel were revealed.

The message. "Not as pleasing men." They did not gear their preaching to a favourable reception. Compare Galatians 1:10, "For do I now seek to satisfy men or God? Or do I seek to please men? If I were yet pleasing men, I were not Christ's bondman" (JND).

The motive. "Not as pleasing men, but God, which trieth our hearts." This reminds us of the words of the Lord Jesus, "He that sent me is with me: the Father hath not left me alone; for I do always those things that please him." Paul served in view of the judgment seat of Christ, when motives would be examined. See 1 Corinthians 4:5.

To sum up, Paul refers in this verse to responsibility entrusted to him ("as we were allowed of God to be put in trust with the gospel"), and responsibility discharged by him ("even so we speak"). He did this habitually, not now and then. This is developed in vv.5-6: "For neither at any time used we flattering words, as ye know, nor a cloke of covetousness; God is witness: nor of men sought we glory, neither of you, nor yet of others, when we might have been burdensome, as the apostles of Christ." Because they sought to please God, they did not resort to "flattering words" or a "cloke of covetousness." Paul studiously avoided all personal advantage.

They avoided personal gain from wrong motives, v.5. "For neither at any time used we flattering words ('flattering discourse', JND), as ye know, nor a cloke of covetousness." W.E. Vine defines "flattery" (*kolakia* is only used here) as follows: "words which flattery uses, not simply as an effort to give pleasure, but with motives of self interest". The expression, "flattering words" or "flattering discourse" (JND), describes a preacher given to slick eloquence in order to win the hearts of his hearers, whom he can then exploit to his own advantage. (Just like Absalom! See 2 Samuel 15:1-6). Hence Paul continues: "nor a cloke of (or, 'for') covetousness", or "nor with a pretext for covetousness" (JND). A cloak (see also John 15:22) covers other clothing, and it is sadly possibly for preachers to cover their true motives, in this case a desire for pecuniary gain. Notice that Paul appeals to witnesses on earth ("as **ye** know") and in heaven ("**God** is witness") to attest his genuine motives for preaching the gospel. The Thessalonians could bear witness that Paul and his colleagues did not use "flattering words", and God could bear witness that they did not use "a cloke of covetousness."

They avoided personal gain from right motives, v.6. The words, "nor of men sought we glory", evidently refer to financial help since, Paul continues: "when we might have been burdensome, as the apostles of Christ." W.E. Vine comments: "The word "glory" probably stands, by metonymy, for material gifts, an honorarium, since in human estimation glory is usually expressed in things material". They had the right to material support, see 1 Corinthians 9, but did not exercise their claim. The Macedonian believers were far from affluent. See 2 Corinthians 8:1-4. But the refusal of Paul and his colleagues to seek financial

Chapter 2

support did not curtail their ministry at Thessalonica, or lessen their love for the new converts. This brings us to

b) Their pastoral care, vv.7-12
In this section, we must notice **(i)** their gentleness (vv.7-8); **(ii)** their labour (v.9); **(iii)** their example (vv.10-12). Very clearly, Paul did not think that the conversion of the Thessalonians meant that his work there was over! He laboured "among" them (v.7).

i) Their gentleness, vv.7-8
"But we were gentle among you, even as a nurse cherisheth her children: so being affectionately desirous of you, we were willing to have imparted unto you, not the gospel of God only, but also our own souls, because ye were dear unto us." Paul and his colleagues went beyond the brief of a professional nurse. He uses the figure of a nursing mother: "as a nurse would cherish her own children" (JND). Paul went beyond the bounds of faithfulness and duty. A nursing mother has a deep personal interest in all that concerns the child. The lives of mother and child are inextricably bound together, and the true pastor not only imparts the message, he imparts himself. "We were willing to have imparted unto you, not the gospel of God only, but also our own souls, because ye were dear unto us." The true pastor is not only anxious to see people saved, he is deeply concerned with their spiritual growth. The pastor is involved in his teaching: it is not merely intellectual instruction, but loving concern for those involved. It involves complete deployment of time and interest, just like a mother! It has been nicely said, that if men turned from idols in Chapter 1, then they turned from idleness in Chapter 2. Paul and his colleagues certainly did not go to Thessalonica to get: they went to give! Paul describes their ministry in most significant language.

- "We were **gentle.**" That is, as opposed to "burdensome" in v.6. The word *(epios)* is only used here and in 2 Timothy 2:24, "the servant of the Lord must not strive; but be gentle unto all men." We should remember that hardness is not necessarily faithfulness! The servants of the Lord should be 'gentlemen' in every sense of the word! The gentleness of Paul's ministry is demonstrated in v.9: the apostles refrained from either accepting or requesting material support, "because we would not be chargeable unto any of you." They laboured "night and day" to make this possible.

- "As a **nurse** cherisheth her children." This is the only occurrence of the word *(trophos)* in the New Testament, but it was used widely elsewhere in connection with the feeding and rearing of children. Associated words meaning to nourish (*anatrepho* and *trepho*) occur in Acts 7:20-21; 12:20.

- **Cherisheth** her children." The word *(thalpo)* means to keep warm. It also occurs in Ephesians 5:29. W.E. Vine states that in the Septuagint Version of the Old Testament (the Greek Old Testament), the word occurs in Deuteronomy 22:6 in connection with a bird on the nest, warming and protecting her eggs.

- "**Affectionately desirous** of you." The expression *(homeiromai)* only occurs here. It means, "to have a strong affection for, a yearning after" (W.E.Vine).

ii) Their labour, v.9
"For ye remember, brethren, our labour and travail: for labouring night and day, because we would not be chargeable unto any of you, we preached unto you the gospel of God." See also 2 Thessalonians 3:8.

We must notice that although their desire not to be "burdensome" involved ongoing ("night and day") hard manual labour ("labour and travail"), they never lost sight of their main task: "we preached unto you the gospel of God." "Labour" *(kopos)* means toil resulting in weariness", and "travail" *(mochthos)* means painful effort. But they never 'took their eye off the ball!'

iii) Their example, vv.10-12
"Ye are witnesses, and God also, how holily and justly and unblameably we behaved ourselves among you that believe: as ye know how we exhorted and comforted and charged every one of you, as a father doth his children, That ye would walk worthy of God, who hath called you unto his kingdom and glory." Paul says three things about the servants ("holily...justly...unblameably") and three things about their service ("exhorted...comforted....charged").

For the second time, Paul calls on earthly and heavenly witnesses to attest their character. Compare v.5. But we can look at it differently. "Ye are witnesses": that is, outwardly; "and God also": that is, inwardly. The three adverbs tell us how we should behave: **"holily"** before God, **"justly"** (righteously) before men, **"unblameably"** as to ourselves.

But these three verses emphasise that their personal behaviour gave moral authority to their teaching at Thessalonica. They behaved "holily and justly and unblameably" as they "exhorted and comforted and charged" the believers there. The apostles not only urged them to "walk worthy of God" (v.12): they showed them how it should be done! They did not resemble the scribes and Pharisees who "say, and do not" (Matt. 23:1-3), but rather the Lord Jesus who "began both to do and teach" (Acts 1:1). Notice that they did three things:

- *"Exhorted."* It means to 'stir up', and was addressed to those who had lost their keen edge. We all flag sometimes, and need stirring up.

- *"Comforted."* The word *(paramutheomai)* means 'to encourage', and was addressed to the faint-hearted.

- *"Charged."* The word *(martureo)* means 'to bear witness' or 'to testify', and was addressed to those in danger of wavering.

We must notice, not only what they said ("exhorted...comforted...charged"), but how they said it: "as ye know **how** we exhorted and comforted and charged every one of you." Compare Isaiah 50:4. We must also notice that Paul ministered to "every one of you." That is, to each believer according to their spiritual need. He didn't generalise. He got to know each believer and their needs. We have noted his ministry as a 'nursing mother.' Now we must notice his ministry as a father. The 'babes in Christ' are growing up, and need a father's firmness! The emphasis is on teaching, and on the responsibilities of the converts. Notice how Solomon "exhorted... comforted...charged" his son: trace the occurrences of "my son" in Proverbs. But remember that a father can be tender as well. See Psalm 103:13.

The object is clearly stated: "That ye would walk worthy of God, who hath called you unto his kingdom and glory." Whilst the word "walk" can be understood in other ways, it does convey the idea of steady progress. It is not a case of 'run' or 'sprint', and then 'flag' or 'crawl', but consistent progress. The lofty standard of these verses is explained by the finale: "called unto his kingdom and glory." "His kingdom" suggests divine rule in our lives, and "his glory" suggests divine reward. However, it seems more likely that both refer to the future. Compare 2 Peter 1:11. We should "walk worthy of God" now, in view of our responsibilities in connection with the coming kingdom of our Lord Jesus Christ. We should live now in view of an 'abundant entry into the kingdom.'

READ CHAPTER 2:13-20

"Ye are our glory and joy"

In our previous study, we noticed that 1 Thessalonians 2 can be divided into three sections: *(1)* the responsibilities of the preachers (vv.1-12): how the gospel of God was conveyed to them; *(2)* the response of the hearers (vv.13-16): how the word of God was received by them; *(3)* the renewal of fellowship (vv.17-20): how the servants of God desired to be with them.

1) THE RESPONSIBILITIES OF THE PREACHERS, vv.1-12
We have already considered this section, and noticed *(a)* their responsibilities in gospel preaching (vv.1-6), and *(b)* in pastoral care (vv.7-12). This brings us to:

2) THE RESPONSE OF THE HEARERS, vv.13-16
This section tells us how the gospel was received by them, and we must notice that *(a)* they acknowledged its authority (v.13a); *(b)* *they* experienced its power (v.13b); *(c)* they incurred its reproach (vv.14-16).

There was nothing half-hearted about Paul's thanks to God for their conversion. "For this cause also thank we God without ceasing." Compare 1:2, "We give thanks to God always for you all." There was nothing half-hearted about Paul's desire to see them again. "We...endeavoured the more abundantly to see your face with great desire" (v.17). In fact, there was nothing half-hearted about Paul in any direction!

a) They acknowledged its authority, v.13a
"For this cause also thank we God without ceasing, because, when ye received (*paralambano*, 'to receive from another') the word of God which ye heard of us, ye received (*dechomai,* to accept) it not as the word of men, but as it is in truth, the word of God." We should notice the emphasis on "the word of God." W.E. Vine explains that the first occurrence of "received" refers to the ear, and the second, adding the idea of appropriation, to the heart. We must notice *(i)* that the preachers felt its authority and *(ii)* that the hearers felt its authority:

i) The preachers felt its authority

"The word of God which ye heard of us." This emphasises the divine origin of the message ("the word of God"), and the human channel through which it was communicated ("which ye heard of us"). It was not the message of the servants! Paul and his companions had no desire to make a name for themselves. The preachers felt the weight of the message, and faithfully imparted it at Thessalonica.

ii) The hearers felt its authority

They "received it not as the word of men, but as it is in truth, the word of God." The Thessalonians felt its weight, and recognised its authority. (The men of Nineveh received the word of God in the same way: read Jonah 3:5). Notice the emphasis on "received." James reminds us that we are to "receive with meekness the engrafted word, which is able to save your souls" (James 1:21). Paul refers to the God-given authority of the word of God in 1 Corinthians 14:37; 1 Thessalonians 4:2.

b) They experienced its power, v.13b

"Which effectually worketh also in you that believe." The present continuous tense is used here. Having been saved through the preaching of the word of God, they continued to experience its power in their lives. The expression "effectually worketh" translates the word *energeo*, which means "to put forth power, be operative, to work" (W.E. Vine).

c) They incurred its reproach, vv.14-16

Paul knew that the word of God operated in their lives by the reproach they incurred. "The word of God, which effectually worketh also in you that believe. *For* ye, brethren, became followers of the churches of God which in Judaea are in Christ Jesus: for ye also have suffered like things of your own countrymen, even as they have of the Jews." After all, if there had been no change in their lives, they would not have been persecuted! Their adversity was evidence that they had submitted to the word of God. We must notice *(i)* Their fellowship with others (v.14), and *(ii)* The ferocity of the persecution (vv.15-16).

i) Their fellowship with others, v.14

"Ye, brethren, became followers of the churches of God which in Judaea are in Christ Jesus: for ye also have suffered like things of your own countrymen, even as they have of the Jews." We must notice the following:

- **"The churches of God."** Compare Galatians 1:2. The expressions "church of God" and "churches of God" refer to local autonomous churches.

- **"In Judaea."** This does not imply federation. It emphasises fellowship. The assembly at Thessalonica had not become linked with the "churches of God in Judaea by some kind of federation. They had become "followers" (imitators) of the assemblies in Judaea in their suffering. "For ye also have suffered like things of your own countrymen, even as they have of the Jews". It was a fellowship in suffering. But there was an even greater fellowship. It was:

- **"In Christ Jesus."** Their spiritual life was beyond the ability of men to destroy. It was vested in "Christ Jesus": in the risen ascended and exalted Lord Jesus. The expression "in Christ Jesus" occurs elsewhere. See, for example, "The promise of life which is *in Christ Jesus*" (2 Tim. 1:1); "His own purpose and grace, which was given us *in Christ Jesus* before the world began" (2 Tim. 1:9); "Faith and love which is *in Christ Jesus*" (2 Tim. 1:13); "Be strong in the grace that *is in Christ Jesus*" (2 Tim. 2:1); "The salvation which is *in Christ Jesus*" (2 Tim. 2:10); "All that will live godly *in Christ Jesus* shall suffer persecution" (2 Tim. 3:12). The expression occurs some forty times in the New Testament.

Suffering is the usual accompaniment of faith in Christ, See 3:3, "For yourselves know that we are appointed thereunto". Compare John 16:4. Here, then, was final proof of the effectiveness of the word of God which they had received: it enabled them to stand in times of testing. They were ready to suffer.

ii) The ferocity of the persecution, vv.15-16
Paul himself had been involved in this (see Acts 9), but now experienced it himself. Notice his words, "have persecuted us" or "have driven us out by persecution" (JND). The tense here signifies a particular past event. Paul refers to Acts 17:5-9. We should notice:

- **The persecution they inflicted, v.15.** "Who both killed the Lord Jesus (the awesomeness of what they had done), and their own prophets, and have persecuted us; and they please not God, and are contrary to all men." They had a history of rejecting divine testimony. "The Lord Jesus...their own prophets... us." The word "contrary" is used to describe 'an opposing wind' (W.E. Vine) in Matthew 14:24; Mark 6:48. Paul and his colleagues, unlike the Jews, *did* please God. See 2:4. The religious Jews, allegedly waiting for their Messiah, rejected the gospel, whereas pagan Gentiles received it! See 1:9.

- **The prohibition they imposed, v.16a.** "Forbidding us to speak to the Gentiles that they might be saved". See Acts 13:45, "But when the Jews saw the multitudes (at Antioch), they were filled with envy, and spake against those things which were spoken by Paul, contradicting and blaspheming"; Acts 17:13, "But when the Jews of Thessalonica had knowledge that the word of God was preached of Paul at Berea, they came thither also, and stirred up the people"; Acts 22:22, "And they gave him (Paul) audience unto this word ('I will send thee far hence unto the Gentiles')", and then shouted "away with such a fellow from the earth: for it is not fit that he should live." It was intolerable to the Jews that Gentiles could be blessed without Judaism. Jonah evidently felt the same!

- **The punishment they incurred, v16b.** "To fill up their sins alway: for the wrath is come upon them to the uttermost." See Matthew 23:32, "Ye are the children of them which killed the prophets. Fill ye up then the measure of your fathers. Ye serpents, ye generation of vipers, how can ye escape the damnation of hell?" Compare Genesis 15:16, "But in the fourth generation they shall come hither again: for the iniquity of the Amorites is not yet full." The word *anapleroo* ('fill up') means to 'fill completely.' Their crowning sin was to prevent Gentiles from hearing the Gospel.

We should notice that the words, "for the wrath is come upon them", are rendered 'But the wrath is come upon them' (RV). If we take this in the sense of the prophetic perfect, it stresses the inevitability of judgment. But bearing in mind the presence tense here (compare Romans 1:18), Paul is emphasising that judgment is **already** resting on the nation. They have been set aside, albeit temporarily, by God. We know, of course, that this judgment will intensify, until it reaches its climax in the day of "Jacob's trouble." For "wrath", see 1:10; 5:9. The words "to the uttermost" *(eis telos)* remind us of John 13:1, where the Lord Jesus loved "his own" to 'the uttermost' ("unto the end", AV). Here we have a people upon whom "wrath" is come: but in v.12, we have a people called to "his kingdom and glory". The word "wrath" *(orge)* denotes a "settled or abiding condition of mind" (W.E. Vine).

3) THE RENEWAL OF FELLOWSHIP, vv.17-20
"But we, brethren, being taken from you for a short time in presence, not in heart, endeavoured the more abundantly to see your face with great desire." There are three things to note in this paragraph: *(a)* his affection for them (v.17a); *(b)* his attempts to see them (vv.17b-18); *(c)* his assurance of seeing them (vv.19-20).

a) His affection for them, v.17a
"But we, brethren, being taken from you for a short time in presence, not in heart" or, literally, 'in face, not in heart'. The Thessalonians were subject to the

hatred of their "own countrymen", but they were assured of Paul's love. See 2:8. We should notice that s**eparation did not erode affection**. The expression 'absence makes the heart grow fonder' does not always apply. Sometimes it is more like, 'out of sight, out of mind.' But not with Paul! We should also notice that **leaving them was akin to bereavement**. The words, "being taken from you", are literally, 'being bereaved of you.' This accords with the similes in vv.7, 11. The word *aporphanizomai* means "to be rendered an orphan" (W.E. Vine). The Lord Jesus said, "I will not leave you comfortless *(orphanos)*" (John 14:18).

b) His attempts to see them, vv.17b-18
"We...endeavoured the more abundantly to see your face with great desire. Wherefore we would have come unto you, even I Paul, once and again; but Satan hindered us." As we have already noticed, there was nothing half-hearted about Paul. The words "endeavoured...abundantly...great desire" make this very clear! He did not treat his absence lightly. The word "endeavoured" *(spoudazo)* is often rendered 'diligent' and means "to hasten to do a thing, to exert oneself" (W.E. Vine). The word "hindered" *(enkopto)* was "used of impeding persons by breaking up the road, or by placing obstacles sharply in the path" (W.E. Vine).

Paul's desire to "see your face", recalls 2 John 12 and 3 John 14. The apostle would rather "speak face to face" than write! In Acts 20, the elders from Ephesus sorrowed "most of all...that they should see his face no more" (v.38). The redeemed shall "see his face; and his name shall be in their foreheads" (Rev. 22:4).

The expression, "even I Paul", probably refers to the fact that Timothy had returned to Thessalonica (3:1-2), and they must not think that Paul's absence betokened some lack of desire on his part. It does seem likely that he is rebutting a charge that he had lost interest in them. Paul had been hindered, possibly by the bond or security taken of Jason. See Acts 17:9.

Notice that Paul refers to "Satan." This is appropriate. "Satan" *(Satanas)* means 'adversary.' The name is interpreted in Zechariah 3:1, "And he showed me Joshua the high priest standing before the angel of the Lord, and Satan standing at his right hand to **resist** him." But Satan's opposition was turned to the benefit of the believers at Thessalonica, and to our benefit as well. Paul could not go in person to Thessalonica, so he wrote two epistles to the assembly there, and we have them in our Bible. They tell us a great deal about the coming of the Lord! Satan was therefore defeated by his own opposition!

c) His assurance of seeing them, vv.19-20

"For what is our hope, or joy, or crown of rejoicing (glorying: *kauchesis*)? Are not even ye in the presence of our Lord Jesus Christ at his coming? For ye are our glory and joy." (Compare James 4:16, where the word *kauchesis* is used in a totally different way). Paul asks two questions here, and the second answers the first! His "hope...joy...crown of rejoicing" was the sight of his dear Thessalonian brethren "in the presence of ('before', RV) our Lord Jesus Christ at his coming." That would be a greater reward than "the chaplet of laurel with which earthly victors were crowned" (W.E. Vine).

Satan might have prevented him from seeing them **at that time**, but he could not prevent him from seeing them **then!** Satan might have hindered the coming of **Paul**, but he cannot hinder the coming of the **Lord!** Paul's desire to see them would certainly be fulfilled then. In this connection, we should notice the following:

- **Paul was certain about the Lord's coming**. He had no doubts about it! He refers to "his coming" without any further argument. The word rendered "coming" (*parousia*) means 'coming, arrival, and subsequent presence.' This is the first occurrence of the word in Paul's writings.

- **Paul laboured in view of the Lord's coming**. His object was that there should be men and women in heaven! In her hymn, *The sands of time are sinking*, Anne Ross Cousin put it like this:

> Oh! If one soul from Anwoth
> Meet me at God's right hand,
> My heaven will be two heavens,
> In Immanuel's land.

But Paul had far more in mind than their presence in heaven. He laboured with the object that there should be men and women there who had "walked worthy of God" (2:12), and who had 'walked' and 'pleased' Him (4:1).

- **Paul expected to see and recognise them at the Lord's coming**. "Are not even ye in the presence of our Lord Jesus Christ at his coming?" The word "ye" is in a place of emphasis. They were the subjects of his deep interest and affection. It is another manifestation of Paul's parental heart. See, again, vv.7, 11, 17.

Notice, finally, that while Paul found great joy in the Thessalonians as he thought about the future (v.19), he also found great joy in them on earth! (v.20). He mentions "hope" in v.19, where he speaks about the coming of the Lord Jesus and the judgment seat of Christ, but not in v.20, where he speaks about the present time. Compare 3:9, "For what thanks can we render to God again for you, for all the joy wherewith we joy for your sakes before our God...." See also 2 Thessalonians 1:4.

READ CHAPTER 3:1-8

"Your faith"

The three paragraphs in Chapter 2 have been entitled *(i)* the preacher and his converts (vv.1-6); *(ii)* the parent and his children (vv.7-12); *(iii)* the pastor and his concern, (vv.13-20). As we have seen, Paul's pastoral concern for the Christians at Thessalonica did not cease when he was obliged to leave the city. "But we, brethren, being taken from you for a short time in presence, not in heart, endeavoured the more abundantly to see your face with great desire. Wherefore we would have come unto you, even I Paul, once and again; but Satan hindered us" (2:17-18). His deep concern for them was still there when he reached Athens (via Berea, Acts 17:10-15), from which he sent Timothy to help them: "Wherefore when we could no longer forbear, we thought it good to be left at Athens alone; and sent Timotheus...to establish you, and to comfort you concerning your faith" (3:1-2).

The words, "your faith", occur five times in this chapter (vv.2, 5, 6, 7, 10). In the first four cases, Paul refers to their trust in God. In the last case, he refers, in all probability, to what they believed: 'the faith', or, if you like, the doctrines of 'the faith'. Bearing this in mind, the chapter can be divided as follows: *(1) Concern for their faith (vv.1-5):* "I sent to know your faith, lest by some means the tempter have tempted you, and our labour be in vain" (v.5). *(2) Confirmation of their faith (vv.6-8):* "Timotheus...brought us good tidings of your faith and charity" (v.6). *(3) Completion of their faith (vv9-13):* "night and day praying exceedingly that we might see your face, and might perfect that which is lacking in your faith" (v.10). There are alternative headings! How about: *Timothy's responsibility (vv.1-5):* "we...sent Timotheus"; *Timothy's report (vv.6-8):* "when Timotheus came"; *Paul's response (vv.9-13):* "we were comforted.....we live.....what thanks can we render to God again for you.....night and day praying exceedingly". However, we'll stay with the original suggestion!

1) CONCERN FOR THEIR FAITH, vv.1-5
The principal points in this section can be summarised as follows: *(a)* the

position of Paul (v.1); **(b)** the person Paul sent (v.2a); **(c)** the purpose of the mission (vv.2b-3a); **(d)** the preparatory teaching (vv.3b-4); **(e)** the possibility of wavering (v.5).

a) The position of Paul, v.1

"Wherefore when we could no longer forbear ('could no longer refrain ourselves', JND), we thought it good (for the Thessalonian believers) to be left at Athens **alone**." Paul uses quite strong language here. The expression, "left...alone" *(kataleipo),* could be rendered 'to leave behind' or 'forsake.' He evidently felt the situation very deeply. Compare 2:17, where the words, "being taken from you" could be used of 'a parentless child, or of childless parents' (*Linguistic Key to the Greek New Testament*). He felt bereaved of them. Paul refers to his hands in 2:9: now he refers to his heart (3:1).

Athens was not the best place to be "left...alone." Paul "saw the city wholly given to idolatry" (Acts 17:16). He could have done with the fellowship of Timothy himself! It seems that Silas was not with him either: see Acts 18:5. He was bereft of fellow-servants. But there was greater need at Thessalonica. We must therefore note Paul's complete unselfishness. Compare Philippians 1:23-24, "I am in a strait betwixt two, having a desire to depart, and to be with Christ; which is far better: nevertheless to abide in the flesh is more needful **for you.** And having this confidence, I know that I shall abide and continue with you all for your furtherance and joy of faith." See also Philemon vv.13-14. This was the very attitude of the Lord Jesus Himself: "Look not every man on his own things (interests), but every man also on the things (interests) of others. Let this mind be in you, which was also in Christ Jesus" (Phil.2:4-5).

Cain's question, "Am I my brother's keeper?" (Gen.4:9) is answered in 1 Corinthians 12:25, "God hath tempered the body together...that there should be no schism in the body; but that the members should have the same care one for another."

> Lord, help me live from day to day,
> In such a self-forgetful way,
> That even when I kneel to pray,
> My thoughts shall be of others.
>
> Others, Lord, yes, others,
> Let this my motto be,
> Help me to live for others,
> That I may live like Thee.

b) The person Paul sent, v.2
Paul "sent Timotheus, our brother, and minister of God, and our fellow labourer in the gospel of Christ." Paul's deep interest and concern for the believers at Thessalonica was expressed, not only by the fact that he sent someone from Athens, but by the fact that it was Timothy. He calls him "our brother, and minister of God" or "God's minister in the gospel of Christ" (RV). (The New Translation (JND) has a lengthy note, with the preface, 'the reading is perplexed').

i) In relation to the saints, Timothy was "our brother." In 2 Corinthians 1:1, he is called 'the brother' (JND & RV margin). This emphasises his true brotherly character. He was a brother indeed! We are told that "a brother is born for adversity", and the believers at Thessalonica were certainly "in adversity (v.4). Timothy was a man who cared about others, enabling Paul to say, "I have no man likeminded, who will naturally (genuinely) care for your state" (Phil. 2:20). He was therefore well qualified to visit Thessalonica. He was the right man to send! That's worth remembering. Some people are not suitable for some tasks! This wasn't the first time that Paul had sent Timothy to help other believers. See 1 Corinthians 4:17. Paul referred to the Corinthians as his "beloved sons" (children), and he sent his "beloved son" (child) to help them. See also Philippians 2:19.

ii) In relation to God, Timothy was a "minister of God." Don't be afraid of the word "minister".It simply means 'one who serves' *(diakonos)*. The emphasis is on service, rather than status. See 1 Corinthians 3:5, "Who then is Paul, and who is Apollos, but ministers by whom ye believed, even as the Lord gave to every man?" Although Timothy was evidently saved through Paul (Acts 16:1 with Acts 14:6-21), he was "a minister of God" in his own right. He was active in Gospel preaching (see Phil. 2:22), and therefore, again, a most suitable man to send to an assembly that was so active in Gospel work.

We should notice that Timothy was commended before he was commissioned. His commission follows, but Paul sent a man of proven character and ability. In the words of Eddie Stobart, 'Only the best will do!' (You won't find him in the Bible!) To sum up: Timothy had a heart for God's people ("our brother") and a heart for God's work ("minister of God"). Do **we** have a heart for God's people, and God's work?

c) The purpose of the mission, V2b-3a
"To establish you, and to comfort you concerning your faith: that no man should be moved by these afflictions." Notice the words "establish" and "comfort."

i) "To establish you." The word *(sterizo)* means 'to strengthen' or 'to make firm.'

It was used for putting in a supporting buttress. This is a most important work. See, for example, Romans 1:11 ("I long to see you, that I may impart unto you some spiritual gift, to the end ye may be **established**"); Romans 16:25 ("Now to him that is of power to **stablish** you according to my gospel"); Acts 15:41 ("And he went through Syria and Cilicia, **confirming** the churches"). If we are not 'established' in Bible teaching, we are liable to be "tossed to and fro, and carried about with every wind of doctrine" (Eph.4:14).

ii) "To comfort you." The word *(parakaleo)* has 'a variety of meanings' (W.E. Vine), including, as here, 'to encourage.' Notice its usage in Acts 15:32, "And Judas and Silas, being prophets also themselves, **exhorted** the brethren with many words, and confirmed them ('established them', as above)."

Paul laid excellent foundations at Thessalonica. Read through both epistles, and note references to his ministry there. You can only conclude that the assembly enjoyed a balanced diet of Bible teaching! But further help was needed. Even at Thessalonica! This reminds us that however well we have been taught in the past, we **cannot dispense with ongoing instruction from the word of God.** This involves "things new and old" (Matt. 13:52). While there are no 'new' doctrines (always be deeply suspicious of anybody who claims 'new light'), there is always plenty of room for exploration and discovery in the Scriptures! But do bear in mind that we need reminding of things we already know! Listen to Peter: "Wherefore I will not be negligent to put you always in **remembrance** of these things, though ye know them, and be established in the present truth...This second epistle, beloved, I now write unto you; in both which I stir up your pure minds by way of **remembrance**" (2 Pet. 1:12; 3:1). Paul therefore sent Timothy to Thessalonica to build on foundations already laid.

We need constant strengthening from the word of God because we are under constant pressure. Timothy was sent "to establish you, and to comfort you concerning your faith: that no man should be **moved** by these afflictions." You can't miss the contrast here: "established...moved." The word "moved" (from *saino*, meaning 'to shake' or 'wag') means to 'disturb, disquiet' (W.E. Vine). The *Linguistic Key to the Greek New Testament* quotes various authorities in saying, "to shake or wag, used especially of a dog wagging the tail to allure, to fascinate, to flatter, to beguile, to draw aside from the right path". The word "afflictions" *(thlipsis)* means 'a pressing, pressure' (W.E. Vine). It is rendered "tribulation" in v.4. This brings us to:

d) The preparatory teaching, vv.3b-4
"For yourselves know that we are appointed thereunto. For verily, when we

were with you, we ***told you before*** ('plainly', RV margin) that we should suffer tribulation; even as it came to pass, and ye know." Paul made no attempt to disguise the consequences of faith in Christ. In this, he followed the example of the Lord Jesus. See John 16:1-4, "These things have I spoken unto you, that ye should not be offended. They shall put you out of the synagogues: yea, the time shall come, that whosoever killeth you will think that he doeth God service...But these things have I told you, that when the time cometh, ye may remember that I told you of them." See also John 16:33; Luke 12:51-53; 1 Peter 4:12. We must remember that "all that will live godly in Christ Jesus shall suffer persecution" (2 Tim. 3:12).

Suffering is the 'norm' in Christian experience. This is the meaning of, "we are appointed thereunto." The word appointed *(keimai)* means, literally, 'to lie.' It is translated "set" in Luke 2:34; Philippians 1:17. Suffering for Christ is a privilege. See Philippians 1:29, "For unto you it is given in the behalf of Christ, not only to believe on him, but also to suffer for his sake". Compare Acts 5:41; James 1:2.

Paul and his colleagues assessed the situation at Thessalonica, and taught accordingly. This is most important. 'To be forewarned is to be forearmed'. Just think about the current climate. There is every reason to believe that pressure is going to be exerted on all who love the Gospel, and endeavour to maintain "all the counsel of God." In the last few days, one of Mr. David Tinkler's school visits (to a Church of England school) has been cancelled by the local vicar, because Mill Lane Chapel does not participate in 'Christians Together in Cheshunt.' Is this the shape of things to come? It looks likely. Be warned.

e) The possibility of wavering, v.5
"For this cause, when I could no longer forbear, I sent to know your faith, lest by some means ('any means', RV) the tempter have tempted you, and our labour be in vain." That is, tempted them successfully. After all, we are all tempted, but we trust not tempted successfully!

Paul's deep concern surfaces again. "When I could no longer forbear". Compare v.1. We would say, 'I couldn't endure it any longer.' Paul could bear lots of things, but he couldn't bear this any more. He wanted to know how they were getting on. "I sent to know your faith." The word *'ginosko'* ("know") means, 'get to know.' Notice that Paul identifies the source of the pressure exerted on the Thessalonians. "Lest by some means the **tempter** have tempted you." Satan was behind the evil men described in 2:14-15. Compare 2:18 ("Satan hindered us"). Satan is not omnipresent, but he is the unseen genius behind every onslaught

Chapter 3

against God's people. He attacked the Lord Jesus: "Then was Jesus led up of the Spirit into the wilderness to be tempted of the devil...and when the **tempter** came to him, he said, If thou be the Son of God, command that these stones be made bread" (Matt. 4:1-3). The word "tempted" *(peirazo)* refers to deliberate trial. In some cases, it means 'to test, try, prove' (W.E. Vine) in a good sense, but here it refers to Satan's attempt to make them deviate from the will of God. James 1:13-15 illustrates both meanings of the word.

Although Paul knew that no labour in the Lord is vain (1 Cor. 15:58), he also knew that his beloved children at Thessalonica were not immune from temptation. There was always the possibility that whilst his visit to Thessalonica was "not in vain" at the time (2:1), relentless pressure could undermine their faith in Christ, and "our labour be in vain." Compare Philippians 2:16. We must never forget that **we** are vulnerable:

> Principalities and powers,
> Mustering their unseen array,
> Wait for thine unguarded hours,
> "Watch and pray."

Only the Lord Jesus was invulnerable. He was "in all points tempted like as we are, yet without sin" (Heb. 4:15).

We now wait with 'bated breath.' What would Timothy discover when he got to Thessalonica? Read on!

2) CONFIRMATION OF THEIR FAITH, vv.6-8
Timothy returned with a smile on his face and a spring in his step! The news was good. Very good! "But now when Timotheus came from you unto us, and brought us good tidings of your faith and charity...we were comforted over you in all our affliction and distress by your faith." Let's look at this section as follows: **(a)** the report of Timothy (v.6); **(b)** the result for Paul (vv.7-8).

a) The report of Timothy, v.6
"But now when Timotheus came from you unto us, and brought us good tidings of your faith and charity, and that ye have good remembrance of us always, desiring greatly to see us, as we also to see you..." We should notice three things:

i) The good tidings. "Timotheus...brought us good tidings of your faith and charity." "Brought us good tidings" translates one word *(euangelizomai)*. Yes, you are quite right: that's where our word 'evangelise' comes from! It means 'cheerful tidings!' W.E. Vine points out that in the Septuagint Version (the Greek translation of the Hebrew Old Testament) it is used of "any message calculated to have a cheering effect on those who receive it". He quotes 1 Samuel 31:9 and 2 Samuel 1:20 in this connection.

We should notice that whilst Timothy spoke about their faith (their confidence in God) and love (their relationship with one another), he did not say anything about their hope. Further instruction was needed here. See v.10 with 4:13-18.

ii) **The good remembrance**. "Ye have good remembrance of us always." The word "remembrance" *(mneia)* is always used in connection with prayer. It is also rendered 'mention.' See Romans 1:9, Ephesians 1:16, 1 Thessalonians 1:2, Philemon v.4, Philippians 1:3 ("I thank my God upon every remembrance of you, always in every prayer of mine for you all making request with joy"), 2 Timothy 1:3 ("without ceasing I have remembrance of thee in my prayers night and day"). Prayer for each other leads to:

iii) **The great desire.** "Desiring greatly to see us, as we also to see you." This is a sure indication of their steadfastness. If they had defected, Paul would have been the last person in the world they would have wanted to see! Some people certainly didn't want to see Paul at Corinth. See, for example, 2 Corinthians 12:15. The more we pray for each other, the more we'll be able to say of each other: "My brethren dearly beloved and longed for" (Phil. 4:1).

b) The result for Paul, vv.7-8
"Therefore, brethren, we were comforted over you in all our affliction and distress by your faith: for now we live, if ye stand fast in the Lord." Paul was helped and encouraged. Notice that when Paul reached Corinth, and "Silas and Timotheus were come from Macedonia" (with good news from Thessalonica), he was "pressed in spirit" ('constrained by the word'), and "testified to the Jews that Jesus was Christ" (Acts 18:5). It does seem that the good news gave impetus to Paul's preaching at Corinth.

Timothy's report was a great encouragement to Paul. He had sent Timothy to encourage ("comfort") them (v.2), and as a result, **he** received encouragement from them! Paul reaped what he sowed. In the nicest sense! He sent to believers who were being afflicted (v.3), and they were a great help to him in **his** affliction (v.7). Paul mentions his "affliction and distress." The first describes what he **received**. See our comments on v.3. The second describes what he **lacked.** The word *(ananke)* is evidently used here with reference to a lack of material things. See also 2 Corinthians 6:4; 12:10.

Do notice the expression, "we were comforted **over you**". W.E. Vine calls it "an expression beautifully in keeping with the simile of 2:7, 'but we were gentle among you, even as a nurse cherisheth her own children'". The figure is repeated in v.8, "For now we live, if ye stand fast in the Lord", or "we live once more" (Lightfoot), or "we enjoy life" (Hogg & Vine). You can almost see the mother giving a big sigh of relief on discovering that the child is not ill after all! Paul's anxiety and concern proved groundless, much to his delight! He could never be charged with a 'couldn't care less attitude.' Every assembly elder should take note!

Let's learn an important lesson from this. Our stability and steadfastness is not only good for us: it is good for others. It will have a salutary effect on our fellow-believers. If you want to bring cheer to your brothers and sisters in Christ, "stand fast in the Lord!" It will enable to the elders to do their work "with joy, and not with grief" (Heb. 13:17). John wrote, "I have no greater joy than to hear that my children walk in truth" (3 John 4).

> Be steadfast, unmoveable,
> By faith stand your ground:
> Let the world not entice you,
> Nor let errors confound.
> For the Lord is your portion,
> His word is your guide.
> Be steadfast, unyielding,
> And turn not aside.

READ CHAPTER 3:9-13

"Night and day praying exceedingly"

As we have noticed, the words, "your faith", occur five times in this chapter (vv.2, 5, 6, 7, 10). In the first four cases, Paul refers to their trust in God. In the last, he evidently refers to the body of Christian doctrine. W.E.Vine puts it like this: "that which, through the premature interruption of his labours as a teacher among them, he had been unable to impart to them". Bearing this in mind, we divided the chapter as follows: *(1) concern for their faith (vv.1-5):* "I sent to know your faith, lest by some means the tempter have tempted you, and our labour be in vain" (v.5); *(2) confirmation of their faith (vv.6-8):* "Timotheus...brought us good tidings of your faith and charity" (v.6); *(3) completion of their faith (vv.9-13):* "night and day praying exceedingly that we might see your face, and might perfect that which is lacking in your faith" (v.10).

1) CONCERN FOR THEIR FAITH, vv.1-5
In our last study, we noted the principal points in this section: *(a)* the position of Paul (v.1); *(b)* the person Paul sent (v.2); *(c)* the purpose of the mission (v.3); *(d)* the preparatory teaching (vv.3-4); *(e)* the possibility of wavering (v.5). The passage has also been divided as follows: *(a)* Paul's anxiety (v.1); *(b)* Paul's action (v.2); *(c)* Paul's anticipation (vv.3-4); *(d)* Paul's apprehension (v.5). Take your pick!

2) CONFIRMATION OF THEIR FAITH, vv.6-8
In our last study, we also noted that the believers at Thessalonica were standing firm under pressure, and we summarised this section as follows: *(a)* the report of Timothy (v.6); *(b)* the result for Paul (vv.7-8). This brings us to

3) COMPLETION OF THEIR FAITH, vv.9-13
Paul and his colleagues prayed "exceedingly that we might see your face, and might perfect that which is lacking in your faith", v.10. As we have noted, the Thessalonians had already received a great deal of instruction, but more was needed.

The section can be divided simply as follows *(a)* their thanksgiving (v.9); *(b)* their prayer (vv.10-13). In connection with the latter, we must notice the consistency of their prayers (v.10) and the content of their prayers (vv.11-13). We must not miss the repetition of "we", "our", and "us" throughout the epistle. Paul does, of course, speak personally (2:18; 3:5; 4:9, 13; 5:1, 23, 27), but generally he uses the plural. This is most interesting and informative. Paul did not seek prominence. He appreciated, enjoyed and valued the fellowship of his fellow-labourers. Just like Daniel! See Daniel 2:17-18. But this did not diminish his authority as an apostle. It is particularly noticeable that Paul speaks in the singular when he introduces teaching. See 4:13; 5:1.

a) Their thanksgiving, v.9

"For what thanks can we render to God again for you, for all the joy wherewith we joy for your sakes before our God...?" This is the third time in this epistle that Paul gives thanks. He gives thanks for their salvation and progress (1:2-4); he gives thanks for their submission to the word of God (2:13); he gives thanks for their steadfastness under pressure (3:9).

Thanksgiving is the proper accompaniment of prayer. We noticed this in 1:2, "We give thanks to God always for you all, making mention of you in our prayers." See Philippians 4:6 ("Be careful for nothing; but in every thing by prayer and supplication with thanksgiving let your requests be made known unto God"); Colossians 4:2 ("Continue in prayer, and watch in the same with thanksgiving"). Paul points out that unregenerate men are unthankful. See Romans 1:21: "When they knew God, they glorified him not as God, neither were **thankful**." See also 2 Tim. 3:2: "For men shall be lovers of their own selves, covetous, boasters, proud, blasphemers, disobedient to parents, **unthankful,** unholy..." In 2 Timothy 3, Paul is evidently referring to religious people: "having a form of godliness, but denying the power thereof" (v.5).

We should be characterised by thankfulness: "Pray without ceasing. In every thing **give thanks**: for this is the will of God in Christ Jesus concerning you" (1 Thess. 5:17-18). We should notice some of the occasions on which the Lord Jesus gave thanks: Matthew 15:36; Mark 8:6; Mark 14:23; Luke 10:21; John 6:11, 23; John 11:41. We must not forget that the Lord "gave thanks" when He instituted the Lord's supper. See Matthew 26:27 and the parallel references in Mark and Luke, together with 1 Corinthians 11:24. The Lord Jesus gave thanks in view of His **death.** He certainly gave thanks "in every thing." Isn't that amazing!

The thanksgiving of Paul, Silas and Timothy reflected their deep inward joy. The steadfastness of the Thessalonians had a salutary effect on them. The burden had been lifted: "For now we live, if ye stand fast in the Lord" (v.8). The words, "For what thanks can we render to God again for you...?", tell us that they found it difficult to fully express their joy. They could not find words which would be equivalent to their joy. Let's notice two things:

i) Our steadfastness will bring joy to others. "For what thanks can we render to God again **for you,** for all the joy wherewith we joy **for your sakes** before our God." The apostle John knew the feeling: "I rejoiced greatly that I found of thy children walking in truth" (2 John 4); "I have no greater joy than to hear that my children walk in truth" (3 John 4). It is the spiritual ambition of every assembly elder to do their work "with joy, and not with grief", Hebrews 13:17.

ii) Our steadfastness will bring glory to God. "For what thanks can we render to God again for you, for all the joy wherewith we joy for your sakes before **our God.**" This reminds us that every spiritual victory is achieved through Him. Paul wrote, "In all these things (tribulation, distress, persecution, famine, nakedness, peril, sword) we are more than conquerors **through him** that loved us" (Rom. 8:37).

> And every virtue we possess,
> And every victory won,
> And every thought of holiness,
> Are **His** alone.

b) Their prayer, vv.10-13
Timothy's "good tidings" did not lessen their prayerful concern. After all, they might have heaved a big sigh of relief, and left it there! We must therefore notice *(i)* the consistency of their prayers (v.10a); *(ii)* the content of their prayers (vv.10b-13).

i) The consistency of their prayers, v.10a
"Night and day praying exceedingly." Paul and his companions laboured "night and day" while at Thessalonica (2:9), and prayed "night and day" while absent from Thessalonica. They certainly exemplified the injunction, "Pray without ceasing!" (5:17), and "Continue (persevere) in prayer" (Col. 4:2). Paul practised what he preached. It has been said that twenty-four of the one hundred and thirty-six verses in 1 & 2 Thessalonians, refer to prayer. (Check it out!). At Ephesus, Paul "ceased not to warn every one night and day with tears" (Acts 20:31). These servants of God were whole-hearted in their

ministry, whatever form it took. Their service for God was certainly not a hobby which could be taken up and put down as fancy took them. It was their very life. But that wasn't all:

"Night and day praying **exceedingly**." The same word *(huperekperissou)* occurs in Ephesians 3:20, "Now unto him that is able to do **exceeding abundantly** above all that we ask or think", and a similar word in 1 Thessalonians 5:13, "Esteem them **very highly** in love for their work's sake." We can easily detect the earnestness and zeal in their prayers. They didn't pray only as a matter of routine. How do **we** pray?

ii) The content of their prayers, vv.10b-13
In this section, we must notice their role in helping them (v.10), and the Lord's work in helping them (vv.11-13). Paul and his companions could help them with further teaching, but only the Lord could enable them "to increase and abound in love one toward another, and toward all men."

- **The role of the servants.** "Night and day praying exceedingly that **we** might see your face, and might perfect that which is lacking in your faith." The words, "that which is lacking in your faith", evidently refer to the body of Christian doctrine. While we are not told what particular matters Paul had in mind, it seems likely that they included future events. Teaching is given on this subject in Chapters 4-5.

While Paul longed to see his spiritual children, he did not have a social visit in mind. Neither was it a case of a 'sentimental journey!' He wanted to help them. The word "perfect" *(katartizo)* does **not** mean 'sinless perfection', or anything like it! It is the word used for mending nets in Matthew 4:21 and Mark 1:19. It occurs in Ephesians 4:11-12, "And he gave some, apostles; and some, prophets; and some, evangelists; and some, pastors and teachers; for the **perfecting** of the saints, for the work of the ministry, for the edifying of the body of Christ." It is used in Galatians 6:1, "Brethren, if a man be overtaken in a fault, ye which are spiritual, **restore** such an one in the spirit of meekness; considering thyself, lest thou also be tempted." The word means "to make fit, to equip, prepare" (W.E. Vine), and its exact use must be determined by the context. It does not always refer to 'running repairs.' In this particular case, Paul refers to the need for further teaching so that the believers at Thessalonica might be "throughly furnished (furnished completely: *exartizo*) unto all good works" (2 Tim. 3:17). We must bear in mind that his ministry at Thessalonica was interrupted by the hasty exit described in Acts 17:10.

All parents worthy of the name are most concerned about the welfare of their children, and do all in their power to prepare them for the future. Paul was no exception. He was deeply concerned for the spiritual well-being and maturity of his spiritual children. Every assembly elder should be intent on the growth and development of the believers amongst whom they labour.

- **The work of the Lord, vv.11-13.** First of all, *in enabling Paul to visit Thessalonica*. While Paul was able to impart further help at Thessalonica, he needed the Lord's help to get there! "Now God himself and our Father, and our Lord Jesus Christ, direct our way unto you" (v.11) or, "But our God and Father himself and our Lord Jesus direct our way to you' (JND). The verb "direct" means 'to make straight' (W.E. Vine), and the verse reminds us that we must always pray about our movements. See James 4:15, "For that ye ought to say, If the Lord will, we shall live, and do this, or that." Paul told the Romans that he made "request, if by any means now at length I might have a prosperous journey by **the will of God** to come unto you", (Rom. 1:10). Remember that the "will of God" overrode Satan's will (see 2:18), and as a result we have 1 & 2 Thessalonians!

The word "direct" is in the singular. This sets aside the normal grammatical law that a verb must agree with its subject in number, in order to stress the unique relationship between the Father and the Son. It emphasises the deity of Christ. He said, "I and my Father are one" (John 10:30). The Jews fully understood His meaning: "For a good work we stone thee not; but for blasphemy; and because that thou, being a man, makest thyself God" (John 10:33). **We** marvel because He, being God, made Himself man!

W.E. Vine points out that "the Thessalonians had been taught to think of the Lord Jesus as One with God, for prayer is addressed conjointly with the Father. It is equally important to notice that while the Lord Jesus is united with the Father in respect of His Godhead, He is distinguished from the Father in respect of His personality" and "The Lord Jesus is associated with God the Father as controller of the ways of men".

The work of the Lord is further seen in enabling the Thessalonians to love one another. Only the Lord could make it possible for Paul to return to Thessalonica, and only the Lord could make them to "increase *(pleonazo)* and abound *(perisseuo)* in love *(agape)* one toward another, and toward all men." This does not imply that they were deficient in their love for each other. Paul makes this clear later in the epistle: "But as touching brotherly

Chapter 3A

love ye need not that I write unto you: for ye yourselves are taught of God to love one another. And indeed ye do it toward all the brethren which are in Macedonia: but we beseech you, brethren, that ye increase *(perisseuo)* more and more" (4:9-10). The verbs "abound" (3:12) and "increase" (4:10) translate the same word. It means, 'to be over and above' (W.E. Vine). The verb "increase" (3:12) means 'to make to abound.' F.F. Bruce *(Expanded Paraphrase of the Epistles of Paul)* renders 3:12 as follows: "And may the Lord make you abound and overflow in love one to another". Are **we** displaying this kind of progress in our relationships with one another? Do **we** ever pray that the Lord will help us to love one another more? There is always room for increasing love to each other. After all, the Lord Jesus did say, "A new commandment I give unto you, That ye love one another; **as I have loved you**, that ye also love one another" (John 13:34). None of us can say that we love one another as He has loved us! So there's plenty of scope for us to love each other more and more!

But that wasn't all. Paul prayed that they would "increase and abound in love one toward another, and **toward all men.**" This was definite and informed prayer. It wasn't a case of 'Lord, bless the Thessalonians', like 'Lord, bless the missionaries in Africa!' The Christians at Thessalonica were under pressure from their fellow countrymen (see 2:14; 3:4; 2 Thess. 1:4), and they were to meet their enemies with love for them! This was the teaching of the Lord Jesus: "Ye have heard that it hath been said, Thou shalt love thy neighbour, and hate thine enemy. But I say unto you, Love your enemies, bless them that curse you, do good to them that hate you, and pray for them which despitefully use you, and persecute you...for if ye love them which love you, what reward have ye? Do not even the publicans the same?" (Matt. 5:43-46). See also Luke 6:32-35.

Paul and his fellow-labourers were examples of their own teaching. Their love for the Thessalonians 'abounded and overflowed.' The teacher practised his own ministry! When he wrote to the Corinthians, Paul had to say, "I will very gladly spend and be spent for you; though the more abundantly I love you, the less I be loved" (2 Cor. 12:15). But that hadn't happened at Thessalonica! Timothy had brought "good tidings" of their faith and love (3:6).

Paul emphasises the importance of the subject, by explaining that "love is not an end in itself, but a means to an end, and that end is holiness" (W.E. Vine). "And the Lord make you to increase and abound in love one toward another... **to the end** he may stablish (*sterizo,* as in 3:2) your hearts **unblameable in holiness** before God, even our Father, at the coming of our Lord Jesus Christ with all his saints." The word "unblameable" means 'deserving no censure.' We learn that love is essential to holiness. Love "one toward another, and toward all men", leads to holy living. This is emphasised in Romans 13:8-10. "Owe no man anything, but to love one another: for he that loveth another hath fulfilled the law...Love worketh no ill to his neighbour: therefore love is the fulfilling of the law." It also reminds us that holiness is not cold and clinical, where everything said and done is meticulously correct. Holiness obviously involves morality and uprightness, but is also warm and vibrant. We should add that "holiness" is far more than 'high moral standards.' "Holiness" is the very character of God Himself. See 1 Peter 1:15-16.

Paul's ministry here is repeated in 2 Thessalonians 3. "But the **Lord** is faithful, who shall stablish you, and keep you from evil. And we have confidence in the **Lord** touching you, that ye both do and will do the things which we command you. And the **Lord** direct your hearts into the love of God, and into the patient waiting for Christ", (vv.3-5) The Lord alone can do all this.

The Lord Jesus makes us to "increase and abound in love one toward another" with the object that He may establish our hearts "unblameable in holiness before God, even our Father, **at the coming** *(parousia)* **of our Lord Jesus Christ** with all his saints." Let's never forget that He is preparing us for the day when He presents us to God in "the beauty of holiness." Do notice that Paul says, "God, even **our Father**." The Lord Jesus wants the Father to have pleasure in His children! We should therefore studiously avoid anything that causes Him displeasure, including lack of love for each other and, therefore, lack of holiness. Let's remember that only what we do in love will be approved at the judgment seat of Christ. If love is missing, the character of God is missing.

T. Ernest Wilson *(What the Bible Teaches – 1 Thessalonians)* points out that "the fact that the word *parousia* (meaning 'presence') is used, and not *apokalupsis* (meaning 'revelation'), surely points to the Rapture.' That is, to the coming of the Lord Jesus **for** His people (described in 1 Thessalonians 4:13-18), as opposed to the coming of the Lord Jesus **with** His people (described in 2 Thessalonians 1:7-10). The concluding words, "at the coming (in the presence) of our Lord Jesus Christ with **all his saints**", may well emphasise that there will be none missing, and prepares the way for more detailed teaching on the subject in 4:13-18. However, the insertion of a comma at the end of v.13, if permissable, gives a different emphasis: "The Lord make you to increase and abound in love...to the end he may stablish your hearts unblameable in holiness before God, even our Father, at the coming of our Lord Jesus Christ, with all his saints". That is, Paul's desire for increasing and abounding love was not only for the believers at Thessalonica, but for "all the saints".

Notice that the Lord's people are described as "saints", meaning 'holy ones.' This is in keeping with the words, "that he may stablish your hearts unblameable in holiness." The subject is developed in Chapter 4:1-8.

READ CHAPTER 4:1-12

"How ye ought to walk and to please God"

Before we commence detailed study of this passage, it might be helpful to look briefly at the structure of Chapters 4-5. In these chapters we have two sections giving practical injunctions, between which lie two sections dealing with the Lord's coming. The sections giving practical instructions (4:1-12 and 5:12-22) both commence with the word "beseech." In the first, Paul deals with our personal conduct, and in the second with our corporate conduct. The sections dealing with the Lord's coming address the subject in relation to dead saints (4:13-18) and living saints (5:1-11).

1 Thessalonians 4 has been called the 'Enoch Chapter!' You can easily see why. "Enoch walked with God: and he was not; for God took him" (Gen. 5:24). This is expanded in Hebrews 11:5, "By faith Enoch was translated that he should not see death; and was not found, because God had translated him: for before his translation he had this testimony, that he pleased God." Put the two passages side by side, and you cannot escape the conclusion that the way to please God is to walk with Him. The word "translated" *(metatithemi)* means 'to transfer to another place' (W.E. Vine). Now read 1 Thessalonians 4. It begins with the words, "Furthermore then we beseech you, brethren, and exhort you by the Lord Jesus, that as ye have received of us how ye ought to **walk and to please God**, so ye would abound more and more" (v.1). There's Enoch! It ends with the words, "Then we which are alive and remain shall be **caught up** together with them (the "dead in Christ") in the clouds, to meet the Lord in the air: and so shall we ever be with the Lord" (v.17). There's Enoch again! It's worth noticing that while "Enoch walked with God: and he was not; for God took him", Noah (who also "walked with God", Gen. 6:9) was present when the Flood came, but he was preserved, and emerged from the Ark to take possession of a cleansed and purged earth. This reminds us that the Lord Jesus will come to take every true believer on earth to heaven before judgment falls on the world, but that afterwards there will be other believers who will be preserved through the years of judgment that will follow, and enter the millennial kingdom of the Lord Jesus Christ.

1 Thessalonians 4 can therefore be divided into two major sections: **(1)** the conduct of saints (vv.1-12); **(2)** the coming of the Lord (vv.13-18).

1) THE CONDUCT OF SAINTS, vv.1-12

The section begins and ends with "walk." It begins with, "Ye have received of us how ye ought to **walk** and to please God" (v.1). It ends with "That ye may **walk** honestly toward them that are without" (v.12). Paul deals with our conduct on earth generally in vv.1-2, and specifically in vv.3-12. In connection with the latter, we must notice **(i)** holiness of life (vv.3-8); **(ii)** harmony of love (vv.9-10); **(iii)** honesty of labour (vv.11-12). Quite clearly, Paul has not turned his attention to new subjects. He is expanding 3:12-13: "And the Lord make you to increase and abound in love one toward another, and toward all men......to the end he may stablish your hearts unblameable in holiness before God, even our Father, at the coming of our Lord Jesus Christ with all his saints." Hence the word "furthermore." Paul now deals with the subjects of love and holiness in the reverse order.

a) Our conduct generally, vv.1-2

"Furthermore then we beseech you, brethren, and exhort you by the Lord Jesus, that as ye have received of us how ye ought to walk and to please God, so ye would abound more and more. For ye know what commandments we gave you by the Lord Jesus." Paul describes our general conduct as 'walking and pleasing God' and we should notice:

i) The character of the appeal

"Furthermore then we beseech you, brethren, and exhort you by the Lord Jesus" (v.1). Paul brings two words together to emphasise the importance of 'walking and pleasing God.' This is the only place in the New Testament where they occur together. The word "beseech" *(erotao)* is often rendered "ask" or "pray", and places 'the petitioner on an equal footing or familiarity with the person to whom the request is made' (W.E.Vine). Hence, it was used by the Lord Jesus in addressing the Father. See John 14:16; 16:26; 17:9, 15, 20 ("pray" in each case). The word "exhort" *(parakaleo)* means to urge someone to pursue a certain course of action. So Paul 'beseeches' them on his own account as one who loves them, but urges them in (AV "by") the Lord Jesus. His exhortation carried the authority of the Lord Jesus, and emphasises our responsibility to obey.

ii) The object of the appeal

"That as ye have received of us how ye ought to walk and to please God, so ye would abound more and more"(v.1). Other translations add "even as ye also do walk" (RV/JND)). Quite obviously, this refers to our day to day living. It is not an option, but an obligation. "How ye **ought** to walk and please God." Compare 2 Timothy 2:4, "No man that warreth entangleth himself with the affairs of this life; that he may please him who hath chosen him to be a soldier." We have already noticed that Enoch 'walked and pleased God' (Gen. 5:22-24; Heb. 11:5). The Lord Jesus, pre-eminently, 'walked and pleased God': "I do always those things that please him" (John 8:29). Compare Romans 15:3. We must remember that "he that saith he abideth in him ought himself also so to walk, even as he walked" (1 John 2:6). As God's people, we should "labour ('make it our aim' or 'be ambitious'), that, whether present or absent, we may be accepted ('well-pleasing') of him" (2 Cor. 5:9). This means that like Paul and his colleagues, we must "speak; not as pleasing men, but God, which trieth our hearts" (1 Thess. 2:4).

Paul was a hard taskmaster! He expected no 'let up' in 'walking and pleasing God!' Rather, "abound more and more." Continual progress is required. We must never think that we 'have arrived!' The same applies to our mutual love as believers (v.10). Compare Proverbs 4:18, "The path of the just is as the shining light, that shineth more and more unto the perfect day."

iii) The consistency of the appeal
"As ye have received of us how ye ought to walk and to please God...for ye know what commandments we gave you by (through) the Lord Jesus" (vv.1-2). The teaching had not changed. The written teaching was consistent with the oral teaching given when Paul was at Thessalonica. The teaching was invested with divine authority. The "commandments" (emphasising again that there is nothing optional about God's word), were given 'through the Lord Jesus.' Compare 1 Corinthians 14:37, "If any man think himself to be a prophet, or spiritual, let him acknowledge that the things that I write unto you are the commandments of the Lord."

b) Our conduct specifically, vv.3-12
In these verses, as we have noticed, Paul deals with three areas of our lives: *(i)* **s**exual relationships (vv.3-8): holiness of life; *(ii)* spiritual relationships (vv.9-10): harmony of love; *(iii)* **s**ecular relationships (vv.11-12): honesty of labour.

i) Sexual relationships, vv.3-8
The section begins and ends with holiness: "For this is the will of God, even your **sanctification**...For God hath not called us unto uncleanness, but unto **holiness.** He therefore that despiseth, despiseth not man, but God, who hath

also given unto us his **holy** Spirit." T.E. Wilson *(What the Bible Teaches – 1 Thessalonians)* points out that "our words, holiness and sanctification, are the same in the original: they mean the same thing. The original word *(hagios)* and its derivatives are applied in a fourfold way to the believer:

- It is God's **purpose** for His children that they should be holy (Rom. 8:29; 1 Cor. 1:2; 1 Peter 1:2; Jude 1).

- It is a **position,** a standing before God, granted immediately on conversion. This is not a gradual change, a progressive work or a moral attribute, but a once-for-all act, like justification (1 Cor.1:30; 6:11).

- It is **practical** and **progressive** throughout the earthly life of the believer (2 Cor. 7:1). This is the work of the Holy Spirit, using the cleansing agency of the Word of God (Eph. 5:26-27; John 17:17).

- It will be **perfected** at the coming of our Lord Jesus Christ with all His saints (1 Thess, 3:13; Jude 24)".

Quite clearly, 1 Thessalonians 4:3, "this is the will of God, even your sanctification", refers to the third of the above: our practical and progressive sanctification. This is applied here to moral conduct, and expressed in a threefold demand:

- **"That ye should abstain (keep yourself from) from fornication" (v.3).** Compare 1 Corinthians 6:13, 18, "Now the body is not for fornication, but for the Lord; and the Lord for the body...Flee fornication. Every sin that a man doeth is without the body; but he that committeth fornication sinneth against his own body." Joseph "fled, and got him out" (Gen. 39:12) when tempted in this way. In the context of this passage, "fornication" refers to **all** unlawful sexual relationships. In passages where it occurs with the word "adultery", "adulteries", or "adulterers" (Matt. 5:32; 19:9; 15:19; 1 Cor. 6:9; Heb. 13:4), it refers to pre-marital unchastity.

The reasons for such teaching here lie in the fact that the Thessalonians had been saved from an idolatrous background (1:9), and immorality is always associated with idolatry. See 1 Corinthians 10:7-8 (citing Exodus 32:4-6); 2 Chronicles 21:11; Acts 15:20, 29; Acts 21:25. They had "turned to God from idols": they were to turn from all that was associated with idolatry as well. The Thessalonians lived in a society where there was constant exposure to such sin. **We** too live in such an environment. We must remember the injunction in

Ephesians 5:3, "But fornication, and all uncleanness, or covetousness, let it not be once named among you, as becometh saints." Hence the significance of 1 Thessalonians 5:23, "The very God of peace sanctify you wholly; and I pray God your whole spirit and soul and *body* be preserved blameless unto the coming of our Lord Jesus Christ." We must make this *our* daily prayer. We are to "pray without ceasing", and you can hardly pray and sin at the same time!

- *"That every one of you should know how to possess his vessel in sanctification and honour" (v.4).* While it is often stated that the word "vessel" here refers to a man's wife (citing 1 Peter 3:7), it seems more likely that Paul refers to the believer's body. After all, men and women are involved. Compare 1 Samuel 21:4-5, "There is no common bread under mine hand, but there is hallowed bread; if the young men have kept themselves at least from women. And David answered the priest, and said unto him, Of a truth women have been kept from us about these three days, since I came out, and the vessels of the young men are holy." (It is only fair to say, however, that v.6 might suggest that Paul refers here to a man's wife). Believers must not use their bodies for immoral purposes, but "possess" them in "sanctification and honour." The word "possess" *(ktaomai)* means to 'bring under control', 'get possession of', or 'have the mastery over.' Notice the word "know": "that every one of you should *know* how to possess his vessel in sanctification and honour." That is, know how to act when tempted by immorality. There are no exceptions. The teaching is addressed to "every one of you."

The power to do this lies in our personal consecration to God. We must "possess" our body in "sanctification and honour." This is positive. "Not in the lust of concupiscence, even as the Gentiles which know not God." This is negative. The power of positive consecration to God will enable us to overcome sinful influences. The word "lust" means 'passion', and the word "concupiscence" means 'uncontrolled desire.' We are not to be overwhelmed by the sinful passion and desire which is characteristic of the Gentiles, "which know not God." They are unregenerate. Saved people are not even to think, let alone act, like unsaved people.

- *"That no man go beyond and defraud his brother in any matter" (v.6)* or "in *the* matter" (JND/RV). It has been suggested, for good reason, that the word "brother" here should be understood in its widest sense. It should not be limited to a Christian "brother", but should include any man. The RV has "that no man transgress, and wrong his brother in the matter". The word "defraud" ('wrong', RV) is translated "get an advantage of us" in 2 Corinthians 2:11, and "make a gain of you" in 2 Corinthians 12:17-18. It is taking from a man what belongs to him, and to him alone. Paul's teaching is clear. He is warning us against overstepping the limits which divide right from wrong, and in particular, the boundary between purity and immorality. It is a specific warning against adultery. The sin of coveting another man's wife.

There are three reasons why we must take heed to the teaching of God's word here, and these are spelt out in vv.6-8:

- ***"Because that the Lord is the avenger of all such" (v.6).*** The word "avenger" *(endikos)* means that He will exact the penalty. Disobedience will bring God's displeasure and judgement. They had been "forewarned" of this. Compare Hebrews 13:4, "marriage is honourable in all, and the bed (the marriage bed) undefiled: but whoremongers (fornicators) and adulterers God will judge." Note that in the case of David and Bathsheba, there was forgiveness (2 Samuel 12:13), but David did not escape the consequences of his sin. He himself said, "he shall restore...fourfold" (v.6), and he paid with four of his children. (Count them up!). Notice that while Paul refers to "God" in vv.3, 5, 7, 8, 9, here he uses "Lord." See also Romans 12:19. This may be due to the fact that in both cases, he is citing an Old Testament passage. See Psalm 94:1. Compare Deuteronomy 32:35-36.

- ***"Because...God hath not called us unto uncleanness, but unto holiness" (v.7).*** Immorality is inconsistent with the call of God. The word 'God' is in the place of emphasis. The calling of God (the divine and effectual call) carries moral implications. The negative is now placed first (compare vv.4-5): "not...unto uncleanness." We cannot therefore continue in our old way of life, particularly in immorality. The positive follows: "but unto holiness."

- ***"Because...God...hath also given unto us his holy Spirit ('Holy Spirit', JND)" (v.8).*** "He ... that despiseth, despiseth not man, but God (compare 1 Samuel 8:7), who hath also given unto us his holy Spirit." The meaning of the word "despise" *(atheteo)* is 'to displace', 'set aside, 'make void', or 'nullify.' We cannot miss the emphasis: "God, who hath also given unto us his **Holy** Spirit." Compare Ephesians 4:30, "Grieve not (by various things including "corrupt communication") the **holy** Spirit of God, whereby ye are sealed unto the day of redemption." See also 1 Corinthians 6:19, "What? Know ye not that your body is the temple of the **Holy** Ghost which is in you, which ye have of God, and ye are not your own?" Just read the preceding verses. The title "Holy Spirit" (1 Thess. 4:8) and "Holy Ghost" (1 Cor. 6:19) have the same background.

Perhaps we could look at this another way, without for one moment contradicting the above, and say that the words, "God, who hath also given unto us his holy Spirit", also remind us that we have not only been **called** to a holy life, but we have been given the capacity, through the Holy spirit to **live** a holy life.

These three reasons for implanting the teaching of God's word have been summed up as follows. We must live holy lives because failure to do so will *infringe divine rights* (v.6), *invite divine wrath* (v.6), and *insult a divine* Person (v.8). This brings us to:

ii) Spiritual relationships, vv.9-10
It has been suggested that so-called love in the world leads to physical compromise, but "brotherly love" will enable us to safeguard the rights of our brethren. It will preserve us from 'going beyond and defrauding our brother.' (v.6). Brotherly love is intolerant of immorality (vv.1-8) and indolence (vv.11-12). Brotherly love and promiscuity cannot co-exist. They are mutually exclusive.

"But as touching brotherly love ye need not that I write unto you (compare 5:1): for ye yourselves are taught of God to love one another" (v.9). This is clear from v.10! "And indeed ye do it toward all the brethren which are in all Macedonia: but we beseech you, brethren, that ye increase more and more." While the Thessalonians needed guidance in connection with sexual purity, they did not have to be told to love one another! The words "brotherly love" occur as a place name in Revelation 3:7, "And to the angel of the church in **Philadelphia** write...". Every assembly ought to be called 'Philadelphia!'. It means 'family love', or 'love of brethren.' The words, "for ye yourselves are **taught of God** to love (from *agape*) one another", indicate that love for one another is an essential part of the new nature. This love is implanted in us by God himself. "We know that we have passed from death unto life, because we love the brethren" (1 John 3:14). We must not think that Paul is implying that love of the Thessalonians was restricted to believers in their own area. The words "in all Macedonia" mean that the Thessalonians loved all the believers with whom they were in contact. Here is another way in which the assembly at Thessalonica was a 'role model' (see 1:7).

While Paul had no need to tell them to love one another, he doesn't leave it there! There must be no standing still in mutual love between believers: "but we beseech (exhort, *parakaleo*) you, brethren, that ye increase more and more." Compare 3:12; 4:1. Do remember that we will never be able to help one another effectively unless we love one another.

iii) Secular relationships, vv.11-12

Brotherly love will preserve believers from 'sponging' on fellow-Christians. These verses warn against the abuse of brotherly love. Paul therefore continues, "and that ye study to be quiet ('seek earnestly to be quiet', JND), and to do your own business, and to work with your own hands, as we commanded you." The word "study" *(philotimeomai)* really means 'to be ambitious' or 'to make it our aim.' It is rendered "labour" in 2 Corinthians 5:9 ("Wherefore we **labour**, that, whether present or absent, we may be accepted of him"), and "strive" in Romans 15:20 ("Yea, so have I **strived** to preach the gospel"). Substitute the word 'ambitious' for "study", "labour", and "strive", and then review **your** ambitions! Are **we** ambitious for God?

We should note the following. To "be quiet" means 'to be at rest.' It means to have orderly and peaceful lives. It means that we cause no disturbance to other people. We are not to be excitable and unstable people. To "do your own business" means to be occupied with your own affairs. We are not to be "busybodies" (2 Thess. 3:11). To "work with your own hands" means to pursue secular employment. Christians are not to be idle people. Compare 2 Thess. 3:10, "For even when we were with you, this we commanded you, that if any would not work, neither should he eat." The previous verses make it clear that Paul and his colleagues were examples of their own teaching. Remember that this is all part of 'walking and pleasing God' (v.1).

Paul gives two reasons for his teaching here. Firstly, "That ye may walk honestly toward them that are without" and, secondly, "That ye may have lack of nothing." The word "honestly" means 'becomingly', 'decently', or 'seemly.' It is so important that we do nothing to invalidate our testimony before unbelievers. Remember that our general conduct, including our attitude to secular work, will reflect on the testimony of our assembly and on the testimony of our fellow-Christians. Our love for our brothers and sisters in Christ should therefore ensure that we do nothing to bring them into disrepute. The second reason needs no explanation. We must be able to support ourselves. 'Spongers' need not apply! This is a particular warning to those "which walk among you disorderly, working not at all", 2 Thessalonians 3:11. Compare Titus 3:8 & 14. We are to "provide things honest *('kalos'*, meaning 'fair, right, honourable') in the sight of all men." The highest possible standards are demanded in our relationships with fellow-Christians, and with non-Christians as well.

READ CHAPTER 4:13-18

"The Lord himself shall descend from heaven with a shout"

We have already noticed that, for good reasons, 1 Thessalonians 4 has been called the 'Enoch Chapter.' In the first place, Paul reminds us how we "ought to walk and to please God" (v.1), just like Enoch, and in the second place we learn that "we which are alive and remain unto the coming of the Lord" will be "caught up" (vv.15, 17), just like Enoch. With this in mind, we divided the chapter into two major sections: *(1)* the conduct of saints (vv.1-12); *(2)* the coming of the Lord (vv.13-18).

1) THE CONDUCT OF SAINTS, vv.1-12
As we have seen, Paul deals here with the sexual, spiritual and secular aspects of our lives, emphasising the need for holiness of life (vv.3-8), harmony of love (vv.9-10), and honesty of labour (vv.11-12).

2) THE COMING OF THE LORD, vv.13-18
Leaving aside the possibility of altering the punctuation, these verses certainly amplify the statement made at the end of Chapter 3 as it stands: "The Lord make you to increase and abound in love...to the end he may stablish your hearts unblameable in holiness before God, even our Father, at **the coming of our Lord Jesus Christ with all his saints**" (v.13). Having stated that every believer will be present when the Lord comes, Paul now explains how this will happen. This was a matter of particular concern for the Christians at Thessalonica, who were evidently under the impression that fellow-believers who had died would not be involved in the Lord's coming. With this in mind, we can divide the section as follows: *(a)* the concern of the Thessalonians (v.13); *(b)* the coming of the Lord (vv.14-17); *(c)* the comfort of the sorrowing (v.18).

a) The concern of the Thessalonians, v.13
"But I would not have you to be ignorant, brethren, concerning them which are asleep, that ye sorrow not, even as others which have no hope." We must notice that they were not concerned for themselves, but for those "which are asleep."

Chapter 4A

Very clearly, the Christians at Thessalonica were **expecting** the Lord Jesus to return. They had "turned to God from idols to serve the living and true God", and were waiting for "his Son from heaven, whom he raised from the dead, even Jesus, which delivered us from the wrath to come" (1:9-10). But what about those believers who had died? It seemed that for them, the happy prospect of the Lord's coming had evaporated. In consequence, their funerals were sad beyond words, and resembled the funerals of unsaved men and women. We must therefore notice how Paul addresses their concern. Even in his preliminary remarks, light begins to shine:

i) Knowledge, not ignorance
"But I would not have you to be **ignorant**, brethren, concerning them which are asleep." As T. Bentley (writing in *Precious Seed*) points out, Paul inserts the heart-warming word, "brethren", to disarm any possible objection to the use of the word "ignorant." He uses a similar form of words in Romans 1:13; 11:25; 1 Corinthians 10:1; 1 Corinthians 12:1; 2 Corinthians 1:8. Bearing in mind that Timothy "brought...good tidings" of their "faith and charity" (3:6), but said nothing about their hope, there can be little doubt that Paul had this in mind when he wrote, "Night and day praying exceedingly that we might see your face, and might **perfect that which is lacking in your faith**" (3:10). He now takes the opportunity to 'perfect that which was lacking in their faith', with particular reference to "them which are asleep."

While 1 & 2 Thessalonians were amongst Paul's earliest letters, and the canon of Scripture was far from complete, we must remember that God has now "given unto us all things that pertain unto life and godliness" (2 Pet. 1:3). We do not have to ask God to **add** to His word. We have to ask God to help us **from** His word! Just like the Psalmist: "Open thou mine eyes, that I may behold wondrous things **out of** thy law", (Psalm 119:18). The Christians at Thessalonica needed new teaching to help them, but **we** must explore God's word for answers to our problems and difficulties. God has told us all that we need to know. "The secret things belong unto the Lord our God: but those things which are revealed belong unto us and to our children for ever" (Deut. 29:29). In view of this, let's explore every part of our Bibles. God doesn't want **us** to be ignorant either. He wants us to enjoy the prospect of the Lord's coming, and everything else as well! It would be tragic if it had to be said of **us,** "My people are destroyed for lack of knowledge" (Hos. 4:6).

ii) Sleep, not death
"But I would not have you to be ignorant, brethren, concerning them which are **asleep**." The authorities tell us that the verb is in the present continuous tense,

and should be rendered either 'them that are lying asleep' or 'them who are falling asleep.' As T. Bentley observes, "the word for "asleep" appears eighteen times in the New Testament, fifteen of which refer to death. See, for example, Mark 5:39". The Lord Jesus referred to death as sleep in relation to a believer in John 11:11.

It is very important to bear in mind that the word asleep refers only to the believer's body. Very clearly, the spirit is not unconscious. When a Christian dies, they are "absent from the body, and...present with the Lord" (2 Cor. 5:8). Paul desired to "depart, and to be with Christ; which is far better" (Phil. 1:23). 'Sleep' is a most appropriate metaphor. W.E. Vine puts it nicely: "The object of the metaphor is to suggest that as the sleeper does not cease to exist while his body sleeps, so the dead person continues to exist despite his absence from the region in which those who remain can communicate with him, and that, as sleep is known to be temporary, so the death of the body will be found to be temporary. Sleep has its waking: death will have its resurrection". This reminds us that resurrection refers also only to the body. See Matthew 27:52, "And the graves were opened; and many bodies of the saints which slept arose, and came out of the graves after his resurrection, and went into the holy city, and appeared unto many." We should also add that the word "sleep" applies to the bodies of unsaved people as well as saved people. See Daniel 12:2, "And many of them that sleep in the dust of the earth shall awake, some to everlasting life, and some to shame and everlasting contempt." We know from Luke 16:19-31, that unsaved people are certainly conscious after death. There is no 'soul sleep' for them either.

iii) Sorrow, not despair
Paul does not say that Christians should not sorrow, but that they "sorrow not, even as others which have no hope." Grieving is a normal and proper human experience which the Lord Jesus shared. See John 11:35. When Stephen died, under a hail of stones, "devout men" carried him to his burial, "and made great lamentation over him" (Acts 8:2). In this connection, it is worth remembering that some believers express their sorrow more than others, and some accept the situation more quickly than others. In every case, God's people should be characterised by thoughtfulness, kindness and sympathy to bereaved fellow-believers.

But we "sorrow not, even as others which have no hope". T.E. Wilson, who served the Lord for many years in Angola, writes as follows: "Pagan sorrow does not characterise the Christian. This can be seen today in places like Central Africa, where the weeping, heart-rending wailing and hysterical tearing of the hair at a pagan funeral is in sharp contrast to the quiet submission and singing of hymns of praise when a Christian goes home to be with the Lord". See also W.E. Vine

Chapter 4A

(Collected Writings - 1 Thessalonians). We "rest in hope of the glory of God" (Rom. 5:2). The Lord Jesus Himself is "our hope" (1 Tim. 1:1). It is a "blessed hope" (Titus 2:13). It has been beautifully said that

> On earth we have the tears without the reason:
> In heaven we'll have the reason without the tears.

Well, if Christians "sorrow not, even as others which have no hope", what **is** the Christian's "hope?" Read on!

b) The coming of the Lord, vv.14-17
We will ponder these precious verses under three headings. *(i)* There is no **doubt** about the welfare of sleeping saints (v.14); *(ii)* There is no **disadvantage** for sleeping saints (v.15); *(iii)* there is no **division** between sleeping and living saints (vv.16-17). Bearing in mind that Paul is addressing a problem in connection with "them which are asleep", notice the occurrence of the word "them" in these verses.

i) No doubt, v.14
"For if we believe that Jesus died (the word 'sleep' is not used in connection with the death of the Lord Jesus) and rose again, even so them also which sleep in Jesus will God bring with him." The resurrection of 'sleeping saints' is guaranteed by the resurrection of the Lord Jesus! There is no doubt about it! This is confirmed by the little expression, "even so." It means, 'in exactly the same way.' This is why Paul does not say 'Lord Jesus': he says "Jesus." This is most important. It emphasises the Lord's humanity. A **Man** went into death and came out of death, and because **that** Man died and rose again, every man or woman who dies trusting in Him will also be raised from the dead to enjoy eternal glory. The scholars point out that the words "sleep in Jesus" should be rendered, 'sleep through *(dia)* Jesus.' This has been variously interpreted. Possibly it means that whilst all the dead "sleep" (see again Daniel 12:2) only the believer 'sleeps through Jesus.' Every believer is assured of a glorious resurrection (unlike the resurrection of the unbeliever) because of the work of the Lord Jesus. His resurrection is the pledge of our resurrection. See 1 Corinthians 6:14; 15:20.

But what about the words, "Even so them also which sleep in Jesus will God **bring with him?**" Does it mean that when the Lord Jesus comes for living believers at the **rapture**, He will bring with Him the spirits of believers who have died, to be reunited with their bodies? Or does it mean that when the Lord Jesus comes to **reign,** He will be accompanied by all the believers who have died, and that Paul is now going to explain that this can happen because they have already been raised from the dead?

Both explanations are popular! But there is a third explanation. The expression "with him" *(sun auto)* does not mean at the same time, but in association with Him. Its meaning is clear from a similar construction in Ephesians 2:5-6: "But God...even when we were dead in sins, hath quickened us together *(sun)* with Christ...And hath raised us up together *(sun)*, and made us sit together *(sun)* in heavenly places in Christ Jesus."

It is important to remember that at this point in the chapter, Paul is referring to the **resurrection** of 'sleeping saints', rather than the **rapture.** (Both are, of course, simultaneous!). "For if we believe that Jesus died and rose again, even so (that is, in like manner) them also which sleep in Jesus will God bring (that is, bring them from the dead) with him." That is, in association with His resurrection. His resurrection is the guarantee of the resurrection of sleeping saints. This is the teaching of 1 Corinthians 15:20-23: "But now is Christ risen from the dead, and become the firstfruits of them that slept... Christ the firstfruits; afterward they that are Christ's at his coming." See also 2 Corinthians 4:14: "Knowing that he who has raised the Lord Jesus shall raise us also with Jesus..." (JND). *Our* resurrection is associated with *His* resurrection.

ii) No disadvantage, v.15

"For this we say unto you by the word of the Lord, that we which are alive and remain unto the coming of the Lord shall not prevent (precede) them which are asleep." The believers at Thessalonica thought their deceased brethren were terribly disadvantaged. Paul now tells them that they have an advantage! That is true generally. After all, they are **already** with Christ which is "far better!" But now we learn that when the Lord comes, the 'sleeping saints' are going to be the vanguard. Certainly not the rearguard! We shall see why in the next two verses. But notice two important statements first:

- **Paul's teaching was divinely-revealed to him.** He spoke "by the word of the Lord." As we shall see later, the Lord Jesus certainly spoke about those "which are alive and remain", and those "which are asleep", but He did not give further details at the time. We must remember that He said, "I have yet many things to say unto you, but ye cannot bear them now. Howbeit when he, the Spirit of truth, is come, he will guide you into all truth" (John 16:12-13). Further details of the Lord's coming were revealed by the Lord to Paul through the Holy Spirit. A.J. Mason *(Ellicott's Commentary)* calls this "a most direct claim to plenary inspiration". Compare 1 Corinthians 11:23. So his teaching rings with absolute certainty. The Lord Jesus has pledged His word. He "cannot lie." It is **His** word! So we have "the word of the Lord" about "the coming of the Lord!" No room for speculation here! Paul relates what the Lord had told him about His coming. Paul refers to the same event in 1 Cor. 15:51, "Behold, I shew you a mystery; We shall not all sleep, but we shall all be changed." A "mystery" is something previously unrevealed, and therefore not found in the Old Testament.

- *Paul's teaching emphasises that we should expect the Lord to come at any time.* "**We** which are alive and remain unto the coming of the Lord." See also v.17. Paul knew later that he would die. See 2 Timothy 4:6. Peter knew that he would die. The Lord told him personally. See John 21:18-19. But we have no such assurance! Our proper hope is to "wait for his Son from heaven." Just like the Thessalonians.

iii) No division, vv.16-17
Paul now describes the coming of the Lord Jesus to receive His people. "For the Lord himself shall descend from heaven with a shout, with the voice of the archangel, and with the trump of God: and the dead in Christ shall rise first: then we which are alive and remain shall be caught up **together with them** in the clouds, to meet the Lord in the air: and so shall we ever be with the Lord." There is so much here! Let's try to look at it like this:

- **The return**. "For the Lord himself shall descend from heaven (*ouranos*) with a shout, with the voice of the archangel, and with the trump of God." For a start, why not make a list of passages containing the word "himself." For example, Luke 24:15, Hebrews 2:14 etc. He will come "himself." The Jewish exiles will be gathered later by angelic power. "He shall send his **angels** with a great sound of a trumpet, and **they** shall gather together his elect from the four winds" (Matt. 24:31). In John 14, the Lord Jesus describes His coming from His standpoint: in 1 Thessalonians 4, Paul describes His coming from our standpoint.

John 14:3	**1 Thessalonians 4:16-17**
"I will come again................"	"The Lord himself shall descend from heaven with a shout."
To "receive you unto myself...."	"To meet the Lord in the air."
"That where I am, there ye may be also."	"So shall we ever be with the Lord."

The coming of the Lord will be accompanied by three things. "A shout...the voice of the archangel...the trump of God."

The "shout." It is a shout of command *(keleusma).* W.E. Vine explains that it is akin to *keleuo,* meaning 'to command.' Quite clearly, His shout of command will be irresistible, and reminds us that when the Lord Jesus "cried with a loud voice, Lazarus, come forth", there was an immediate response: "And he that was dead came forth" (John 11:43-44). Compare John 5:28. But to whom is the "shout" here addressed? Is it also to the dead? Read on!

The "voice of the archangel." Scholars tell us that "the shout" and "the voice of the archangel" are one and the same. It can be translated, 'The Lord himself shall descend from heaven with a shout, in **(en)** the voice of the archangel', or 'in archangel's voice', or 'with archangel's voice' (JND). This does not mean that the archangel (only Michael is given this title) will shout (!), but that the Lord's shout will have the character of the 'archangel's voice.' But why "the voice of (the) archangel?" The answer evidently lies in Jude v.9: "Michael the archangel, when contending with the devil...disputed about the body of Moses." We learn, therefore, that Satan claims the bodies of men. This is why he is called, "him that had the power of death." (Death receives the bodies of men: hell, that is, hades, receives the souls of men: see Revelation 1:18, 20:13). But the power of Satan will be incapable of preventing the resurrection of the saints when the Lord Jesus returns. In addition to Jude v.9, we should read the references to Michael in Daniel 10:13, 21; 12:1-2, and Revelation 12:7. In all cases, the archangel prevails. The Lord Jesus will prevail: hence the expression "with the voice of (the) archangel." Only believers will hear this shout!

The "trump of God." This is "the last trump" of 1 Corinthians 15:52. We must not confuse this with the seventh trumpet in Revelation 11:15. This will signal the end of the seven 'trumpet judgments' on earth. In the Old Testament, silver trumpets (Numbers 10) were blown for four reasons, and while they have no immediate connection with "the last trump", their use certainly reminds us of four things that will happen when the Lord comes. They were blown to gather the people (vv.3-4); they were blown to initiate movement (vv.5-6); they were blown to signal victory (v.9); they were blown at times of rejoicing (v.10). Now apply all that to "the last trump!"

- *The resurrection.* "The dead in Christ shall rise first." The wording is important. Not 'the dead in Jesus', or the 'dead in the Lord', but "the dead **in Christ.**" Bearing in mind that "God hath made that same Jesus, whom ye have crucified, both Lord and Christ", this means that believers are destined to share His glory. He is "the firstfruits" (1 Cor. 15:23). But the expression, "the dead in Christ", has another significance. J.J. Stubbs puts it like this: "This phrase, often used by the apostle in his epistles, refers to the spiritual union of believers with Christ. God sees every believer 'in Christ'". This term refers to the **standing** of a believer, not to the **state** of a believer. We should notice the difference in the New Testament between the terms, "in Christ", and, "in the Lord." The former speaks of **position,** while the latter speaks of **condition.**' This is most important in connection with what follows:

- **The rapture**. "Then we which are alive and remain shall be **caught up** together with them in the clouds, to meet the Lord in the air." As W.E. Vine points out, the word, "then", marks the order of events, but does not necessarily imply any interval. We must remember that all this will happen "in a moment, in the twinkling of a eye." The words, "caught up" *(harpazo),* are used of Philip in Acts 8:39 ("caught away"), of Paul in 2 Corinthians 12:2, 4, and of the "man child" in Revelation 12:5. It occurs in John 10:12 (AV "catcheth": JND 'seize'), and in John 10:28-29 (AV "pluck": JND 'seize'). The word signifies 'to carry off by force.' It is a force that cannot be resisted. Satan is called "the prince of the power of the air" (Eph. 2:2), but he could not stop the ascension of the Lord Jesus, and he will not be able to impede our translation to heaven either!

The Lord Jesus spoke about the resurrection and rapture of His people in John 11:25-26, "I am the resurrection and the life: he that believes on me, though he have died, shall live; and every one who lives and believes on me shall never die" (JND). Compare 1 Corinthians 15:51, "we shall not all sleep, but we shall all be changed." 1 Corinthians 15 deals with the resurrection in detail, but not the rapture. 1 Thessalonians emphasises the rapture. We are going to "meet the Lord!" Hallelujah!

- **The reunion**. "Then we which are alive and remain shall be caught up together **with them** in the clouds, to meet the Lord in the air." The dead (v.16) and the living (v.17), will together "meet the Lord," and be for ever "with the Lord."

> Friends will be there I have loved long ago;
> Joy like a river around me shall flow;
> Yet, just a smile from my Saviour, I know.,
> Will through the ages be glory for me.

c) The comfort of the sorrowing, v.18
No wonder Paul says, "Wherefore comfort (encourage) one another with these

words!" The chapter therefore begins ("exhort") and ends, with encouragement. Rightly understood the coming of the Lord Jesus is an incentive to us all to 'walk and please God' in holiness of life, harmony of love, and honesty of labour (vv.1-12).

It has been nicely said that in 1 Corinthians 15, the saints are still on earth! The subject is resurrection not rapture. In 1 Thessalonians 4 the saints are in the air, but not in heaven. In John 14, the saints are in the Father's house!

"Even so, come, Lord Jesus".

READ CHAPTER 5:1-11

"Sudden destruction"

1 Thessalonians 5 clearly divides into two major sections. They can be broadly entitled **(1)** preservation from the day of the Lord (vv.1-11), and **(2)** preservation from spiritual disorders (vv.12-28).

1) PRESERVATION FROM THE DAY OF THE LORD, vv.1-11
We now reach the second of the two sections in the epistle which describe the Lord's return. Whilst, as we shall see, they deal with different phases of His coming, they both end in the same way. The first (4:13-18) concludes with the words, "Wherefore comfort (encourage) one another with these words", and the second (5:1-11) with the words, "Wherefore comfort (encourage) yourselves together..." There is, however, a difference of emphasis. In Chapter 4, Paul writes about the Lord's coming in connection with Christians who have died, but in Chapter 5, he writes about the Lord's coming in connection with Christians who are alive. In the first case, he assures them that believers who die will not miss the Lord's coming. In the second, he assures them that believers who are alive will not pass through the judgments associated with "the day of the Lord."

It is quite clear that Paul distinguishes clearly between the events in Chapter 4, and the events in Chapter 5. Having said, "I would not have you to be ignorant, brethren" in connection with the former (4:13), he now says, "But of the times and seasons, brethren, ye have no need that I write unto you. For yourselves know perfectly that the day of the Lord so cometh as a thief in the night" (5:1-2). We can put it like this:

- ***In Chapter 4***, he deals with people destined for blessing.
- ***In Chapter 5***, he deals with people subject to judgment.

- ***In Chapter 4***, he deals with people removed from the world.
- ***In Chapter 5***, he deals with people remaining on earth.

- **In Chapter 4**, he deals with a welcome event.
- **In Chapter 5**, he deals with an unwelcome event.

- **In Chapter 4**, he deals with unending joy.
- **In Chapter 5**, he deals with inescapable travail.

We can divide the passage as follows; *(a)* their consciousness of "the times and the seasons" (v.1); *(b)* the coming of "the day of the Lord" (vv.2-3); *(c)* the character of the believer (vv.4-5); *(d)* their conduct as "children of the day" (vv.6-8); *(e)* the certainty of deliverance from "wrath" (vv.9-10); *(f)* their continuance in mutual fellowship (v.11).

a) Their consciousness of "the times and the seasons", v.1
"But of the times and seasons, brethren, ye have no need that I write unto you." The very expression "times and seasons" (it also occurs in Genesis 1:14) makes it clear that Paul is describing earthly events. The word "times" (*chronos*) is indicative of duration, and the word "seasons" *(kairos)* is indicative of character. It is used in Acts 3:19. This is a distinct change from the setting in 4:13-18. The same expression occurs in Acts 1:6-7, "Lord, wilt thou at this time restore again the kingdom to Israel? And he said unto them, It is not for you to know the times or the seasons, which the Father hath put in his own power." We should remember that the Lord Jesus is not saying here that they shouldn't know **about** "the times and the seasons", but that they should not be concerned about the **commencement** of the "times and seasons." There was no necessity for Paul to write about future events on earth for two reasons:

- He had given them **previous teaching** on the subject. See 2 Thess. 2:5, "Remember ye not, that, when I was yet with you, I told you these things?" They knew "perfectly that the day of the Lord so cometh as a thief in the night" (v.2). This is quite different from his teaching about the coming of the Lord in Chapter 4. While they were expecting the Lord to come (1:10), they needed further teaching on the subject, and Paul introduces this with the words, "this we say unto you by the word of the Lord." This was something entirely new. The Lord Jesus introduced the subject in John 11:25-26 and 14:1-3 (see our previous study), but added, "I have yet many things to say unto you, but ye cannot bear them now. Howbeit when he, the Spirit of truth, is come, he will guide you into all truth...and he will shew you things to come" (John 16:12-13).

- These events were **predicted in the Old Testament**, where "the day of the Lord" (v.2) is frequently mentioned. The Old Testament has nothing to say about the coming of the Lord for believers as described in 1 Thessalonians 4. Hence, "Behold, I shew you a *mystery:* we shall not all sleep, but we shall all be changed" (1 Cor.15:51). A "mystery" is something "which in other ages was *not* made known unto the sons of men, as it is *now* revealed unto his holy apostles and prophets by the Spirit" (Eph. 3:1-5). Paul is writing here about the church, but notice his definition of a "mystery".

b) The coming of "the day of the Lord", vv.2-3
"For yourselves know perfectly that the day of the Lord so cometh as a thief in the night. For when they shall say, Peace and safety; then sudden destruction cometh upon them, as travail upon a woman with child; and they shall not escape."

Notice the word "perfectly" *(akribos)* means 'accurately.' It also occurs in Acts 18:26, "And he (Apollos) began to speak boldly in the synagogue: whom when Aquila and Priscilla had heard, they took him unto them, and expounded unto him the way of God more perfectly." It is very important to be accurate in understanding the Scriptures, and in teaching them. While we all have a long way to go here, we should at least make it our objective!

Now, a little revision. The expression, "the day of the Lord", reminds us that we do need to distinguish between various 'days' mentioned in the New Testament. There are four:

- *'Man's day'.* See 1 Corinthians 4:3, where "man's judgment" (AV) is better translated, 'man's day'. We live, at the moment, in 'man's day'.

- *"The day of Jesus Christ"*, elsewhere called "the day of Christ" (Phil. 1:10; 2:16); "the day of our Lord Jesus Christ" (1 Cor. 1:8); "the day of the Lord Jesus" (1 Cor. 5:5; 2 Cor. 1:14), and "that day" (2 Tim. 4:8). These passages all refer to the Lord's coming and to His review and reward of our work for Him. This will take place in heaven.

- *"The day of the Lord".* Unlike "the day of Christ", this refers to events on earth, and includes divine judgment on wicked men, together with the millennial reign of the Lord Jesus. See 1 Thess. 5:2. and 2 Thess. 2:2, where it is very important to notice the translation, "that ye be not soon shaken in mind...as that the day of the Lord is present" (RV/JND). The Old Testament prophecies abound with references to "the day of the Lord".

- *"The day of God".* This expression occurs in 2 Peter 3:12, and refers to the eternal state.

Zephaniah describes "the day of the Lord" as follows: "The great day of the LORD is near, it is near, and hasteneth greatly, even the voice of the day of the LORD: the mighty man shall cry there bitterly. That day is a day of wrath, a day of trouble and distress, a day of wasteness and desolation, a day of darkness and gloominess, a day of clouds and thick darkness" (Zeph. 1:14-15). Malachi describes it as "the great and terrible day of the LORD" (Mal. 4:5). Here, the **commencement** of the period is emphasised: "the day of the Lord so **cometh** as a thief in the night." Two figures are used:

- **"As a thief in the night".** First of all, **the event will be unexpected.** "For yourselves know perfectly that the day of the Lord so cometh as a **thief in the night**." Compare 2 Peter 3:10, "But the day of the Lord will come as a thief in the night; in the which the heavens shall pass away with a great noise, and the elements shall melt with fervent heat, the earth also and the works that are therein shall be burned up." The dissolution of creation will take place at the **end** of "the day of the Lord." While "the day of the Lord" will commence before the Lord Jesus returns to earth as the great Warrior-King (Rev. 19:11-21), His actual coming is described in similar terms. See Revelation 16:15, "Behold, I come as a thief." It therefore follows that -

Secondly, **the world will be unprepared.** "When they shall say, Peace and safety (like the false prophets: see, for example, Jeremiah 6:14); then **sudden destruction** cometh upon them." While, once again, Paul is describing the commencement of "the day of the Lord", the actual return of the Lord to bring these judgments to a conclusion, is described in the same way. See Matthew 24:37-45. "For as in the days that were before the flood they were eating and drinking, marrying and giving in marriage, until the day that Noe entered into the ark, and **knew not** until the flood came, and took them all away; so shall also the coming of the Son of man be...But know this, that if the goodman of the house had known in what watch the **thief** would come, he would have watched, and would not have suffered his house to be broken up. Therefore be ye also ready: for in such an hour as ye think not the Son of man cometh". Compare Luke 21:34, "Take heed to yourselves, lest at any time your hearts be overcharged with surfeiting, and drunkenness, and cares of this life, and so that day come upon you **unawares**". When the Lord's coming is described as a thief, it is always in connection with judgment. See Revelation 3:3.

Divine judgment will fall on the world when it is least expected. There will be "Peace and safety." This suggests that ultimately, the outstanding conflicts will be resolved, and humanity will breathe a huge sigh of relief. The world will enter a period symbolised in Revelation 6 by the rider on a white horse who will impose peace by his ability to deliver destruction through the air (v.2). But he will be followed by the rider, carrying a "great sword", who will abolish peace (v.4). He will be followed by two further riders symbolising famine (vv.5-6) and death (v.8).

- *"As travail upon a woman with child."* "When they shall say, Peace and safety; then sudden destruction cometh upon them, as travail upon a woman with child; and they shall not **escape**." This stresses that the judgments connected with the "day of the Lord" will be **inescapable**.

The figure of a travailing woman is used particularly of Israel. See Jeremiah 30:5-7, "Ask ye now, and see whether a man doth travail with child? Wherefore do I see every man with his hands on his loins, as a **woman in travail**, and all faces are turned into paleness? Alas! For that day is great, so that none is like it: it is even the time of Jacob's trouble; but he shall be saved out of it." See also Micah 5:3, "Therefore will he give them up, until the time that she which travaileth hath brought forth." Compare Revelation 12:1-5.

c) *The character of the believer, vv.4-5*
We must notice the contrast: "When **they** shall say, Peace and safety; then sudden destruction cometh upon **them**, as travail upon a woman with child; and **they** shall not escape. But **ye**, brethren, are not in darkness (which is when the thief comes), that that day should overtake **you** as a thief. Ye are all the children of light, and the children of the day: **we** are not of the night, nor of darkness."

The judgment described in vv.2-3 will fall upon men and women in "darkness." Quite obviously, the word is used in a bad sense. It describes men and women alienated from God. See, for example, Ephesians 5:8 ("For ye were sometimes **darkness**, but now are ye light in the Lord"); 1 Peter 2:9 (God has called us "out of **darkness** into his marvellous light"); John 3:19 ("Men loved **darkness** rather than light, because their deeds were evil"); John 8:12 ("I am the light of the world: he that followeth me shall not walk in **darkness**, but shall have the light of life"). The "sudden destruction" is **not** therefore applicable to believers. They are "the children of light, and the children of the day." They are "**not** of the night, **nor** of darkness." This is emphasised by the inclusion of the little word "for" in the New Translation (JND): 'But ye, brethren, are not in darkness, that that day should overtake you as a thief: **for** all ye are sons of light and sons of day: we are not of night nor of darkness."

This is true of every believer; hence "ye are *all* the children of light, and the children of the day." This is confirmed in v.9, "For God hath not appointed *us* to wrath (the wrath of the "day of the Lord"), but to obtain salvation by our Lord Jesus Christ." Divine wrath will fall upon men and women "in darkness", not upon "sons of light and sons of day" (JND). We do not belong to the sphere of darkness. The expression 'son of' means 'having the nature of' or, 'having the character of.' 'Sons of light' describes what we *are*: we are "light in the Lord". 'Sons of day' describes where we *move*: we "walk as children of light" (Eph. 5:8).

d) Our conduct as "children of the day", vv.6-8
"Therefore let *us* not sleep, as do others; but let *us* watch and be sober. For *they* that sleep sleep in the night; and *they* that be drunken are drunken in the night. But let *us*, who are of the day, be sober, putting on the breastplate of faith and love; and for an helmet, the hope of salvation." Notice how Paul continues to differentiate between 'sons of night' (our expression) and 'sons of day.' It is a question of "us" and "they." But, as usual in the Bible, Paul now addresses the present in the light of the future. He says in effect, 'Since you don't belong to the sphere of darkness, with its sleep and drunkenness, don't behave as if you do!' We are to have "no fellowship with the unfruitful works of darkness" (Eph. 5:11). He gives us three exhortations:

- **"Let us watch"**. We are to be spiritually alert and aware. We are not to sleep. See, for example, Ephesians 5:14, "Awake thou that sleepest, and arise from the dead, and Christ shall give thee light. See then that ye walk circumspectly, not as fools, but as wise". We need to be alert in connection with false teachers: "Also of your own selves shall men arise, speaking perverse things, to draw away disciples after them. Therefore **watch**..." (Acts 20:30-31). We all need to "**watch** and pray" (Matt. 26:41). We need to be alert in prayer: "Continue in prayer, and **watch** in the same with thanksgiving" (Col. 4:2). See also 1 Corinthians 15:13.

- **"Be sober"**. Yes, it does mean, 'to be free from the influence of intoxicants', and it is difficult to escape the conclusion that Paul is contrasting literal drunkenness in v.7, with literal sobriety in v.8. But if alcohol can cloud judgment, and impair balance, then the 'heady wine' of popularity, or position, or prominence, can impair our sound judgment and disturb our spiritual balance. It can result in self-assertiveness, excitability, and insobriety of language and behaviour. Compare 2 Timothy 4:5, "But thou, be sober ("watch", AV) in all things" (JND). Read Romans 13:11-14.

- *"Putting on the breastplate...helmet"*. The tense (aorist) means 'put on and keep on the breastplate of faith and love; and for an helmet, the hope of salvation.' This will enable us to be "sober." Paul is quoting from Isaiah 59:17 here: "For he (the Lord) put on righteousness as a breastplate, and an helmet of salvation upon his head; and he put on the garments of vengeance for clothing, and was clad with zeal as a cloke." The New Testament refers to the Christian's armour in Romans 13:12 ("the armour of light"); Ephesians 6: 13 ("the whole armour of God"), and 2 Cor. 6:7 ("the armour of righteousness").

We should notice that **the heart must be protected**. This involves "the breastplate of faith and love." Faith is Godward, and love is manward. Faith and love give protection to the heart. Then we should notice that the **head must be protected:** "for an helmet, the hope of salvation." This is selfward. The Thessalonians needed this helmet in view of false teaching about the Lord's coming. See 2 Thessalonians 2:1-2, "Now we beseech you, brethren, by the coming of our Lord Jesus Christ, and by our gathering together unto him, that ye be not soon shaken **in mind,** or be troubled, neither by spirit, nor by word, nor by letter as from us, as that the day of Christ ('the day of the Lord', JND) is at hand ('is present', JND). For "the hope of salvation", see 1 Peter 1:3-5.

T. Bentley puts it nicely: "Faith here denotes dependence, while love suggests devotion. Hope signifies deliverance. The Christian's defence is sure for he is sufficiently guarded by the three virtues of faith, love and hope". Compare 1:3, "your work of faith, and labour of love, and patience of hope in our Lord Jesus Christ." See also Philippians 4:7. The "hope of salvation" is now explained:

e) The certainty of deliverance from "wrath", vv.9-10
"For God hath not appointed us to wrath, but to obtain salvation by our Lord Jesus Christ, who died for us, that, whether we wake or sleep, we should live together with him." We should notice at least three things here:

- **The statement.** "God hath not appointed us to wrath." As already noted, this refers to the divine wrath which will fall on the world in the dark and dreadful "day of the Lord". Paul refers to this in 1:9-10, "For they themselves shew of us what manner of entering in we had unto you, and how ye turned to God from idols to serve the living and true God; and to wait for his Son from heaven, whom he raised from the dead, even Jesus, which delivered us from the wrath to come ('our deliverer from the coming wrath', JND)". The "wrath" in v.9 is the "sudden destruction" of v.3.

- **The salvation.** "To obtain salvation by our Lord Jesus Christ." This refers, not to salvation from sin, but to salvation from the "day of the Lord." This salvation will be accomplished by the coming of the Lord Jesus described in 4:13-18. Paul refers to this again in 2 Thessalonians 2:1-2, "Now we beseech you, brethren, by the **coming** of our Lord Jesus Christ, and by **our gathering together unto him**, that ye be not soon shaken in mind, or be troubled, neither by spirit, nor by word, nor by letter as from us, as that the day of Christ ('the day of the Lord', JND) is at hand ('is present', JND).

- **The basis.** "Who died for us, that, whether we wake or sleep, we should live together with him." The basis of our salvation from coming wrath on earth, is the death of the Lord Jesus. The 'rapture' is an integral part of our unmerited salvation secured by the Lord's death. Participation in the 'rapture' does not depend on our spiritual attainment, but solely on His work at Calvary. This is why Paul says, "whether we wake or sleep, we should live together with him." This does not mean, whether we are dead or alive, but whether we are alert and expectant, or lax and indifferent. The word "sleep" here *(katheudo)* is quite different to the word "sleep" *(koimaomai)* in 4:14. Whatever our spiritual condition, we will leave this world when the Lord comes, and "live together with him." ("So shall we ever be with the Lord", 4:17). But this does not mean that we can live as we please. Remember that "we must all appear before the judgment seat of Christ; that every one may receive the things done in the body, according to that he hath done, whether it be good or bad" (2 Cor. 5:10).

f) Their continuance in mutual fellowship, v.11
"Wherefore (with such a message of hope) comfort (encourage) yourselves together, and edify (build up) one another, even as also ye do." It's easier to break up than build up. Paul had no intention of letting these Christians slow down. They were to keep up the good work! Compare 4:10.

READ CHAPTER 5:12-28

"The very God of peace sanctify you wholly"

We have noticed that 1 Thessalonians 5 divides into two major sections, which can be broadly entitled **(1)** preservation from the day of the Lord (vv.1-11), and **(2)** preservation from spiritual disorders (vv.12-28).

1) PRESERVATION FROM THE DAY OF THE LORD, vv.1-11

The section can be summed up with the words, "For God hath not appointed us to wrath, but to obtain salvation by our Lord Jesus Christ, who died for us, that, whether we wake or sleep, we should live together with him" (vv.9-10). The "wrath" in question is the "sudden destruction" (v.3) of the "day of the Lord" (v.2). The Lord Jesus is 'our deliverer from the coming wrath' (1:10 JND). This brings us to the second section of the chapter, and to the concluding passage in the epistle.

2) PRESERVATION FROM SPIRITUAL DISORDERS, vv.12-28

The section refers to various disorders. For example, disunity is implied by the injunction, "And be at peace among yourselves" (v.13). Then there are "unruly" people (v.14). The apostle's prayer, "I pray God your whole spirit and soul and body be preserved blameless unto the coming of our Lord Jesus Christ" (v.23), reminds us of the ever-present danger of immorality. We may divide the passage as follows: **(a)** appreciation (vv.12-13); **(b)** ministration (v.14); **(c)** exhortation (vv.15-22); **(d)** sanctification (vv.23-24); **(e)** salutation (vv.25-28).

a) Appreciation, vv.12-13

"And we beseech you, brethren, to know them which labour among you, and are over you in the Lord, and admonish you; and to esteem them very highly in love for their work's sake. And be at peace among yourselves."

Although the word "elders" is not used, there can be no doubt that Paul refers to them here. The words, "which labour among you, and are over you in the Lord, and admonish you", make this clear. It has been suggested that Paul does not use the words, "elders" or "overseers", because this was a young church, but the suggestion is not convincing! He introduces his teaching with the words "we beseech ('beg', JND) you, brethren." Compare 4:1. The word "beseech" *(erotao)* means 'to ask on equal terms', not from one of lesser position. The words, "know them", mean 'recognise them', not just 'know who they are!' They are to be recognised by their "labour." Paul deals *(i)* with the responsibilities of elders in the assembly, and *(ii)* with the recognition of elders by the assembly:

i) The responsibilities of elders
"Know them which labour among you, and are over you in the Lord, and admonish you." We should notice three things here:

- **"Which labour among you."** The word "labour" *(kopiao)* means 'laborious toil.' It occurs in 2:9, "For ye remember, brethren, our labour and travail." It is a work, not a position! Shepherding God's people involves time and effort. Notice the words, "among you." The elders should be present, not away. Compare 1 Peter 5:1-2, "The elders which are *among you* I exhort…feed the flock of God which is *among you*, taking the oversight thereof".

- **"Which…..are over you in the Lord."** This means, 'which take the lead among you in the Lord.' So they are not elected by a democratic process. They are not co-opted by other elders. They are divinely-appointed: "over you *in the Lord*." See Acts 20:28, "Take heed therefore unto yourselves, and to all the flock, over the which ('in the which', JND) the Holy Ghost hath made you overseers". We must remember, too, that we are all subject to the lordship of Christ. Everything we do should be "in the Lord."

The Scriptures have a great deal to say about 'rule'. There is **self rule**: "He that is slow to anger is better than the mighty; and he that **ruleth** his spirit than he that taketh a city" (Prov. 16:32)." There is **home rule**: "One that **ruleth** well *(proistemi*, meaning 'to conduct', 'stand before', 'or attend', JND) his own house" (1 Tim. 3:4-5). There is **assembly rule**: "Let the elders that **rule** well *(proistemi)* be counted worthy of double honour, especially they who labour in the word and doctrine" (1 Tim. 5:17). There is **state rule**: "For **rulers** *(archon)* are not a terror to good works, but to the evil" (Rom. 13:3).

- **"Which…admonish you."** The word "admonish" *(noutheteo)* means to warn or reprove, particularly in view of things which are wrong. It occurs again in v.14, "**warn** them that are unruly." See also Acts 20:31, "Therefore watch, and remember, that by the space of three years I ceased not to **warn** every one night and day with tears".

ii) The recognition of elders

"Esteem them ('regard them', JND) very highly in love for their work's sake." So the assembly is to "know them", and "esteem them very highly." The word "esteem" *(hegeomai)* means "to lead, then to lead before the mind" (W.E. Vine). The words, "very highly", mean "exceedingly", and are rendered in that way in 3:10, "Night and day praying exceedingly that we might see your face." It could be rendered 'over and abound', or 'abundantly.' But that is not all. It is "esteem them very highly **in love.**" So it is not grudging acceptance of their leadership, or even, simply, acceptance of their leadership. On the other hand, elders must see to it that they earn the love of the assembly. It is, "esteem them very highly in love for their **work's sake."**

In this connection, we should notice the following: "Esteem them" (1 Thess. 5:13); "remember them" (Heb. 13:7); "obey them" (Heb. 13:17); "salute them" (Heb. 13:24). The words "that have the rule *(hegeomai)* over you" in Hebrews 13, mean 'those that stand before so as to lead you', or 'those that guide you.'

Paul adds, "And be at peace among yourselves." This can be taken as a general exhortation addressed to the entire assembly, since it follows a request to the whole assembly in v.13. Friction and resentment can arise when elders have occasion to warn and rebuke. Joseph's advice to his brethren as they set out for Canaan is applicable to us all: "See that ye fall not out by the way" (Gen. 45:24) or "Do not quarrel on the way' (JND). See Romans 12:18. It could, however, refer to strife arising from desire for leadership. Compare Mark 9:49-50: "have salt in yourselves, and have peace one with another." Note the context, the Lord Jesus was dealing with a dispute amongst the disciples, "who should be the greatest" (Mark 9:33-34).

b) Ministration, v.14

While Paul again prefaces his remarks with "brethren" (compare vv.1, 4, 12, 25), it does seem likely that he is speaking particularly to the assembly elders who "labour among you, and are over you in the Lord" (v.12). He now refers to their work in more detail: "Now we exhort you, brethren, warn them that are unruly, comfort the feeble minded, support the weak, be patient toward all men." Paul was able to do this as a shepherd himself. See Acts 20:17-35, where he refers to his teaching "publickly, and from house to house", involving "tears, and temptations....bonds and afflictions." He ceased not to "warn every one night and day with tears." He was therefore able to address the needs of God's people. Notice the wide variety of need. Circumstances vary, and different problems have to be addressed in different ways. Wisdom and discretion are needed. The work of elders in this way does not hit the headlines. It is, in the main, quiet and unobtrusive.

i) "Warn them that are unruly"

The word "warn" *(noutheteo)* means 'to put in mind', or 'admonish'. The word "unruly" *(ataktos)* means 'not keeping in step' or 'not keeping rank.' Paul refers here to people who were irresponsible and lacking self-discipline. This has particular reference to idle believers. See 2 Thessalonians 3:10-11: "we hear that there are some which walk among you **disorderly** *(ataktos)* working, not at all, but are busybodies."

ii) "Comfort the feeble minded"

The expression "feeble minded" *(oligopsuchos)* describes people who are 'fainthearted': anxious, discouraged, despondent. See Deuteronomy 20:8. This happens so often when pressure takes its toll, resulting in despondency. Perhaps this refers, here, particularly to people who had lost sight of the Lord's return. They are not to be condemned, but encouraged. The word "comfort" *(paramutheomai)* means 'to soothe', or 'cheer up.' It is used in connection with bereavement in John 11:19, "And many of the Jews came to Mary and Martha, to comfort them concerning their brother." In order to do this, they were "with her in the house" (John 11:31). Compare 1 Corinthians 14:3; Philippians 2:1; 1 Thessalonians 2:11; This ministry involves time and interest.

iii) "Support the weak"

The word "support" *(antechomai)* means 'to keep close to' or 'to hold to.' The "weak" are to be lifted up. The Lord's people can be weak in a variety of ways:

- **They can be weak in conscience.** See Romans 14:1, "Him that is weak in the faith receive ye, but not to doubtful disputations." Paul refers here to believers who are imperfect in faith and understanding with regard to dietary laws etc. See also Romans 15:1.

- **They can be weak in body.** See Acts 20:35, "I have shewed you all things, how that so labouring ye ought to support the weak, and to remember the words of the Lord Jesus, how he said, It is more blessed to give than to receive."

- **They can be weak in spirit (resolve).** The Lord's people sometimes need 'propping up.' See, for example Joash who reigned well "all the days of Jehoiada", but who went sadly wrong after Jehoiada's death. See 2 Chronicles 24:12-22. Lot needed constant support from Abraham. The word "weak" can describe people who have made little or no spiritual progress, and are "carried about with every wind of doctrine." These cases try the patience of all. No wonder Paul says

iv) "Be patient toward all men"
The word "patient" *(makrothumeo)* means long-tempered in the face of provocation. It involves self-restraint. It means waiting with a purpose: not 'putting up with it.' Patience is active and intelligent.

The work described above demands men like David, of whom it is written, "From following the ewes great with young he brought him to feed Jacob his people, and Israel his inheritance. So he fed them according to the **integrity of his heart**; and guided them by the **skilfulness of his hands**" (Psalm 78:72).

c) Exhortation, vv.15-22
Paul now includes all believers in a series of exhortations, which can be divided as follows: *(i)* exhortations in connection with others (v.15); *(ii)* exhortations in connection with ourselves (vv.16-18); *(iii)* exhortations in connection with the assembly (vv.19-22).

- *In connection with others, v.15.* "See that none render evil for evil unto any man; but ever follow that which is good, both among yourselves, and to all men." We may look at this **negatively**: "See that none render evil for evil unto any man." We should not be people who practise 'tit for tat.' The Lord Jesus is our example: "Who, when he was reviled, reviled not again; when he suffered, he threatened not" (1 Pet. 2:23). He exemplified His own teaching in Matthew 5:44. Moses did not "render evil for evil" when provoked by Israel. He was "very meek, above all the men which were upon the face of the earth" (Num.12:3). David did not "render evil for evil" when faced with the animosity and hatred of Saul. Joseph did not "render evil for evil" when his brothers applied for corn in Egypt. It is very sad when people try to 'level old scores.' God says, "their sins and iniquities will I remember no more," but some Christians appear to have longer memories than God Himself!

Then we make look at this **positively**: "But ever follow that which is good, both among yourselves, and to all men." The word "follow *(dioko)* means 'to pursue earnestly', or 'to press on. See Philippians 3:6, "Concerning zeal, **persecuting** the church." The word "good" *(agathos)* means 'beneficial to others.' Notice the consistency here: "both among yourselves, **and** to all men."

- *In connection with ourselves, vv.16-18.* "Rejoice evermore. Pray without ceasing. In every thing give thanks: for this is the will of God in Christ Jesus concerning you." So we are to be joyful, prayerful, and thankful:

Joyful. "Rejoice evermore" or "Rejoice always" (JND). Compare Philippians 4:4. We should all be members of the tribe of Judah! Judah means 'praise', and it is most interesting that Judah leads the way on so many occasions in both Old and New Testaments. For example, Judah led the way when the children of Israel marched through the wilderness (Num. 10:14). Judah led the way in the second campaign against the Canaanites (Judges 1:1-2). Judah is the first tribe mentioned in Revelation 7:4-8.

Prayerful. "Pray without ceasing *(proseuchomai)*." As we have noted before, W.E. Vine illustrates this with reference to a papyrus discovered in Egypt: "An old papyrus letter, lately discovered in Egypt (he was writing in 1914) but written as far back as the Apostles' days, speaks of an 'incessant cough'. Thus not uninterrupted prayer, but constantly recurring prayer is the thought here".

Thankful. "In every thing give thanks: for this is the will of God (see also 4:3) in Christ Jesus concerning you." Do notice that Paul says, "In **every thing** give thanks." This means that we are to be thankful in difficult times as well as in good times. We are not to be like the heathen ("neither were thankful", Rom. 1:21) or like the apostates ("unthankful", 2 Tim. 3:2).

- *In connection with the assembly, vv.19-22.* "Quench not the Spirit. Despise not prophesyings. Prove all things; hold fast that which is good. Abstain from all appearance of evil." Where **individuals** are concerned, it is "Grieve not the holy Spirit of God" Eph. 4:30). There is an orderly development in these exhortations:

"Quench not the Spirit." The word "quench" carries the idea of extinguishing a fire. It can be applied generally. See, for example 4:8, "He therefore that despiseth, despiseth not man, but God, who hath also given unto us his Holy Spirit." However, the context here suggests that Paul is teaching that there should be opportunity for all gifts to be exercised in the assembly. Every encouragement should be given in this direction. W.E. Vine suggests that it means "to quench the Spirit in another". Bearing in mind the following exhortation, "despise not prophesyings", it could have a particular meaning. See 1 Corinthians 14:29-32. "Let the prophets speak two or three, and let the other (JND 'others') judge. If anything be revealed to another that sitteth by, let the first hold his peace." Those who received communications from God must be allowed to pass them on. Hence:

*"**Despise not prophesyings**."* The word "despise" means to 'regard as of no account.' This does seem to amplify the previous exhortation. The gift of prophecy was necessary whilst the Scriptures were incomplete. The prophets received direct revelations from God. Now we have the completed Scriptures. The prophets have given place to the teachers, who draw attention to what the Scriptures say: they do not add to them. There is a solemn warning at the end of the Bible to any who would either add to the Scriptures, or subtract from them. See Revelation 22:18-19. We do not have the gift of prophecy today, but we do have Bible teaching. We can therefore legitimately say, 'despise not teaching.'

*"**Prove all things**."* The connection is clear: 'Do not lightly esteem prophecies; **but** prove all things' (JND). Ministry was to be tested. The word "prove" *(dokimazo)* mans to 'test with a view to approval.' Christians are not to be gullible. They need 'good Berean blood flowing through their veins' (J. Harrison). "They (the Bereans) received the word with all readiness of mind, and searched the scriptures daily, whether those things were so." (Acts 17:11). Similarly, Christians are to "try the spirits" (1 John 4:1). Quite obviously, John refers here to the spirit controlling a man who professes to teach the word of God. God's people in the Old Testament were to "prove all things." See Isaiah 8:20, "To the law and to the testimony: if they speak not according to this word, it is because there is no light in them." But having 'proved all things' we are to:

*"**Hold fast that which is good**."* Note the words "hold fast" (*katecho*: 'hold firmly') and "good" (*kalos:* what is intrinsically good). But

*"**Abstain from all appearance of evil**"* or "hold aloof from every form of wickedness" (JND). We must, of course, apply this generally, but in context it does appear to refer to evil teaching. See, for example, 1 Corinthians 12:1-3, "Now concerning spiritual gifts ('manifestations', JND) brethren, I would not have you ignorant...Wherefore I give you to understand, that no man speaking by the Spirit of God calleth Jesus accursed: and that no man can say that Jesus is the Lord, but by the Holy Ghost." In the first case, we have the "appearance of evil", and in the second "that which is good."

But after all these injunctions and after all this teaching, it remains that it is not the actual teaching that keeps and preserves. It is God Himself. Hence Romans 16:25, "Now to **him** that is of power ('that is able', JND) to stablish you according to my gospel, and the preaching of Jesus Christ", and Jude v.24, "Now unto **him** that is able to keep you from falling." This brings us to:

d) Sanctification, vv.23-24

"And the very God of peace sanctify you wholly; and I pray God your whole spirit and soul and body be preserved blameless unto the coming of our Lord Jesus Christ. Faithful is he that calleth you, who also will do it" or "Now the God of peace **himself** sanctify you wholly..." (JND/RV). He alone can carry out the work of our entire sanctification. It is our sanctification which will make possible the fulfilment of the injunctions in the previous verses.

Notice the expression, "the very God of peace." See also Romans 15:33, 16:20, Philippians 4:9, Hebrews 13:20. In the context of 1 Thessalonians 5, the words, "the very God of peace" take on a specific meaning in view of the disorders previously mentioned. The scope of our sanctification is expressed as follows: "And...your whole **spirit** and **soul** and **body** be preserved blameless unto the coming of our Lord Jesus Christ." In this connection, we should note the following;

- **The body is not the man.** Believers who have 'fallen asleep' are "absent from the body, and...present with the Lord" (2 Cor. 5:8). When Paul refers to "visions and revelations", he is unable to say whether he was in the body, or "out of the body" (2 Cor. 12:1-3). We normally say, 'body, soul and spirit', but God places the spirit first. As Wm. MacDonald *(Believer's Bible Commenatary)* observes: "In the original creation, the spirit was of first importance, the body last. Sin reversed the order: man lives for the body, and neglects the spirit. When we pray for one another, we should follow the biblical order, putting spiritual welfare before physical needs".

- **The body is an essential part of the man**. The redeemed are not perfected until the resurrection. No man will be, ultimately, without his body.

- **Spirit and soul represent the spiritual element in man**. The body is animated by soul and spirit.

- **Body and spirit can be separated. Soul and spirit can only be distinguished.** "Spirit" describes the life we have from God, enabling us to approach and worship

Him. "Soul" describes the life we have from God, giving us the ability to perceive, reflect, feel, desire: in fact, self-consciousness.

Paul's prayer was therefore, that they might be preserved, *(i)* in the realm of the spirit: that is, in their worship and prayer life; *(ii)* in the realm of the soul: that is, in the realm of their desires and emotions; *(iii)* in the realm of their body: that is, in physical purity. Hence Paul's warnings against immorality. The word "blameless" signifies 'beyond accusation.' It is often said that with the spirit, we have God-consciousness, with the soul we have self-consciousness, and with the body, we have world-consciousness.

Paul prayed that the believers at Thessalonica would be "preserved blameless *unto* the coming of our Lord Jesus Christ" or "*at* the coming of our Lord Jesus Christ" (JND), suggesting that this refers to our appearance at the judgment seat of Christ. See 2 Corinthians 5:10. The words, "Faithful is he that calleth you, who also will do it", remind us that God, Who has called us to holiness (1 Pet. 1:15-16), is able to "sanctify you wholly." He is able to 'present us faultless before the presence of his glory with exceeding joy' (Jude 24). Salvation and sanctification are His work. Preachers and teachers have no ability in themselves to do this.

e) *Salutation, vv.25-28*

"Brethren, pray for us. Greet all the brethren with an holy kiss. I charge you by the Lord that this epistle be read unto all the holy brethren. The grace of our Lord Jesus Christ be with you. Amen".

We should notice the *"**holy** kiss"* and the *"**holy** brethren."* This is in accordance with their entire sanctification (v.23). The epistle was to be read aloud. All were to hear what Paul had to say. We must remember that "the Bible is for all Christians, not for some inside circle or privileged class. All its truths are for all the saints" (Wm. MacDonald). We need its teaching in order to implement the exhortations in vv.14, 21.

2 THESSALONIANS

by
John M Riddle

READ CHAPTER 1:1-4

"Your faith groweth exceedingly"

As we noted in connection with 1 Thessalonians, preachers frequently refer to the assembly at Thessalonica as 'a model church.' This description is based on the words, "Ye were ensamples *(tupos)* to all that believe in Macedonia and Achaia" (1:7). Paul also speaks equally highly of them in 2 Thessalonians: "we ourselves glory in you in the churches of God for your patience and faith in all your persecutions and tribulations that ye endure" (1:3-4). They certainly displayed some excellent features. Just think again of their "work of faith, and labour of love, and patience of hope in our Lord Jesus Christ" (1 Thess.1:3). Just think of their mutual love (1 Thess. 4:9)

But this doesn't mean that the 'model' was perfect! External and internal problems needed to be addressed. In the case of the Thessalonians, unrelenting persecution brought a new problem (2 Thess. 2:1-2), and an existing problem needed further attention. Compare 1 Thess. 5:14 and 2 Thess. 3:6-15. Please don't think that we will ever be free from problems!

This brings us to 2 Thessalonians, and by way of introduction, we must notice: *(1)* the circumstances of the epistle, and *(2)* the contents of the epistle.

1) THE CIRCUMSTANCES OF THE EPISTLE
We have already recalled that in the First Epistle, Paul 'remembered without ceasing' their "work of **faith**, and labour of **love**, and patience (endurance) of **hope** in our Lord Jesus Christ" (1:3). Other people noticed these three things as well. See 1:9-10. Of the three, their "patience of hope" needed strengthening. When Timothy returned from Thessalonica, he brought "good tidings of your faith and charity" (1 Thess. 3:6), but no reference is made to hope. When Paul wrote the Second Epistle, he gave thanks that "your **faith** groweth exceedingly, and the **charity** of every one of you all toward each other aboundeth" (1:3), but hope is not mentioned. Their "hope" needed strengthening for two reasons:

i) In the First Epistle, we learn that the Christians at Thessalonica were deeply concerned about fellow-believers who were "asleep" (4:13). This is the way in which the Bible describes "the dead in Christ" (4:16). Stephen was "stoned", but he "fell asleep" (Acts 7:59-60). He was amongst those that "sleep in Jesus" (1 Thess. 4:14). Paul therefore points out that these believers would not be disadvantaged in any way, for at the return of the Lord Jesus, "the dead in Christ shall rise first: then we which are alive and remain shall be caught up together with them in the clouds, to meet the Lord in the air: and so shall we ever be with the Lord." In view of this Paul adds, "Wherefore comfort (encourage) one another with these words" (1 Thess. 4:16-18).

The distinctive hope of the church in Chapter 4 is set against the Old Testament expectation of the "day of the Lord" in Chapter 5, and we learn that "God hath not appointed us to wrath, but to obtain salvation by our Lord Jesus Christ, who died for us, that, whether we wake or sleep, we should live together with him" (1 Thess. 5:9-10).

ii) In the Second Epistle, we learn that the persecuted Christians at Thessalonica were reeling under teaching that the dreadful events of the 'day of the Lord' (AV "day of Christ") had burst upon them. See 2:1-2. This contradicted teaching in the First Epistle. See 5:1-11. Paul is therefore obliged to write: "That ye be not soon shaken in mind, nor troubled, neither by spirit, nor by word, nor by letter, as (if it were) by us, as that the day of the Lord is present" (JND/RV). Their persecution had been equated with the "sudden destruction" and "wrath" of 1 Thessalonians 5:3, 9.

Paul therefore reminded them that this could not be the case, because the 'day of the Lord' would be preceded by two events. **Firstly**, by the Lord's coming for the church: see 2:1, "Now we beseech you, brethren, by the coming of our Lord Jesus Christ, and by our gathering together unto him, that ye be not soon shaken in mind, or be troubled" and, **secondly**, by certain recognisable events on earth: see 2:3-4. "For that day shall not come, except there come a falling away first, and that man of sin be revealed, the son of perdition." In passing, notice that the Thessalonians, who had "turned to God from idols", are now told that a man himself would become an idol! Compare 1 Thess. 1:9 with 2 Thess. 2:4.

To sum up, hope was at a low ebb in the First Epistle on account of **'sleeping saints'**, and at a low ebb in the Second Epistle on account of **living saints.** In the first case, they were distressed because it seemed that the dead would miss the rapture. In the second, they were distressed because it seemed that the living were passing through the 'great tribulation.' Hence, 2 Thessalonians was written to restore hope in the pre-tribulation return of Christ. In view of this Paul prays, "Now our Lord Jesus Christ himself, and God, even our Father, which hath loved us, and hath given us everlasting consolation and good **hope** through grace, comfort (encourage) your hearts, and stablish you in every good word and work" (2:16-17).

2) THE CONTENTS OF THE EPISTLE
It is often asserted, with good reason, that Second Epistles emphasise *(a)* end times, *(b)* the work of the enemy, *(c)* the correction of false teaching. Compare 2 Timothy and 2 Peter.

The Epistle can be summarised as follows: **Chapter 1**, the revelation of the Lord Jesus: "The Lord Jesus shall be revealed from heaven with his mighty angels" (v.7); **Chapter 2**, the revelation of the man of sin: "That day shall not come, except there come a falling away first, and that man of sin be revealed" (v.3); **Chapter 3**, the rebuking of disorderly conduct: "Now we command you, brethren, in the name of our Lord Jesus Christ, that ye withdraw yourselves from every brother that walketh disorderly" (v.6). We can now give attention to the details of the Epistle.

CHAPTER 1
The chapter may be analysed as follows: *(1)* their example to the churches of God (vv.1-4); *(2)* the righteousness of the judgment of God (vv.5-10); *(3)* their worthiness of the calling of God (vv.11-12).

1) THEIR EXAMPLE TO THE CHURCHES OF GOD, vv.1-4
"We are bound to thank God always for you, brethren, as it is meet, because your faith groweth exceedingly, and the charity of every one of you all toward each other aboundeth; so that we ourselves **glory in you in the churches of God** for your patience and faith in all your persecutions and tribulations that ye endure" (vv.3-4).

While Paul did not keep a "league table", some churches certainly brought him more pleasure than others. The "churches of Galatia" brought him great distress: "I marvel that ye are so soon removed from him that called you into the grace of Christ unto another gospel" (Gal. 1:6). Paul was able to "glory" in the Thessalonians, but the Corinthians gloried in themselves (1 Cor. 4:7) in spite of their glaring deficiencies! Would **our** local assembly bring Paul pleasure? Or, and more to the point, does our local assembly bring the **Lord** pleasure?

Chapter 1

The believers at Thessalonica were marked by consistency and progress. How about **our** assembly? Are **we** marked by these features, and since assemblies are made up of individuals, how about us **personally?**

Paul's introductions to the First and Second Epistles are very similar. But a little revision, and repetition, will not go amiss! We should notice:

a) The writer, v.1
The Epistle was written, of course, by Paul. See 3:17, "The salutation of Paul with mine own hand, which is the token in every epistle: so I write." But he associates others with him. Hence, "Paul, and Silvanus, and Timotheus, unto the church of the Thessalonians in God our Father and the Lord Jesus Christ: Grace unto you, and peace, from God our Father and the Lord Jesus Christ."

Paul, Silas and Timothy had all laboured and suffered at Thessalonica (Acts 17:10-14), and it was therefore appropriate that all three should greet the assembly. It was a well-balanced trio: Paul was an apostle; Silas was one of "the chief men among the brethren" (Acts 15:22), and a prophet (Acts 15:32); Timothy was a younger man (1 Timothy 4:12), and a teacher (1 Timothy 1:3). Paul doesn't seek prominence, and exclude others. We should notice the wording: "**we** are bound to thank God always for you...**we** ourselves glory in you in the churches of God...**we** pray always for you" (vv.3, 4, 11). There was a balance of age and experience. Older and younger believers should always be willing to work together. Younger believers should value the help and experience of older believers, and older believers should give every encouragement to younger believers.

Once again, Paul does not mention his apostleship. It was still unnecessary for him to do so. There was no doctrinal error at Thessalonica, and there was no need to emphasise his authority. It was quite different in "the churches of Galatia." See Galatians 1:1. But Paul continued to have every reason to rejoice over the assembly at Thessalonica, and wrote to encourage them. He did not standardise the introduction to his epistles, but 'tailored' his approach to suit the circumstances at the time.

b) The readers, v.1
Like the First Epistle, this letter is addressed, not to 'the church at Thessalonica' (compare "the church of God which is at Corinth": "the churches of Galatia"), but to "the church of the Thessalonians." This is unique to the Thessalonian Epistles. As we said before, this possibly reflects Paul's special interest in every believer.

They were his spiritual children. He had tended them as "a nurse (nursing mother) cherisheth her (own) children", and had "exhorted and comforted and charged" every one of them, "as a father doth his children" (1 Thess. 2:7, 11).

The "church of the Thessalonians" was located in two places. It was, obviously, at Thessalonica, but it was, equally, in "God our Father and the Lord Jesus Christ."

i) It was on earth, and in time. It was "the church of the **Thessalonians**." This reminded them of their earthly and local responsibilities. With this in mind, they were commanded "that if any would not work, neither should he eat" and that they were not to be "weary in well doing" (3:10-12).

ii) It was in heaven, and in eternity. The church was "in God **our** Father and the Lord Jesus Christ." The First Epistle has "in God **the** Father." The change emphasises the tenderness of God. Increasing pressure made this more precious. It also stresses the union of Jew and Gentile. As believers at Thessalonica, they were subject to harm and danger. As believers "in God our Father and the Lord Jesus Christ", their spiritual security was beyond harm and danger. They were shielded and protected from "every evil work." The words, "**in** God our Father and the Lord Jesus Christ", emphasise the impossibility of separation from them, and the intimacy of union with them. Selah! It emphasises the dignity and sanctity of the local church. But as we have noticed, while they were "in God our Father and the Lord Jesus Christ", they were not immune from tribulation. In fact, it was because of this that they were the **particular focus** of Satan's attack.

The title, "God our **Father**", emphasises His love. The title, **"Lord** Jesus Christ", emphasises His authority. It occurs eleven times in the epistle.

c) The greeting, v.2
The well-known words, "grace unto you, and peace", remind us that the Lord Jesus brought us grace (Titus 2:11), and left us peace (John 14:27). The order is important. It is "grace...and peace", not 'peace...and grace!' There could not be peace apart from grace. Peace is the result of grace! "Grace" is a big word in the Bible! It is rendered "benefit" in 2 Corinthians 1:15, and reminds us that every benefit we enjoy, and every ability we possess, comes from the throne of God. Our resources are not located on earth. We do not serve God with the "wisdom of words", or the "wisdom of the wise", or with "the wisdom of this world" (1 Cor. 1:17, 19, 20), but "according to the grace that is given to us" (Rom. 12:6).

The greeting comes jointly from "God our Father" and "the Lord Jesus Christ", emphasising the Saviour's deity. The characteristic greeting amongst Greeks was 'Rejoice!' (*chairete*), but Paul uses "grace" *(charis)*. The characteristic greeting amongst Jews was 'Peace!' (*shalom*). See Matthew 10:12-13, Luke 10:5.

d) The thanksgiving, vv.3-4

"We are bound to thank God always for you, brethren, as it is meet, because that your faith groweth exceedingly, and the charity of every one of you all toward each other aboundeth." Paul had said, "in every thing give thanks" (1 Thess. 5:18): now he practises it again! Compare 1 Thessalonians 1:2; 3:9. The word "bound" *(opheilo)* indicates a duty: a debt to discharge. It occurs again in 2:13. The word "meet" *(axios)* means 'befitting' or 'worthy.'

The substance of his thanksgiving follows: "Because that your faith groweth exceedingly, and the charity of every one of you all toward each other aboundeth." **Faith** is Godward, and **love** is saintward. See also 1 Thessalonians 3:6.

i) "Your faith groweth exceedingly." ("Groweth exceedingly" translates one Greek word, *huperauxano*; from *auxano*, to grow). Paul has a great deal to say about their faith in the First Epistle. See, for example, 3:2, "to establish you, and to comfort you concerning your **faith**"; 3:5, "I sent to know your **faith**, lest by some means the tempter have tempted you"; 3:6, "Timotheus...brought us good tidings of your **faith**"; 3:7, "we were comforted over you in all our affliction and distress by your **faith**." Now he tells us that it was growing! Not just growing, but 'growing exceedingly!' How did he know? After all, we cannot see faith! The answer lies in v.4. Paul knew that their faith was growing by their steadfastness under intensifying pressure. Growing persecution was matched by growing "patience and faith." Although they were in "the eye of the storm", they continued to trust in God. Adversity facilitates, not hinders, faith. Had the Thessalonians succumbed to pressure, Paul would have been obliged to record their weakened faith.

This recalls the teaching of James that "faith without works is dead" (James 2:26). Notice his observation, "Shew me thy faith without thy works, and I will shew thee my faith by my works" (James 2:18). Compare Mark 2:5, "When Jesus **saw** their faith". See also Luke 7:50, "And he said to the woman, Thy faith hath saved thee; go in peace." Only the Lord Jesus could see her faith. But her devotion to the Lord Jesus proved its existence. In fact, when the Lord Jesus justified the woman in the eyes of Simon, He pointed to her **works**. But when He sent the woman away in peace, He pointed to her **faith**. On this same principle, Barnabas **saw** "the **grace** of God" (Acts 11:23).

ii) "The love of every one of you all toward each other aboundeth." ("Aboundeth" translates *pleonazo*). Note the personal emphasis. Paul's prayer in the first epistle had been abundantly answered: "And the Lord make you to increase and abound *(pleonazo)* in love one toward another" (1 Thess. 3:12). Paul's appeal in the first epistle had been abundantly met: "But as touching brotherly love ye need not that I write unto you: for ye yourselves are taught of God to love one another. And indeed ye do toward all the brethren which are in all Macedonia: but we beseech you, brethren, that ye increase more and more" (1 Thess. 4:9-10).

So their faith was growing "exceedingly", and their love to each other was "abounding." Could this be said about **us**? Is **our** faith in God growing,? Are **we** increasing in love for each other? A right attitude towards God will be accompanied by a right attitude towards each other. Bearing in mind the circumstances of the Thessalonians, we learn that opposition casts us more upon God, and draws us closer to each other. Here, then, we have an assembly not only continuing but growing in spiritual stature. We shall see shortly that tribulation is not only beneficial for the present (vv.3-4): it is also beneficial for the future. See vv.5-6.

The healthy spiritual life of the believers at Thessalonica enabled Paul to "glory in you in the churches of God for your patience and faith in all your persecutions and tribulations that ye endure." W.E. Vine comments on the word, "ourselves", as follows: the word "occupies a place of emphasis, thereby implying, first, that others had reported the progress of the church at Thessalonica, and, second, that this progress was so marked that the men who had laid the foundation of the work, and who might, therefore, have been expected to maintain a degree of reticence about it, were constrained to break even so good a rule". We can be sure that Paul did not indulge in self-glory! (The word *enkauchaomai* means 'boast'). He gloried, or boasted, in the grace of God that enabled the Thessalonians to make such progress. They were marked by "patience" (*hupomone,* meaning 'endurance') and "faith". The first denotes their attitude to the trials themselves. The second denotes their relationship with God in the trials.

The word "persecutions" *(diogmos)* focuses on man's hostility and hatred towards believers. The word "tribulations" *(thlipsis)* focuses on their injury and distress. Note that in v.4, the "tribulation" originates in men, but in v.6, it originates in God: "Seeing it is a righteous thing with God to recompense **tribulation** to them that trouble you." The Lord's people should expect tribulation. This was taught by the Lord Jesus ("In the world ye shall have tribulation", John

16:33), and by the apostle Paul ("For verily, when we with you, we told you before that we should suffer tribulation" (1 Thess. 3:4: see also Acts 14:22). The word "endure" *(anechomai)* means 'to bear up.'

The tribulation here is akin to 1 Peter 5:8, "Your adversary the devil, as a roaring lion, walketh about, seeking whom he may devour". We must remember, however, that this is not the only weapon in Satan's armoury. He also uses deceit and deception. See 2 Thess 2:3: "Let no man deceive you by any means." An assembly can be subject to Satanic attack in one way, and if that fails, he will employ other means. Notice his strategy at Thessalonica in this way. The believers there were marked by "patience", and both Paul (Rom. 5:3-4) and James (1:2-3) tell us that "patience" leads to hope. But not in this case! Satan could see that tribulation only produced growth, so he endeavoured to stop it by introducing false teaching (see 2:1-2), with the intention of robbing the saints of their hope. Paul now addresses this problem.

READ CHAPTER 1:5-12

"The Lord Jesus shall be revealed from heaven"

In our first study, we suggested that this chapter can be divided as follows: **(1)** their example to the churches of God (vv.1-4); **(2)** the righteousness of the judgment of God (vv.5-10); **(3)** their worthiness of the calling of God (vv.11-12).

1) THEIR EXAMPLE TO THE CHURCHES OF GOD, vv.1-4

The Christians at Thessalonica had certainly proved that "all that will live godly in Christ Jesus shall suffer persecution" (2 Tim. 3:12). Paul refers to their sufferings in v.4: "We ourselves glory in you in the churches of God for your patience and faith in all your persecutions and tribulations that ye endure". Their "patience and faith" in the face of such gale force adversity enabled him to use them as an example of the power and grace of God.

But was this all? Their suffering seemed rather pointless if this was the case. After all, it was all very well for Paul to use them as an example, but that didn't help **them!** Unless there was another explanation, their endurance under trial seemed purposeless. Their opponents seemed to have it all their own way, and there was no divine intervention on their behalf. Paul now proves that this was far from true, which brings us to:

2) THE RIGHTEOUSNESS OF THE JUDGMENT OF GOD, vv.5-10

Paul answers these questions by explaining, **(a)** that their endurance under suffering was preparing them for future responsibility (v.5) and **(b)** that their suffering would be avenged by the Lord Jesus Himself (vv.6-10).

Their endurance of "persecutions and tribulations" was "a manifest token of the righteous judgment of God, that ye may be counted worthy of the kingdom of God, for which ye also suffer: seeing it is a righteous thing with God to recompense tribulation to them that trouble you." There are two ways in which these verses can be understood.

i) That the words, "that ye may be counted worthy of the kingdom of God, for which ye also suffer", are a parenthesis, and that the main subject is the judgment of God upon those who oppose the Gospel. We can illustrate this by using brackets: "Which is a manifest token of the righteous judgment of God (that ye may be counted worthy of the kingdom of God, for which ye also suffer) seeing it is a righteous thing with God to recompense tribulation to them that trouble you." In this case, their sufferings were the guarantee that God would intervene in judgment on their adversaries.

ii) That their endurance of "persecutions and tribulations" was "a manifest token of the righteous judgment of God" in **allowing them to suffer**, because He was preparing them for the future. In due course, He would execute righteous judgment on those who afflicted them. For the purposes of this study, we will adopt this suggestion.

a) God is righteous in allowing suffering, v.5
"Your persecutions and tribulations that ye endure: which is a manifest token of the righteous judgment of God, **that ye may be counted worthy of the kingdom of God, for which ye also suffer**." (Notice that Paul does not say 'made worthy', but "counted worthy"). Paul demonstrates that far from being unjust, their persecution had a distinct purpose in God's plan for them. Notice that it is not the "persecutions and tribulations" which constitute the "manifest token of the righteous judgment of God", but their **endurance** of the "persecutions and tribulations". This proved their fitness for future responsibility. The believers at Thessalonica were showing the very qualities of faithfulness and reliability needed for service in the coming kingdom. Compare 1 Thessalonians 2:12, "That ye would walk worthy of God, who hath called you unto his kingdom and glory." Peter refers to an 'abundant entrance' into "the everlasting kingdom of our Lord and Saviour Jesus Christ" (2 Pet. 1:11).

We must not forget that "the saints shall judge (administer) the world", and "judge (administer) angels" (1 Cor. 6:1-3). So their endurance of "persecutions and tribulations" was a "manifest token" *(endeigma,* meaning 'proof') to **them** of "the righteous judgment of God." He had not made a mistake in putting them through these trials. They were suffering now in the interests of the "kingdom of God", where they would reign with Christ. See Romans 8:17 and 2 Timothy 2:12. (Notice that in Philippians 1:28, the steadfastness of God's people under trial is "an evident token of perdition" to their adversaries of coming judgment. The word "token" there is *endeixis,* meaning 'a declaration').

It has been said that 'the brightest steel is forged in the hottest fire.' We learn then that God uses present suffering to produce people of proven ability to administer His kingdom. As W.W. Wiersbe observes, "God doesn't waste suffering in the experience of His people". The qualities of "patience and faith" are developed in adversity.

b) God is righteous in avenging suffering, vv.6-10

Since they were suffering for "the kingdom of God", it was "a righteous thing with God to recompense tribulation to them that trouble you." He would deal with their persecutors. God who says, "Vengeance is mine; I will repay" (Rom. 12:19), will act on behalf of His people. The very instigators of tribulation would suffer tribulation themselves. We must notice four things here: *(i)* the time (v.7); *(ii)* the terror (vv.7-8); *(iii)* the tribulation (vv.8-9); *(iv)* the triumph (v.10).

i) The time, v.7

"Seeing it is a righteous thing with God to recompence tribulation to them that trouble you *(thlibo*, to afflict); and to you who are troubled *(thlibo)* rest with us, **when the Lord Jesus shall be revealed from heaven** with his mighty angels". Those who have persecuted His people will experience the wrath of the Lord Jesus, and see His glory in the very people they persecuted! See v.10: "he shall come to be glorified in his saints, and to be admired in all them that believe". At the moment, the Lord Jesus is persecuted in His saints: "Saul, Saul, why persecutest thou *me*?" (Acts 9:4). But He will then be "glorified in his saints." It is "a righteous thing with God to recompence tribulation to them that trouble you", not only because they were suffering unjustly, but because they were suffering in God's interests.

Notice that the enemies of God's people will receive **"recompence"**, but God's people will enjoy **"rest!"** The meaning of the verse becomes clear if we use brackets like this: "Seeing it is a righteous thing with God to recompence tribulation to them that trouble you (and to you who are troubled rest with us) when the Lord Jesus shall be revealed from heaven with his mighty angels." The Lord Jesus is 'our deliverer from the coming wrath' (1 Thess. 1:10, JND). He said, "Verily, verily, I say unto you, He that heareth my word, and believeth on him that sent me, hath everlasting life, and shall not come into condemnation (judgment); but is passed from death unto life" (John 5:24).

The word "recompence" *(antapodidomi)* means 'to give in return for', or 'to give back as an equivalent'. The expression "rest **with us**", reminded the Thessalonians that although Paul was not present in their city, and subject to persecution there, he was not exempted from affliction. He lists his afflictions in 2 Corinthians 11:21-33.

ii) The terror, vv.7-8

"The Lord Jesus shall be revealed from heaven with his mighty angels, in flaming fire taking vengeance on them that know not God, and that obey not the gospel of our Lord Jesus Christ". These are solemn words. We must notice the following:

- **"Shall be revealed from heaven."** The word "revealed" *(apokalupto)* means 'uncovered' or 'unveiled': to become visible. At present, the Lord Jesus is veiled by the heavens. But John "saw heaven opened" to reveal Him (Rev. 19:11). The Lord Jesus was last seen **publicly** being taken down from the cross. He will next be seen **publicly** coming down from heaven.

- **"With his mighty angels."** Compare Matthew 13: "The enemy that sowed them is the devil; the harvest is the end of the age; and the reapers are the angels...the Son of man shall send forth his angels...the angels shall come forth, and shall sever the wicked from among the just, and shall cast them into the furnace of fire" (vv.39, 41, 49, 50). Compare Matthew 16:27, "For the Son of man shall come in the glory of his Father with his angels". See also Revelation 14:14-20, "And I looked, and behold a white cloud, and upon the cloud one sat like unto the Son of man...and another angel came out of the temple...And another angel...And another angel."

The Lord Jesus, who refused twelve legion of angels in Gethsemane, will come "with his mighty angels." On earth, He was "seen of angels." They witnessed his humility: "And there appeared an angel unto him from heaven, strengthening him" (Luke 22:43). See also Luke 2:8-15. At His birth, the angels went "away... **into** heaven." At His revelation, they will come with Him **from** heaven." As we have already noted, He will be accompanied by the saints as well (v.10). See also Zechariah 14:5, where the word, "saints", means 'holy ones', and probably includes holy men and holy angels. It is used of both. See Deuteronomy 33:2-3, where angels are described in v.2, and the nation of Israel in v.3.

- **"In flaming fire."** Compare Isaiah 66:15, "For, behold, the Lord will come with fire, and with his chariots like a whirlwind, to render his anger with fury, and his rebuke with flames of fire"; Psalm 50:3, "Our God shall come, and shall not keep silence: a fire shall devour before him." Fire is a symbol of the righteousness and holiness of God. See Hebrews 12:29. God's judgment against sin reflects His own character.

The suffering believers at Thessalonica were therefore reminded of the majesty and power of God. Their adversaries appeared to have the upper hand, but He was in absolute control of the situation, and when the time was right, He would intervene in "power and great glory" (Matt. 24:30). This must have given them great reassurance in their difficult circumstances.

iii) The tribulation, vv.8-10

These verses describe, in most solemn language, how God will "recompence tribulation" to those who persecute His people: "taking vengeance on them that know not God, and that obey not the gospel of our Lord Jesus Christ: who shall be punished with everlasting destruction from the presence of the Lord, and from the glory of his power." We should notice the following:

- **"Taking vengeance."** W.E. Vine points out that the word "vengeance" (*ekdikesis*, from *dike,* meaning justice) is, literally, 'out of justice' (that which proceeds out of justice): "not, as often with human vengeance, out of a sense of injury, or merely out of a feeling of indignation". He continues, "The judgments of God are holy and right (Rev. 16:7), and free from any element of self-gratification or vindictiveness". See Obadiah v.15: "As thou hast done, it shall be done unto thee: thy reward shall return upon thine own head."

His vengeance is directed against two classes of people. Firstly, "On them that know not God" and secondly, On them "that obey not the gospel of our Lord Jesus Christ." In both cases, it is willing ignorance. W.E. Vine explains this as follows: "Two classes are intended, as the repetition of the article shows. The first of these includes all Gentiles who have refused such knowledge of God as is to be had from the light of nature, cp. Acts 10:34, Rom. 2:10-15". (Compare 1 Thessalonians 4:5, "Even as the Gentiles which know not God"). "The second includes all, Jews and Gentiles, who, having heard the gospel, refused to submit to the claims of God therein declared, cp. Acts 17:32-33". Quite obviously, there is no such thing as 'a second chance.' Notice that Paul does not catalogue human sin: he simply points out the solemnity of rejecting the gospel.

We should never cease to thank God for His grace and mercy that resulted in our "obedience of faith" (Rom.16:26). "But God be thanked, that ye were the servants of sin, but ye have obeyed from the heart that form of doctrine which was delivered you" (Rom. 6:17). Do notice that we have "the **gospel** of our Lord Jesus Christ" in 1:8; "the **glory** of our Lord Jesus Christ" in 2:14; "the **grace** of our Lord Jesus Christ" in 3:18.

- **"Punished with everlasting destruction."** This is the outcome of divine judgment: "Who shall be punished with everlasting destruction from the presence of the Lord, and from the glory of his power." The word "punish" *(dike)*, as already noted, means 'what is right', and is closely associated with *dikaios,* meaning 'righteous.' The punishment will be absolutely just. The words, "everlasting destruction", do not mean cessation of existence, but everlasting **ruin.** The word "destruction" *(olethros)* means, "not the destruction of being, but of well-being: not annihilation, the putting an end to the existence of a person or thing, but its ruin so far as the purpose of its existence is concerned" (W.E. Vine). Compare Revelation 14:11, "And the smoke of their torment ascendeth up for **ever and ever**: and they have no rest day or night, who worship the beast, and whosoever receiveth the mark of his name." See also John 3:36, "He that believeth on the Son hath everlasting life: and he that believeth not the Son shall not see life; but the wrath of God **abideth on him**." Quite obviously the wrath of God cannot 'abide' on someone who does not exist.

This involves total exclusion from "presence (*prospon*: face or countenance) of the Lord and from the glory of his power." It means, complete and irrevocable banishment from His personal presence, and from the sphere in which He will display "the glory of his power." This means "outer darkness" where there will be "weeping and gnashing of teeth" (Matt. 25:30). But not for the saints:

iv) The triumph, v.10
"When he shall come to be glorified in his saints, and to be admired in all them that believe (because our testimony among you was believed) in that day". Disobedient sinners will be excluded from "the **glory** of his power", but the Lord Jesus will be "**glorified** in his saints." So, the 'revelation' of the Lord Jesus (the time when He returns to earth from heaven) will bring judgment on unbelievers, and glory for believers:

- **From the standpoint of the unsaved**. That is, those that "know not God, and that obey not the gospel of our Lord Jesus Christ." For them, He will come "in flaming fire taking vengeance."

- **From the standpoint of the saved.** That is, those who believed the gospel: "because our testimony among you was believed." For them, He will come "to be glorified in his saints, and to be admired in all them that believe...in that day." Our great hope is to meet the Lord Jesus in the air (1 Thess. 4:17), and then to return with Him to earth. It will be wonderful to "behold" his glory (John 17:24): it will be wonderful to be glorified with Him (Rom. 8:17); it will be wonderful when our bodies are "fashioned like unto his glorious body ('His body of glory')" (Phil. 3:21). But this goes further: we will display His glory to a wondering world. Our bodies will be vehicles through which the world will see the glory of the Lord Jesus. The word "admire" *(thaumazo)* means 'to wonder at' or 'marvel.' W.E. Vine defines it as "mingled surprise and admiration".

> The heavens shall glow with splendour;
> But brighter far than they,
> The saints shall shine in glory,
> As Christ shall them array;
> The beauty of the Saviour
> Shall dazzle every eye,
> In the crowning day that's coming
> By-and by.

We must not forget that the Lord Jesus should be seen in our lives **now**. See v.12.

3) THEIR WORTHINESS OF THE CALLING OF GOD, vv.11-12

Future events are never taught in a vacuum. It has been said that 'the timetable for the future is always accompanied by the tasks for the present'. The Old Testament prophets certainly addressed the present in the light of the future, and this principle is equally clear in the New Testament. Paul now raises practical issues.

We should notice, first of all, that teaching and prayer are not divorced. Having told them that their present circumstances were part of God's training programme for future responsibility, he now prays for them. It is right to pray that unsaved people will hear and understand the Gospel. The Bible teacher must also pray that God's people will be blessed and helped through hearing Bible teaching. Since it was God's will that they should be "counted worthy of the kingdom of God" (v.5), Paul now prays God will accomplish this in their lives: "Wherefore also we pray always for you, that our God would count you worthy of this calling, and fulfil all the good pleasure of his goodness, and the work of faith with power: that the name of our Lord Jesus Christ may be glorified in you, and ye in him, according to the grace of our God and the Lord Jesus Christ." We should notice at least three things here:

i) **What he wanted God to impute to them.** "That our God would **count** you worthy of this calling" or "That our God would count you worthy of your calling" (RV). We could never be **made** worthy of the calling described in v.10. After all, we are, at best, "unprofitable servants" (Luke 17:10). Paul evidently had in mind their future reward here. He therefore prays that God would reward them as if they were worthy of their calling. This is true of all rewards. As W.E.Vine explains, God will not reward us "according to the actual attainment, or to the work accomplished, but according to the riches of His grace in Christ". After all, He gives us the ability to serve Him, and we are completely dependent on Him for any success in service. See 1 Corinthians 3:5-7.

ii) What He wanted God to accomplish in them. Paul wanted God to accomplish two things in their lives:

- "That our God...will fulfil **all the good pleasure of (his) goodness**." The word "pleasure" *(eudokia)* means 'good pleasure', or 'desire.' W.E. Vine points out that apart from Matthew 19:17, and its parallels in the other Gospels, the word "goodness" *(agathosune)* is never used of God. This, together with the fact that the words, "the work of faith", could only be used of men, strongly suggests that Paul refers here to the desires of the Thessalonians themselves. There is nothing more satisfying than to know that our highest spiritual desires are being fulfilled. See Psalm 37:4, "Delight thyself also in the Lord; and he shall give thee the desires of thine heart."

- "That our God...will fulfil all the good pleasure of (his) goodness, and **the work of faith with power.**" He prays here that all service undertaken by them in faith would be attended by divine power. This is relevant to us all. We undertake service for God in faith. We trust in Him. We can therefore pray for His power to make our service effective.

iii) What he wanted the Lord Jesus to receive. "That the name of our Lord Jesus Christ may be glorified in you, and ye him, according to the grace of God and the Lord Jesus Christ." That is, that His name might be glorified in us **now**, as we will be glorified in Him in the **future.** How can this happen? Only "according to the grace of our God and the Lord Jesus Christ." The word "grace" points to the infinite resources which are available to help us bring glory to the Lord Jesus.

READ CHAPTER 2:1-5

"Be not soon shaken in mind"

Chapter 1 describes the **revelation of the Lord Jesus**: "the Lord Jesus shall be revealed (*apokalupto*: meaning 'uncovering' or 'unveiling') from heaven with his mighty angels, in flaming fire taking vengeance on them that know not God, and that obey not the gospel of our Lord Jesus Christ" (vv.7-8). Chapter 2 describes the **'revelation' of the "man of sin."** The word "revealed" *(apokalupsis)* occurs three times in the passage (vv.3, 6, 8).

Chapter 2 commences with believers "shaken in mind.....troubled" (v.1), but having dealt with the cause of their disturbance and distress, Paul prays that they will enjoy "everlasting consolation and good hope through grace" (vv.16-17). With this in mind, we may divide the chapter as follows: **(1)** the concern at Thessalonica (vv.1-2); **(2)** the coming of the man of sin (vv.3-12); **(3)** the consolation of God's people (vv.13-17).

1) THE CONCERN AT THESSALONICA, vv.1-2
We should notice **(a)** the response to their concern (v.1); **(b)** the reason for their concern (v.2).

a) The response to their concern, v.1
The chapter opens with some very unhappy believers! "Now we beseech you ('beg you', JND), brethren, by the coming of our Lord Jesus Christ, and by our gathering together unto him, that ye be not soon shaken in mind, or be troubled, neither by spirit, nor by word, nor by letter as from us, as that the day of Christ is at hand". Paul wastes no time at all in tackling the problem. It arose because they had lost sight of the Lord's coming! The urgency of the situation is conveyed by the word "beseech" *(erotao)*. It is often translated 'ask.' Paul was deeply concerned about their spiritual welfare.

This accounts for the absence of "hope" in the thanksgiving at the beginning of the epistle. "We are bound to thank God always for you, brethren, as it is meet, because your faith groweth exceedingly, and the charity (love) of every one of you all toward each other aboundeth" (1:3) But what had happened to their "hope?" It was there originally. See 1 Thessalonians 1:3: "Remembering without ceasing your work of faith, and labour of love, and patience of **hope** in our Lord Jesus Christ." Quite clearly, they thought that the Lord had left them to endure the unutterable horrors of the "day of the Lord." It had been put to them that they were suffering because 'the day of the Lord is now present' (RV) rather than "the day of Christ is at hand" (AV). In consequence, their "hope" had faded. Paul therefore commences by reminding them that the Lord Jesus was coming back before these events took place.

This is the first part of Paul's twofold answer to their problem. Here, he cites the coming of the Lord Jesus for His people (v.1). Later, he cites the coming of the "man of sin" (v.3).

i) **The coming of the Lord Jesus.** "The coming *(parousia)* of our Lord Jesus Christ, and…our gathering together unto him" (v.1). (Do notice that Paul does not say 'our coming **with** Him!'). The word *"by"* here is italicised, and should be omitted. The "coming of our Lord Jesus Christ" and "our gathering together unto him" are one event. Paul describes this in 1 Thessalonians 4:13-18. We call this 'the **rapture**.' (The word *harpazo* means to 'snatch' or 'catch away'). It assures us that "God hath not appointed us to wrath (the "wrath" of the "day of the Lord"), but to obtain salvation by our Lord Jesus Christ, Who died for us, that, whether we wake or sleep, we should live together with him" (1 Thess. 5:9-10):

> On that bright and golden morning when the Son of Man shall come,
> And the radiance of His glory we shall see;
> When from every clime and nation He shall call His people home –
> What a gathering of the ransomed that will be!

Do remember, by the way, that in the New Testament the coming of "the Son of man" refers to His public return, not to the rapture. (But don't stop singing the hymn!), If the Lord's coming in v.1 refers, as many teach, to His public return after the fearful judgments of the "day of the Lord", and therefore after the great tribulation, then it did nothing to quieten the minds of the believers at Thessalonica. They were still "shaken in mind" and "troubled." After all, they were well aware that He would come to reign. But that was no consolation to them as they faced, as they thought, the prospect of living in the world subject to unprecedented divine judgment. Paul therefore reminds them of previous teaching by saying, "Now we beseech you, brethren, by the coming of our Lord Jesus Christ, and by our gathering together unto him, that ye be not soon shaken in mind." They had been taught about the rapture, and should not, therefore, have been deceived into thinking that they were in the "day of the Lord."

ii) The coming of the "man of sin". Here is Paul's second reason why the believers at Thessalonica were not in "the day of the Lord." The awful judgments of that period would be preceded by clearly defined events, including the appearance of "that man of sin...the son of perdition". Paul deals with this in vv.3-12.

b) The reason for their concern, v.2
As we have noted above, the believers at Thessalonica were disturbed by the suggestion that they could be actually living in the period described as 'the day of the Lord' (v.2, JND). Perhaps we ought to remind ourselves at this juncture of the various 'days' in the New Testament. See our remarks in connection wth 1 Thessalonians 5:2-3. The "day of the Lord" will be a period of "sudden destruction" and "wrath" (1 Thess. 5:3, 9). Zephaniah describes the "day of the Lord" as follows: "That day is a day of wrath, a day of trouble and distress, a day of wasteness and desolation, a day of darkness and gloominess, a day of clouds and thick darkness" (Zeph. 1:15).

Paul uses two words to describe their state of mind. *(i)* "Shaken" *(saleuo)* meaning 'agitated', or 'unsettled.' W.E. Vine explains that it was used, primarily, of "the action or stormy winds, waves, etc." *(ii)* "Troubled" *(throeo)* comes from a word meaning 'a tumult' *(throos),* and therefore means 'disturbed.' According to JND (see his margin) it means "shaken from a steady and soberly judging mind". Their agitation had evidently begun quite quickly after receiving the First Epistle, in which Paul refers to the visit of Timothy "to establish you, and to comfort you concerning your faith: that no man should be moved by these afflictions" (1 Thess. 3:2-3). Hence, "that ye be not **soon** shaken in mind, or be troubled..." Compare Galatians 1:6. Their concern had been caused particularly by a ***forged letter:*** "by letter as from us" (v.2). This raises at least three important issues:

i) **False teaching undermines peace of mind.** It causes uncertainty and distress. Sound teaching brings joy and assurance, even when we are under pressure. The Thessalonians had "received the word in much affliction, with ***joy*** of the Holy Ghost" (1 Thess. 1:6). Like the New Testament prophet, the Bible teacher speaks "to edification (he builds up), and exhortation (he stirs up), and comfort (he cheers up)" (1 Cor. 14:3). False teaching does none of these things. Look what happened at Thessalonica!

ii) False teaching contradicts apostolic teaching. We must not diverge from original teaching! In this case, the suggestions of the false teachers contradicted **written** teaching given in 1 Thessalonians 4-5. Paul directs them to this in saying, "Now we beseech you, brethren, by the coming of our Lord Jesus Christ, and (by) our gathering together unto him." It also contradicted **oral** teaching. See v.5: "Remember ye not, that, when I was yet with you, I told you these things?" Galatians 1: 8-9 emphasises the lesson.

iii) False teaching is often surreptitious. It is not 'all square, and above board.' On the contrary, it is downright deceitful (v.3). Notice how Paul describes the letter: "by letter as from us." Sound teaching will 'stand the light of day.' It doesn't need craft and stealth. The Lord Jesus said, "I spake openly to the world; I ever taught in the synagogue, and in the temple, whither the Jews always resort; and in secret have I said nothing" (John 18: 20). False teachers are furtive. Read Galatians 2:4, 2 Peter 2:1, Jude 4. Paul assures them that he had not written the letter in question. All his letters bore his signature. See 3:17, "The salutation by the hand of me Paul, which is the mark in every letter; so I write" (JND).

The false teachers had evidently gone about their business in three ways: "That ye should be not soon shaken in mind, or be troubled, neither by **spirit**, nor by **word**, nor by **letter** as from us." The word **"spirit"** refers to people. See 1 John 4:1-3: "Beloved, believe not every spirit, but try the spirits whether they are of God." This refers, obviously, not to some ghostly apparition, but to a person. "Try the spirits" means test the spiritual powers that control the man. W.E. Vine defines "spirit" as "those who claimed to be depositaries of spiritual gifts". By **"word"**, Paul refers to verbal teaching, and **"letter"** obviously refers to written teaching. Compare v.15: "Therefore, brethren, stand fast, and hold the traditions which ye have been taught, whether by **word** (a verbal message), or our **epistle**". A forged letter referring to the "day of the Lord" suggests a Jewish author. After all, the Jews knew far more about the "day of the Lord" than anybody else!

This brings us to the second reason why they should not be "shaken in mind" and "troubled":

2) THE COMING OF THE MAN OF SIN, vv.3-12
In this section, Paul reminds them (see v.5) that "the day of the Lord" would be

preceded by certain clearly-defined events, including the appearance of "the man of sin." As we shall see, his name indicates that he will be the embodiment of evil. He will be Satan's masterpiece. He will be the final world ruler before the establishment of the millennial kingdom. He will be marked by total opposition to God. He will blaspheme God, and relentlessly persecute God's people. Note the repetition of "revealed" (vv.3, 6, 8). We must now notice the following:

a) The conditions preceding the man of sin, v.3

"Let no man deceive you by any means (for example, by "spirit…word…letter as from us"): for that day shall not come, except there come a falling away first" or "the apostasy *(apostasia)* have first come" (JND). We must notice the definite article here: it is '**the** apostasy', or '**the** falling away.' Since no further explanation is given here, we must conclude that the details were known to the Thessalonians. See vv5-6. In Acts 21:21, the word *apostasia* is translated "forsake."

The "falling away" is the total abandonment of the word of God, and total rejection of God Himself. It is man's final and deliberate 'No' to God. The seed sown in Genesis 3:1-5 reaches its ultimate fruition. In the garden of Eden, the serpent said: "Hath God said…ye shall not surely die." Now we have the final result. Various passages in the New Testament describe conditions at the end-time. See, for example, 2 Peter 3:3-4, "There shall come in the last days scoffers, walking after their own lusts, and saying, Where is the promise of his coming". Read Jude 14-15, "Behold, the Lord cometh with ten thousands of his saints, to execute judgment upon all, and to convince all that are ungodly among them of all their ungodly deeds which they have ungodly committed, and of all their hard speeches which ungodly sinners have spoken against him". Read 2 Timothy 3:1 "This know also, that in the last days perilous times shall come. For men shall be lovers of their own selves, covetous, boasters, proud, blasphemers…." Read Matthew 24:24, "For there shall arise false Christs, and false prophets, and shall shew great signs and wonders; insomuch that, if it were possible, they shall deceive the very elect." These passages combine to paint a picture of conditions at the end-time, which will reach their zenith in '**the** falling away', or '**the** apostasy.'

But, as we shall see, mankind must have an object of worship. If they reject the **true** God, then they will accept a **false** god. See vv.10-11. People who receive "not the love of the truth, that they might be saved", will "believe a lie" (literally, 'the lie'). This is solemn beyond words: men and women who reject God's word, will believe the lie of Satan. The following verses describe the man who will claim to be God:

b) The character of the man of sin, v.3
He is called, "that man of sin...the son of perdition." His character is described in v.3, and his actions are described in v.4.

i) He is that ***"man*** of sin." As W.E. Vine points out, the word "man" *(anthropos)* is only used of a human being, and therefore the expression, "man of sin", cannot be read as sin personified. Here is Satan's answer to "the man Christ Jesus" (1 Tim. 2:5). The Jews accused the Lord Jesus of blasphemy: "For a good work we stone thee not; but for blasphemy; and because that thou, being a man, makest thyself God" (John 10:33). The Lord Jesus did not 'make himself' God. He was, and is, God! Christians alter their statement, and say with wonder, 'Thou, being God, makest thyself man!' The "man of sin" will claim to be God. He will sit "in the temple of God, shewing himself that he is God" (v.4).

ii) He is "that man of ***sin***". This suggests that he will be a man "over whom sin will have absolute dominion". He will be "the willing and efficient instrument of sin". (W.E. Vine). The word "sin" translates *hamartia*, meaning 'a missing of the mark', but other readings give *anomia*, meaning 'a breaking of law.' The word *anomia* is used in v.7 ("mystery of ***iniquity***"), and in v.8 ("that **Wicked**"). He has therefore been described as 'the man of lawlessness': he will be 'without law altogether'. Either way, he will be the incarnation of evil. We cannot escape the contrast between "the man of sin", and the Lord Jesus Who could say, "Which of you convinceth (convicteth) me of sin?" (John 8:46). When He was born, it was said, "That holy...which shall be born of thee shall be called the Son of God" (Luke 1:35). He "did no sin" (1 Pet. 2:22), He "knew no sin" (2 Cor. 5:21) and "in him is no sin" (1 John 3:5). The Lord Jesus is called "the Holy One and the Just" (Acts 3:14). See also Acts 7:52; 22:14.

iii) He is ***"the son of perdition"***. The word "perdition" *(apoleia)* means 'destruction', and indicates his destiny. He is fitted for destruction. The expression is used of Judas Iscariot. See John 17:12. W.E. Vine puts it like this: "If 'man of lawlessness' refers to character, then 'son of perdition' refers to the proper destiny of one, who, like Judas, must 'go to his own place' (Acts 1:25)". We must now consider the question of his identity.

c) The claims of the man of sin, v.4
"Who opposeth and exalteth himself above all that is called God, or that is worshipped; so that he as God sitteth in the temple of God, shewing himself that he is God."

The precise identity of the "man of sin" has been thoroughly debated. Some able Bible teachers assert that he is the first "beast" of Revelation 13 (see vv.1-10). Other equally able Bible teachers assert that he is the second "beast" in the chapter (vv.11-17). It is important to ensure that discussion does not generate more heat than light! It is not a crucial issue. Interesting, but not crucial! Very clearly, at the end-time, Satan will endeavour to replicate the Godhead. We learn from Revelation 13, that Satan ("the dragon") will endeavour to counterfeit the Father; the Beast (that is, "the first beast", v.12) will counterfeit the Son; the False Prophet (Rev. 16:13: that is, the second "beast "of Revelation 13) will counterfeit the Holy Spirit.

The Scriptures assign design, plan, purpose and initiative to the Father. See, for example, 1 John 4:14, "the Father sent the Son to be the Saviour of the world." The Lord Jesus, the Son of God, reveals the Father, and implements His will and purposes. See, for example Colossians 1:18, 2 Corinthians 1:20, Ephesians 1:10. The ministry of the Holy Spirit is to engage our minds and hearts with the Lord Jesus. See, for example, John 15:26, 16:13-15. Now compare the roles of the Dragon, the Beast, and the False Prophet in Revelation 13. The Dragon takes the initiative, and gives the Beast "his power, and his seat, and great authority" (v.2). The Beast achieves the object of the Dragon by securing for him the worship of the world (v.4). The False Prophet takes steps to ensure that "the earth and them which dwell therein...worship the first beast, whose deadly wound was healed" (v.12).

In view of the fact that the work of the False Prophet is to ensure the supremacy of the Beast, it does seem that it is the Beast himself who is described in 2 Thessalonians 2. The "man of sin" is the supreme object of worship. Compare the following:

- **Revelation 13: 5-8,** "And there was given unto him a mouth speaking great things and blasphemies; and power was given unto him to continue forty and two months. And he opened his mouth in blasphemy against God, to blaspheme his name, and his tabernacle, and them that dwell in heaven. And it was given unto him to make war with the saints, and to overcome them: and power was given unto him over all kindreds, and tongues, and nations. And all that dwell upon the earth shall worship him, whose names are not written in the book of life of the Lamb slain from the foundation of the world."

- **2 Thessalonians 2:4,** "Who opposeth and exalteth himself above all that is called God, or that is worshipped; so that he as God sitteth in the temple of God, shewing himself that he is God." Notice, in passing, clear reference to the rebuilding of the temple in Jerusalem.

His opposition to "all that is called God, or that is worshipped", includes the destruction of the "great whore that sitteth upon many waters" (Rev. 17:1). She is described as, "MYSTERY, BABYLON THE GREAT, THE MOTHER OF HARLOTS AND ABOMINATIONS OF THE EARTH" (Rev. 17:5), and represents the amalgam of all world religion. The "great whore" is the final form of the Ecumenical Movement. Notice, too, that Revelation 17 also describes His opposition to the Lord Jesus. "These (the ten part kingdom of the beast) shall make war with the Lamb", but to no avail: "and the Lamb shall overcome them: for he is Lord of lords, and King of kings" (Rev. 17:14). The Beast will oppose every religious system: idolatrous and otherwise. We know that the beast will "speak great words against the most High, and shall wear out the saints of the most High, and think to change times and laws" (Dan. 7:25), and "cause the sacrifice and the oblation to cease" (Dan. 9:27).

The Lord Jesus referred to him as follows: "I am come in my Father's name, and ye receive me not: if another shall come in his own name, him ye will receive" (John 5:43). The "man of sin" casts his shadow before him. See 1 John 4:3 "And every spirit that confesseth not that Jesus Christ is come in the flesh is not of God: and this is that spirit of **antichrist** (meaning, not only 'against Christ', but 'instead of Christ'), whereof ye have heard that it should come; and even now already is it in the world".

The fact he sits in "the temple of God, shewing himself that he is God" does not infer that he will be there all the time. It will be the business of the False Prophet to ensure that he is worshipped at all times, and for this purpose he will command worship for "the image of the beast" (it is called "the abomination of desolation" in Matt. 24:15) which will be erected in the temple precincts. Refusal to worship the image will incur the death penalty. Daniel and his friends knew all about this! Read Daniel chs. 3 and 6.

It could be objected that since the 'first beast' in Revelation is evidently a Gentile (he rises "up out of the sea", which suggests the Gentile nations), under no circumstances could he be recognised and accepted as the rightful occupant of the temple. Against this, we notice that "the beast" will **impose** himself upon Jew and Gentile alike, and so far as the former are concerned, he will "change times and laws", and "cause the sacrifice and oblation to cease" (Dan. 7:25, 9:27).

One final note: we never know when past teaching will prove useful. Don't forget v.5!

READ CHAPTER 2:6-17

"Then shall that Wicked be revealed"

In our last study, we divided this chapter as follows: *(1)* the concern at Thessalonica (vv.1-2); *(2)* the coming of the man of sin (vv.3-12); *(3)* the consolation of God's people (vv.13-17). The Chapter commences with believers "shaken in mind...troubled" (v.1), but having dealt with the cause of their disturbance and distress, Paul prays that they will enjoy "everlasting consolation and good hope through grace" (vv.16-17).

1) THE CONCERN AT THESSALONICA, vv.1-2

The believers at Thessalonica had been told that their intense suffering was evidence that they were living in "the day of the Lord." Paul therefore corrects this error: "Now we beg you, brethren, by the coming of our Lord Jesus Christ and our gathering together to him, that ye be not soon shaken in mind, nor troubled, neither by spirit, nor by word, nor by letter, as (if it were) by us, as that the day of the Lord is present" (JND). The first reason why these believers were not in "the day of the Lord" was because the Lord Jesus would come before the commencement of that period. The second reason follows:

2) THE COMING OF THE MAN OF SIN, vv.3-12

In this section, Paul reminds them ("remember ye not, that, when I was with you, I told you these things", v.5) that the "day of the Lord" would be preceded by certain clearly-defined events, including the appearance of the "man of sin". We have already noted the following:

a) The conditions preceding the man of sin, v.3

"Let no man deceive you by any means: for that day shall not come, except there come a falling away first." God will be totally rejected. It is called, "**the** apostasy" (JND).

b) The character of the man of sin, v.3

He is described as "that man of sin" and "the son of perdition." The first indicates that he will be the personification of evil, and the second indicates his destiny. He is fitted for destruction.

c) The claims of the man of sin, v.4
"Who opposeth and exalteth himself above all that is called God, or that is worshipped; so that he as God sitteth in the temple of God, shewing himself that he is God." This brings us to:

d) The control on the man of sin, vv.6-7
"And now ye know what withholdeth *(katecho,* to restrain) that he might be revealed in his time. For the mystery of iniquity doth already work: only he who now letteth *(katecho)* will let ('only there is he who restrains now', JND), until he be taken out of the way." These verses emphasise two kinds of activity.

i) **Evil activity**. "The mystery of iniquity doth already work." A "mystery" *(musterion)* is something that lies beyond human understanding, and can therefore only be known to man by divine revelation. Hence, as W.E. Vine points out, the word occurs in conjunction with such expressions as 'made known', 'revealed' (Eph. 3:3-5), 'made manifest' (Rom. 16:26, Col. 1:26), 'shew', (1 Cor. 15:51). This definition will help us to understand "the mystery of iniquity", or 'lawlessness' *(anomia)*. W.E. Vine continues to be most helpful: "Lawlessness is not necessarily confusion and disorder: the idea intended is that it is the aim of the Devil and of 'the spiritual hosts of wickedness in the heavenly places' (Eph. 6:11-12), to overthrow the Divine government". Quite obviously, men and women in general, and politicians and statesmen in particular, have no conception of Satan's intention. The very idea would be greeted with scorn and derision. Hence the description, "the **mystery** of iniquity." Very clearly, every divine institution is under concerted attack. Witness the attacks on God's ordinance of marriage, the divine concept of family life, the role of the "powers that be" (Rom. 13:1-2), and the distinctive roles of men and women. The sin of Sodom has almost become the norm in society. God's laws are blatantly ignored and rejected, and tragically, so-called 'churchmen' often lead the way. The "mystery of iniquity" operated when Paul wrote 2 Thessalonians, and it is 'sweeping the field' today. Satan has one grand objective, and that will be fulfilled in the emergence of "the man of sin." But his dominance will be limited to three and a half years. The "mystery of inquity" is Satan's answer to the "mystery of godliness" (1 Tim.3:16).

ii) **Divine activity**. At the moment, Satan's activity is restrained. The "man of sin" has not yet emerged, and cannot do so until the restraining power is removed.

There is considerable debate over the nature of this restraint. In this connection, we must notice that both the neuter and masculine genders are used. "And now ye know **what** withholdeth that he might be revealed in his time. For the mystery of iniquity doth already work: only **he** who now letteth will let, until he be taken out of the way." The words, "**what** witholdeth", indicate that **something** is restraining or hindering the emergence of the "man of sin", and the words, "**he** who now letteth", indicate that **someone** is involved in the restraint.

Very clearly, the restraint described here is ongoing. It existed at the time of writing, and will continue to exist until it is removed. It therefore exists today. The restraint has been variously explained. Some suggest that it is the authority vested in the "higher powers". See Romans 13:1-3: "there is no power but of God: the powers that be are ordained of God." When Paul wrote 2 Thessalonians, "the powers that be" were represented by the authority of the Roman Empire. But while the efficiency and authority of the Roman Empire cannot be doubted, it did not control evil. Woe to any Christian who did not burn incense to Caesar! Human government has facilitated evil, and, sadly, we have only to think of legislation passed by the British parliament in recent years to prove the point. Others suggest that the 'restrainer' is Satan himself, who is waiting for the right time to introduce "the man of sin", through whom he will endeavour to control the world. But this does not agree with the passage, which makes it clear that the 'restrainer' himself will be removed. The removal of the restraint does not free the world of Satan's activity. Quite the contrary! The suggestion reminds us that "if a house be divided against itself, that house cannot stand!" (Mark 3:25). We must look elsewhere for the answer.

As we have noted, the words, "**what** withholdeth", indicate that **something** is restraining or hindering the emergence of the "man of sin", and the words, "**he** who now letteth", indicate that **someone** is involved in the restraint. The close connection between the two reminds us of the close connection between the church and the Holy Spirit. The coming of the Holy Spirit on the day of Pentecost marked the commencement of the church, and the intimacy of the relationship is stressed in the final appeal to mankind, "The Spirit and the bride say, Come" (Rev. 22:17) Bearing in mind, therefore, that the "falling away" and consequent events will follow the rapture of the church, the present restraint is evidently exercised by the Holy Spirit in the church.

We must notice in this connection that the Lord's people are "the salt of the earth" (Matt. 5:13). Just as the strata of rock salt preserve the earth from corruption, so the Lord's people, the church, have a restraining influence on the progress of sin, although the "mystery of iniquity" is now proceeding rapidly. But the church in itself cannot restrain. This is achieved by the power of the Holy Spirit in the church. In this connection, we should notice:

i) The "wicked one" is a person, and he acts in the power of Satan. He wields immense spiritual power. The restrainer must therefore also be a Person with superior power in the spiritual realm.

ii) To achieve restraint, the restrainer must, of necessity, be a member of the Godhead. He must be stronger than the "man of sin", and stronger than Satan.

iii) These qualifications can only belong to the Spirit of God. The Lord Jesus described His restraining work in John 16:7-11: "And when he is come, he will reprove (convict) the world of sin, and of righteousness, and of judgment." It is in the context of Satanic activity that John writes: "Greater is he that is in you, than he that is in the world" (1 John 4:4).

The words, "until he be taken out of the way", do not mean that the Holy Spirit will be removed from the earth with the church, when the Lord Jesus returns "with a shout, with the voice of the archangel, and with the trump of God" (1 Thess. 4:16). But He will be taken 'out of the midst' so far as His present ministry is concerned, in order that "he (the man of sin) might be revealed in his time." He will certainly be present on earth during this period. See, for example, Revelation 5:6, "the seven Spirits of God sent forth into **all the earth**." In the Old Testament, the Holy Spirit did not indwell men and women permanently, as He does now. He empowered servants of God for specific tasks, and for limited periods, and this will evidently be resumed after the church has been taken to heaven. This brings us to:

e) The consuming of the man of sin, v.8
"And then shall that Wicked (*anomos*: 'the lawless one') be revealed (*apokalupto*: 'unveiled' as in vv.3, 6: see 1:7), whom the Lord shall consume (*analisko*: 'to use up' or 'to spend up') with the spirit of his mouth, and shall destroy with the brightness of his coming." When the Lord Jesus was *en route* to Jerusalem, the Samaritans refused to receive him, causing the disciples to say, "Lord, wilt thou that we command fire to come down from heaven, and consume (*analisko*) them, even as Elias did?" The Lord Jesus replied: "Ye know not what manner of spirit ye are of. For the Son of man is not come to destroy men's lives, but to save them" (Luke 9:51-56). But in 2 Thessalonians 2, that day has now ended, and divine judgment must fall on His enemies.

The words, "Whom the Lord shall consume with the spirit of his mouth", meaning, 'with the breath of his mouth', cite Isaiah 11:4, "He shall smite the earth with the rod of his mouth, and with the breath of his lips shall he slay the wicked." Compare Revelation 19:15-21, "And out of his mouth goeth a sharp sword, that with it he should smite the nations...and the remnant were slain with the sword of him that sat upon the horse, which sword proceeded out of his mouth: and all the fowls were filled with their flesh."

The Psalmist reminds us that "By the word of the Lord were the heavens made; and all the host of them by the breath of his mouth" (Psalm 33:6). "The wicked" whom He will slay "with the breath of his lips" will therefore be no match for Him!

The word "destroy" *(katargeo)* means "to reduce to inactivity" (W.E. Vine). It is used in Hebrews 2:14, where it is often translated 'brought to naught.' It does not mean loss of being, but loss of well-being. The words, "with the brightness (*epiphaneia,* meaning, 'shining forth') of his coming *(parousia)*", recall Matthew 24:27, "As the lightning cometh out of the east, and shineth even unto the west; so shall also the coming of the Son of man be."

At His trial, the Lord Jesus "answered nothing" (Matt. 27:12). Now He speaks. After three and half years of "speaking great things and blasphemies", and having "opened his mouth in blasphemy against God" (Rev. 13:5-6), the "man of sin" is silenced by the Lord Jesus.

f) The craft of the man of sin, vv.9-10
"Even him, whose coming is after the working of Satan with all power and signs and lying wonders, and with all deceivableness of unrighteousness in them that perish; because they received not the love of the truth, that they might be saved." The word "coming" *(parousia)* "denotes both arrival and consequent presence" (W.E. Vine). Our English word 'energy' comes from the word rendered "working" (*energia).*

The words, "after the working of Satan" should be compared with Revelation 13:2 ("The dragon gave him his **power** *(dunamis)*, and his seat, and great authority"), and 13:4 ("And they worshipped the dragon which gave **power** *(exousia)* unto the beast"). See also Daniel 8:24, which describes the same evil person, "And his **power** shall be mighty, but **not** by his own power."

The expression, "deceivableness of unrighteousness", means 'deceit of unrighteousness.' The "man of sin" will have no scruples about the methods he uses to deceive men and women. He will follow his dark master, of whom the Lord Jesus said: "He...abode not in the truth, because there is no truth in him. When he speaketh a lie, he speaketh of his own: for he is a liar, and the father of it" (John 8:44). The Lord Jesus is "the way, and the **truth,** and the life." In every way, the "man of sin" will endeavour to counterfeit the Lord Jesus. He was "a man approved of God...by miracles and wonders and signs" (Acts 2:22). The same three words are used in Hebrews 2:4, "God also bearing them witness, both with signs and wonders, and with divers miracles, and gifts of the Holy Ghost, according to his own will." Satan will endeavour to replicate this with his own "power and signs and lying wonders." See Revelation 13:12-15, which describe the power of the False Prophet (the second "beast" in Revelation 13): "He exerciseth all the power of the first beast before him...And he doeth great wonders, so that he maketh fire come down from heaven on the earth in the sight of men, and deceiveth them that dwell on the earth by the means of those miracles which he had power to do in the sight of the beast; saying to them that dwell on the earth, that they should make an image to the beast, which had the wound by a sword, and did live. And he had power to give life (breath) unto the image of the beast, that the image of the beast should both speak, and cause that as many as would not worship the image of the beast should be killed."

The Lord Jesus warned His disciples about "false Christs, and false prophets" who would show "great signs and wonders; insomuch that, if it were possible, they shall deceive the very elect" (Matt. 24:24). The "great signs and wonders" mentioned by the Lord Jesus, are called "lying wonders" here. Those who are tricked by the "lying wonders", are described as "them that perish." W.E. Vine states that the verb corresponds with the noun in v.3 ("son of perdition"), and continues, "Antichrist and his deluded supporters, since they share a common character and shall share a common doom, are appropriately described by the same term". We should be so grateful to God for His grace. We **have** "received... the love of the truth." We **are** "saved." Otherwise, we would share the doom of the "man of sin." More follows:

g) The consequences of belief in the man of sin, vv.11-12
"And for this cause God shall send them strong delusion, that they should believe a lie (literally, '**the** lie', W.E. Vine: 'what is false' JND): that they all might be damned (judged, *krino*) who believed not the truth, but had pleasure in unrighteousness." Notice the deliberate choice: "they received not the love of the truth (v.10)...who believed not the truth" (v.12)". Once again, we should be thankful to God that **we** have "believed...the truth". When men and women reject the truth, they become vulnerable to lies, and in this case, the most fearful

lies the world has ever seen. The choice is stark: either accept the Lord Jesus Christ, "the true God, and eternal life" (1 John 5:20), or accept the Antichrist. See John 5:43. It is either "love of the truth" or "pleasure in unrighteousness." Compare Romans 1:32. W.E. Vine comments with great solemnity: "Distaste for the truth leads to its rejection. God in retributive justice sends a working of error to those who love error, this they gladly accept, yielding themselves to it, and co-operating with it, until they are overtaken by the climax in which the righteous judgment of God is expressed". This brings us to:

3) THE CONSOLATION OF GOD'S PEOPLE, vv.13-17
In the concluding section of the chapter, we should notice *(a)* Paul's thanksgiving (vv.13-14); *(b)* Paul's exhortation (v.15); *(c)* Paul's prayer (vv.16-17).

a) Paul's thanksgiving, vv.13-14
"But we are bound to give thanks alway to God for you, brethren beloved of the Lord, because God hath from the beginning chosen you to salvation through sanctification of the Spirit and belief of the truth: whereunto he called you by our gospel, to the obtaining of the glory of our Lord Jesus Christ."

The contrast could not be more vivid. In vv.11-12, we have people who will be judged because they will "believe a lie" and who "believed not the truth." In v.13, we have people who are saved through "belief of the truth." In the first case, it is the result of Satanic delusion. In the second case, it is the result of the work of the Spirit of God. In the first case, people will experience divine judgment. In the second, people will enjoy the "glory of our Lord Jesus Christ." Extending this, on the one hand, we have people who will have "pleasure in unrighteousness": on the other, people established in "every good word and work" (v.17).

These are astounding verses. They begin with God's love. "But we are bound to give thanks alway to God for you, brethren **beloved of the Lord**", and continue with reference to the way in which the entire Godhead is involved in our salvation and eternal blessing. We must therefore notice:

*i) "**God** hath from the beginning chosen you to salvation."* God's choice (v.13) took place in eternity: His calling (v.14) took place in time. The expression, "from the beginning", must be understood with reference to such passages as 1 Corinthians 2:7 ("But we speak the wisdom of God in a mystery, even the hidden wisdom, which God ordained before the world unto our glory"); Ephesians 1:4 ("According as he hath chosen us in him before the foundation of the world"); 2 Timothy 1:9 ("Who hath saved us, and called us with an holy calling, not according to our works, but according to his own purpose and grace, which was given us in Christ Jesus before the world began").

ii) "Through sanctification of the **Spirit** and belief of the truth." Very clearly, "the sanctification of the Spirit is associated with the choice, or election, of God: it is a divine act preceding the acceptance of the Gospel by the individual" (W.E. Vine). Notice the parallel passage in 1 Peter 1:2, "Elect according to the foreknowledge of God the Father, through **sanctification of the Spirit**, unto obedience and sprinkling of the blood of Jesus Christ." Both passages emphasise God's part, and our part in salvation. For us, "belief of the truth" and "obedience" were involved. But God took the initiative in our salvation. There is far more to salvation than 'the choice we made!'

iii) "Whereunto he called you by our gospel, to the obtaining of the glory of **our Lord Jesus Christ**". That is the purpose of salvation: we are going share the glory of the Lord Jesus. We have been predestinated "to be conformed to the image of his Son, that he might be the firstborn among many brethren" (Rom. 8:29).

> And is it so! we shall be like Thy Son,
> Is this the grace which He for us hath won?
> Father of glory! (thought beyond all thought)
> In glory to His own blest likeness brought.

What an encouragement for the Gospel preacher. God uses His servants in accomplishing His eternal purposes! "Whereunto he called you by **our gospel**." See 1 Thessalonians 1:5.

b) Paul's exhortation, v.15

"Therefore, brethren, stand fast, and hold the traditions which ye have been taught, whether by word, or our epistle." In view of the teaching of the chapter (note the "therefore"), the believers at Thessalonica were to be no longer "shaken in mind" (v.2), but to "stand fast, and hold the traditions." The word "traditions" *(paradosis)* means 'a handing down' or 'a handing on.' It refers to divinely-given teaching. See Jude v.3: "the faith which was once delivered *(paradidomi*: to 'transmit', or 'hand over') unto the saints." It is important to remember that New Testament teaching did not originate with the apostles. They received it from God, and conveyed it by oral and written teaching. See, for example, Galatians 1:11-12.

We must never forget that Bible teaching is intended to have an effect in our lives. In the first place, it should impart stability. Hence the exhortation, "Stand fast." The believers at Thessalonica were under pressure, and the assurance "of the sovereign grace of God in their election, and of its certain issue in glory" (W.E. Vine), was a double incentive to steadfastness. In the second place, they were to "hold" (*krateo:* 'exert strength upon', meaning 'grasp firmly') teaching already given. We must not be 'forgetful hearers' (James 1:25). It was because they had evidently forgotten previous teaching (see v.5), that they had become "shaken in mind."

c) Paul's prayer, vv.16-17

"Now our Lord Jesus Christ himself, and God, even our Father, which hath loved us, and hath given us everlasting consolation (compare 1:9: "everlasting destruction") and good hope through grace, comfort your hearts, and stablish you ('encourage your hearts, and establish you', JND) in every good word and work."

These verses are full of important lessons. We should notice that Paul refers to the "Lord Jesus Christ" before "God, even our Father." See also 2 Corinthians 13:14. This, of course, emphasises the deity of the Lord Jesus, and it has been suggested that He is placed first since "it is by the grace of the Son that the revelation of the Father is made" (W.E. Vine). Compare Matthew 11:27. Notice, too, that Paul says, "our Lord Jesus Christ **himself**." He is going to come for us personally (see 1 Thess. 4:16), but we have His personal help now. We could never "stand fast, and hold the traditions" (v.15) without His help!

The prayer with which the chapter ends was not just pious sentiment. Paul's desire that they should enjoy divine encouragement ("comfort your hearts"), and stability ("stablish you in every good word and work"), could be fulfilled because:

i) **God loved them.** Compare 2 Peter 3, where the apostle uses the word "beloved" four times (vv.1, 8, 14, 17) when describing adverse circumstances at the end-time. When the going gets tough, as well as at other times, we must 'keep ourselves in the love of God' (Jude v.21).

ii) **God had bestowed eternal blessing on them.** He "hath given us everlasting consolation *(paraklesis)*". They were experiencing temporary adversity: they could look forward to 'eternal comfort.' Compare Romans 8:18 and 2 Corinthians 4:17-18. Those who persecuted them could only look forward to eternal judgment. See 1:9.

iii) **God had given them "good hope through grace."** There was no uncertainty about it. It was a good hope. W.E. Vine explains this as follows: "The hope is said to be good because of its cheering and sustaining effect on him who cherishes it". Their "good hope" was rooted in the return of the Lord Jesus described in v.1: "the coming of our Lord Jesus Christ, and...our gathering together unto him".

READ CHAPTER 3:1-5

"The Lord direct your hearts into the love of God"

As we have seen, the believers at Thessalonica were enduring "persecutions and tribulations" (1:4), and in order to help and encourage them, Paul has described two future events: *(i)* the revelation of the Lord Jesus (Chapter 1) and *(ii)* the revelation of the "man of sin" (Chapter 2).

i) The revelation of the Lord Jesus
In Chapter 1, Paul assures the assembly at Thessalonica that their current sufferings were not without purpose: their steadfastness under pressure was preparing them for responsibility in the coming kingdom of God. He also assures them that God would deal with all who persecute His people. He will "recompense tribulation to them that trouble you." The Lord Jesus will take "vengeance on them that know not God, and that obey not the gospel of our Lord Jesus Christ." See vv.9-10.

In view of the revelation of the Lord Jesus, Paul **prays** that they might be counted "worthy of this calling" ***now.*** They were to behave in a manner which was worthy of the prospect described in v.10, "when he shall come to be glorified in his saints, and to be admired in all them that believe."

ii) The revelation of the man of sin
In Chapter 2, Paul assures the assembly that they could not be passing through the "day of the Lord" since two things must take place before that period begins. Firstly, "the coming of our Lord Jesus Christ, and...our gathering together unto him" (v.1), and secondly, the emergence of the "man of sin" (v.3). He will ultimately be destroyed when the Lord returns: "whom the Lord shall consume with the spirit of his mouth, and shall destroy with the brightness of his coming" (v.8).

In view of this, Paul **gives thanks** that while all would be "damned (judged) who believed not the truth", God had destined every believer "to the obtaining of the glory of our Lord Jesus Christ". He therefore urges them to "stand fast" and "hold the traditions" (vv.13-17).

Having dealt with their disturbance and distress, caused particularly by a forged letter (2:2), Paul prays, "Now our Lord Jesus Christ himself, and God, even our Father, which hath loved us, and hath given us everlasting consolation and good **hope** through grace, comfort your hearts, and stablish you in every good word and work" (vv.16-17). Hope was missing in 1:3, where Paul refers only to their faith and love.

Having addressed their circumstances in the light of the **future**, Paul now deals with their circumstances in the light of **present** responsibility. In the first place, he emphasises that believers should be **praying** people, and in the second, that they should be **working** people.

With this in mind, the chapter may be divided into three major sections; **(1)** external persecution (vv.1-5): this was caused by "unreasonable and wicked men" (v.2); **(2)** internal problems (vv.6-15): these were caused by "some which walk ... disorderly" (v.11); **(3)** final benediction and greeting (vv.16-18).

1) EXTERNAL PERSECUTION, vv.1-5

The section begins with prayer for **him** ("Finally, brethren, pray for us"), and ends with prayer for **them** ("the Lord direct your hearts into the love of God, and into the patient waiting for Christ"). He asks them to pray for **him**, in view of the persecution which he was experiencing (vv.1-2), and he prays for **them** in view of the persecution which they were experiencing (vv.3-5). We should notice Paul's request to them (vv.1-2), his assurance about them (vv.3-4), and his desire for them (v.5).

a) Persecution against Paul, vv.1-2

Do notice the order in Paul's prayer request: **(i)** "**that** the word of the Lord may have free course, and be glorified ('run and be glorified', JND)" (v.1); **(ii)** "**that** we may be delivered from unreasonable and wicked men" (v.2). This raises the question of the relationship between our prayers and the will of God. We know that "if we ask any thing according to his will, he heareth us" (1 John 5:14). But in view of the fact that "known unto God are all his works from the beginning of the world" (Acts 15:18), why are our prayers necessary? Part of the answer lies in the fact that God involves us in His purposes. See, for example, 2 Corinthians 1:10-11: "God...who delivered us from so great a death, and doth deliver: in whom we trust that he will yet deliver us; ye also **helping together by prayer** for us". It is a great privilege to share God's desires, and in a wonderful way, He merges our prayers, as directed by the Holy Spirit, and His own will.

We must notice that Paul's principal concern was for the progress of God's word, rather than his own personal comfort.

i) He asks them to pray for the progress of God's word
We might have expected Paul to ask them to pray, above all things, for his deliverance from persecution. But that was not at the top of the list of his priorities. He asks them to pray, first of all, "*that* the word of the Lord may have free course ('run'), and be glorified" (v.1). Compare Ephesians 6:19-20. Paul put the interests of the Gospel first.

Paul's great desire was for the 'free and rapid progress' of the Gospel. (Read Psalm 147:15). He had every confidence in the power of God's word. See, for example, 2 Timothy 2:9, "The word of God is not bound." The messenger was in prison, but not the message! This is beautifully illustrated in Philippians 1:12: "But I would ye should understand, brethren, that the things which happened unto me have fallen out rather unto the furtherance of the gospel." Compare Acts 13:48, "And when the Gentiles heard this, they were glad, and glorified the word of the Lord." God's word was glorified as its power was displayed in their lives.

But we need look no further than Thessalonica for an illustration of the 'free and rapid progress' of the Gospel. Paul had no need to look elsewhere: "As it is *with you*". He was thinking of the progress of the Gospel in their lives. See 1 Thessalonians 1:6-10, "And ye became followers of us, and of the Lord, having received the word in much affliction, with joy of the Holy Ghost: so that ye were ensamples to all that believe in Macedonia and Achaia. For from you sounded out the word of the Lord..." The word of the Lord 'ran' in them, and through them! Since Paul evidently wrote 2 Thessalonians from Corinth, he is praying for a similar effect there, and his prayer was certainly answered for "many of the Corinthians hearing believed, and were baptized" (Acts 18:8).

We must not let this pass without examining *our* priorities. Paul was more concerned about God's interests and the salvation of other people, than he was with his own comfort. How about *us?*

ii) He asks them to pray for his personal deliverance
"*That* we may be delivered from unreasonable and wicked men." While his personal safety is placed second, that is not to say that it was unimportant. Notice

the order of the so-called 'Lord's prayer' (more accurately, the 'disciples' prayer') in Matthew 6:9-13. It begins with three petitions for God's glory: "Hallowed be **thy** name. **Thy** kingdom come. **Thy** will be done." These are followed by three petitions (or four, if you separate the last two) for our blessing: "Give **us** this day our daily bread. And forgive **us** our debts…And lead **us** not into temptation, but deliver **us** from evil."

The word "unreasonable" means 'out of place', and designates men 'capable of outrageous conduct' (W.E. Vine). The revised text has **"these** men", which refers, in all probability, to a definite class of people. That is, the Jews. See 1 Thessalonians 2:14-16, "Ye also have suffered like things of your own countrymen, even as they (the churches of God in Judaea) have of the Jews: who both killed the Lord Jesus, and their own prophets, and have persecuted us; and they please not God, and are contrary to all men: forbidding us to speak to the Gentiles that they might be saved." See Acts 17:5 and 18:12-16. However, this could refer to all men. See, again, 1 Thessalonians 2:14, where Paul refers to their "own countrymen."

Some have suggested that the meaning is that "all men have not **the** faith", but that hardly seems a necessary observation. It seems more in keeping to understand the meaning as 'few have faith.' See Romans 10:16, "Lord, who hath believed our report?" Not many had received the message.

b) Persecution against the Thessalonians, vv.3-5
After thinking briefly of himself, and his own dangers, Paul returns to the Thessalonians, and their dangers. Paul does not become immersed in self-pity or self-occupation. Once again, he acts as a 'nursing mother cherishing her own children' (1 Thess. 2:7). We must notice **(i)** the faithful God (v.3) and **(ii)** faithful saints (vv.4-5). Paul was assured about the faithfulness of the Lord, and of the saints.

i) The faithful God, v.3
"But the Lord is faithful, who shall stablish you, and keep you from evil". We should notice the contrast between faithless men ("All men have not faith"), and the faithful God ("The Lord is faithful"). The text can read, 'not all have faith; faithful, however, is the Lord' (vv.2-3). Compare 2 Tim. 4:16-17: "no man stood with me…the Lord stood with me."

He is faithful in every way. Here are some verses to encourage a delightful study of His faithfulness: "God is **faithful**, by whom ye were called unto the fellowship of his Son" (1 Cor. 1:9); "God is **faithful,** who will not suffer you to be tempted above that ye are able" (1 Cor. 10:13); "**Faithful** is he that calleth you, who also will do it" (1 Thess. 5:24); "Wherefore in all things it behoved him to be made like unto his brethren, that he might be a merciful and **faithful** high priest in things pertaining to God" (Heb. 2:17); "Wherefore let them that suffer according to the will of God commit the keeping of their souls to him in well doing, as unto a **faithful** Creator" (1 Pet. 4:19).

The faithfulness of the Lord here is emphasised in two ways: "who shall stablish you, and keep you from evil":

- *"Who shall stablish you"*, meaning, 'who shall 'stay you up', 'steadfastly set you', or 'fix you.' That is, by His word, by His power, and by His presence. The word *sterizo* comes from *sterix,* a prop. It occurs in 1 Thess. 3:2, 13; 2 Thess. 2:17.

- *"And keep you from evil"*: 'guard *(phulasso)* you from the evil (one).' As in 2 Peter 2:5, "And spared not the old world, but saved *(phulasso)* Noah the eighth person", and John 17:12, "I kept them in thy name." This could refer to evil generally or, more probably, to Satan as 'the evil one.' Compare 1 Thessalonians 2:18; 3:5. See also 1 John 5:18.

We must notice that Paul does not say that we will be guarded against persecution and adversity, but against surrendering our faith, and losing our testimony. These are the great objectives of Satan. See Luke 22:31.

If the "Lord is faithful", then Paul anticipated that His people at Thessalonica would be faithful too. This brings us to:

ii) *Faithful saints, vv.4-5*
"And we have confidence in the Lord touching you, that ye both do and will do the things which we command you." We should notice:

- That Paul's confidence did not lie in the Thessalonian believers themselves, but in the enabling grace and power of the Lord Jesus. "And we have confidence **in the Lord** touching you." Compare Philippians 1:6, "Being confident of this very thing, that he which hath begun a good work in you will perform it until the day of Jesus Christ." See Galatians 5:10, "I have confidence in you through the Lord" or "I have confidence to you-ward in the Lord' (RV).

- That Paul did not deal in optional extras. "That ye both do and will do the things which we **command** (*parangello*) you." While the next section of the chapter commences with the words, "Now we command (*parangello*) you, brethren" (v.6), and makes two further references to commandments (vv.10, 12), it seems more likely that Paul refers here to his teaching in general. This includes 1 Thessalonians 4:2, 11, and 2 Thessalonians 2:15. Compare 1 Corinthians 14:37, "If any man thinketh himself to be a prophet, or spiritual, let him acknowledge that the things that I write unto you are the commandments (*entole*) of the Lord."

It is important to notice that Paul commends the believers at Thessalonica ("we have confidence in the Lord touching you, that ye both do and will do the things which we command you"), before he proceeds to give them commandments in vv.6, 10. As we shall see, Paul is about to ask the assembly at Thessalonica to deal with disorderly conduct amongst them, but his instructions are given in the right atmosphere. It is all too easy to cause damage by saying the right thing in the wrong way.

In all their circumstances, where men were determined to harm them, Paul prays that they may never lose sight of God's love, and never lose sight of the Lord's coming. "And the Lord direct your hearts into the love of God, and into the patient waiting for Christ":

- **"The Lord direct your hearts into the love of God."** The word "direct" *(kateuthuno)* occurs in Luke 1:79: "to **guide** our feet into the way of peace." It means 'to make straight', and suggests the removal of every obstacle and distraction. W.E. Vine defines the word "heart" as a figure "for the hidden springs of personal life".

When, like the Thessalonians, we are under pressure, we must never forget that God loves us. Peter reminds his readers of God's love for them when anticipating the arrival of the "scoffers, walking after their own lusts, and saying, Where is the promise of his coming?" (2 Pet. 3:3-4). In this context, he uses the word "beloved" four times (2 Pet. 3:1, 8, 14, 17). Adversity, whatever form it takes, can make us question God's love. We must 'keep ourselves in the love of God.' We sing:

> His love in times past forbids me to think
> He'll leave me at last in ruin to sink.
> Each sweet Ebenezer I hold in review
> Confirms His good pleasure to see me right through.

- **"Into the patient waiting for Christ"** or "Into the patience of Christ.' (RV/JND). On this basis, we could conclude that Paul is urging the believers at Thessalonica to be patient as Christ was patient. See Hebrews 12:2, "Looking unto Jesus... who for the joy that was set before him endured the cross, despising the shame, and is set down at the right hand of the throne of God." Compare Revelation 3:10, "thou hast kept the word of my patience", although commentators differ in their interpretation of this verse. However, the AV rendering which, according to W.E. Vine, is a paraphrase, does make excellent sense in the context of the Thessalonian epistles! Paul commented on their "patience of hope in our Lord Jesus Christ" in 1 Thessalonians 1:3.

In this passage, we have "the word of the Lord (v.1), the faithfulness of the Lord (v.3), confidence in the Lord (v.4), and the direction of the Lord (v.5).

READ CHAPTER 3:6-18

"Busybodies"

We have already noticed that this chapter can be divided into three sections: *(1)* external persecution (vv.1-5); *(2)* internal problems (vv.6-15); *(3)* final benediction and greeting (vv.16-18).

1) EXTERNAL PERSECUTION, vv.1-5
This section deals with persecution against Paul himself (vv.1-2), and persecution against the Thessalonians (vv.3-5). In this connection, Paul asks them to pray **for him**, and then he prays **for them**. It is noteworthy that in Paul's personal request for prayer, he places the progress of the word of God before his personal deliverance from "unreasonable and wicked men."

2) INTERNAL PROBLEMS, vv.6-15
The problem concerns 'disorderly brethren' (vv.6, 11). The necessity for the teaching in these verses is set out in v.11; "We hear that there are some which walk among you disorderly, working not at all, but are busybodies." The word "disorderly" *(ataktos)* is a military term meaning 'out of rank', hence 'undisciplined.' The word also occurs in v.7, where it is used in a negative sense: "we behaved not ourselves disorderly among you." It is rendered "unruly" in 1 Thessalonians 5:14; "warn them that are unruly."

We are not told why these 'disorderly brethren' were reluctant to work. According to T.W. Smith (*What the Bible Teaches: 2 Thessalonians),* some have suggested that it was because of "their overwhelming occupation with the Lord's return: others say that it was due to the initial excitement and buoyancy of their conversion". Both suggestions seem highly unlikely! In view of the fact that the Cretans had been described by one of their own prophets as "always liars, evil wild beasts, lazy gluttons" (Titus 1:12, JND), Paul urges the Christians there to "maintain good works for necessary uses ('profess honest trades', AV margin)" (Titus 3:14). The words 'profess honest trades' probably convey the sense, even if it is not an exact translation! Christians should not be 'work-shy' people.

Thessalonica evidently had its fair share of people like that. They are called "lewd fellows of the baser sort" (hangers about in the market place) in Acts 17:5. There is some truth in the proverb that 'the devil finds work for idle hands to do.' It's worth adding that in assembly work, busy Christians are usually the least troublesome. They just haven't got time to cause disruption! Most trouble comes from the people who stand on the touch-lines! Energy in the Lord's work promotes fellowship: idleness promotes strife!

These verses can be analysed as follows: *(a)* the command to the assembly (v.6); *(b)* the example to the assembly (vv.7-10; *(c)* the disruption of the assembly (vv.11-13; *(d)* the action by the assembly (vv.14-15).

a) The command to the assembly, v.6

"Now we command you, brethren, in the name of our Lord Jesus Christ, that ye withdraw yourselves from every brother that walketh disorderly, and not after the traditions which he received of us." We have already discussed the circumstances that necessitated this particular teaching, and noted the meaning of "disorderly." We must, however notice *(i)* the authority; *(ii)* the action.

i) The authority

Disruption in the assembly is a serious matter, and Paul exercises his apostolic authority in dealing with the matter. "Now we **command** you, brethren, in the name of our Lord Jesus Christ." In this connection, we should notice the following:

- The assembly is not the place where saints, including the elders, do as they please. It is a place where the word of God is obeyed. Paul **commands** them "in the name of our Lord Jesus Christ." There are no 'optional extras' here.

- The assembly is the place of settled order. Paul refers to "the tradition which he ('they', RV) received of us". We have already discussed "the traditions." See 2:15, "Therefore, brethren, stand fast, and hold the traditions which ye have been taught, whether by **word**, or our **epistle**." Paul's reference here to "the tradition which he received of us", therefore includes his **oral** ministry ("by word") on the subject (see 3:10), and his written ministry ("our epistle"): see 1 Thessalonians 4:11-12: "And that ye study to be quiet, and to do your own business, and to work with your own hands, as we commanded you." Both oral and written ministry had evidently been ignored. The 'disorderly brethren' were not acting ignorantly, but wilfully. This was most serious, and accounts for his stronger language here than in 1 Thessalonians 4.

- The assembly is not to countenance disorderly conduct. It should be marked by godliness of behaviour, as well as sound doctrine. Note the expression, "The doctrine which is according to godliness" (1 Tim. 6:3). What we **say** may be right, but are **we** right?

ii) The action
"That ye **withdraw yourselves** from every brother that walketh disorderly." The word "withdraw" *(stello)* means, literally, 'to bring together', or 'gather up', and was used of furling sails. It signifies to shrink, or draw back, from a person or thing. It is translated 'avoiding' in 2 Corinthians 8:20. Note Galatians 2:12, "he (Barnabas) withdrew *(hupostello)* and separated himself." The expression "withdraw yourselves" does not imply excommunication. This is only applicable in most serious cases. See 1 Corinthians 5:11-13, where the guilty party is described as "that wicked person." The misconduct described in 2 Thessalonians 3 was to be met by the withdrawal of the usual friendly relations in the assembly. This is amplified in vv.14-15: "If any man obey not our word by this epistle, note that man, and have no company with him, that he may be ashamed. Yet count him not as an enemy, but admonish him as a brother."

b) The example to the assembly, vv.7-10
"For yourselves know how ye ought to follow us: for we behaved not ourselves disorderly among you; neither did we eat any man's bread for nought; but wrought with labour and travail night and day, that we might not be chargeable to any of you: not because we have not power, but to make ourselves an ensample unto you to follow us. For even when we were with you, this we commanded you, that if any would not work, neither should he eat." In vv.7-9 we have **practice,** and in v.10, we have **precept.**

The words, "for yourselves know", reminded the Thessalonians, not only of the 'traditions', that is, of the oral teaching given, but of the conduct of Paul and his colleagues. **Precepts** were supported by **practice.** Compare 1 Thessalonians 2:5-9. "For neither at any time used we flattering words, as ye know, nor a cloke of covetousness; God is witness: nor of men sought we glory, neither of you, nor yet of others, when we might have been burdensome, as the apostles of Christ…For ye remember, brethren, our labour and travail: for labouring night and day, because we would not be chargeable unto any of you, we preached unto you the gospel of God." We should note the following:

i) Practice, vv.7-9
- Paul and his colleagues deliberately surrendered their right to support (see

1 Corinthians 9) for two reasons. In the first place, the Macedonian believers (Thessalonica was in Macedonia) were impoverished. See 2 Corinthians 8:1-3. Hence his words, "we might have been burdensome, as the apostles of Christ... we would not be chargeable unto any of you." Secondly, Paul and his colleagues refused support at Thessalonica in order to set them an example. They worked hard (notice the words, "labour and travail": "travail" means 'painful effort') "night and day, that we might not be chargeable to any of you: not because we have not power, but to make ourselves **an ensample unto you to follow us.**"

Paul did the same at Corinth, but for different reasons. See 2 Corinthians 12:16, "But be it so, I did not burden you: nevertheless, being crafty, I caught you with guile." (He is evidently quoting his accusers here). Paul anticipated opposition at Corinth, and gave no opportunity for his critics to accuse him of financial gain. This leads to:

- Paul anticipated future problems, and took steps to ensure that he set them a good example, as well as giving them good teaching. Notice that the section is bound together by the expression, "follow us" (vv.7, 9). The two occurrences are like two book-ends! This wasn't the only area in which Paul anticipated future problems. See 1 Thessalonians 3:4, "For verily, when we were with you, we told you before that we should suffer tribulation; even as it came to pass, and ye know."

This raises at least two issues. First, how do we read **our** present circumstances? How do **we** see the future? Just think about the legislation announced in Parliament on Monday, 30th June, 2002. It seems unbelievable that a once so-called Christian country should deliberately ignore Romans 1:26-27. It does not need much imagination to visualise the problems which loom for all who love the word of God, and refuse to compromise its teaching. Secondly, we must remember that what we do now has a profound influence on the future. What kind of influence is our present conduct going to have on other Christians, perhaps the next generation of Christians, in the future? A bad example now might prove ruinous to someone in later life. Who would have thought that events described in Exodus. 32:1-6 would have had repercussions over five hundred years later? See 1 Kings 12:28. Even the language was the same "These be thy gods, O Israel, which brought thee up out of the land of Egypt."

ii) Precept, v.10
"For even when we were with you, this we **commanded** you, that if any would not work, neither should he eat." The practice gave moral authority to the precept. Paul and his colleagues lived by their own teaching. The Lord Jesus

censured the religious leaders for their inconsistency. "They say, and do not" (Matt. 23:1-3). He was completely consistent: "The former treatise *(logos)* have I made, O Theophilus, of all that Jesus began both to do and teach" (Acts 1:1). James had the moral right to say, "count it all joy when ye fall into divers temptations", James 1:2. See Acts 5:40-42.

The purpose of work is indicated in Genesis. Adam was placed in the garden of Eden, "to dress it and to keep it" (Gen. 2:15). Even in his unfallen state, he was to be occupied, and he was certainly to be occupied in his fallen state: "In the sweat of thy face shalt thou eat bread" (Gen. 3:19). Sinful man needs to be fully occupied, for obvious reasons! Christians are to be industrious, and occupy their time properly. Layabouts need not apply! See Ephesians 6: 5-6; Colossians 3:22-24; Titus 2:9-10. Do notice that even secular work is to be undertaken "as to the Lord." That should make us first-class employees! Christianity should not be a society which encourages 'spongers'. "Poor saints" are in a totally different category. See, for example, Acts 11:29: Romans 15:26. Do remember that, amongst other things, our wages (or salaries, pensions, pocket money) enable us to support the Lord's work. We rob God if we are too lazy to work. Perhaps we should add that unemployment does not necessarily mean laziness.

c) The disruption of the assembly, vv.11-13
"For we hear that there are some which walk among you disorderly, working not at all, but are busybodies."

Notice, "we hear". Not all that Paul heard about them was good! Compare 1 Corinthians 11, "I praise you.....I praise you not" (vv.2, 17). W.E. Vine explains that there is a play on words here which cannot be reproduced in a literal translation. To paraphrase: 'some that are not busy people, but are busybodies', or, 'some who are not busied in their own business, but are overbusied in that of others.' Compare 1 Timothy 5:13, "And withal they learn to be idle, wandering about from house to house; and not only idle, but tattlers also and busybodies, speaking things which they ought not."

Paul addresses these people directly: "Now them that are such we command and exhort by our Lord Jesus Christ, that with quietness they work, and eat their own bread." We should notice that the authority of the Lord Jesus Himself is invoked. Notice the words, "command and exhort." He gives the command and urges them to obey it. He urges "quietness", as opposed to the noisy activities of the busybodies. Verse 12 is addressed to ungodly 'activists!'. Verse 13 is addressed to godly 'activists': "But ye, brethren, be not weary in well doing."

d) The action by the assembly, vv.14-15
"And if any man obey not our word by this epistle, note that man, and have no company with him, that he may be ashamed. Yet count him not as an enemy, but admonish him as a brother."

Having said, "we command and exhort", Paul now indicates what must happen if this is ignored and rejected: "Note that man, and have no company with him, that he may be ashamed." Compare v.6. This signifies the withdrawal of friendly relations, and is intended to impress the 'disorderly brethren' with the thorough disapproval of the assembly. "Have no company with him, that he may be ashamed." The object is to produce better conduct. Verse 15 emphasises that since he is a brother, he is not to be treated with hostility. The man is not opposed to Christ. The motive for such action is brotherly love, which seeks to gain him.

3) FINAL BENEDICTION AND GREETING, vv.16-18
Paul concludes the epistle with a benediction (v.16), and a greeting (vv.17-18). "Now the Lord of peace himself give you peace always by all means. The Lord be with you all. The salutation of Paul with mine own hand, which is the token in every epistle: so I write. The grace of our Lord Jesus Christ be with you all. Amen."

a) The benediction, v.16
"Now the Lord of peace himself (again: "himself": see 2:16 etc) give you peace always by all means. The Lord be with you all." The title, "Lord of peace", is most appropriate in view of the persecution they were experiencing. We should notice:

i) The gift. His peace. "Now the Lord of peace himself give you peace always by all means" or "But the Lord of peace himself give you peace continually in every way" (JND). In 1 Thessalonians 5:23, Paul refers to the "God of peace." (See also Romans 15:33). Here, he refers to the "Lord of peace."

ii) The giver. His presence. "The Lord be with you all." We can rejoice in His words, "I will never leave thee, nor forsake thee." We can enjoy His peace and His presence in the midst of persecution.

b) The salutation, vv.17-18
"The salutation of Paul with mine own hand; which is the token in every epistle: so I write". As we have already noticed, the necessity for this remark arose from the forged letter to which Paul refers earlier: "That ye be not soon shaken...by letter as from us" (2:2). Here, Paul authenticates the epistle.

"The grace of our Lord Jesus Christ be with you all. Amen." All three chapters end with "grace". Compare 1:12 and 2:16. Notice emphasis upon "all" here. As W.E. Vine observes, "While he had commended some and censured others, the final word of benediction is for all". He commences and concludes the epistle in the same way: "Grace unto you...the grace of our Lord Jesus Christ be with you all."